COHEN & COHEN

OCT 1999

SPECIALIST IN CHINESE EXPORT PORCELAIN AND WORKS OF ART

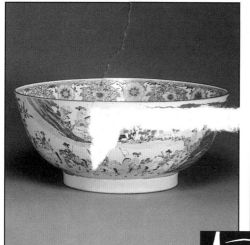

An unusual famille rose punch bowl depicting the Dutch Embassy to Peking, c.1730.

A very rare tureen with the Arms of Joaquim Inacio Da Cruz Sobral, Portuguese market, c.1775.

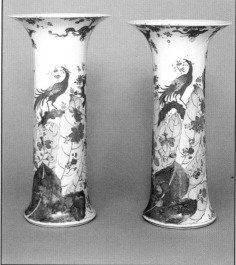

A rare famille rose covered cistern decorated with "The Archer" after a design by Cornelis Pronk, c.1740.

A fine and large pair of 'tobacco leaf' beaker vases, c.1770.

MILLER'S
Chinese & Japanese Antiques
BUYER'S GUIDE

MILLER'S CHINESE & JAPANESE ANTIQUES BUYER'S GUIDE

Created and designed by
Miller's
The Cellars, High Street
Tenterden, Kent, TN30 6BN
Tel: 01580 766411
Fax: 01580 766100

Contributing Editor: Peter Wain
Project Editor: Jo Wood
Editorial Assistants: Catherine Carson-Parker, Shirley Reeves
Production Assistants: Gillian Charles, Kate McDonald, Léonie Sidgwick
Advertising Executive: Elizabeth Smith
Advertising Assistant: Melinda Williams
Designers: Kari Reeves, Shirley Reeves
Advertisement Designer: Simon Cook
Indexer: Hilary Bird
Additional Photographers: Ian Booth, Roy Farthing, Robin Saker

First published in Great Britain in 1999
by Miller's, a division of Mitchell Beazley,
imprints of Octopus Publishing Group Ltd,
2–4 Heron Quays, London E14 4JB

© 1999 Octopus Publishing Group Ltd

A CIP catalogue record for this book is
available from the British Library

ISBN 1-84000-127-5

Film output by Perfect Image, Hurst Green, E. Sussex
Colour origination by Pica Colour Separation Overseas Pte Ltd, Singapore
Printed and bound by Toppan Printing Co (HK) Ltd, China

Miller's is a registered trademark of
Octopus Publishing Group Ltd

MILLER'S
Chinese & Japanese Antiques
BUYER'S GUIDE

Contributing Editor

Peter Wain

Project Editor

Jo Wood

HOW TO USE THIS BOOK

I t is our aim to make this guide easy to use. In order to find a particular item, turn to the contents list on page 5 to find the main heading, for example, Japanese Ceramics. Having located your area of interest, you will see that larger sections have been sub-divided by subject. If you are looking for a particular factory, maker, or object, consult the index, which starts on page 316.

Koros • Tea & Coffee Ware • JAPANESE CERAMICS 171

Koros

A decorated and enamelled lozenge-shaped *koro*, with pierced cover, signed 'Etsuseki', c1890, 5in (12.5cm) high.
£1,800–2,000 *MER*

A Satsuma *koro* and cover, decorated in enamels and gilt, on 3 elephant head feet, Meiji period, 36½in (92.5cm) high.
£3,500–3,800 *S*

A Satsuma earthenware *koro* and cover, the sides painted with a border of flowers, slight damage, signed 'Dai Nihon, Tojiki Goshigaisha, Ryozan', below the Yasuda company trademark, Meiji period, 5½in (14cm) wide.
£4,500–5,000 *S(S)*

A Satsuma earthenware *koro* and cover, painted with chrysanthemums, peonies and dianthus among clouds, on 3 bracket feet, cover pierced and with bud finial, 19thC, 7in (18cm) high, with wood stand.
£3,500–4,000 *S(S)*

A Satsuma earthenware *koro*, with metal cover, damaged and repaired, Meiji period, 6in (15cm) high.
£1,300–1,500 *S(S)*

A *koro* and cover, painted and gilt with a coiled dragon above foaming waves, the sides with floral medallions, signed 'Kinkozan zo', late 19thC, 2in (5cm) high.
£200–220 *CSK*

Tea & Coffee Ware

An Arita blue and white silver-mounted coffee pot and cover, the loop handle decorated with scrolling foliage, porcelain late 17thC, mounts 19thC, 13in (33cm) high.
£2,000–2,500 *CAm*

Tea & Coffee Ware
During the Momoyama period (1568–1600) the tea ceremony was consolidated and refined, and tea wares were produced at such pottery centres as Bizen, Seto, Kyoto, Hagi, Karatsu and Satsuma. Extant tea wares from this period are rare and among the most prized Japanese ceramics; they must be accompanied by a full and accurate provenance if they are not to be confused with numerous later copies.

A Kyoto earthenware kettle, painted in enamels and gilding, on a seeded gilt ground, spout repaired, painted mark, Meiji period, 5in (12.5cm) high.
£500–600 *Bon*

r. A blue and white teapot and cover, decorated with *ho-o* birds, by Makuzu Kozan, late 19thC, 8in (20.5cm) wide.
£1,600–1,800 *C*

An Imari teapot and cover, decorated in underglaze blue, iron-red, green and yellow, slight damage, Edo period, c1700, 4¾in (12cm) high.
£2,600–3,000 *S(S)*

Caption
provides a brief description of the item including the maker's name, medium, date, measurements and in some instances condition.

Italicised words
for an explanation of italicised words, please refer to the Glossary on page 313.

Price Guide
price ranges are worked out by a team of trade and auction house experts, and are based on actual prices realised. Remember that Miller's is a PRICE GUIDE not a PRICE LIST and prices are affected by many variables such as location, condition, desirability and so on. Don't forget that if you are selling it is quite likely you will be offered less than the price range. Price ranges for items sold at auction tend to include the buyer's premium and VAT if applicable.

Information Box
covers relevant collecting information on factories, makers, care, restoration, fakes and alterations.

Source Code
refers to the 'Key to Illustrations' on page 8 which contains details of where the item was photographed.

CONTENTS

ACKNOWLEDGEMENTS

The publishers would like to acknowledge the great assistance given by the following consultants

PETER WAIN, CONTRIBUTING EDITOR, is a leading specialist in Chinese and Japanese ceramics and works of art. He lived in Hong Kong for several years, and is a frequent visitor to China. He has written numerous books and articles, has broadcast on radio and television and given many lectures both in the UK, the USA and Australia. At present he is researching a major new book on Chinese porcelain. As well as being Chairman of the Oriental Vetting Committee for the Olympia Internatioanl Fine Arts and Antiques Fairs, he is a member of the British Antique Dealers' Association and the Oriental Ceramics Society.

NEIL DAVEY is Senior Specialist in the Japanese Art Department at Sotheby's, London, where he has been since 1958. He is the author of *Netsuke*, a comprehensive study based on the M. T. Hindson collection, co-author of *The Garrett Collection, Netsuke, Inro, Lacquer* at Evergreen House, John Hopkins University, Baltimore, Maryland, and author of numerous articles on *netsuke*, lacquer ware and collecting. He has given lectures on these subjects in Europe and the USA, including the Victoria & Albert Museum, London, the Asian Art Museum, San Francisco, the Lowe Art Museum, Miami, and the Honolulu Academy of Arts, Hawaii.

ROBERT KLEINER is a leading authority on Chinese snuff bottles. He has written several books and articles on the subject, curated and organised many important museum exhibitions including those in the British Museum and the Hong Kong Museum of Art, and lectured worldwide on both snuff bottles and other areas of Chinese art. After ten years in the Chinese Department at Sotheby's, London, he set up his own consultancy in Chinese art and snuff bottles in 1989, based in Old Bond Street, London.

MAX RUTHERSTON joined Sotheby's, London, in 1979, working with impressionist and modern 19th-century European and Russian pictures. In 1987 he left the firm to run his own gallery and business, dealing mostly in modern British pictures. He then rejoined Sotheby's in 1992, where he is now Director of the Japanese Department.

LINDA WRIGGLESWORTH established her antique Chinese, Tibetan and Korean costume and textiles business in Mayfair, London, in 1978. Her focused approach to the subject has gained her the reputation of being one of the foremost authorities worldwide. Her company has published several catalogues illustrating her annual international exhibitions, and in 1991 she wrote *Imperial Wardrobe* with Gary Dickinson, historian in Chinese history and philosophy.

JOHN CULLIS has been a dealer in English and European antique furniture for 27 years. His introduction to Chinese furniture during a trip to the interior of China three years ago proved inspirational. Since then he has spent long periods of time travelling through China and South East Asia establishing contacts, finding pieces and increasing his knowledge. In 1998, he opened his shop Kite in London.

ROY BUTLER is Senior Partner at Wallis & Wallis, the internationally renowned auctioneers of militaria and arms and armour. He is also a director of the Militaria Antique Arms Fair, held in London since 1967, founder of the Military Heritage Museum, and has appeared on numerous television programmes on antiques. As well as being a life member of Friends of the Royal Navy Museum, and of HMS *Warrior,* he is working on a book, *Relics of Nelson's Navy.*

Front cover illustrations, from top left:

A *huanghuali* yoke-back armchair, the back splat with carved *shou* character, 17thC. **£1,200–1,500** *S(NY)*
An ivory and lacquer snuff bottle, Qianlong mark, late 19thC, 3in (7.5cm) high. **£7,000–8,000** *S(NY)*
A Japanese basket-seller and boy, signed 'Jogyoku', 19thC, 10¼in (26cm) high. **£1,000–1,500** *CSK*
A Satsuma earthenware vase, by Seikozan, signed, Meiji period, 6in (15cm) high. **£1,800–2,200** *S*
A gilt-bronze mythical beast, repaired, Han Dynasty, 11in (28cm) long. **£245,000–280,000** *S*
A lacquer three-case inro, with ceramic *ojime* and wood *netsuke*, 19thC, 3¾in (9.5cm) high. **£5,200–5,800** *S(NY)*
A pair of blue and white jars and cover, Qing Dynasty, 24in (61cm) high. **£8,000–9,000** *S(NY)*
A blue dragon robe and embroidered dragon banner, 19thC. **£3,500–4,500** *S(NY)*

Don't Throw Away A Fortune!
Invest In
Miller's Price Guides

Please send me the following editions

❏ **Miller's Antiques Price Guide 1999** – £22.50
❏ **Miller's Pine & Country Furniture Buyer's Guide** – £18.99
❏ **Miller's Clocks & Barometers Buyer's Guide** – £18.99
❏ **Miller's Collectors Cars Price Guide 1999/2000** — £19.99
❏ **Miller's Classic Motorcycles Price Guide 1999/2000** – £14.00

If you do not wish your name to be used by Miller's or other carefully selected organisations for promotional purposes, please tick this box ❏

I enclose my cheque/postal order for £.................post free (UK only)
Please make cheques payable to *Octopus Publishing Group Ltd*
or please debit my Access/Visa/Amex/Diners Club account number

Expiry Date............/............

NAME *Title   Initial   Surname*

ADDRESS

Postcode

SIGNATURE

Photocopy this page or write the above details on a separate sheet and send it to **Miller's Direct, 27 Sanders Road, Wellingborough, Northants, NN8 4NL** *or telephone the Credit Card Hotline 01933 443863.*
Lines open from 9:00 to 5:00. Registered office: Michelin House, 81 Fulham Road, London, SW3 6RB.
Registered in England number 3597451

KEY TO ILLUSTRATIONS

Each illustration and descriptive caption is accompanied by a letter code. By referring to the following list of Auctioneers (denoted by *) and dealers (•) the source of any item may be immediately determined. Inclusion in this edition in no way constitutes or implies a contract or binding offer on the part of any of our contributors to supply or sell the goods illustrated, or similar articles, at the prices stated. Advertisers in this year's directory are denoted by †.

If you require a valuation for an item, it is advisable to check whether the dealer or specialist will carry out this service and if there is a charge. Please mention Miller's when making an enquiry. Having found a specialist who will carry out your valuation it is best to send a photograph and description of the item to the specialist together with a stamped addressed envelope for the reply. A valuation by telephone is not possible. Most dealers are only too happy to help you with your enquiry; however, they are very busy people and consideration of the above points would be appreciated.

AAV * Academy Auctioneers & Valuers, Northcote House, Northcote Avenue, Ealing, London W5 3UR Tel: 0181 579 7466

AG * Anderson & Garland (Auctioneers), Marlborough House, Marlborough Crescent, Newcastle-upon-Tyne, Tyne & Wear NE1 4EE Tel: 0191 232 6278

AH * Andrew Hartley, Victoria Hall Salerooms, Little Lane, Ilkley, Yorkshire LS29 8EA Tel: 01943 816363

ALB • Albany Antiques Ltd, 8-10 London Road, Hindhead, Surrey GU26 6AE Tel: 01428 605528

ALL * Allen & Harris, Bristol Auction Rooms, St John's Place, Apsley Road, Clifton, Bristol, Glos BS8 9737201

AnE • The Antiques Emporium, The Old Chapel, Long Street, Tetbury, Glos GL8 8AA Tel: 01666 505281

ART • Artemesia Antiques, 16 West Street, Alresford, Hants Tel: 01962 732277

ATo Adrienne Turner. Tel: 01442 878460

AVA • Admiral Vernon Antique Gallery, Portobello Road, London W11 2QB

AWH • Amherst Antiques, 23 London Road, Riverhead, Sevenoaks, Kent TN13 2BU Tel: 01732 455047

Bea * 1 Southernhay West, Exeter, Devon EX1 1JG Tel: 01392 219040

Bon * Bonhams, Montpelier Street, Knightsbridge, London SW7 1HH Tel: 0171 393 3994

Bon(C)* Bonhams, 65–69 Lots Road, Chelsea, London SW10 0RN Tel: 0171 393 3900

BRU • Brunel Antiques, Bartlett Street Antiques Centre, Bath, Somerset BA1 2QZ Tel: 01225 310457

BWe * Biddle & Webb Ltd, Ladywood Middleway, Birmingham, West Midlands B16 0PP Tel: 0121 455 8042

C * Christie, Manson & Wood Ltd, 8 King Street, St James's, London SW1Y 6QT Tel: 0171 839 9060

C(HK)* Christie's Hong Kong, 2203-5 Alexandra House, 16–20 Chater Road, Hong Kong Tel: (852) 2521 5396

C(S) * Christie's Scotland Ltd, 164–166 Bath Street, Glasgow, Scotland G2 4TG Tel: 0141 332 8134

CAG • Canterbury Auction Galleries, 40 Station Road West, Canterbury, Kent CT2 8AN Tel: 01227 763337

CAI • No longer trading

CAm * Christie's Amsterdam BV, Cornelis Schuystraat 57, 1071 JG Amsterdam, Holland Tel: (3120) 57 55 255

CAT • Lennox Cato, 1 The Square, Edenbridge, Kent TN8 5BD Tel: 01732 865988

CDC * Capes Dunn & Co, The Auction Galleries, 38 Charles Street, off Princess Street, Gt Manchester M1 7DB Tel: 0161 273 6060/1911

ChC • Christopher Clark, The Fosse Way, Stow-on-the-Wold, Glos. Tel: 01451 830476

CNY * Christie, Manson & Wood International Inc, 502 Park Avenue, (including Christie's East), New York, NY 10022 USA Tel: 212 546 1000

CS • Christopher Sykes, The Old Parsonage, Woburn, Milton Keynes, Bucks MK17 9QM Tel: 01525 290259

CSK * Christie's South Kensington Ltd, 85 Old Brompton Road, London SW7 3LD Tel: 0171 581 7611

DA * Dee, Atkinson & Harrison, The Exchange Saleroom, Driffield, Yorkshire YO25 7LJ Tel: 01377 253151

DAN • Andrew Dando, 4 Wood Street, Queen Square, Bath, Somerset BA1 2JQ Tel: 01225 422702

DDM * Dickinson Davy & Markham, Wrawby Street, Brigg, Humberside DN20 8JJ Tel: 01652 653666

DN * Dreweatt Neate, Donnington Priory, Donnington, Newbury, Berkshire RG13 2JE Tel: 01635 31234

DUB * Dubey's Art & Antiques, 807 N. Howard Street, Baltimore, MD 21201, USA Tel: 001 410 383 2881

E * Ewbank, Burnt Common Auction Rooms, London Rd, Send, Woking, Surrey GU23 7LN Tel: 01483 223101

EL * Eldreds, Robert C Eldred Co Inc, 1475 Route 6A, East Dennis, Massachusetts 0796, USA 02641 Tel: 001 508 385 3116

FBG * Frank H. Boos Gallery, 420 Enterprise Ct, Bloomfield Hills, Michigan 48302 USA Tel: 001 248 332 1500

GAK * G. A. Key, Aylsham Salerooms, 8 Market Place, Aylsham, Norfolk NR11 6EH Tel: 01263 733195

GAZE * Thomas Wm. Gaze & Son, Diss Auction Rooms, Roydon Road, Diss, Norfolk IP22 3LN Tel: 01379 650306

GBr • Geoffrey Breeze Antiques, 6 George Street, Bath, Somerset BA1 2EH Tel: 01225 466499

GC * Geering & Colyer, Hawkhurst, Kent. Fine Art Department no longer trading

GD • Gilbert & Dale, The Old Chapel, Church Street, Ilchester, Nr Yeovil, Som BA22 8LN Tel: 01935 840464

GeW •† Geoffrey Waters Ltd, F1 to F6 Antiquarius Antiques Centre, 135–141 King's Road, London SW3 4PW Tel: 0171 376 5467

GH * Gardiner Houlgate, The Old Malthouse, Comfortable Place, Upper Bristol Road, Bath, Avon BA1 3AJ Tel: 01225 447933

GHa • No longer trading.

GM * See **MEA**

GOR * Gorringes Auction Galleries, 15 North Street, Lewes, Sussex BN7 2PD Tel: 01273 472503

GRG • Gordon Reece Gallery, Finkle Street, Knaresborough, Yorkshire HG5 8AA Tel: 01423 866219

GSP • Graves, Son & Pilcher, Hove Street, Hove, Sussex BN3 2GL Tel: 01273 735266

GVA • Geoffrey Vann Arcade, Portobello Road, London W11 2QB

HAM * Hamptons Antique & Fine Art Auctioneers, Baverstock House, 93 High St, Godalming, Surrey GU7 1AL Tel: 01483 423567

HCH * Hobbs & Chambers, Market Place, Cirencester, Glos GL7 1QQ Tel: 01285 642420

HDS * HY Duke & Son, Fine Art Salerooms, Dorchester, Dorset DT1 1QS Tel: 01305 265080

HOLL * Dreweatt Neate Holloways, 49 Parsons Street, Banbury, Oxfordshire OX16 8PF Tel: 01295 253197

HSS * Phillips, 20 The Square, Retford, Nottinghamshire, DN22 6XE Tel: 01777 708633

J&L * No longer trading

JH * Jacobs & Hunt, 26 Lavant Street, Petersfield, Hampshire GU32 3EF Tel: 01730 233933

JHW • John Howkins, 1 Dereham Road, Norwich, Norfolk NR2 4HX Tel: 01603 627832

KOT • Stephen Joseph Kotobuki. Tel: 01493 780918

L * Lawrence Fine Art Auctioneers, South Street, Crewkerne, Somerset TA18 8AB Tel: 01460 73041

LAY * David Lay ASVA, Auction House, Alverton, Penzance, Cornwall TR18 4RE Tel: 01736 361414

LG * No longer trading

LHA * Lesley Hindman Auctioneers, 215 West Ohio Street, Chicago, Illinois, IL 60610 USA Tel: 001 312 670 0010

LR • Leonard Russell, 21 King's Avenue, Mount Pleasant, Newhaven, Sussex Tel: 01273 515153

LRG * Lots Road Galleries, 71 Lots Road, London SW10 Tel: 0171 351 7771

LT * Louis Taylor Auctioneers & Valuers, Britannia House, 10 Town Road, Hanley, Stoke-on-Trent, Staffordshire ST1 2QG Tel: 01782 214111

LW * Lawrences Auctioneers, Norfolk House, 80 High Street, Bletchingley, Surrey Tel: 01883 743323

MA • No longer trading

MEA * Mealy's, Chatsworth Street, Castle Comer, Co. Kilkenny, Republic of Ireland Tel: 00 353 564 1229

MER •† Mere Antiques, 13 Fore Street, Topsham, Exeter, Devon EX3 OHF Tel: 01392 874224

MGM * Bonhams West Country, Devon Fine Art Auction House, Dowell Street, Honiton, Devon EX14 8LX Tel: 01404 41872

MJB * Michael J Bowman, 6 Haccombe House, Netherton, Newton Abbot, Devon TQ12 4SJ Tel: 01626 872890

MN * No longer trading

MSW * Marilyn Swain Auctions, The Old Barracks, Sandon Road, Grantham, Lincs NG31 9AS Tel: 01476 568861

N * Neales, 192–194 Mansfield Road, Nottingham, Notts NG1 3HU Tel: 0115 962 4141

N(A) * Amersham Auction Rooms, 125 Station Road, Amersham, Bucks HP7 OAH Tel: 01494 729292

Nam • V. Namdar, Stand B22, Gray's Mews, 1–7 Davies Mews, London W1 Tel: 0171 629 1183

ORI •† Oriental Gallery. Tel: 01451 830944

OT Old Timers, Box 392, Camp Hill, PA 17001-0392 USA Tel: 001 717 761 1908

P * Phillips, 101 New Bond Street, London W1Y OAS Tel: 0171 629 6602

P(Ch) * Phillips Chichester, Baffins Hall, Baffins Lane, Chichester, Sussex PO19 1UA Tel: 01243 787548

P(EA) * Phillips, 32 Boss Hall Road, Ipswich, Suffolk 1P1 59J Tel: 01473 740494

P(HSS) * See **HSS**

P(M) * Phillips, Eaton Place, 114 Washway Road, Sale, Manchester M33 7RF Tel: 0161 962 9237

P(N) * Phillips, Fine Art Auctioneers, Whitefriars House, 52 Fishergate, Norwich, Norfolk NR3 1SE Tel: 01603 616426

P(Re) * See **P(M)**

P(S) * Phillips Fine Art Auctioneers, 49 London Road, Sevenoaks, Kent TN13 1AR Tel: 01732 740310

PC Private Collection

PCh * Peter Cheney, Western Road Auction Rooms, Western Road, Littlehampton, Sussex BN17 5NP Tel: 01903 722264/713418

POA * Proud Oriental Auctions, Proud Galleries, 5 Buckingham St, London WC2N 6BP Tel: 0171 839 4942

POR • Portobello Road Market, London W11 2QB

RBA •† Roger Bradbury Antiques, Church Street, Coltishall, Norfolk NR12 7DJ Tel: 01603 737444

RBB * Russell, Baldwin & Bright, Ryelands Road, Leominster, Hereford HR6 8NZ Tel: 01568 611122

RHa • Robert Hall, 15c Clifford Street, London W1X 1RF Tel: 0171 734 4008

RID * Riddetts of Bournemouth, 26 Richmond Hill, The Square, Bournemouth, Dorset Tel: 01202 555686

RIT * Ritchie Inc, D. & J. Auctioneers & Appraisers, 288 King Street East, Toronto, Ontario, Canada M5A 1K4 Tel: 416 364 1864

S * Sotheby's, 34–35 New Bond Street, London W1A 2AA Tel: 0171 293 5000

S(Am) * Sotheby's Amsterdam, Rokin 102, Amsterdam, Netherlands 1012 KZ Tel: 31 20 550 2200

S(HK) * Sotheby's, Li Po Chun Chambers, 18th Floor, 189 Des Vouex Rd, Hong Kong Tel: 852 524 8121

S(NY) * Sotheby's, 1334 York Avenue, New York USA, NY 10021 Tel: 001 212 606 7000

S(S) * Sotheby's Sussex, Summers Place, Billingshurst, Sussex RH14 9AD Tel: 01403 833500

SIG • Sigma Antiques, Water Skellgate, Ripon, Yorkshire, HG4 1BH Tel: 01765 603163

SK * Skinner Inc, The Heritage On The Garden, 63 Park Plaza, Boston, MA 02116, USA Tel: 001 617 350 5400

SK(B) * Skinner Inc, 357 Main Street, Bolton, MA 01740, USA Tel: 001 508 779 6241

SLN * Sloan's, C. G. Sloan & Company Inc, 4920 Wyaconda Road, North Bethesda, MD 20852, USA Tel: 001 301 468 4911

SPU • Spurrier-Smith Antiques, 28, 39 & 41 Church Street, Ashbourne, Derbyshire DE6 1AJ Tel: 01335 343669

SSW • Spencer Swaffer, 30 High Street, Arundel, Sussex BN18 9AB Tel: 01903 882132

SW • No longer trading

SWO * G. E. Sworder & Sons, 14 Cambridge Road, Stansted Mountfitchet, Essex CM24 8BZ Tel: 01279 817778

TAR • Lorraine Tarrant Antiques, 23 Market Place, Ringwood, Hampshire BH24 1AN Tel: 01425 461123

Wai • Peter Wain. Tel: 01630 638358

WeH • Westerham House Antiques, The Green, Westerham, Kent TN16 1AY Tel: 01959 561622

WHB * William H. Brown, Ashford House, Saxmundham, Suffolk IP17 1AB Tel: 01728 603232

WL * Wintertons Ltd, Lichfield Auction Centre, Wood End Lane, Fradley, Lichfield, Staffordshire WS13 8NF Tel: 01543 263256

WLi • Wakelin & Linfield, PO box 48, Billingshurst, Sussex RH14 OYZ Tel: 01403 700004

WW * Woolley & Wallis, Salisbury Salerooms, 51–61 Castle Street, Salisbury, Wiltshire SP1 3SU Tel: 01722 424500

A Selection of Chinese Dynasties & Marks

Early Dynasties

Neolithic	10th – early 1st millennium BC	Tang Dynasty	AD 618–907
Shang	16th Century–c1050 BC	Five Dynasties	AD 907–960
Zhou	c1050–221 BC	Liao Dynasty	AD 907–1125
Warring States	480–221 BC	Song Dynasty	AD 960–1279
Qin	221–206 BC	*Northern Song*	AD 960–1127
Han	206 BC–AD 220	*Southern Song*	AD 1127–1279
Six Dynasties	AD 222–589	Xixia Dynasty	AD 1038–1227
Wei Dynasty	AD 386–557	Jin Dynasty	AD 1115–1234
Sui Dynasty	AD 581–618	Yuan Dynasty	AD 1279–1368

Ming Dynasty Marks

Hongwu
1368–1398

Yongle
1403–1424

Xuande
1426–1435

Chenghua
1465–1487

Hongzhi
1488–1505

Zhengde
1506–1521

Jiajing
1522–1566

Longqing
1567–1572

Wanli
1573–1619

Tianqi
1621–1627

Chongzhen
1628–1644

Qing Dynasty Marks

Shunzhi
1644–1661

Kangxi
1662–1722

Yongzheng
1723–1735

Qianlong
1736–1795

Jiaqing
1796–1820

Daoguang
1821–1850

Xianfeng
1851–1861

Tongzhi
1862–1874

Guangxu
1875–1908

Xuantong
1909–1911

Hongxian
1916

CHINESE MOTIFS & MARKS

Butterflies: alleged to have a lifespan of 70 or 80 years, butterflies are symbolic of longevity, and are said to represent the spirits of ancestors.

Qilins: mythological beasts, sometimes similar to unicorns, seen as a symbol of grandeur, happiness and joy. It is said that they tread lightly, crushing nothing underfoot and leaving no footprints.

Cranes: symbolic of longevity, and said to be a mode of transport for the Eight Immortals.

Dogs of Fo: Buddhist guardian lions, often playing with a brocaded ball.

Dragons: in Chinese mythology, the dragon is the lord of the skies and bringer of rain. It also is the symbol of goodness, strength and fertility. It is thought that the five-clawed dragon represented the emperor, and four-and three-clawed dragons represented the descent of social status.

Eight Buddhist Emblems: most commonly found on Ming and later ceramics:
Wheel, Conch Shell, Umbrella, Canopy, Lotus, Vase, Paired Fish, and Endless Knot.

Eight Daoist Emblems: the attributes of the Eight Immortals.

Eight Immortals: three were historical characters, five were legendary. They were as follows: Zhungli Quan, He Xiangu, Lan Zaihe, Zao Guozhiu, Han Xiangzi, Li Tieguai, Lu Dongbin, and Zhang Gualao. They are often associated in decoration with Shou Lao, the Star God of Longevity.

Fish: emblems of wealth or abundance. Pairs of fish symbolise marital bliss and harmony.

Horses: represent speed and perseverance.

Phoenixes: emblematic of the empress, also symbolising the warmth of the sun, the harvest and fertility.

Chrysanthemum: represents the 10th month of the lunar calendar, joviality and retirement from public office.

Lingzhi: sacred fungus, symbolic of longevity.

Lotus: emblematic of the 7th month and summer, symbolising happiness in maturity.

Peony: popular in blue and white decoration, representing the 3rd month in the lunar calendar, emblematic of spring, symbolising love and affection, beauty, wealth, honour and happiness.

Prunus: emblematic of the 1st month and winter.

Shou: often found on blue and white wares, symbolises longevity.

The Three Friends, also known as the **Three Friends of Winter**: prunus, pine and bamboo, symbolising winter and longevity, and male qualities. Also symbolic of Daoism, Buddhism and Confusianism.

Willow Trees: said to keep away the influence of evil.

JAPANESE PERIODS & MARKS

Jomon period (Neolithic)	circa 10,000–100 BC	Muromachi (Ashikaga) period	1333–1568
Yayoi period	circa 200 BC–200 AD	Momoyama period	1568–1600
Tumulus (Kofun) period	200–552 AD	Edo (Tokugawa) period	1600–1868
Asuka period	552–710 AD	Genroku period	1688–1703
Nara period	710–794 AD	Meiji period	1868–1911
Heian period	794 AD–1185	Taisho period	1912–1926
Kamakura period	1185–1333	Showa period	1926–1989

Japanese dynastic or reign marks were not used before the 19th century. From c1640 potters often borrowed Chinese Ming reign marks, particularly those of Chenghua and Xuande. Other marks are mainly commendatory or benevolent, for example *fuku* (happiness):

The Kyoto seal mark for Yabu Meizan (1853–1934):

The mark used on many Noritake Nippon wares (c1911–21); 'M' is for Morimura:

CHINESE PRONUNCIATION

Standard (Mandarin) Chinese was, until recently, transcribed into western script according to the Wade-Giles system, devised early this century. This system has now been superseded by the Pinyin system, which tends to give more easily understood phonetic sounds to the Chinese words being represented. Since many books still follow the Wade-Giles system, the comparison given below should help in developing a pronunciation of Chinese terms that is acceptable and can be used with reasonable confidence.

The Sounds

Wade-Giles	Pinyin	Pronounced
ch	zh or j	as in **j**eans
ch'	ch or q	as in **ch**eap or crin**g**e
hs	x	as in **sh**ell
j	r	as in **r**age
k	g or k	as in **g**orse or **c**ore
p	b	as in **b**orn
p'	p	as in **p**our
t	d	as in **d**oor
t'	t	as in **t**orn
ts, tz	z	as in roa**ds**
ts', tz'	c	as in **ts**etse

A Selection of Words

Wade-Giles	Pinyin	Wade-Giles	Pinyin
An hua	anhua	Ching-te Chên	Jingdezhen
Pa Hsien	Baxian	Chi chou	Jizhou
pi	bi	chüeh	jue
Pu Tai	Budai	Chun yao	Junyao
ch'ih lung	chilong	ling chih	lingzhi
Ts'u chou	Cizhou	Lung-ch'üan	Longquan
Te Hua	Dehua	mei-p'ing	meiping
ting	ding	nien tsao	nianzao
Ting yao	Dingyao	ch'i-lin	qilin
Tou ts'ai	doucai	Ju yao	Ruyao
Fukien	Fujian	ju-i	ruyi
Kuan Ti	Guandi	san ts'ai	sancai
kuang	guang	t'ao-t'ieh	taotie
Kuangtung	Guangdong	wu ts'ai	wucai
Kuan yao	Guanyao	yen-yen	yanyan
Kuan yin	Guanyin	ying ch'ing	Yingqing
Honan	Henan	I Hsing	Yixing
chia	jia	Yüeh yao	Yueyao
Chien yao	Jianyao	chung	zhong

INTRODUCTION

Although trade links existed between China and the Roman Empire, it was not until the establishment of the Silk Route through the Central Asian deserts that luxurious and exotic Asian artefacts came to be much admired and sought-after in the West. In the 16th century, the rise of the East India companies produced a dramatic increase in the amount of goods imported into the West from China and Japan. Between 1604 and 1657 the Dutch East India Company alone shipped more than three million pieces of Chinese porcelain. From 1657 the company turned its attention to Japan, from where equally large amounts of porcelain were exported. From 1715 onwards, with the establishment of the Canton *hongs* (warehouses), up to 12 Western countries were importing goods from the East. Large amounts of beautiful ceramics, furniture, paintings, carved ivory, silver, cloisonné enamel, fans, lacquer ware and mother-of-pearl were exported (often acting as ballast in ships) to supplement the main trades of tea and silk.

The active 18th-century trade declined dramatically in the first six decades of the 19th, due to the increase in home manufacture and the imposition of punitive import duties to protect the home market. This all changed when, in 1860, the summer palace of the Chinese Emperor was sacked and looted by French and English troops retaliating for the excesses of the Taiping Rebellion. For the first time, the splendours of the Imperial Court were seen by an appreciative western public, and the magnificent Imperial porcelains and works of art were eagerly sought by western collectors who had previously only seen export wares. This stimulated a general demand for eastern works of art, further fuelled by the success of the Chinese and Japanese stands at the late 19th-century international exhibitions. Large quantities of Japanese and Chinese works of art were imported by fashionable stores such as Liberty's in London, and small exquisite carvings (*okimono*), fine enamel vases and intricate Satsuma pottery wares were eagerly bought by appreciative western collectors during the 'golden age' of Japanese export art (circa 1880–1930).

The mixture of art, refined technical skill and often great age continue to make Chinese and Japanese antiques very desirable to the western collector. Availability and variety mean that there is something to suit every taste and pocket. It is therefore very important that collectors try to aim for the best of their chosen field within their budget. Ten good pieces will ultimately give more satisfaction and pleasure than 100 mediocre pieces. Don't be afraid to 'trade up' – most reputable dealers will be only too pleased to take back items purchased from them against a piece of higher value.

The choice of collecting fields is personal, determined largely by motive: is the collection an investment, for academic study, purely aesthetic, or a mixture of all three? Fakes and copies exist in quantity and may easily deceive the most discerning collector. It is therefore advisable to purchase items from a reputable dealer who is a member of a national trade association which offers guarantees, or from auction houses that offer similar guarantees.

If buying for investment, the condition of the object is very important. Minor damage may not greatly affect the value of antiquities, but can reduce the value of later ceramics and works of art by up to 90 per cent. Look for fine artistry and workmanship, rarity, condition and authenticity, and don't be taken in by fashionable (and often ephemeral) collecting trends.

In China, recent irresponsible and illegal excavation of historical sites has produced a flood of antiquities on to the world market, thus greatly affecting prices. A good Tang Dynasty pottery horse can now be bought for a quarter of what it would have fetched 12 to 15 years ago, and only exceptional pieces can still achieve record prices. World financial trends also greatly affect value. The recent downturn in the Far Eastern economy has resulted in the cancellation of auction sales or very poor results in those that did take place. However, upper levels of the market have remained buoyant, (with most items of $100,000 or more), with the middle market suffering the most.

Chinese furniture is still going up in price as collectors compare quality with relatively low prices. However, large quantities of provincial country furniture are being imported into the West, most of which is of little consequence due to its poor quality, complete refinishing and altered forms. Good paintings, particularly 20th-century examples, also continue to attract high prices as more collectors come into this field. These must only be bought from reputable sources due to the large number of fakes. The very best of the fine Japanese Meiji period *objets d'art* are still very much in demand and will continue to rise in value in the near future. Top-quality 20th-century examples in all media are well worth considering; they will soon belong to 'the last century' and will be viewed in a different light.

In this book we have tried to show a good selection of Chinese and Japanese antiques suitable for collecting. It is a buyer's guide, and not a definitive statement on individual values. Each piece has to be looked at on its own merit.

CHINESE BLUE AND WHITE CERAMICS

B lue and white porcelain is one of the greatest contributions the Chinese have made to world art, and it enjoys a keen appreciation and demand by the international art market. A Chenghua period (1465–87) small blue and white jar with floral motif made a record price of HK$13 million in a Christie's Hong Kong sale of Chinese art in 1991.

The earliest blue and white porcelain was produced in the 8th century AD by the craftsmen of Xiaohuangzi village of Gong County in Henan Province, using cobalt blue imported from Persia. The beautiful blue and white porcelain known today was not perfected until the Yuan Dynasty (1279–1368), when large groups of craftsmen from kilns in Cizhou, Hebei Province, fled the northern war areas and migrated to Jingdezhen in Jiangxi Province in the south. There they continued their established painting skills, using local high-temperature firing techniques and locally mined *luoping* cobalt to produce the porcelain that was to make Jingdezhen famous. Their only criterion was perfection. Production costs being of no concern (and with Court artists involved in the design of patterns) many masterpieces appeared, incorporating traditional motifs and designs influenced by the Persian culture.

During the middle Ming period the supply of imported cobalt stopped, and the local *pitang* cobalt was used. It was calcined and refined to remove impurities, and gave a bright, pure blue without the iron 'black' spots of the earlier periods. Towards the end of the Ming Dynasty (1368–1644), the Europeans began to have influence in the Far East. In 1558 the Macao peninsula was granted to the Portuguese. Blue and white ware was exported to Europe, thus starting the great passion for this fine porcelain, which continues to this day. In 1603 the Dutch captured the Portuguese carrack *Santa Caterina,* and its cargo of fine porcelain, known as *kraak porselein*, was auctioned in Amsterdam, amid great excitement. With the subsequent founding of the Dutch East India Company, there was a huge expansion in the export trade. A good example of *kraak porselein* can still be bought for £400–600.

During the Transitional period (1620–83) Imperial orders diminished and the potters of Jingdezhen had to search for new markets. New shapes, exceptionally good glazes and a high standard of painting all combined to produce a fine range of porcelain, which was much admired in the West. The prices for good Transitional wares range from £1,500–8,000. Some of the best blue and white export porcelain was produced during the second half of the reign of Emperor Kangxi (1662–1722). During this 'golden age' of blue and white production vast quantities of high-quality porcelain were made for the European market and can still be purchased for a relatively modest amount today. A small, perfect wine cup may cost £100, while a large, complete garniture may cost up to £20,000. In the second half of the 18th century huge amounts of blue and white tableware were exported to the West, used as ballast in the holds of tea clippers. This 'Nanking' porcelain, named after the port on the Yangtze river from which it was shipped, was made particularly famous by the sale in 1986 of the 'Nanking cargo' in Amsterdam. Nanking blue and white porcelain can be purchased for as little as £30 for a saucer; any piece from the 'Nanking cargo' carries a small premium.

MING DYNASTY
Bowls & Dishes

A blue and white *kraak porselein* deep dish, Ming Dynasty, 13in (33cm) diam.
£1,000–1,200 *ORI*

l. A blue and white foliate dish, painted in a pencilled style with a design of foaming and swirling waves, dotted with flowerheads, a double-headed eel-form fish to the centre, small rim chip and frits, Jiajing mark, 17thC, 6½in (16.5cm) diam.
£1,000–1,200 *C*

A set of 4 blue and white bowls, damaged, Ming Dynasty, 5½in (14cm) diam.
£350–450 *CSK*

Did You Know?

Distinguishing features of *kraak porselein* are the radial marks on the base. These are known as 'chatter' marks because it is said that the potters gossiped among themselves, rather than concentrating on their work.

A large blue and white saucer dish, Jiajing six-character mark in a line below the rim exterior and of the period, 19½in (49.5cm) diam.
£13,000–15,000 *C*

A blue and white saucer dish, painted in inky blue tones to the interior with a striding five-clawed dragon amidst fire and cloud scrolls, the exterior painted with dragons, encircled Jiajing six-character mark and of the period, 10in (25.5cm) diam.
£7,000–8,000 *C*

A blue and white dish, painted with a leaping carp, chipped and cracked, six-character Jiajing mark and of the period, 8in (20.5cm) diam.
£1,800–2,000 *C*

A blue and white saucer dish, hair crack, encircled Wanli six-character mark and of the period, 6½in (126.5cm) diam.
£1,200–1,400 *C*

An Annamese blue and white bowl, the centre painted with a fish, the exterior with 2 dragons, late 16th/early 17thC, 6in (15cm) diam.
£350–400 *Bea*

A blue and white shaped deep dish, Wanli period, 14½in (37cm) diam.
£1,200–1,400 *CSK*

l. A pair of blue and white *kraak porselein* bowls, one repaired, chips, Wanli period, 14in (35.5cm) diam.
£2,000–2,500 *C*

A blue and white bowl, fritted, cracked, encircled mark '*fu gui jia qi*', late 16thC, 15in (38cm) diam, with fitted box.
£2,000–2,500 *C*

The mark translates as 'fine vessel for the rich and honourable'.

r. A blue and white *kraak porselein* bowl, fritted, Wanli period, 14½in (37cm) diam.
£1,800–2,200 *CSK*

Two blue and white dishes, each painted to the centre with a flowerhead and cell pattern, Tianqi period, 8½in (21.5cm) diam.
£1,200–1,400 *CSK*

l. A blue and white *lianzu* bowl, boldly painted in deep underglaze blue tones with 'heaping and piling' on the interior, the exterior with a frieze of narrow petal flutes , minor damage, Xuande period, 8in (20.5cm) diam.
£22,000–24,000 *S(HK)*

r. A pair of *kraak porselein* dishes, with grasshopper designs, Wanli period, 6in (15cm) diam.
£800–1,000 *ORI*

A blue and white fruit bowl, the exterior painted in strong underglaze blue, with darker 'heaping and piling' effect, the interior glazed white, frit on rim, Xuande mark and of the period, the mark written in a line below the rim, 11½in (29cm) diam.
£82,000–90,000 *S*

These distinctive Ming bowls appear to have been made for a very short time, as they all have the Xuande reign marks below the rim. They were painted in a number of different designs, including flower scrolls, such as tree peony, rose, stylised lotus or lingzhi fungus. Although experts are uncertain of their exact use it has been suggested that these shallow bowls with 'finger thick' walls served scholars as brush washers. They may also have been used for playing dice in the palace, or for cricket fights, popular in the Ming Dynasty, for which the extreme thickness of the bowls would render them ideal for a battle!

Boxes

A blue and white box and cover, painted with a dragon, cover restored, encircled six-character Jiajing mark and of the period, 6½in (16.5cm) diam.
£1,500–2,000 *C*

A blue and white five-lobed box, damaged, Wanli mark and of the period, 5½in (14cm) diam.
£10,000–12,000 *S(HK)*

l. A pierced blue and white box and cover, the cover with a scene of 16 boys, Wanli mark and of the period, 12½in (32cm) wide.
£50,000–55,000 *S(HK)*

Censers

l. A Transitional blue and white tripod censer, painted vividly with Daoist Immortals and monks, Jiajing six-character mark, c1640, 7½in (19cm) diam.
£4,000–5,000 *C*

A blue and white tripod censer, cracked, Wanli/Tianqi period, 7in (18cm) diam.
£1,000–1,200 *CSK*

l. A blue and white tripod censer, Ming Dynasty, 10in (25.5cm) diam.
£500–550 *CSK*

A blue and white lobed tripod censer, with S-shaped handles, painted with panels of seated Immortals, Ming Dynasty, 4¼in (11cm) high.
£700–800 *CSK*

Cups

A blue and white stem-cup, painted in bright tones, cracked and restored, Zhengde six-character mark in a line to the foot interior and of the period, 6½in (16.5cm) diam.
£4,500–5,000 *C*

A Transitional blue and white stem-cup, 17thC, 3½in (9cm) diam.
£800–1,000 *Wai*

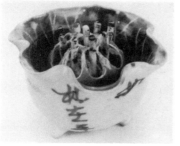

A Transitional blue and white tripod surprise cup, modelled in the shape of a lotus leaf, the exterior with a poem, mid-17thC, 2½in (6.5cm) diam.
£1,200–1,500 *CAm*

A Transitional blue and white cup, on tall spreading foot, painted with a bird in flight beside pine, prunus and bamboo, incised collector's mark, c1650, 6in (15cm) high.
£1,200–1,500 *C*

l. A Transitional blue and white stem-cup, painted with a bird on a peony branch, insects and a butterfly, with an incised foliate band below the rim, c1650, 5in (12.5cm) high.
£3,700–4,500 *C*

Ewers & Kendi

A blue and white *kendi*, the body decorated with flowering lotus sprays, restored, early Ming Dynasty, 4½in (11.5cm) high.
£5,500–6,000 *S(NY)*

A blue and white ewer, minor fritting, early 17thC, 7½in (19cm) diam.
£2,500–3,500 *C*

A blue and white *kraak*-type *kendi*, Wanli period, 7½in (19cm) high.
£1,200–1,400 *CSK*

A blue and white *kendi*, Wanli period, 7½in (19cm) high.
£1,300–1,500 *Bea*

A blue and white *kendi*, painted with fish below a band of flowerheads and lappets at the shoulder, chipped and cracked, Wanli period, 7in (17.5cm) high.
£2,000–2,500 *CSK*

A blue and white *kendi*, damaged, Ming Dynasty, 6in (15cm) high.
£1,000–1,100 *CSK*

A blue and white *kendi*, delicately potted, Wanli period, 7in (17.5cm) high.
£2,500–3,000 *C*

A blue and white *kendi*, painted with alternating panels of peonies and horses above foaming waves, the neck with prunus, some fritting, Wanli period, 8½in (21.5cm) high.
£700–800 *CSK*

A blue and white *kraak porselein kendi*, modelled as a frog, its mouth forming the spout, some fritting, Wanli period, 7in (17.5cm) high.
£10,000–12,000 *C*

A Transitional blue and white serpent-stretcher metal-mounted ewer, painted on both sides, mounts Indonesian or Near Eastern and later, 15in (38cm) high.
£2,500–3,000 *C*

A Transitional blue and white ewer, painted with flowersprays, 9in (23cm) high.
£1,000–1,200 *WHB*

A Transitional blue and white ewer, with short spout and 4 lug mask handles, restored, cover missing, 14in (35.5cm) high.
£1,200–1,500 *CSK*

Flatware

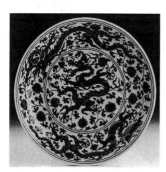

A blue and white dragon dish, with rounded sides and flaring rim, painted in strong tones with a five-clawed dragon amid a lotus meander and flame scrolls, surrounded by 2 striding dragons, the reverse with similar dragons above *ruyi* lappets, slight damage, Zhengde four-character mark and of the period, 9½in (24cm) diam.
£28,000–33,000 *C*

It is unusual to find a Zhengde dish of this size and design, which is seen as one of the trademarks of this period.

Buying Tips

When buying Chinese porcelain, there are certain facts to be considered. Firstly, the condition of the piece is important. This affects the price considerably, as a very good piece with a hairline crack or small chip can be reduced in value by up to two-thirds. The rarity of the item is also important. Rare items fetch considerably more than their common counterparts. Most of the high prices for Chinese porcelain come from the Hong Kong salerooms. The Far Eastern buyer tends to collect the pieces made by the Chinese potters for their own internal market, rather than export ware made for the European trade.

A blue and white saucer, cracked, Xuande mark and of the period, 4½in (11.5cm) diam.
£20,000–25,000 *S(NY)*

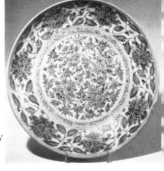

r. A blue and white dish, centrally painted with 4 peony heads, minutely fritted, c1500, 20in (51cm) diam.
£2,000–2,500 *C*

A blue and white saucer dish, painted in underglaze blue, extensively restored, early Ming Dynasty, 16in (40.5cm) diam.
£4,000–5,000 *S*

A blue and white Swatow dish, painted with phoenix and foliage within a border of scattered flowers, slight damage, 16thC, 11in (30cm) diam.
£300–350 *CSK*

A Swatow dish, painted in white slip on a light blue ground with flowers and leaves, the well with 4 floral motifs with a floral scroll, 16thC, 15in (38cm) diam.
£2,300–2,500 *S*

A blue and white saucer dish, Jiajing six-character mark and late in the period, 14in (35.5cm) diam.
£2,000–2,500 *C*

A blue and white saucer dish, the exterior painted with a frieze of boys at play, the interior with similar theme, slight damage, Jiajing six-character mark and of the period, 5½in (14cm) diam.
£4,400–4,800 *C(HK)*

A blue and white saucer dish, the interior painted with 3 *lingzhi* and cloud scrolls, slight damage, drilled six-point collector's mark on base, Wanli mark and of the period, 7in (18cm) diam.
£4,200–4,700 *S(HK)*

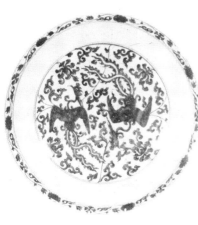

r. A *kraak porselein* blue and white charger, decorated with birds, fruits and flowers, restored, Wanli period, 18½in (47cm) diam.
£780–820 *S(Am)*

l. A blue and white saucer dish, painted within a double circle, the border with stylised trailing flowers, the reverse with 6 cranes divided by stylised clouds, 16thC, 17in (43cm) diam.
£2,000–2,500 *CSK*

A blue and white dish, damaged, Wanli period, 17in (43cm) diam.
£500–700 *CSK*

A blue and white *kraak porselein* dish, repaired, Wanli period, 20in (51cm) diam.
£1,000–1,200 *CSK*

A blue and white saucer dish, with lobed floral rim, each moulded lobe with a floral spray, the exterior with emblems, minor fritting, Wanli period, 8½in (21.5cm) diam.
£1,200–1,500 *C*

A blue-ground dish, firing crack, Jiajing mark and of the period, 13in (33cm) diam.
£75,000–80,000 *S(HK)*

This is an extremely rare and attractive Imperial saucer dish from the early 16thC.

A blue and white saucer dish, painted with scrolling pencilled lotus washed in a greyish-blue, Wanli six-character mark and of the period, 6in (15cm) diam, in a fitted box.
£2,500–3,000 *C*

A blue and white dish, chipped, late 16thC, 16½in (42cm) diam.
£1,500–2,000 *C*

A blue and white *kraak porselein* dish, minor fritting, Wanli period, 19½in (49.5cm) diam, with fitted box.
£3,000–3,500 *C*

Two blue and white saucer dishes, fritted, Wanli period, 8in (20cm) diam.
£1,000–1,100 *C*

A Swatow blue and white dish, painted with a roundel of 2 deer in a landscape, the everted rim with trellis pattern, wave pattern and panels of stylised flowers, rim chips, c1600, 16in (40.5cm) diam.
£650–750 *CSK*

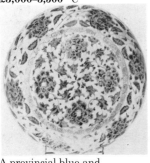

A provincial blue and white saucer dish, c1600, 16½in (42cm) diam.
£2,000–2,500 *CSK*

A blue and white *kraak porselein* dish, fritted and cracked, c1620, 18½in (47cm) diam.
£2,500–3,000 *C*

A blue and white *kraak porselein* dish, small chips to rim, Wanli period, 14in (35.5cm) diam.
£1,500–2,000 *C*

A blue and white *kraak* dish, Wanli period, 11½in (29cm) diam.
£700–800 *CSK*

r. A blue and white saucer dish, painted with a central roundel of a vase, the border with butterflies in flight among flowering and fruiting branches, fritted, Xuande mark, Wanli period, 11in (28cm) diam.
£800–1,000 *CSK*

A blue and white *kraak porselein* dish, painted in vivid blue tones at the centre, within a band of trellis and cell pattern divided by half flowerheads, the well decorated with quatrefoil lappets of flowers and fruit below the foliate rim, the exterior with similar lappets, fritted, Wanli period, 18in (45.5cm) diam.
£4,000–4,500 *C*

A blue and white dish, painted within a well of trailing foliage, the border with alternate panels of travellers in landscapes, minor frits, c1630, 14in (35.5cm) diam.
£2,000–2,500 *CSK*

A blue and white dish, with scroll border, early 17thC, 8in (20.5cm) diam.
£500–600 *WW*

A blue and white moulded saucer dish, made for the Japanese market, Chenghua six-character mark, Tianqi period, 8½in (21.5cm) diam.
£1,200–1,500 *CAm*

A Transitional blue and white dish, painted with a warrior and 2 dignitaries on a terrace, damaged, mid-17thC, 19in (48.5cm) diam.
£2,500–3,000 *CAm*

Five blue and white *kraak* plates, each painted variously to the centre, minor chips, Wanli period, 8½in (21.5cm) diam.
£800–1,000 *CSK*

A pair of blue and white saucer dishes, decorated with geese on a riverbank, Chongzhen period, 6in (15cm) diam.
£800–1,000 *C*

A blue and white saucer dish, the exterior with 5 lotus sprays, encircled six-character mark, mid-17thC, 6in (15cm) diam.
£1,000–1,500 *CAm*

A blue and white *Shonsui*-type dish, with wavy brown dressed rim, painted with alternate panels of cell pattern, bamboo and cloud scrolls, the reverse with flowerheads and scrolling foliage, Chenghua mark, Chongzhen period, 8in (20.5cm) diam.
£800–1,000 *C*

r. A Transitional blue and white saucer dish, painted with a ferocious *qilin* breathing flames, the base with four-character mark, c1650, 14in (35.5cm) diam.
£1,400–1,800 *C*

Did You Know?

The peak of blue and white porcelain art was reached at the beginning of the Ming Dynasty (1368–1644), with the establishment of the Imperial kilns at Jingdezhen.

A Transitional blue and white shallow dish, the centre painted with deer in a landscape, the rim with a band of insects, flowers and foliage, 2 hair cracks, minor glaze chipping to rim, 17½in (44.5cm) diam.
£400–600 *Bea*

Jars

l. A pair of blue and white oviform jars and domed covers, painted with figures standing in continuous rocky landscapes below bands of leaves at the shoulders, Yuan/early Ming Dynasty, 5in (12.5cm) high.
£600–700 *CSK*

A blue and white oviform jar and domed cover, Yuan/early Ming Dynasty, 5½in (14cm) high.
£800–1,000 *CSK*

A blue and white jar, decorated in vivid underglaze blue, the flat unglazed base spotted with orange and brown, Ming Dynasty, 12in (30.5cm) high.
£3,500–4,000 *S*

A blue and white jar, fritted, mid-17thC, 18in (45.5cm) high.
£2,500–3,000 *C*

A Transitional blue and white oviform jar, painted in inky blue tones with a continuous scene from *Sanguo Yanyi*, with *anhua* bands, c1640, 12in (30.5cm) high.
£3,500–4,000 *C*

l. A blue and white *kraak porselein* jar and cover, c1650, 6½in (16.5cm) high.
£1,200–1,500 *Wai*

A blue and white jar, painted around the sides in vivid underglaze blue, neck replaced, firing cracks from base, Jiajing mark and of the period, 15½in (39.5cm) high.
£7,000–8,000 *S*

A blue and white baluster jar, with metal-bound rim, Jiajing six-character mark and of the period, 13in (33cm) high.
£8,000–10,000 *C*

A blue and white oviform jar, painted in bright tones, with dot lappets at the foot and cloud and pendant dot lappets at the shoulder, the tapering neck with stylised wave motifs, restored, Jiajing six-character mark and of the period, 9in (23cm) high.
£8,000–10,000 *C*

A blue and white jar, neck reduced, Jiajing six-character mark in a double square and of the period, 4½in (11.5cm) high.
£2,000–2,500 *C*

l. A blue and white baluster jar, painted with flowers below *ruyi* heads and key-pattern at the shoulder and short neck, 16thC, 4in (10cm) high.
£500–600 *CSK*

A blue and white jar, painted in underglaze blue of brilliant tone, the short neck with a diaper band, reserved with barbed *shou* characters, the base unglazed, exterior wear, Jiajing/Wanli period, 19in (48.5cm) high.
£18,000–22,000 S

A blue and white jar, decorated with a scene of an Immortal in a continuous landscape, minor fritting at rim, Wanli mark and of the period, 4in (10cm) high.
£4,000–5,000 S(HK)

A Swatow blue and white jar, painted in greyish-blue tones, 17thC, 10½in (26.5cm) high.
£2,500–3,000 C

r. A blue and white quatrefoil jar, painted overall with scrolling peonies and leaves below a band of key fret to the neck, damaged, 17thC, 7in (17.5cm) high.
£250–300 CSK

A blue and white jar, painted on a cell ground with 4 lion mask handles, base restored, cracks, Wanli period, 13½in (34.5cm) high.
£1,300–1,500 C

A blue and white jar and cover, slight damage, Ming Dynasty, 18½in (47cm) high.
£2,800–3,400 S

A Transitional blue and white jar and cover, glaze scratched, rim crack, c1640, 10in (25.5cm) high.
£800–1,000 CSK

A blue and white jar, painted with a bird perched on rock between peony and chrysanthemums, above a band of whorl pattern, Wanli period, 8½in (21.5cm) high.
£1,200–1,400 C

A blue and white baluster jar and cover, painted with 4 oval scenes illustrating Daoist influenced stories, damaged, Tianqi period, c1625, 19in (48.5cm) high.
£3,800–4,200 C

Covered Jars

All jars were originally supplied with covers. Many covers were very loose and badly fitted and have subsequently been lost. Having the original cover can increase the value of a jar by up to thirty per cent.

A Transitional blue and white oviform jar, rim interior with shallow chip, c1650, 9½in (24cm) high.
£2,500–3,000 C

A Transitional blue and white oviform jar, painted with 2 *qilins* beside rockwork and plaintain on a terrace, rim crack, c1643, 10in (25.5cm) high, with wooden cover.
£2,000–2,500 *C*

A Transitional blue and white jar and cover, decorated beneath a band of leaves on the neck, the cover decorated with 3 figures on a terrace, cover restored, vase cracked, c1650, 12in (30.5cm) high.
£2,000–2,500 *C*

A Transitional oviform jar, c1640, 11⅜in (29cm) high.
£1,500–2,000 *C*

A Transitional blue and white jar, decorated with flowers and leaves, damaged, 10in (25.5cm) high.
£400–500 *CSK*

A blue and white jar, damaged, 17thC, 16in (40.5cm) high.
£1,000–1,200 *CSK*

A blue and white baluster jar, painted with a continuous garden scene below stylised clouds or *lingzhi* scrolls, reserved on a dense diaper ground around the slightly flaring neck, firing cracks to shoulder, Ming Dynasty, 14in (35.5cm) high.
£25,000–30,000 *C*

Vases

l. A blue and white vase, encircled Jiajing six-character mark and of the period, 9½in (24cm) high.
£1,500–2,000 *C*

A blue and white vase, painted in strong blue tones, the neck with foliate scrolls, rim chip, c1500, 5in (12.5cm) high.
£1,200–1,500 *C*

r. A blue and white jar, reserved on dense diaper cell ground above a border of lappets to the foot, copper band fitted to the damaged neck, Wanli period, 15in (38cm) high.
£750–1,000 *Bon*

A blue and white double gourd painted vase, below a band of stiff leaves to the neck, cracked, Wanli period, 11½in (29cm) high.
£200–300 *CSK*

A blue and white pear-shaped vase, *yuhuchunping*, painted with flowerheads, the rim with silver gilt mount, Jiajing four-character mark and of the period, 13in (33cm) high.
£3,300–3,700 *C*

l. A blue and white *gu*-shaped vase, painted in inky-blue tones, base missing, Wanli six-character mark at the rim and of the period, 28½in (72.5cm) high.
£3,500–4,000 *C*

A blue and white *meiping*, damaged, Wanli period, 17½in (44.5cm) high.
£1,000–1,200 *C*

A blue and white *kraak* bottle vase, painted with panels of leaping horses and flowering shrubs below a band of lappets, glaze fault, Wanli period, 11in (28cm) high.
£1,000–1,200 *CSK*

A blue and white double gourd vase, Wanli period, 10½in (26.5cm) high.
£1,200–1,500 *Bea*

A double gourd vase, painted in underglaze blue with sprays of camellia and peony, body cracks, 16thC, the red enamel probably later, 13½in (34.5cm) high.
£1,000–1,500 *C*

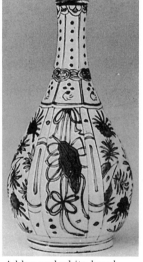

A blue and white *kraak*-style bottle vase, painted with alternating panels of precious objects and flowers issuing from rockwork, damaged and repaired, Wanli period, 12in (30.5cm) high, on a wooden stand.
£400–450 *CSK*

A pair of blue and white *kraak porselein* double gourd vases, moulded and decorated on the exterior, one neck cracked and chipped, Wanli period, 12in (30.5cm) high.
£3,500–4,000 *C*

A Transitional blue and white sleeve vase, decorated in underglaze blue, the base unglazed, slight wear, 19in (48.5cm) high.
£3,000–3,500 *S*

Two Transitional blue and white bottle vases, the tall flaring neck painted with flowersprays, one with 2 insects in flight, c1640, 13½in (34.5cm) high.
£3,500–4,000 *C*

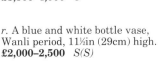

r. A blue and white bottle vase, Wanli period, 11½in (29cm) high.
£2,000–2,500 *S(S)*

A pair of blue and white vases, *meiping*, minor fritting, Wanli/Tianqi period, 10½in (26.5cm) high, with wooden stands and fitted boxes.
£4,500–5,500 *C*

A Transitional blue and white vase and cover, damaged, 18½in (47cm) high.
£2,000–2,500 *CSK*

A Transitional rouleau vase, decorated in underglaze blue with a continuous river landscape, the neck with flowering prunus, cracked, late Ming Dynasty, 19in (48.5cm) high.
£1,300–1,500 *DN*

A Transitional blue and white ovoid vase, cover missing, 9½in (24cm) high, with a stand.
£1,400–1,800 *CSK*

A pair of *kraak porselein* vases, late Ming Dynasty, 4½in (11.5cm) high.
£160–180 *HCH*

A Transitional blue and white vase, decorated with ducks, a kingfisher and flowering plants, 10in (25.5cm) high.
£1,500–2,000 *DN*

A blue and white double gourd vase, painted on the lower body with a scene from the Romance of the Three Kingdoms, frits at rim, Chongzhen period, 13½in (34.5cm) high.
£3,500–4,000 *C*

A Transitional blue and white *gu*-shaped vase, slight rim chip, 8½in (21.5cm) high.
£800–1,000 *Bon*

A Transitional blue and white vase, with non-matching cover, 17thC, 10in (25.5cm) high.
£650–800 *Bon*

r. A Transitional blue and white vase, rim frits, c1650, 8in (20.5cm) high.
£1,200–1,500 *C*

Transitional Blue and White Porcelain

The Transitional period bridges the Ming and Qing Dynasties (c1620–60). This high-quality porcelain is distinguished by its well-made shapes and high standard of painting. The glaze is exceptionally good. The decoration runs freely over the surface and there is often a finely incised border above and below the main decoration.

A Transitional blue and white beaker vase, rim polished, foot rim fritted, c1650, 8½in (21.5cm) high.
£800–1,200 *C*

Miscellaneous

A blue and white *kraak porselein* bottle, frit chip and firing crack to rim, Wanli period, 11in (28cm) high.
£750–900 *C*

A pair of blue and white pear-shaped bottles, painted with panels of flowering shrubs below hanging tassels and lappets, Wanli period, 5½in (14cm) high.
£1,000–1,200 *CSK*

A blue and white drum-shaped brush holder, painted in pale underglaze blue, minor cracks, c1500, 4½in (11.5cm) diam.
£1,000–1,200 *CNY*

A blue and white brush rest, moulded in high relief, firing cracks around base, Wanli six-character mark and of the period, 6½in (16.5cm) wide.
£8,500–10,000 *S(HK)*

A Transitional blue and white candlestick, restored, 13in (33cm) high, on a wooden base, drilled.
£4,500–5,500 *CSK*

A Transitional blue and white brush pot, painted with 2 scholars admiring the moon and stars, c1650, 7½in (19cm) high.
£1,800–2,200 *C(HK)*

A blue and white jardinière, vividly painted in bright blue tones, Wanli period, 13in (33cm) diam.
£4,000–4,500 *C*

A blue and white figure of Guanyin, damaged, Wanli period, 16in (40.5cm) high.
£1,400–1,600 *C*

A blue and white jardinière, damaged, Jiajing six-character mark and of the period, 16½in (42cm) diam.
£6,500–7,000 *C*

r. A blue and white pierced two-tiered stand, painted with blue wash outlines, cracked and chipped, Zhengde period, 10in (25.5cm) high.
£2,000–2,200 *C*

l. A blue and white garden seat, with lion mask handles, some restoration, Wanli period, 15in (38cm) high.
£2,600–3,000 *C*

A blue and white memorial tablet, with fifteen-line inscription, Jiajing mark and of the period, 12in (30.5cm) high.
£2,500–3,000 *C*

QING DYNASTY

In order to distinguish Ming porcelain from the later Qing wares it is necessary to appreciate the technical rather than the decorative differences between the two. The Qing decorators frequently copied ancestral designs with great accuracy, therefore making it difficult to attribute certain pieces. With certain exceptions Ming porcelain is more heavily glazed, giving a blue or green tint. Rarely is the glaze evenly applied, and if carefully examined one can detect runs and dribbles of excess glaze. Most Qing wares are covered in a glaze of uniform thickness. The Kangxi potters achieved a pure white appearance by only coating the vessel in a thin and even wash. The reigns of Yongzheng and Qianlong did, however, witness some pieces that were deliberately covered in a thick glaze in order to emulate the early 15th-century porcelains.

Other signs of age can be found on footrims: those on Ming wares were generally knife-pared and little effort was made to remove the facets left by the blade; most, if not all, Qing pieces were smoothed after the trimming. The footrims on Ming dishes or bowls are for the most part higher than Qing examples; those on Ming wares will generally manifest a narrow orange zone abutting the edge of the glaze, caused by the presence of iron in the porcelain.

Later Chinese wares tended to be mass-produced for export, often to specific demands from traders. It is on these items that potters frequently used the marks of earlier dynasties. This was not the work of a faker, since the Chinese believed they should venerate the skills of previous generations. Accordingly, they marked a piece with the reign-mark of the Emperor they wished to honour.

Bowls

A blue and white bowl and cover, with metal handles and finial, Kangxi period, 8in (20.5cm) high.
£850–1,000 CSK

A blue and white bowl, with rounded sides and slightly everted rim, painted to the exterior with birds, under a sky with a star constellation, small chip, Kangxi six-character mark and of the period, 8in (20.5cm) diam.
£1,700–2,000 C

A blue and white moulded foliate stem bowl, Kangxi period, 8in (20.5cm) diam.
£1,000–1,200 C

A blue and white dragon and phoenix bowl, Kangxi six-character mark and of the period, 5½in (14cm) diam.
£4,500–5,000 C

l. A blue and white moulded foliate bowl, reserved on a diaper pattern ground at the rim, chips, crack and restoration, seal mark to the base, Kangxi period, 13⅓in (34cm) diam.
£1,300–1,500 C

A blue and white bowl, the exterior decorated with panels of flowers beneath a diaper border, the interior with a deer, crane and other longevity symbols, artemisia mark, Kangxi period, 10¼in (26cm) diam.
£700–800 WW

A large blue and white bowl, painted overall with various fish, Kangxi period, 21in (53.5cm) diam.
£4,500–5,000 S

A blue and white bowl, painted on the exterior with *ruyi* lappets, the interior with a central peony roundel beneath a band of trellis and swastika reserved with cartouches, rim frits, the base with square seal mark, Kangxi period, 14in (35cm) diam.
£1,700–2,000 C

Brush Pots

A blue and white brush pot, decorated with a continuous river landscape, on 3 cloud scroll feet, Kangxi period, 8in (20cm) high.
£1,700–1,900 *DN*

A blue and white brush pot, painted in bright blue tones with a scene of a scholarly gathering, rim firing crack, early Kangxi period, 7in (18cm) diam.
£3,000–3,500 *C*

A blue and white brush pot, 2 panels painted in rich blue, Kangxi period, 5½in (13.5cm) high.
£1,800–2,200 *C*

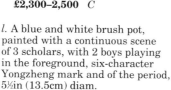

A blue and white brush pot, painted with *qilong* among scrolling foliage, fritted, Kangxi four-character mark and of the period, 7in (18cm) high.
£1,500–2,000 *CSK*

A blue and white brush pot, painted with a continuous landscape, the base with 3 short bracket feet, Kangxi period, 8½in (22cm) diam.
£2,300–2,500 *C*

A blue and white brush pot, painted with a mythical beast seated among censers, vases of lotus, precious objects, *ruyi* sceptres, scrolls and bowls of fruit, fritting, Kangxi period, 6in (15cm) high.
£800–1,000 *CSK*

l. A blue and white brush pot, painted with a continuous scene of 3 scholars, with 2 boys playing in the foreground, six-character Yongzheng mark and of the period, 5½in (13.5cm) diam.
£45,000–50,000 *S(HK)*

Candlesticks

A pair of blue and white silver-shaped candlesticks, one stem restored, Qianlong period, 7½in (19cm) high.
£2,000–2,500 *C*

A blue and white candlestick, made for the Middle Eastern market, with tapering ribbed neck, painted overall with bands of stylised calligraphy, early 18thC, 6½in (16.5cm) high.
£500–600 *CSK*

A pair of blue and white silver-shaped candlesticks, painted with ladies and deer in landscapes, with borders of stylised foliage, one damaged, Qianlong period, 9in (23cm) high.
£2,000–2,500 *CSK*

Cups

l. A Chinese export blue and white

l. A Chinese export blue and white teabowl and saucer, painted with Neptune and attendants, 18thC, saucer 4½in (11.5cm) diam.
£650–800 *CSK*

A blue and white teabowl and saucer, from the 'Nanking' cargo, c1750, saucer 4½in (12cm) diam.
£90–120 *CAm*

Flatware

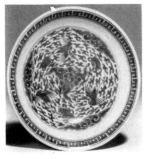

A blue and white cup, painted with the Eight Immortals and their attributes, *Shoulao* riding a deer and *Xiwangmu* on a phoenix, rim chip restored, Yongzheng six-character mark and of the period, 4in (10cm) diam.
£1,000–1,500 *C*

l. A blue and white saucer dish, minor rim chips, four-character mark '*yu tang jia qi*' within a double circle, 17thC, 14in (35.5cm) diam.
£1,500–2,000 *C*
The mark reads 'fine vessel for jade hall'.

A blue and white saucer dish, six-character mark, early Kangxi period, 7in (18cm) diam.
£700–900 *C*

A pair of blue and white dishes, fritting at rims, one small chip, blue leaf mark within a double circle, Kangxi period, 13½in (34.5cm) diam.
£2,000–2,500 *C*

A set of 6 Chinese export blue and white dishes, Kangxi period, 5in (12.5cm) diam.
£800–1,000 *Wai*

Two blue and white Japanese style plates decorated in the manner of Frederik van Frytom copying a Dutch Delft original, the pattern traditionally known as Deshima Island, one chipped, one fritted, one with imitation Japanese spur marks, late 17th/early 18thC, 7½in (19cm) diam.
£800–1,000 *C*

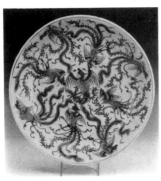

A blue and white dish, painted overall with phoenix, the underside with the Eight Precious Things, slight damage, Kangxi period, 15in (38cm) diam.
£500–550 *CSK*

A blue and white *Rotterdam Riot* plate, painted with a scene representing the demolished house of Jacob van Zuylen, 2 small rim chips, Chenghua six-character mark, Kangxi period, 8in (20cm) diam.
£1,200–1,600 *CSK*

A dish in the form of a peach with short-lipped upright sides, painted in underglaze blue heightened in copper red, the base underglazed, cracked from firing fault in rim, Kangxi period, 10in (25.5cm) diam.
£1,500–2,000 *S*

A pair of blue and white fluted dishes, with barbed rims, 2 small cracks, Chenghua six-character marks, Kangxi period, 8in (20.5cm) diam.
£500–700 *CSK*

Two blue and white armorial plates, rim chips, Kangxi period, 10in (25.5cm) diam.
£2,500–3,000 *C*

A blue and white plate, painted with 2 ladies within a trellis pattern border reserved with panels of fruit, Kangxi six-character mark and of the period, 8in (20.5cm) diam.
£800–1,000 *CSK*

A blue and white saucer dish, Chenghua mark, Kangxi period, 6in (15cm) diam.
£200–300 *Wai*

A blue and white saucer dish, with slightly flared rim painted, chipped, Kangxi period, 16in (40.5cm) diam.
£500–600 *CSK*

Fifteen blue and white plates, each painted with a central flower-spray medallion within a dense panel of flowers and foliage, most with small chips or frits, Kangxi period, 10in (25.5cm) diam.
£800–1,100 *CSK*

r. A blue and white deep dish, painted at the centre, reserved on a key-pattern ground in the well and at the foliate border, fritted, encircled Kangxi six-character mark and of the period, 13½in (34cm) diam.
£1,700–2,200 *C*

r. A pair of blue and white saucer dishes, Chenghua six-character marks, Kangxi perod, 6in (15cm) diam.
£1,000–1,200 *CSK*

A blue and white deep moulded dish, painted with stylised scrolling flowers and leaves, small restoration, Kangxi period, 19½in (49.5cm) diam.
£1,000–1,200 *CSK*

A blue and white dish, painted at the centre and reserved on a key pattern ground within a foliate rim, fritted, Kangxi six-character mark and of the period, 13½in (34.5cm) diam.
£2,200–2,700 *C*

A blue and white charger, painted with prunus trees, bamboo and *lingzhi*, cracked and rim ground, Kangxi period, 22in (56cm) diam.
£1,000–1,200 *CSK*

A blue and white saucer dish, Kangxi period, 13⅛in (33.5cm) diam.
£2,500–3,000 *C*

A set of 4 Chinese blue and white deep dishes, with everted rims painted to the centres and borders with fruit sprays, Kangxi period, 7½in (19cm) diam.
£1,000–1,500 *CSK*

r. A pair of blue and white moulded deep plates, each painted at the centre with a crab among shells and water fronds, below a deep moulded border with wavy rim painted with fish, the reverse with further sprays, Kangxi period, 8in (20.5cm) diam.
£1,500–2,000 *C*

A blue and white dish, small rim chips, cracks to base, Chenghua mark, Kangxi period, 15in (38cm) diam.
£1,800–2,000 *C*

Two enamelled and underglaze blue and white armorial plates, painted at the centre with the gilt cypher 'S.W.' on a central underglaze blue medallion beneath a simple coat-of-arms at the plain border, rim crack, star crack, gilding worn, Kangxi period, largest 14in (35cm) diam.
£1,200–1,500 *C*

The arms are those of Winder, seated originally in Cumberland.

l. A blue and white dish, with underglaze copper-red, painted to the interior with a sage and attendant, below a three-line inscription, rim crack, minute glaze chip, early Kangxi period, 10in (25.5cm) diam.
£2,000–2,500 *C*

A blue and white dish, decorated with fruit-sprays, on double foot rim, restored crack, Kangxi period, 14½in (37cm) diam.
£1,000–1,500 *C*

A blue and white bowl, with underglaze copper-red, haircrack sealed, underglaze blue mark to base, Kangxi period, 8in (20.5cm) diam.
£2,000–2,500 *C*

A blue and white saucer dish, with a commendation mark, Kangxi period, 9½in (24cm) diam.
£650–800 *Wai*

A pair of blue and white saucer dishes, boldly painted on a scale-pattern ground, Kangxi period, 15in (38cm) diam.
£1,200–1,500 *C*

A blue and white foliate saucer dish, painted in inky-blue tones, chips to rim, Chenghua six-character mark, Kangxi period, 6½in (16.5cm) diam.
£900–1,000 *C*

A blue and white dish, fritted, leaf mark, Kangxi period, 20in (51cm) diam.
£5,000–6,000 *C*

l. A set of 12 blue and white plates, some damage, 18thC, 9in (23cm) diam.
£850–1,000 *CSK*

A pair of blue and white saucer dishes, centrally painted below trellis ground floral panels at the compass points, slight damage, Kangxi period, 14in (35.5cm) diam.
£1,300–1,500 *C*

A pair of blue and white saucer dishes, painted with The Arbour pattern after a design by Cornelis Pronk, one with chips, c1735, 9in (22.5cm) diam.
£4,500–5,500 *C*

r. A blue and white dish, painted in the early Ming style, Yongzheng period, 13in (33cm) diam.
£1,000–1,200 *C*

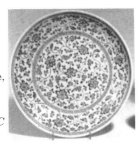

Cornelis Pronk

Cornelis Pronk was appointed by the Dutch East India Company in 1734 as a designer. He only worked for a brief period (possibly just 3 years). His two most famous designs are The Parasol and The Doctor's Visit to the Emperor.

A pair of blue and white saucer dishes, painted in the Ming style, one small rim chip, encircled Yongzheng character marks and of the period, 7½in (19.5cm) diam.
£2,500–3,000 *C*

A blue and white European subject plate, painted with *La Dame au Parasol*, after Cornelis Pronk, c1737, 8½in (21.5cm) diam.
£2,500–3,000 *C*

l. A blue and white deep dish, decorated with trailing floral border, the centre with figures in a landscape and pagodas, c1750, 15in (38cm) diam.
£400–450 *WW*

A blue and white armorial dish, painted at the centre with a gilt coat-of-arms with a sepia squirrel beneath a coronet, Qianlong period, 15in (38cm) wide.
£4,000–5,000 *C*

The arms are those of Sichterman, the family of the Dutch Governor of Bengal between 1734 and 1744.

A pair of blue and white octagonal plates, painted with fishermen before pagodas in a mountainous river landscape, minor restoration and rim frits, Qianlong period, 13½in (33.5cm) diam.
£300–350 *CSK*

A blue and white dish, painted with exotic fish swimming among lotus heads and water plants within a band of flowers and foliage, the border with broad clusters of peony and stylised flowers, rim chips and frittings, c1750, 17½in (44.5cm) diam.
£6,000–6,500 *CAm*

A blue and white saucer, painted in Ming style with a lotus bouquet surrounded by a composite floral scroll and a classic band at the rim, Qianlong seal mark and of the period, 4¾in (12cm) diam.
£5,000–6,000 *S(HK)*

A pair of Nanking blue and white sauceboat stands, c1760, 8in (20cm) wide.
£250–300 *DAN*

A pair of blue and white meat dishes, Qianlong period, 14in (35.5cm) wide.
£1,500–2,000 *LG*

A blue and white dish, painted with figures and birds beside a willow tree on a rocky terrace, Qianlong period, 17½in (45cm) diam.
£1,000–1,200 *C*

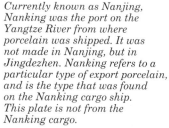

A blue and white Nanking plate, c1760, 13½in (34.5) diam.
£350–400 *Wai*

Currently known as Nanjing, Nanking was the port on the Yangtze River from where porcelain was shipped. It was not made in Nanjing, but in Jingdezhen. Nanking refers to a particular type of export porcelain, and is the type that was found on the Nanking cargo ship. This plate is not from the Nanking cargo.

A Nanking platter, decorated in blue with a river scene, c1760, 13in (33cm) wide.
£160–175 *BRU*

l. A Chinese export blue and white meat dish, with central decoration, late 18thC, 16in (40.5cm) wide.
£250–350 *DN*

A blue and white shaped dish, Qianlong period, 10in (25.5cm) diam. **£320–360** *LG*

A Nanking cargo dish, with rosette and keyhole border, the centre decorated with a scene of pagodas and a figure on a bridge, 18thC, 16½in (42cm) wide. **£240–270** *GAK*

A blue and white saucer dish, the centre painted in iron-red with a bold displaying dragon against a background of foaming wares, the well painted in iron-red with clawed dragons against clouds, damaged and repaired, Qianlong seal mark and of the period, 19in (48cm) diam. **£1,800–2,500** *L*

A blue and white saucer dish, the interior painted with a five-clawed dragon, the reverse with similar striding dragons, Qianlong seal mark and of the period, 6½in (16.5cm) diam. **£3,000–3,500** *C(HK)*

A porcelain dish, with everted rim, painted in the centre with sailing boats on a river between rocks and pagodas, 18thC, 14in (35.5cm) diam. **£500–600** *HCH*

A blue and white bowl, pencilled at the centre with scholars before a pavilion on a terrace, rim slightly polished, seal mark on base, 18thC, 15½in (39cm) diam. **£1,500–2,000** *C*

r. A Chinese blue and white shallow basin, painted to the centre with a standing lady among flowers, Xuande six-character mark, 18thC, 11½in (29cm) diam. **£2,000–2,500** *CSK*

A pair of blue and white warming dishes, each painted with a pagoda in a riverside garden, Qianlong period, 11in (28cm) diam. **£450–600** *Bea*

A set of 15 blue and white plates, painted with fishing boats before pagodas in rocky river landscapes, damaged, Qianlong period, 9in (23cm) diam. **£700–850** *CSK*

r. A pair of blue and white meat dishes, painted with precious objects on rockwork among peonies and willow, within borders of butterflies and geometric patterns, Qianlong period, 12in (30.5cm) wide. **£400–500** *CSK*

Three blue and white dishes, rim chips and fritting, Qianlong period, 15in (38cm) diam.
£1,000–1,200 *C*

r. A blue and white dragon dish, painted in the centre in deep underglaze blue with a large leaping dragon enclosing a *shou* character, chip on rim, Qianlong seal mark and of the period, 17½in (45cm) diam.
£5,000–6,000 *S*

A blue and white deep dish, painted at the centre below a band of trellis pattern at the border, the exterior with 3 flowersprays, Qianlong period, 17in (43cm) diam.
£1,200–1,700 *C*

A pair of blue and white plates, painted at the centre with peony and bamboo, the rim with a band of scrolling foliage, Qianlong period, 13½in (34cm) diam.
£800–1,000 *C*

A blue and white charger, painted within a border of stylised pomegranates and floral designs, Qianlong period, 21¼in (54cm) diam.
£1,200–1,400 *CSK*

A set of 10 blue and white plates, with foliate rims, minor damage and rubbing, Qianlong period, 9½in (24cm) diam.
£3,000–3,500 *CSK*

A blue and white saucer dish, painted with Ming-style scrolling flowers, leaves and whorl patterns, rim chip restored, Qianlong period, 14½in (37cm) diam.
£1,000–1,200 *CSK*

A blue and white deep dish, rim chip, Qianlong period, 19in (48.5cm) diam.
£700–800 *CSK*

Locate the Source

The source of each illustration can be found by checking the code letters at the end of each caption with the Key to Illustrations on page 8.

l. A blue and white saucer, from the 'Nanking' cargo, Qianlong period, 4½in (11.5cm) diam.
£90–120 *ART*

A pair of blue and white meat dishes, painted with figures on bridges before buildings and shrines, Qianlong period, 18in (46cm) wide.
£500–600 *CSK*

r. A Chinese export blue and white serving dish, the centre painted with a Dutch coastal view, Qianlong period, 18in (45.5cm) wide. **£600–700** *Bon*

A blue and white meat dish, painted within a cell-pattern border reserved with panels of flowers, and later decorated iron-red and gilt, small rim chips, one restored, Qianlong period, 15in (38cm) wide. **£450–550** *CSK*

A blue and white and underglaze copper red deep dish, Qianlong seal mark and of the period, 14in (35.5cm) diam. **£6,000–7,500** *C*

A blue and white dish, painted with a sampan moored at a promontory, Qianlong period, 22in (56cm) diam. **£1,600–1,800** *C*

A pair of blue and white foliate dishes with raised central bosses, Qianlong period, 12in (30.5cm) diam. **£600–800** *CSK*

A blue and white quatrefoil dish, raised on 4 narrow tab feet, spur marks, Daoguang seal mark and of the period, 6¼in (16cm) wide. **£3,200–3,500** *S(HK)*

A blue and white saucer dish, painted in the early Ming style, the deeply cut foot unglazed, Qianlong period, 15½in (39cm) diam. **£2,000–2,500** *C*

A blue and white *shou* character dish, with the Eight Daoist emblems, Jiaqing mark and of the period, 5½in (14cm) diam. **1,000–1,200** *Wai*

These emblems are the attributes of the Eight Immortals, which often appear on Qing Imperial porcelain. They are the Fan, the Sword, the Gourd, the Castanets, the Flower Basket, the Bamboo tubes and rods (a kind of drum), the Flute and the Lotus.

> **Miller's is a price GUIDE not a price LIST**

A pair of blue and white dishes, one cracked, both chipped, Daoguang seal mark and of the period, 7in (18cm) diam. **£500–700** *CSK*

r. A blue and white saucer dish, painted to the interior with scrolling lotus, small rim chips, Daoguang seal mark and of the period, 8in (20.5cm) diam. **£400–600** *CSK*

A blue and white saucer dish, the interior decorated within a double line border repeated around the rim, the underside with similar phoenix and clouds, Xianfeng mark and of the period, 6½in (16.5cm) diam.
£1,700–2,200 *S*

A blue and white saucer dish, the interior painted with the Three Friends, the exterior with a continuous band of figures, slight damage, Tongzhi six-character mark and of the period, 7in (17.5cm) diam.
£750–850 *CSK*

A blue and white dish, the centre painted with a dragon chasing a flaming pearl, the underside similarly decorated, slight damage, Guangxu six-character mark and of the period, 7in (17.5cm) diam.
£250–350 *CSK*

Garden Seats

A pair of blue and white garden seats, painted with peonies and scrolling foliage, 19½in (49.5cm) high.
£2,000–2,500 *CSK*

A blue and white barrel-shaped garden seat, 19in (48.5cm) high.
£600–700 *CSK*

A blue and white hexagonal garden seat, with foliate decoration, late 19thC, 18½in (47cm) high.
£450–500 *DA*

l. A blue glazed pierced garden seat, moulded in white relief, 19thC, 20in (50cm) high.
£600–800 *C*

Jardinières

A blue and white jardinière, with everted rim, decorated with figures in a landscape, marked, Kangxi period, 7¼in (18.5cm) diam.
£1,800–2,000 *S(Am)*

r. A blue and white low jardinière, painted with a band of scrolling lotus at the foot and key pattern at the rim, 18thC, 21in (53.5cm) diam.
£3,500–4,500 *C*

A blue and white jardinière, base pierced, Kangxi period, 9in (23cm) diam.
£900–1,200 *C*

A blue and white deep jardinière, painted with a continuous scene figures in a landscape, slight damage, Kangxi period, 20in (51cm) high, on a later English carved giltwood stand.
£6,500–7,000 *C*

A blue and white porcelain jardinière, decorated with panels of landscape vignettes alternating with peonies, lotus and chrysanthemums, 18thC, 9in (23cm) diam.
£1,500–1,800 *Bon*

A blue and white jardinière, painted with pavilions and pagodas among pine and willow in a continuous riverscape, damaged and restored, Qianlong period, 24in (61cm) diam.
£2,500–3,000 *C*

A blue and white jardinière, painted with 5 four-clawed dragons among clouds above breaking waves at the foot and below a bat and cloud band at the rim, 19thC, 18½in (47cm) diam, on a wooden stand.
£1,500–2,000 *C*

A pair of blue and white jardinières, each painted with 2 four-clawed dragons, one cracked, 19thC, 24½in (62cm) diam.
£6,000–7,000 *C*

A pair of blue and white jardinières, painted with panels below a band of leaves and key pattern at the border, the bases pierced, rim chip, glaze bubbles, late 19thC, 17½in (44.5cm) diam.
£3,500–4,000 *C*

A pair of blue and white jardinières, painted within key pattern and archaistic dragon bands, small chips, 19thC, 11in (28cm) diam.
£1,500–1,800 *C*

l. A pair of blue and white jardinières, painted on the exterior in mirror image with scholars and young boys, below a *ruyi* collar, the flat rim with a band of scrolling foliage, fritted, one base restored, 19thC, 18½in (47cm) high.
£3,500–4,000 *C*

Jars

l. Two blue and white broad oviform jars, each painted with 3 shaped panels of *qilin* on a 'cracked-ice' pattern ground, reserved with sprays of prunus, Kangxi period, 8in (20.5cm) high, with pierced wood covers.
£1,000–1,200 *CSK*

A blue and white jar, painted in inky-blue tones, the neck with a band of leaves, base unglazed, minor rim fritting, Kangxi period, 16½in (41.5cm) high.
£2,500–3,000 *C*

r. A pair of blue and white jars, with silver metal covers, Kangxi period, 7in (18cm) high.
£800–900 *ORI*

Two blue and white baluster jars, freely painted, one neck with minor damage, Kangxi period, 13in (33cm) high.
£1,500–1,800 *C*

A blue and white jar and lid, containing a pebble from the sea-bed, from the *Vung Tau* cargo, c1690, 7½in (18.5cm) high.
£1,350–1,500 *SPU*

A blue and white jar and related domed cover with bronze Buddhistic lion finial, painted with a continuous scene of ladies at literary pursuits in a fenced garden of prunus, bamboo and willow, the cover with boys playing in a garden, damaged, finial replaced, 17thC, 25½in (65cm) high.
£1,800–2,000 *CSK*

A blue and white ginger jar, painted with a continuous scene of deer and cranes among pine issuing from rockwork, cover missing, Kangxi period, 8½in (21cm) high.
£700–800 *CSK*

A pair of blue and white square jars, with white metal-mounted necks, edges chipped, body crack, Kangxi period, 10½in (26.5cm) high.
£700–800 *C*

A blue and white oviform jar, painted with 4 panels alternately depicting figures in mountainous riverscapes and archaistic vessels among precious emblems, reserved on a trellis-pattern ground between *ruyi* lappets at the foot and shoulder, Kangxi period, 12½in (32cm) high, with wood cover.
£3,000–3,500 *C*

A pair of blue and white jars, painted in a bright blue, Kangxi period, 8½in (21.5cm) high, with wood covers and stands.
£2,500–3,000 *C*

Jars

Jars were originally used for food storage, but are now mainly decorative.

A blue and white ginger jar and cover, painted on a cracked ice ground, cover riveted, Kangxi period, 9in (23cm) high.
£350–400 *WHB*

A pair of blue and white square tea jars and covers, the borders with trellis pattern and *ruyi* lappets at the corners, chipped, one cover damaged, Kangxi period, 11½in (29.5cm) high.
£5,000–6,000 *C*

l. A blue and white baluster jar, painted with Buddhistic lions playing with brocade balls below a border of emblems, Kangxi period, 12½in (31.5cm) high.
£1,800–2,000 *CSK*

A blue and white baluster jar and cover, painted with a cloud collar reserved with scrolling peony on a blue washed ground above flower-sprays and lappets at the foot, Kangxi period, 15½in (39.5cm) high.
£2,500–3,000 *C*

A pair of blue and white jars, painted with quatrefoil panels of archaistic vessels and emblems, on 'cracked-ice' pattern grounds reserved with prunus heads, Kangxi period, 7½in (19cm) high, with wood covers and stands. **£600–700** *CSK*

A blue and white baluster jar, painted with birds in flight, cracks, glaze chip to shoulder, early Kangxi period, later replacement cover, 19½in (49.5cm) high. **£3,000–3,500** *CSK*

A blue and white ginger jar and cover, with a 'cracked-ice' pattern ground enriched with prunus heads between bands of fret pattern at the foot and on the shoulder, Kangxi period, 12in (40.5cm) high. **£2,000–2,500** *C*

A blue and white oviform jar, decorated in vivid blue tones, foot with glaze flake, Kangxi period, 7½in (19cm) high, with wood cover. **£1,800–2,000** *C*

A pair of blue and white jars and covers, decorated in inky cobalt blue, Kangxi period, 12in (30.5cm) high. **£4,500–5,000** *N*

Prunus Blossom Jars

One of the most famous decorations on jars from the Kangxi period is prunus blossom. The jars were beautifully decorated with sprigs of white plum blossom against a blue and white 'cracked ice' ground, and were frequently copied in later periods.

A blue and white jar and cover, cracked and restored, Kangxi period, 20½in (52cm) high. **£1,800–2,000** *C*

A pair of blue and white soft-paste miniature jugs and covers, the covers and handles pierced, minute chips, jade character mark, Kangxi period, 4in (10cm) high. **£1,800–2,000** *CAm*

A blue and white baluster jar, with flaring neck and twin moulded ring handles, Kangxi seal mark, 19thC, 12in (30.5cm) high. **£400–500** *CSK*

A blue and white ginger jar and pierced wood cover, painted with interlocking chrysanthemum heads and *shou* symbols between lappet border, Kangxi period, 8½in (21.5cm) high.
£170–220 *CSK*

A blue and white jar, painted in a pencilled style with 2 five-clawed dragons, each chasing a flaming pearl among cloud and fire scrolls, Qianlong seal mark and of the period, 7⅞in (19.5cm) high.
£4,500–5,500 *C*

A blue and white jar, the domed cover with Buddhistic lion finial, glaze cracks, cover chipped, late Qianlong period, 18in (45.5cm) high.
£800–1,000 *CSK*

A blue and white baluster jar and cover, decorated in underglaze blue, damaged, 18thC, 23in (58.5cm) high.
£1,000–1,200 *DN*

A blue and white square tea jar, painted with pagodas and boats in a rocky wooded river landscape, cracked, c1800, 12½in (32cm) high.
£1,200–1,500 *CSK*

A pair of blue and white jars with shallow domed covers, decorated with foliate panels of scholars' utensils and floral sprays, one foot rim chipped, 19thC, 13in (33cm) high.
£1,800–2,200 *C*

Jugs

A blue and white jug and cover, painted with panels of ladies in fenced gardens, alternating with scrolling lotus, 17thC, 8½in (21cm) high.
£250–300 *CSK*

A blue and white cider jug and cover, with Buddhistic lion finial and entwined branch handle, painted with the Trench Mortar pattern, and a band of Fitzhugh pattern to the neck, restored, 18thC, 11in (28cm) high.
£600–800 *CSK*

The Trench Mortar pattern was also used by various English factories, including Spode and New Hall.

A blue and white barrel-shaped cider jug and cover, with Buddhistic lion finial, painted with fishermen and pavilions in a rocky river landscape, damaged, 18thC, 11½in (28.5cm) high.
£800–1,000 *CSK*

Teapots

r. A blue and white barrel-shaped teapot and flat cover, with Buddhistic lion finial and rope twist handle and spout, painted with panels of vessels and emblems, Kangxi period, 6½in (16.5cm) wide.
£600–800 *CSK*

A blue and white teapot and cover, with *torii*-shaped handle, painted with 2 panels, cover fritted, hairline crack to spout, Kangxi period, 10½in (26.5cm) high.
£2,000–2,200 *C*

A blue and white two-spouted teapot and cover, restored, Kangxi period, 6in (15cm) high.
£1,400–1,700 *CSK*

A blue and white soft paste teapot and domed cover, painted with chrysanthemums issuing from pierced rockwork between cell-pattern borders, chip to spout, Qianlong period, 5½in (14cm) high.
£350–380 *CSK*

Tureens

A blue and white soup tureen and cover, Qianlong period, 10½in (26.5cm) wide.
£2,200–2,500 *LG*

A blue and white tureen and cover, frits to the handles, 18thC, 10½in (26.5cm) wide.
£1,400–1,800 *C*

A blue and white soup tureen and cover, with pomegranate knop, painted with a river landscape, Qianlong period, 12½in (32cm) wide.
£1,200–1,400 *WHB*

A pair of blue and white bombé tureens and covers, one painted in slightly darker tones than the other, one cover restored, late 18thC, 14½in (37cm) wide.
£2,500–3,000 *C*

A blue and white tureen, cover and stand, with boar's head handles, decorated with peony and other flowersprays between scrolling borders, Qianlong period, 13½in (34.5cm) wide.
£2,500–3,000 *CSK*

A blue and white tureen, cover and stand, with boar's-head handles, pomegranate finial, minor damage, late 18thC, 12in (30.5cm) wide.
£1,500–2,000 *P(S)*

A blue and white tureen and cover, with foliate knop and rabbit-head handles, knop repaired, Qianlong period, 14in (35.5cm) wide.
£600–800 *Bon*

Did You Know?

The value of a tureen is increased considerably if it has its original stand.

r. A blue and white tureen and stand, the related domed cover with pomegranate finial and boar's-head handles, some chips, Qianlong period, stand 15in (38cm) wide.
£1,000–1,200 *CSK*

A blue and white soup tureen, cover and shaped stand, with lion mask handles and Buddhistic lion's-mask finial, painted with scattered flowersprays within borders of further flowers, trellis pattern and cell pattern, Qianlong period, stand 15in (38cm) wide.
£2,000–2,500 *CSK*

A blue and white tureen and domed cover, with pomegranate finial and boar's-head handles, painted with figures and buildings in a rocky river landscape, within a border of flowers and foliage, finial chipped, Qianlong period, 13in (33cm) diam.
£1,500–2,000 *CSK*

The unusual shape of this tureen accounts for its high value.

l. A blue and white exportware tureen and cover, with animal heads handles, the cover with a lion dog knop, painted with a pagoda under a pine tree and figures on a bridge, Qianlong period, 12in (30.5cm) wide.
£800–1,000 *S(S)*

A blue and white tureen, cover and stand, with boar's-head handles and pomegranate finial, painted with a landscape scene, stand damaged, Qianlong period, stand 15in (38cm) wide.
£1,000–1,200 *CSK*

l. A blue and white tureen and cover, with branch finial, boar's head handles and decorated with a river landscape, Qianlong period, 14in (35.5cm) wide.
£800–1,000 *AH*

A blue and white tureen and domed cover, the handles modelled as masks with feathered headdresses, Qianlong period, 14in (35.5cm) wide.
£2,000–2,500 *CSK*

A blue and white lobed tureen and cover, with pierced finial and boar's-head handles, painted with lotus flowers and foliage within whorl-pattern borders, cover restored, 18thC, 11in (28cm) wide.
£800–1,000 *CSK*

A Chinese export blue and white tureen, with gilt decoration and monogrammed armorial-type shields, 18thC, 14½in (37cm) wide.
£1,100–1,200 *EL*

r. A blue and white tureen and domed cover, with fruit spray finial and hare's-head handles, painted with stags in river landscapes, the cover with peonies, 18thC, 11½in (29cm) wide.
£600–800 *CSK*

Two blue and white vegetable tureens and domed covers, with strawberry finials, painted with fishermen in mountainous river landscapes, early 19thC, 9in (23cm) wide.
£800–1,000 *CSK*

Vases

l. A blue and white sleeve vase, the rim brown dressed, Kangxi period, 15½in (39.5cm) high.
£1,500–2,000 *C*

A blue and white bottle vase, painted with peonies between leaf lappets at the foot and lower part of the neck below stiff leaf lappets rising towards the rim, early 18thC, 16in (40.5cm) high.
£2,000–2,500 *C*

A powder blue glazed rouleau vase, gilt to one side, the other with a faint inscription below emblem cartouches at the shoulder and *shou* characters dividing swastikas at the neck, Kangxi period, 18in (45.5cm) high.
£2,000–2,500 *C*

A blue and white *yanyan* vase, base pierced, Kangxi period, 18in (45.5cm) high.
£1,600–1,800 *C*

A pair of blue and white moulded vases, painted with flowers on a diaper ground, between moulded lotus leaves at the shoulder, one cracked, some fritting, Kangxi period, 10½in (26.5cm) high.
£1,200–1,500 *C*

l. A powder blue vase, decorated and gilt with shaped panels, 18thC, 18in (45.5cm) high.
£2,000–2,500 *CSK*

A blue and white vase, Kangxi period, 9½in (24cm) high.
£1,000–1,200 *Wai*

A pair of blue and white baluster vases, drawn with shaped panels of leafy branches above rockwork, Kangxi period, the silver cover Sheffield 1897, 9½in (24cm) high.
£1,800–2,200 *CSK*

l. A pair of blue and white *gu*-shaped beaker vases, painted on the central section with 2 *taotie* masks on a trellis-pattern ground, one rim with hairline crack, Kangxi period, 10in (25.5cm) high.
£1,500–1,800 *C*

A blue and white vase, Kangxi period, 6in (15cm) high.
£800–1,000 *Wai*

A blue and white bottle vase, with garlic neck, Kangxi period, 17½in (44.5cm) high.
£3,000–3,500 *C*

l. A blue and white *gu*-shaped beaker vase, foot chip restored, rim with one small chip, encircled Chenghua six-character mark, Kangxi period, 18½in (47cm) high.
£2,000–2,500 *C*

Did You Know?

Very little Kangxi porcelain for export bears the Kangxi reign mark. Pieces bearing a four-character Kangxi mark (Da Qing being omitted) are often found, and are invariably late 19thC copies.

For further information on Chinese Dynasties and marks please refer to the charts on pages 10 and 11.

A pair of blue and white square bottle vases, some glaze fritting, 17thC, 10½in (26.5cm) high.
£1,800–2,200 *CSK*

A blue and white vase, painted with prunus and pine, cracked, Kangxi period, 18½in (47.5cm) high.
£500–600 *CSK*

Two blue and white square vases, painted on each side with an audience scene below birds among lotus scrolls on the sloping shoulder, one chip restored, impressed Xuande four-character marks, Kangxi period, 11½in (29cm) high.
£2,700–3,200 *C*

A blue and white vase, restored, Kangxi period, 18in (45.5cm) high.
£1,500–1,800 *CSK*

A set of 3 blue and white bottle vases, damaged, Kangxi period, 9½in (24cm) high.
£2,000–2,500 *CSK*

A pair of blue and white vases, with pierced foliate handles, the necks painted with birds among flowers, Kangxi period, 9½in (24cm) high.
£5,000–6,000 *CSK*

l. A pair of blue and white vases, with 6 panels decorated with flower designs, Kangxi period, 8in (20.5cm) high.
£700–800 *ORI*

A blue and white baluster vase, decorated in shallow relief with a magnolia tree, slight damage, Kangxi period, 17¼in (44cm) high.
£3,500–4,000 *S(HK)*

A pair of blue and white vases and covers, the sides decorated with panels of figures and flowering branches, each neck and foot with panels of antiques, finials missing, damaged, Kangxi period, 15in (38cm) high.
£4,500–5,000 *DN*

A blue and white vase, with squat body and tall sloping neck, foot crack, possibly restuck, Qianlong seal mark and of the period, 19½in (49.5cm) high.
£6,500–7,500 *C*

A blue and white vase, painted with flowers and lotus panels, neck crack, Qianlong mark and of the period, 11in (28cm) high.
£7,000–8,000 *C*

An underglaze blue and copper red vase, with fixed ring handles, painted with *ruyi* lappets at the neck and with a band of pendant stiff leaves at the foot, Qianlong period, 6in (15.5cm) high.
£4,000–5,000 *C*

A blue and white vase, painted with stylised lotus, with moulded archaistic fretwork handles, restored, Qianlong seal mark and of the period, 17½in (44.5cm) high.
£2,500–3,000 *C*

A pair of blue and white vases and covers, moulded with panels painted with river landscapes on a raised dot ground, restored, Qianlong period, 17½in (44.5cm) high.
£6,500–7,500 *C*

A blue and white baluster vase and cover, painted with flowers and gilt, Qianlong period, 16½in (42cm) high.
£1,800–2,000 *CSK*

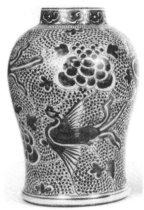

A pair of blue and white vases and covers, with knop finials, necks reduced, damaged, Qianlong seal marks and of the period, 19in (48cm) high.
£5,000–6,000 *C*

A blue and white bottle vase, late Qianlong/Jiaqing period, 17in (43cm) high.
£2,000–2,500 *C*

A blue and white vase, painted with large phoenix among rising peony on a scale-pattern ground, 18thC, 13½in (34cm) high.
£1,200–1,500 *C*

l. A blue and white vase, Qianlong seal mark and of the period, 20½in (52cm) high.
£62,000–68,000 *S*

This vase is thought to have been presented by Queen Mary to Sir Ralph Harwood, KCB, KCVO, and to have come from the Royal Collection at Windsor Castle.

A pair of blue and white baluster vases, decorated in underglaze blu with temple landscapes, within shagreen borders, gilt scrolling pierced handles to neck, Qianlong period, 14in (35.5cm) high.
£1,500–1,750 *J&L*

Two blue and white baluster vases and covers, one neck restored, one with small rim chip and cover chipped, Qianlong period, 15in (38cm) high.
£1,300–1,600 *C*

A blue and white vase, decorated in Ming style, Qianlong period, 13in (33cm) high.
£1,600–1,800 *Wai*

A blue and white five-piece garniture, four-character Kangxi marks, 19thC, 15in (38cm) high.
£4,000–5,000 *C*

A blue and white vase, painted with a dignitary and attendants receiving 3 officials on a walled terrace, 19thC, 7½in (44.5cm) high.
£650–750 *Bon*

A pair of blue and white vases, each low baluster body filled with leaf-shaped landscape panels in insect medallions in a lotus-scroll ground, under a broad neck with bell-shaped mouth, one rim chipped, 19thC, 17in (43.5cm) high.
£1,200–1,500 *S(S)*

A blue and white tulip vase, painted overall with scrolling flowers and foliage below bands of lappets, 19thC, 10in (25.5cm) high.
£600–700 *CSK*

l. Two blue and white vases, decorated with figures in landscapes, 19thC, 12½in (32cm) high.
£180–200 each *BRU*

l. A blue and white bottle vase, painted in Ming style, Daoguang seal mark and of the period, 14½in (36.5cm) high.
£7,000–8,000 *C*

A set of 12 Chinese *kraak porselein* dishes, slight damage, Wanli period, 8½in (21.5cm) diam.
£5,800–6,500 *C*

A set of 10 Chinese *kraak porselein* dishes, each painted with a pair of deer in a landscape, slight damage, Wanli period, 8½in (21.5cm) diam.
£3,500–4,000 *C*

A Japanese Nabeshima dish, decorated with flowers, on a tall tapering foot with 'comb' design, 18thC, 8in (20.5cm) diam.
£12,000–14,000 *S*

A Chinese *meiping*, painted with a *lingzhi* scroll, Ming Dynasty, c1430, 13in (33cm) high.
£17,500–18,500 *S*

A Chinese Ming-style moon flask, each shoulder with a scroll handle, Qianlong seal mark and of the period, 19½in (49.5cm) high.
£50,000–55,000 *C*

A Chinese Ming-style pear-shaped vase, Qianlong seal mark and of the period, 12in (30.5cm) high.
£10,000–12,000 *C*

A Chinese Ming-style moon flask, with *ruyi*-head handles, some damage, Qianlong seal mark and of the period, 9½in (24cm) high.
£5,200–6,000 *C*

A Chinese Ming-style pear-shaped vase, body cracked, Qianlong seal mark and of the period, 11½in (29cm) high.
£10,000–12,000 *C*

A Chinese Ming-style bottle vase, restored, Qianlong seal mark and of the period, 14½in (37cm) high.
£2,000–2,500 *C*

A Chinese pear-shaped faceted vase, decorated with panels of flowers, Yuan Dynasty, 11½in (24.5cm) high.
£9,000–10,000 *S*

A Chinese blue and white dish, the reverse
with 2 birds in flight, minor fritting,
Wanli period, 18½in (47cm) diam.
£5,000–6,000 *C*

A Chinese blue and white box and cover, with dragons
chasing flaming pearls, minor cracks, cover restored, Wanli
six-character mark and of the period, 12in (30.5cm) wide.
£6,000–7,500 *C*

A Chinese blue and
white jar, encircled
Jiajing six-character
mark and of the period,
5in (12.5cm) diam.
£16,000–18,000 *C*

A Chinese hexagonal dish, painted in the
centre with 2 herons, the sides with fish,
frogs and crustacea, Tianqi/Chongzhen
period, 8in (20.5cm) diam, in a fitted box.
£7,000–8,000 *C*

A Chinese blue and
white magnolia vase,
Kangxi period,
18in (46cm) high.
£10,000–12,000 *C*

A Chinese blue and white armorial
pilgrim flask, with emblems of
Leon and Castille for Spain, c1590,
12in (30.5cm) high.
£80,000+ *C*

A Chinese blue and white saucer dish,
encircled Wanli six-character mark and of
the period, 7in (18cm) diam, in a fitted box.
£6,500–8,000 *C*

r. A Chinese
Transitional
blue and white
brush pot,
painted with
military scene,
incised rim,
c1640, 8in
(20.5cm) high.
£4,500–5,000 *C*

A Chinese provincial storage jar, glaze damaged and small chips, Ming Dynasty, 16thC, 6in (15cm) high.
£70–80 *AnE*

A Chinese provincial bowl, painted with a pair of sinuous dragons, Ming Dynasty, c1600, 5in (12.5cm) diam.
£100–115 *AnE*

Two Chinese *kraak porselein* bottle vases, cracked, Wanli period, tallest 12½in (32cm) high.
£1,500–2,000 *C*

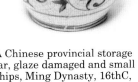

A Chinese rose-water sprinkler, with brass-mounted top, made for the Middle Eastern market, 18thC, 8½in (21.5cm) high.
£550–600 *AnE*

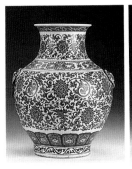

Two Chinese Ming-style *gu* vases, painted with dragons amid clouds, Wanli six-character marks, 19thC, 32½in (82.5cm) high.
£6,500–7,000 *C*

A Chinese Willow pattern spoon tray, applied with gilt in Europe, mid-19thC, 5in (12.5cm) wide.
£75–100 *AnE*

A Chinese Karonic vase, with Islamic inscription, Zhengde mark and of the period, 3½in (9cm) high, and another vase, 17thC.
£4,500–5,000 *C*

A pair of Chinese Ming-style *hu* vases, with moulded *taotie* mask handles, one restored, Qianlong seal mark, 19thC, 19½in (49.5cm) high.
£7,000–8,000 *C*

A Chinese baluster vase and cover, restored, on a European giltwood stand, damaged, Kangxi period, 61½in (156cm) high.
£11,000–13,000 *S*

A Chinese bulb planter, painted with a scene of scholars and attendants in a mountain and river landscape, Kangxi period, 9in (23cm) diam.
£800–1,000 *AnE*

A Japanese Arita garniture, comprising 3 jars and covers and 2 beaker vases, each painted with a continuous scene of trailing clouds and *ho-o* birds on rocks, peonies and pomegranates, damaged and restored, late 17thC, jars 21½in (54.5cm) high.
£34,000–36,000 *C*

A pair of Chinese yellow glazed bowls, one cracked, Qianlong seal marks and of the period, 4½in (11.5cm) diam.
£12,000–14,000 *C*

r. A Canton *famille rose* punchbowl, early 19thC, 21in (53.5cm) diam.
£2,500–3,000 *C*

A Chinese *famille rose* punchbowl, painted with figures, Qianlong period, 15in (38cm) diam.
£2,500–3,000 *C*

A Chinese blue and white bowl, encircled Wanli six-character mark and of the period, 6in (15cm) diam.
£7,000–9,000 *C*

A Chinese blue and white dragon bowl, star crack, Zhengde four-character mark in underglaze blue within a double circle and of the period, 6in (15cm) diam.
£30,000–35,000 *CNY*

A pair of Chinese blue and white bowls, painted with flying phoenix, some damage, encircled Jiajing six-character marks and of the period, 5in (12.5cm) diam, in fitted boxes.
£1,500–1,800 *C*

A Chinese copper-red glazed bowl, with finely pitted glaze, rim chip, Yongzheng mark within a double circle and of the period, 6in (15cm) diam.
£1,500–1,800 *CNY*

A Neolothic painted pottery basin.
£10,000–12,000 *CNY*

A pair of Chinese *famille verte* dragon and phoenix bowls, Qianlong seal marks and of the period, 5½in (14cm) diam, in fitted boxes.
£22,000–25,000 *C*

A Chinese blue and white incense burner and cover, depicting Liu Hai riding on the back of his mythical three-legged toad, chipped, mid-17thC, 4½in (11.5cm) long.
£8,000–10,000 *C*

A Japanese Kakiemon teabowl, decorated in enamels and gilt, the interior with a five-pointed floret, c1680, 3in (7.5cm) diam.
£1,000–1,200 *C*

Shonzui Wares

Shonzui wares are named after Gorodaiyu Wu Shonzui, a Japanese potter who is reputed to have made the first Japanese porcelain in the early 16thC. Shonzui is said to have gone to Jingdezhen in China in 1510 and to have studied there for five years before setting up a kiln in Arita, Hizen Province. In the middle of the 17thC a group of tea ceremony wares was exported from China to Japan, probably made to special order and bearing the spurious mark 'Made by Gorodaiyu Wu Shonzui'. These rare wares are of the finest quality porcelain with painting of a high standard. They have been much imitated and faked and are often confused with *kometsuke* porcelains made at Jingdezhen with Japanese-inspired designs made specifically for export to Japan.

A Chinese blue and white display dish, rim chipped, late Wanli period, 13½in (34.5cm) diam, in a wooden box.
£16,000–18,000 *C*

A Shonzui-style blue and white serving dish, *fu* seal mark, Chongzhen period, 8in (20.5cm) diam, in a wooden box.
£3,500–4,000 *C*

A Shonzui-style blue and white serving dish, encircled Chenghua six-character mark, Chongzhen period, 9in (23cm) diam, in a wooden box.
£3,500–4,000 *C*

A Shonzui-style blue and white serving dish, rim frits, Tianqi period, 8in (20.5cm) diam, in a wooden box.
£2,000–2,500 *C*

r. A Chinese *famille verte* saucer dish, painted with an English coat-of-arms below a royal crown and inscription, some damage, Kangxi period, 13½in (34.5cm) diam.
£6,000–7,000 *C*

A Shonzui-style enamel serving dish, *fu* mark within a double square, Chongzhen period, 8in (20.5cm) diam.
£3,500–4,000 *C*

r. A Chinese moulded dish, the veins in raised relief within line borders and reserved in white, foot-rim chipped, Yongzheng mark in underglaze blue within a double circle and of the period, 13in (33cm) diam.
£25,000–28,000 *CNY*

Five Chinese serving plates, rim frits, Tianqi/
Chongzhen period, 6½in (16.5cm) diam, in a wood box.
£3,000–3,500 *C*

Five Chinese serving plates, chips and frits,
Tianqi period, 6in (15cm) diam, in a wood box.
£3,200–3,600 *C*

An Imari charger, Genroku
period, 21⅛in (54.5cm) diam.
£4,500–5,000 *C*

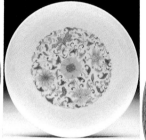

A pair of *doucai* dishes,
enamels rubbed, 18thC,
6in (15cm) diam.
£12,000–15,000 *CNY*

A Chinese *famille rose* eggshell deep plate,
Yongzheng period, 8½in (21.5cm) diam,
in a box.
£15,000–17,000 *C*

l. A Chinese blue
and white cup stand,
Wanli mark within
a double circle and
of the period,
6in (15cm) diam.
£3,500–4,500 *CNY*

A five-piece *famille rose* garniture,
decorated with Buddhist emblems,
restored and damaged, iron-red
Qianlong six-character seal marks,
19thC, beakers 11in (28cm) high.
£6,500–8,000 *C*

A Chinese *famille rose*
plaque, mid-18thC,
16½in (42cm) diam.
£2,000–2,500 *AG*

r. A Chinese *famille
rose* dish, mid-18thC,
15in (38cm) diam.
£2,500–3,000 *AG*

An Imari garniture, decorated in enamels and
gilt on underglaze blue, small cracks, Genroku
period, the mounts later, vases 17in (43cm) high.
£8,000–10,000 *C*

Three Chinese blue and white eggshell month cups, painted with various flowers for December, September and January, cracked, Kangxi mark and of the period, 3in (7.5cm) diam.
£2,000–2,200 *CNY*

A *doucai* cup, painted with chickens, Kangxi period, 3½in (9cm) diam.
£15,000–18,000 *C*

Five Japanese painted sake cups, one repaired, one cracked, mid-17thC.
£3,000–4,000 *C*

A set of 5 Chinese blue and white cups, rim frits, encircled Jiajing six-character marks, Chongzhen period, 3in (7.5cm) diam.
£2,500–3,000 *C*

A Chinese blue and white stem cup, painted in underglaze blue with a continuous scene, the interior with a central medallion surrounded by a foliate diaper border at the rim, 16thC, 5½in (14cm) diam.
£8,000–10,000 *CNY*

A pair of Chinese yellow and blue glazed libation cups, Daoguang period, 4½in (11.5cm) wide, in a fitted cloth box.
£1,800–2,000 *CNY*

A pair of Chinese blue and white saucer dishes, rim chip, Jiajing mark and of the period, 6in (15cm) diam.
£16,000–18,000 *CNY*

A Chinese *kometsuke* style serving dish, firing cracks, 17thC, 9in (23cm) wide, in a wood box.
£4,500–5,500 *C*

A set of 6 Chinese blue and white *mukozuke*, one with underglaze blue Chenghua six-character mark, Chongzhen period, 5½in (14cm) wide.
£3,300–4,000 *C*

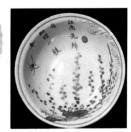

A set of 5 Chinese enamelled *mukozuke*, with scalloped borders and brown rims, rim frits, four-character seal marks, Chongzhen period, 5½in (14cm) diam, in a wood box.
£5,000–6,000 *C*

l. A Chinese *famille verte* dish, damaged, Kangxi period, 12½in (32cm) diam.
£4,500–5,500 *C*

A set of 6 Chinese *mukozuke*, each painted with an underglaze blue Tang poem, rim frits, Tianqi period, 5½in (14cm) diam, in a wooden box.
£4,500–5,500 *C*

A Chinese *yenyen* vase, decorated with deer and 2 cranes, Kangxi period, 18½in (47cm) high.
£5,000–6,000 *S(HK)*

A Chinese tripod ewer and cover, the spout in the form of a chicken's head, chipped, Qianlong period, 6in (15cm) wide.
£3,500–4,000 *S(HK)*

A pair of Chinese Lotus Pond saucers, with low rounded sides, painted with a band of mandarin ducks, spots on rim, Yongzheng marks and of the period, 4⅓in (11.5cm) diam.
£14,500–16,000 *S(HK)*

A pair of Chinese underglaze blue bowls, each decorated with cranes, the interior with a medallion enclosing a fruiting peach tree, one with short firing mark under glaze, Yongzheng marks and of the period, 6in (15cm) diam.
£38,000–42,000 *S(HK)*

A Chinese blue and white bowl, the exterior painted with the Three Friends and branches, light wear, Yongzheng mark and of the period, 7½in (19cm) diam.
£3,000–3,500 *S(HK)*

A pair of Chinese dragon jardinières, each decorated with dragons amid cloud and flame scrolls, small glaze cracks, Daoguang mark and of the period, 8½in (21.5cm) diam.
£7,500–8,500 *S(HK)*

A Chinese blue and white dish, the interior painted with a Daoist scene of an Immortal, attendants and Shoulao, the exterior with floral sprigs, kiln grit and glaze pooling, Wanli period, 6½in (16.5cm) diam.
£2,500–3,500 *S(HK)*

A Chinese underglaze blue jar, decorated with lotus flowers and stems, Yongzheng mark and of the period, 4⅓in (11.5cm) high.
£9,500–10,500 *S(HK)*

A soft-paste vase, painted with a temple hall and buildings, Qing Dynasty, 15½in (39.5cm) high.
£2,000–2,500 *S(HK)*

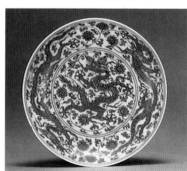

A pair of Chinese blue and white butter lamps, the interior decorated with lotus flower medallions, the exteriors with characters, lotus flowers and leafy stems, Qianlong seal marks and of the period, 6in (15cm) diam.
£15,000–16,000 *S(HK)*

A Chinese saucer dish, painted with a dragon leaping among scrolling lotus, rim chipped, Zhengde mark and of the period, 8in (20.5cm) diam.
£7,000–8,000 *S(HK)*

A pair of baluster jars and covers, damaged, Kangxi period, 15in (38cm) high.
£8,000–10,000 *C*

l. Mark on base of brush washer, *shown below left.*

A pair of Chinese painted vases and covers, replacement gilt Buddhistic lion finials, firing fault and fritted, Kangxi period, 32in (82cm) high.
£30,000–33,000 *C*

A Japanese Arita dish, painted with monogram 'VOC', late 17thC, 15½in (39.5cm) diam.
£6,500–8,000 *S*

A Chinese mantel garniture, comprising 3 rectangular vases and a pair of *gu*-form beakers, slight damage, c1710, largest 13½in (34cm) high.
£4,800–5,200 *S(NY)*

A Chinese foliate brush washer, with flaring lobed sides, Xuande six-character mark and of the period, 6in (15cm) diam.
£625,000–650,000 *Bon*

A Chinese five-piece garniture, comprising 3 baluster vases and 2 *gu*-form beaker vases, minor restorations, Kangxi period, largest 22in (56cm) high.
£22,000–26,000 *C*

A Japanese Arita octagonal tureen and cover, damage and restored, late 17thC, 12½in (32cm) high.
£6,500–8,000 *C*

A Chinese finely painted dish, the centre with the Three Friends of Winter, damaged and restored, Yongle period, 13½in (34cm) diam.
£22,000–25,000 *S*

l. A pair of Chinese baluster jars and covers, each painted with quatrefoil panels, with knop finials, minor damage, Kangxi period, 13in (33cm) high.
£4,500–6,000 *C*

A Japanese Arita jar, decorated with the Three Friends, a bridge and a waterfall, damaged, c1700, 20½in (52cm) high.
£4,000–4,500 *S*

A set of 8 Chinese *famille rose* figures of Daoist Immortals, holding their appropriate attributes, one head restored, some extremities chipped, c1800, 8½in (21.5cm) high.
£4,500–5,500 *C*

A pair of celadon ground and gilt candlesticks, rim chipped, Qianlong seal mark and of the period, 11in (28cm) high.
£3,500–4,000 *C*

A pair of Chinese *famille rose* armorial dishes, the centres painted with European style landscapes, possibly of Fort St George, India, damaged, c1745.
£4,500–5,500 *Bon*

A pair of Chinese blue and white garden seats, each with 2 sides centrally pierced with interlocking cash, within a band of scrolling lotus, c1800, 19in (48.5cm) high.
£3,000–3,500 *C*

A pair of Chinese export models of hawks, the wings and tails detailed with sepia feather markings, restored, Qianlong period, 11in (28cm) high.
£23,000–25,000 *C*

A set of 4 Chinese *famille rose* erotic panels, each elaborately painted with lovers in a pavilion, with a terrace, a garden and a chamber, mid-Qing Dynasty, 8 x 5in (20.5 x 12.5cm), in wooden frames.
£8,000–9,000 *C*

A Chinese *famille rose* turquoise ground vase, painted with iron-red bats in flight, repaired, Qianlong seal mark, 27in (68.5cm) high.
£12,000–14,000 *C*

A pair of Chinese export glazed models of cockerels, painted with iron-red bodies, head extremities restored, c1800, 11in (28cm) high.
£6,000–7,000 *C*

A pair of Chinese *famille rose* Tobacco Leaf tureens and covers, with flowerhead handles and pomegranate finials, painted with overlapping coloured leaves scattered with flowersprays and peonies, one spare cover, one tureen with handles missing, chipped, Qianlong period, 12in (30.5cm) wide.
£5,500–6,500 *C*

Twenty-four Chinese blue and white plates, painted with peonies below flowering pomegranate branches, within a band of trellis pattern, c1750, 9in (23cm) diam.
£4,000–5,000 *C*

A pair of Chinese jars and covers, painted with dragons in pursuit of flaming pearls, below bands of Buddhistic emblems within *ruyi* heads and scrolls, rim chip, Qianlong six-character seal marks and of the period, 8in (20.5cm) high. **£16,000–18,000** *C*

A *doucai* saucer dish, with eight Buddhistic emblems, Qianlong seal mark and of the period, 20½in (52cm) diam. **£35,000–40,000** *C*

A pair of Chinese neo-classical *famille rose* urns and covers, in the style of Marieberg faïence, one restored, one cover chipped, gilding rubbed, Qianlong period, 16in (40.5cm) high. **£5,500–6,500** *C*

A pair of Chinese *famille rose* vases and covers, decorated in Mandarin palette, restored, Qianlong period, 20in (51cm) high. **£8,000–9,000** *C*

A pair of Chinese *famille rose* vases and covers, painted with figures on a turquoise ground, minor restoration, Qianlong period, 18in (45.5cm) high. **£8,000–10,000** *C*

Two Chinese *famille rose* plates, each painted with The Doctor's Visit, attributed to Cornelis Pronk, c1735, 9in (23cm) diam. *l.* slight wear, **£4,000–5,000** *r.* **£9,500–10,500** *C*

l. A pair of Chinese export armorial basins, enamelled in colours, small rim chips, one with hairline crack, c1745, 15in (38cm) diam. **£6,000–7,000** *C*

r. A Chinese export unrecorded documentary shipping bowl, inscribed 'Elizabeth Cook 1747' and 'William Hillyard 1747', enamel restored, 10in (25.5cm) diam. **£12,000–14,000** *C*

A Chinese *rose/verte* dish, painted with figures in a walled garden, the rim with landscape panels on a green ground with peonies and magnolias, rim restored, Yongzheng period, 21⅛in (54.5cm) diam.
£14,000–16,000 *C*

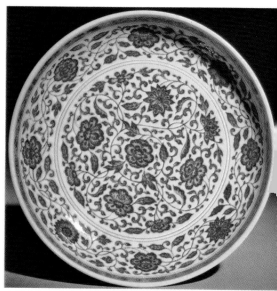

A Chinese yellow ground saucer dish, painted with blue and white flowers on leafy stems, the exterior similarly painted, glazing flaw, Yongzheng six-character mark and of the period, 8½in (21.5cm) diam.
£34,000–36,000 *C*

A Chinese *famille rose* punchbowl, painted with hunting scenes, cracked, late Qianlong period, 16in (40.5cm) diam.
£9,000–10,000 *C*

A Chinese garniture of 5 blue and white vases, 3 with covers, each decorated with a peach-shaped panel of a pavilion, one cover renewed, some restoration, early 18thC, vases 17½in (44.5cm) high.
£6,500–8,000 *C*

A Chinese blue and white jar, each lobe painted with gourds, Yongzheng six-character mark and of the period, 3½in (9cm) high.
£6,500–8,000 *C*

A Chinese export armorial neo-classical punchbowl, painted after a European engraving in the manner of Bartolozzi, the interior with a coat-of-arms, some damage and rubbing, c1790, 22in (56cm) diam.
£8,000–10,000 *C*

l. A Louis XVI ormolu-mounted *famille rose* pot pourri vase, the porcelain Yongzheng period, 5½in 14cm) high.
£4,000–5,000 *C*

r. A Chinese Imari armorial shaving bowl, painted in underglaze blue, iron-red and gilt at the centre, 2 rim chips restored, c1720, 11in (28cm) diam.
£3,000–3,500 *C*

A Chinese pilgrim bottle, rim cracked, Qianlong seal mark and of the period, 18½in (47cm) high, fitted box.
£35,000–40,000 *CHK*

A pair of Chinese *famille rose* vases, one repaired, late Qing Dynasty, 32½in (82.5cm) high.
£8,000–10,000 *CNY*

A Chinese five-piece garniture, comprising 3 vases and covers and 2 beaker vases, damage and restorations, Kangxi period, baluster vases 17½in (44cm) high.
£12,000–13,000 *C*

A Chinese garniture of *famille verte* vases, cracked and restored, Kangxi, beakers 10½in (26cm) high.
£8,000–10,000 *C*

A Chinese *famille rose* vase, Jiaqing mark, 11in (28cm) high.
£12,000–15,000 *CHK*

A Japanese Kinkozan enamelled vase, signed, late 19thC, 12½in (31cm) high.
£6,000–7,000 *C*

Garnitures

At the end of the 17thC, William and Mary renovated Hampton Court and filled it with imported Chinese and Japanese porcelain. The obvious place for display were chimneypieces, but cabinets and purpose-built stands and shelves were also used. The fashion quickly spread throughout 18thC Europe and many thousands of garnitures were imported.

As with all Chinese and Japanese ceramics, the value of a garniture is reflected by size, quality, condition and being complete with covers where intended. Most garnitures consist of three covered vases and two open trumpet-shaped vases.

A *famille rose* vase, Qianlong mark, 25in (63.5cm) high.
£7,000–8,000 *CHK*

A Chinese *famille rose* baluster vase, iron-red Qianlong seal mark and of the period, 7½in (19cm) high.
£26,000–30,000 *CHK*

l. A Chinese *Ge*-type glazed Cong form vase, Qianlong seal mark in underglaze blue and of the period, 11½in (29cm) high.
£6,500–8,000 *CNY*

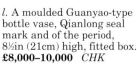

r. A Chinese celadon glazed baluster vase, Qianlong seal mark and of the period, 16in (40cm) high.
£8,000–10,000 *CHK*

A pair of Japanese Imari vases and covers, damaged, Genroku period, 24½in (62cm) high.
£6,500–8,000 *C*

l. A moulded Guanyao-type bottle vase, Qianlong seal mark and of the period, 8½in (21cm) high, fitted box.
£8,000–10,000 *CHK*

Twelve Chinese blue and white chocolate cups and saucers, from the Nanking cargo, each painted with chrysanthemums, bamboo and daisies issuing around a jagged outcrop of rockwork, with elaborate European-style loop handles, c1750, saucers 5in (13cm) diam.
£2,500–3,000 C

A pair of Chinese *famille rose* millefleurs vases, reserved with oval landscape panels, each with figures in boats on a promontory in a wooded river landscape, on brightly enamelled gilt and floral ground, 19thC, 28in (71cm) high.
£3,000–3,500 C

The Lord Mayor of London's enamelled punchbowl, decorated in *famille rose* with views taken from prints of the City of London in the 18thC, cracks stabilised, one area overpainted, c1805, 16in (40.5cm) diam.
£28,000–32,000 C

l. A Chinese blue and white vase and cover, with a seated lady Immortal finial, painted with lotus in leafy meanders, finial restored, 19thC, 40in (101.5cm) high.
£4,000–5,000 C

A pair of Chines *famille rose* celadon ground bottle vases and domed covers, with peach finials, the bodies decorated in bright enamels, trailed white slip and gilding with flying bats, cloud scrolls, floral roundels and Buddhist emblems, beneath spearheads at the rims, one cover and rim restored, early 19thC, 35½in (90cm) high.
£7,000–8,000 C

A pair of Chinese *famille rose* yellow ground fish bowls, moulded and brightly painted in relief with vases of flowers, stands of scholars' utensils, archaistic vessels and scattered flowers, the interiors with swimming carp among water weeds, 19thC, 20in (51cm) diam.
£8,000–10,000 C

A pair of Chinese *famille rose* figures of seated Buddhistic lions, one with a pierced ball beneath its forepaw, the other with a cub, on detachable bases pierced with kidney-shaped apertures, restored, 19thC, 20in (51cm) high.
£3,500–4,000 C

Two Chinese *famille rose* saucer dishes, Yongzheng mark and of the period.
£16,000–18,000 *CNY*

A pair of Chinese dishes, painted with a bust of Queen Anne, Qianlong period, 14in (35.5cm) diam.
£7,000–8,000 *C*

A pair of Chinese *rose/verte* dishes, painted with court ladies and a young boy in a garden, rim frits, Yongzheng period, 15in (38cm) diam.
£12,000–15,000 *CNY*

r. A pair of Chinese dishes, firing crack, Daoguang seal marks and of the period, 7in (18cm) diam.
£3,400–3,800 *C*

A pair of Chinese *famille verte* dishes, the centres pencilled in underglaze blue, rim cracked, Kangxi period, 13in (33cm) diam.
£4,000–5,000 *CNY*

A Chinese Ming-style saucer dish, Yongzheng mark and of the period, 8in (20.5cm) diam.
£4,000–5,000 *C*

l. A pair of Chinese *famille rose* saucer dishes, early 20thC, 7in (18cm) diam.
£1,000–1,200 *Wai*

A Chinese bottle vase, late Wanli period, 7½in (19cm) high, in a wood box.
£8,000–10,000 *C*

A Japanese Kutani bottle, rim restored, c1670, 8in (20.5cm) high.
£12,000–15,000 *C*

A Japanese Arita blue and white bottle vase, c1680, 18½in (47cm) high.
£4,500–5,500 *C*

A Chinese Imperial *famille verte* bowl, Yongzheng Yuzhi marks, 5½in (14cm) diam, in a box.
£80,000–100,000 *C*

A Chinese *famille rose* mythological subject punchbowl, cracked, Qianlong period, c1750, 15½in (39.5cm) diam.
£9,000–12,000 *C*

A Chinese water pot, decorated with copper-red and iron-red flowerheads, rim chips, Kangxi six-character mark.
£22,000–25,000 *CNY*

A Chinese *ru*-type bulb bowl, restored, underglaze blue Qianlong four-character seal mark and of the period, 9in (23cm) wide.
£10,000–12,000 *CNY*

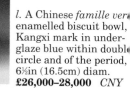

An Imari bowl, decorated with a continuous scene, restored, Genroku period, 15½in (39.5cm) diam.
£4,000–5,000 *C*

l. A Chinese *famille verte* enamelled biscuit bowl, Kangxi mark in underglaze blue within double circle and of the period, 6½in (16.5cm) diam.
£26,000–28,000 *CNY*

A Japanese Kakiemon blue and white bowl, *kin* mark, late 17thC, 8½in (21.5cm) diam.
£5,500–6,000 *C*

r. A Chinese blue and white punchbowl, Kangxi period, 15½in (39.5cm) diam.
£5,000–6,000 *C*

CHINESE POLYCHROME CERAMICS

The use of overglaze enamels was developed at Jingdezhen in the 15th century. Known as *sancai* (three colour), *wucai* (five colour) and *doucai* (opposed or contrasted colours), they were difficult to make and were usually reserved for Imperial wares. A small amount of coloured enamelling was done on the Transitional wares, but it was not until the late Kangxi period that the popular *famille verte* pieces, named after the predominant use of green enamel, were made in large quantities; there were also *famille jaune* (yellow) and the rare *famille noire* (black). Up to the end of the 17th century, any red colouring was produced with a flat iron-red oxide. *Famille rose* enamelling, the opaque pink of which was derived from colloidal gold, was not introduced until circa 1720. It was

one of the few ceramic innovations to have been introduced to China by Europeans, and by the mid-18th century the demand for *famille rose* decoration for export wares almost equalled that for blue and white. Huge *famille rose* dinner services were ordered from Europe, many of which were decorated with a family coat-of-arms or crest. A good quality *famille rose* tea bowl and saucer can still be bought for about £120, although a complete service may cost up to £50,000.

Towards the end of the 17th century, as the East Indies companies increased their trade with Japan, the Chinese potters competed with Arita by producing their own version of the popular Imari pattern. The Chinese version of Imari porcelain is thinner, with a harder, smoother glaze and softer colours.

FAMILLE ROSE
Bottles

A *famille rose* bottle, with underglaze blue garlic neck, painted with figures at leisure, Qianlong period, 10in (25.5cm) high.
£600–700 *CSK*

A *famille rose* moulded bottle, shaped as Liuhai holding a string of cash in both hands, late 18th/early 19thC, 6in (15cm) high.
£450–500 *C*

A *famille rose* bottle, painted in blue enamel on a yellow ground, blue enamelled Qianlong mark, early 20thC, 21½in (54.5cm) high, on a wood stand.
£1,700–2,000 *C*

A *famille rose* bottle vase, painted with magpies among flowering peonies, Qianlong seal mark, 19thC, 21½in (54.5cm) high.
£4,500–5,000 *C*

Bowls

A *famille rose* bowl, the exterior decorated with a ship in full sail, Qianlong period, c1770, 10in (25.5cm) diam.
£500–600 *WW*

A *famille rose* bowl, the exterior painted with 3 poppy blooms in pink, white and iron-red, with leaves in shaded tones of green, the interior with 3 fallen blossoms in pink and white, restored, Yongzheng mark and of the period, 3½in (9cm) diam.
£6,500–7,500 *S*

l. A *famille rose* bowl, painted with a European hunting scene, damaged, Qianlong period, 11in (28cm) diam.
£850–1,000 *CSK*

A *doucai* bowl, painted in enamels with the Eight Daoist Immortals, small rim chip, encircled four-character mark, 18thC, 7½in (18.5cm) diam.
£1,700–2,000 *C*

A *famille rose* punchbowl, delicately painted
with a continuous scene, restored, rim chipped,
early Qianlong period, 15½in (39.5cm) diam.
£3,000–4,000 *C*

A *famille rose* bowl, painted and modelled
in relief on the exterior, the interior with
a central group of flowers, Qianlong period,
11in (28cm) diam.
£800–1,000 *CSK*

A Chinese export *famille rose* bowl,
c1740, 11in (28cm) diam.
£500–550 *DUB*

*When tea and dinner services were
imported into Britain in the 18thC,
the service would have included
a table 'washing bowl', normally
about 11in (28cm) diam. This
was for the hostess to wash the tea
bowls at the table, as the porcelain
was far too expensive to be left for
the servants to wash.*

A *famille rose* armorial dish,
the exterior with a continuous
band of bamboo and flowersprays, rim chips, Qianlong
period, 11½in (29cm) wide.
£1,600–2,000 *C*

A *famille rose* punchbowl, painted
in pink, iron-red, black and gilt,
cracked and repaired, Qianlong
period, 16in (40.5cm) diam.
£1,200–1,500 *CSK*

l. A *famille rose* shell-
shaped dish, painted
with butterflies and
flowersprays below
iron-red and gilt bands,
Qianlong period,
3½in (9cm) wide.
£400–450 *CSK*

A pair of *famille rose*
fish bowls, each
painted with a
continuous scene,
the interior with
fish among aquatic
plants, 19thC,
18in (46cm) diam.
£1,800–2,200 *CSK*

A Chinese export *famille rose* bowl,
the exterior painted with a panel
scene depicting 'The Judgement
of Paris', within gilt and iron-red
borders, Qianlong period,
10½in (26.5cm) diam.
£2,000–2,200 *CNY*

A *famille rose* Mandarin pattern
punchbowl, painted with figures
reserved on a gilt scrolling
ground, cracked, Qianlong
period, 14in (35.5cm) diam.
£2,000–2,500 *C*

A *famille rose* punchbowl, painted
with figures within underglaze blue
floral surrounds, restored, Qianlong
period, 16in (40.5cm) diam.
£1,000–1,500 *C*

A pair of *famille rose* bowls,
with gilt rims, Qianlong seal
mark and of the period,
4¼in (11cm) diam.
£4,500–5,500 *C(HK)*

A *famille rose* and cobalt blue
fish bowl, the interior painted
with carp amid seaweed,
mid-Qianlong period,
24in (61cm) diam.
£10,000–11,000 *S(NY)*

r. A Canton *famille rose* punchbowl, painted within gold key pattern surrounds divided by butterflies, birds, flowers and emblems, restored, Daoguang period, 23in (59cm) diam.
£3,000–4,000 *CSK*

A Canton *famille rose* bowl, painted and gilt with alternating panels of dignitaries, ladies and attendants on terraces before a screen, and birds, butterflies and flowers, on green and gold scroll grounds, mid-19thC, 16in (40.5cm) diam.
£1,000–1,500 *CSK*

A Canton *famille rose* punchbowl, enamelled in the interior, restored, c1830, 20½in (52cm) diam.
£3,000–4,000 *C*

A *famille rose* bowl, the interior painted in underglaze blue with a roundel depicting figures with an ox and birds, Daoguang seal mark and of the period, 6in (15cm) diam.
£2,000–3,000 *S(S)*

A Canton *famille rose* punchbowl, painted with panels of ladies divided by green and gold bands, the interior rim with a gold band, rim restored, Daoguang period, 20in (51cm) diam.
£3,500–4,000 *CSK*

r. A *famille rose* bowl, with ribbed exterior, painted and gilt with figures, the interior turquoise, iron-red Daoguang seal mark, 6in (15cm) diam.
£400–450 *CSK*

A *famille rose* medallion bowl, painted with roundels of flowers and *lingzhi*, on a yellow ground, Daoguang mark and of the period, 6in (15cm) diam.
£2,000–2,500 *CSK*

A Canton *famille rose* punchbowl, decorated with Mandarins, c1830, 16in (40.5cm) diam.
£550–650 *EL*

A Canton *famille rose* punchbowl, painted with panels of figures between flowers and precious objects, the borders with birds and bats on a flower-decorated ground, slight damage, 19thC, 16in (40.5cm) diam.
£1,200–1,700 *S(S)*

A *famille rose* bowl, decorated with phoenix, flower and leaf sprays, hairline crack, Daoguang seal mark and of the period, 8¼in (21cm) diam.
£700–850 *WW*

A pair of *famille rose* bowls, with ruby ground, the interiors plain, Kangxi marks, 19thC, 4½in (11.5cm) diam.
£1,200–1,700 *C*

A Canton *famille rose* bowl, painted and gilt with alternating panels of figures on terraces, birds and butterflies among flowers, damaged, late 19thC, 14⅜in (36.5cm) diam.
£550–650 *CSK*

A Canton *famille rose* punchbowl, the rim with gilt ground, restored, 19thC, 18½in (47cm) high.
£4,000–5,000 *C*

A Canton *famille rose* punch-bowl, painted with a crest beneath the inscription 'Alexander Crawford Rhodes', 19thC, 16in (41cm) diam.
£4,500–5,500 C

A Canton *famille rose* basin, enamelled in the Mandarin palette, heightened in gilt, 19thC, 18½in (47cm) diam.
£2,000–2,200 CNY

A pair of *famille rose* chargers, decorated with flowers and butterflies, 19thC, 14in (35.5cm) diam.
£650–750 LRG

l. A Canton *famille rose* bowl, with gilt and burnt-orange key borders, restored, mid-19thC, with later cast gilt-brass beaded mounts, on a quatrefoil foot, 19in (48.5cm) diam.
£350–550 HSS

A Canton *famille rose* punchbowl, painted and gilt with friezes of figure groups, 19thC, 16in (41cm) diam.
£1,800–2,000 RBB

A Canton *famille rose* bowl, reserved in gold on a celadon ground, the rim painted on a gold ground, 19thC, 8½in (47.5cm) diam.
£2,000–2,500 Bea

A Canton *famille rose* punchbowl, decorated with courtly interiors depicting patriarchs, ladies and servants, 19thC, 20in (51cm) diam.
£2,500–3,000 SLN

Canton famille rose *wares are known as 'rose medallion' wares in the USA.*

A Canton *famille rose* punchbowl, painted with shaped panels of figures on terraces, rim chipped, 19thC, 14in (35.5cm) diam.
£800–1,000 C(S)

A Canton *famille rose* bowl, painted with panels of figures in conversation, the rim painted with birds, insects and flowers, 16in (40.5cm) diam.
£2,000–2,500 Bea

A *famille rose* bowl, Tongzhi mark and of the period, 7in (17.5cm) diam.
£1,600–1,800 Wai

Two *famille rose* bowls, with rounded sides rising to flaring rims with plain interiors, painted to the exterior with flowersprays, both with iron-red Guangzu six-character marks and of the period, 6½in (16.5cm) diam.
£2,500–3,500 C

r. A *famille rose* eggshell porcelain bowl, painted and gilt with a continuous scene, cracked, Qianlong mark, 5½in (14cm) diam.
£150–200 CSK

Cups & Mugs

A *famille rose* tea bowl and saucer, painted with blossoming plants, Yongzheng period, saucer 5in (12.5cm) diam.
£550–650 *CSK*

A *famille rose* wine cup, painted with a peony bearing one pink bloom, beside a yellow chrysanthemum, the reverse with a purple butterfly, the interior white, Yongzheng mark and of the period, 2½in (6.5cm) diam.
£3,800–4,400 *S*

A *famille rose* mug, painted with a coat-of-arms and inscription, restored, c1750, 5½in (14cm) high.
£650–750 *C*

A *famille rose* European subject tea cup and saucer, enamelled with 'The Ascension', Christ in Majesty above a group of Apostles, all on a plain grassy terrace, Yongzheng period, saucer 5in (12.5cm) diam.
£1,800–2,500 *C*

A *famille rose* European subject tea bowl, depicting Water from the Elements, after a design by Albani, early Qianlong period, 2½in (6.5cm) diam.
£700–800 *C*

Famille Rose Wares

Export *famille rose* wares were often decorated with European patterns sent to China via the East Indies companies. Family crests and coats-of-arms were added to these patterns by special order. Most of the important European families ordered special services to be made.

Five *famille rose* semi-eggshell porcelain tea bowls, 4 enamelled with a butterfly and flowersprays and a single bloom to the interior, both Qianlong period, 3½in (9cm) diam, and one larger, 4in (10cm) diam.
£1,500–2,000 *CAm*

A *famille rose* barrel-shaped mug, painted and gilt, Qianlong period, 4½in (11.5cm) high.
£450–500 *CSK*

A *famille rose* shell-shaped cup and stand, painted with sprays of flowers on the moulded dish below a pierced holder, rim chips, Qianlong period, 9in (23cm) wide.
£500–600 *CSK*

l. A *famille rose* tea bowl and saucer, 18thC, saucer 4½in (11.5cm) diam.
£400–450 *DAN*

A Chinese export *famille rose* mug, painted with peonies and a tree hung with berries, Qianlong period, 6½in (16cm) high.
£650–750 *Bea*

A pair of *famille rose* flared libation cups and stands, painted with panels of figures, on grounds of gilt scrolling foliage reserved with small pink panels, within orders of trailing flowers and bamboo, Qianlong period, stands 6½in (16cm) wide.
£1,200–1,500 *CSK*

A *famille rose* cup, painted with a continuous scene of chrysanthemums on a yellow ground, blue enamel Qianlong seal mark, early 20thC, 2½in (6cm) diam.
£350–400 *CSK*

l. A Chinese export mug, decorated in colours, with underglaze blue borders, 6in (15cm) high.
£2,000–2,500 *GC*

A set of 3 *famille rose* bell-shaped mugs, each painted with a large panel of flowersprays flanked by smaller quatrefoil floral panels, on underglaze blue cell pattern grounds, late Qianlong period, largest 5½in (13cm) high.
£1,200–1,400 *CSK*

A pair of *famille rose* beakers, 19thC, 3in (7cm) high, with a matching saucer dish.
£300–400 *HCH*

Figures – Animals

A pair of *famille rose* phoenix, on pierced iron-red rockwork painted with peonies, the birds with multi-coloured feathers, impressed marks, 19thC, 10in (25.5cm) high.
£650–750 *C*

A pair of *famille rose* cockerels, minor damage, 19thC, 6½in (16.5cm) high.
£1,400–1,700 *CSK*

l. A pair of *famille rose* models of *ho-o* birds, brightly decorated and perched on rockwork, 19thC, 11in (28cm) high.
£500–600 *DN*

A pair of *famille rose* pheasants, perched on pierced rockwork, 19thC, 14in (35.5cm) high.
£1,600–2,000 *CSK*

Figures – People

A set of 9 *famille rose* figures of Immortals, on floral bases, holding their various attributes, restored, late Qianlong period, 10in (25.5cm) high.
£4,200–4,700 *C*

A set of 8 *famille rose* figures of Immortals, wearing brightly coloured robes and holding their various attributes, some restoration, late Qianlong period, 9in (23cm) high.
£1,800–2,200 *C*

A pair of *famille rose* models of attendants, wearing lilac robes decorated with cloud scrolls, each holding a jar of peaches, restored, Qianlong period, 9½in (24cm) high.
£1,500–2,000 *CSK*

A pair of *famille rose* figures of dignitaries, holding a *ruyi* sceptre and a peach spray, slight damage and restoration, Jiaqing period, 9¼in (23.5cm) high.
£700–800 *CSK*

A pair of *famille rose* export figures of lady candle holders, each modelled in mirror image holding a *gu*-shaped beaker vase, wearing long robes with full sleeves, hair tied in a topknot, restored, Jiaqing period, 6in (40cm) high.
£4,250–5,000 *CAm*

A *famille rose* figure of a kneeling boy, wearing floral white robe and iron-red breeches, mounted in brass as a table lamp, the porcelain 18th/early 19thC, 12in (30.5cm) high.
£1,000–1,200 *CSK*

Two *famille rose* figures, one modelled as Li Tieguai, wearing black ground floral robes, 12½in (32cm) high, the other as Buddha, damaged, early 19thC, 12in (30.5cm) high.
£1,400–1,800 *C*

r. A *famille rose* model of Buddha, his robes decorated with butterflies among flowers, 19thC, 12in (30.5cm) high, on a wood stand.
£1,800–2,200 *CSK*

Two *famille rose* Daoist Immortal groups, each modelled with the Eight Immortals and Shoulao standing on rockwork and holding their attributes, chipped and repaired, 19thC, 6½in (16cm) high.
£300–350 *CAm*

Flatware

A *famille rose* enamelled plate, the interior painted *en grisaille* and gilt, the border with a blue enamelled Y-pattern ground below a band of scrolling foliage, rim chips, Yongzheng period, 8½in (21cm) wide.
£2,200–2,500 *CAm*

A *famille rose* saucer dish, the interior enamelled, the exterior plain, rim chip, encircled Yongzheng six-character mark and of the period, 8in (20cm) diam.
£3,000–3,500 *C*

A *famille rose* deep plate, painted with yellow and black cockerels among shrubs and rockwork, the pale blue cell pattern border reserved with panels of fruit and flowers, restored, Yongzheng period, 8½in (20.5cm) diam.
£200–300 *CSK*

A pair of *famille rose* dishes, each painted with a yellow and blue bird perched on blue rockwork, within pink patterned wells, borders of flowersprays and rims of iron-red and gilt foliage, one restored, Yongzheng period, 15in (38cm) diam.
£3,000–3,500 *CSK*

A *famille rose* deep saucer dish, painted with butterflies, insects and flowers, the rim gilt, encircled Yongzheng six-character mark and of the period, 21½in (54.5cm) diam.
£9,000–10,000 C

A pair of *famille rose* saucer dishes, painted in iron-red, shaded yellow, pink, white and green, one with 3 cracks, Yongzheng period, 7½in (19cm) diam.
£1,400–1,600 *CAm*

A *famille rose* deep dish, painted at the centre with a phoenix in flight above figures on a terrace, the well with cartouches containing ribboned vases reserved on a trellis pattern and flowerhead ground, Yongzheng period, 12½in (32cm) diam.
£3,500–4,000 *C*

A *famille rose* dish, painted after a design by Francesco Albani, within a gilt floral border, restored, Yongzheng period, 16in (40.5cm) diam.
£3,000–3,500 *C*

A *famille rose* cockerel dish, Yongzheng period, 14½in (37cm) diam.
£2,200–2,500 *C*

l. A set of 6 *famille rose* soup plates, decorated with pink and green diaper pattern, the exterior with iron-red prunus sprigs, Yongzheng period, 9in (23cm) diam.
£2,500–3,500 *WW*

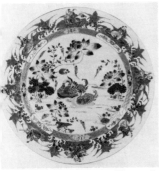

A *famille rose* dish, painted beneath a band of pink trellis pattern, the well reserved with cartouches of precious emblems, the border with the Eight Daoist Immortals, slight rubbing and chip, early Qianlong period, 13½in (34.5cm) diam.
£3,500–4,000 *CAm*

A *famille rose* deep dish, painted with figures in conversation, the everted cell pattern rim reserved with river landscape panels divided by flowers, restored, early Qianlong period, 15½in (39.5cm) high.
£700–800 *CSK*

A pair of *famille rose* armorial plates, painted with a central coat-of-arms below a crest with a lamb bearing the banner of St George, chips, restoration, Qianlong period, 9in (23cm) diam.
£800–1,200 *C*

l. A Chinese meat dish, painted in the Tobacco Leaf palette, the rim painted with gold scrolling design on a brown band, Qianlong period, 15in (38cm) wide.
£2,000–2,200 *Bea*

Three *famille rose* armorial plates, painted with a coat-of-arms, some cracks, Qianlong period, 9in (23cm) diam.
£2,500–3,000 *C*

A pair of *famille rose* armorial dishes, decorated with the arms of the Duke of Grafton, one chipped, Qianlong period, 10in (25.5cm) wide.
£1,000–1,200 *DN*

A *famille rose* dish, brightly enamelled with blue borders, chips to inner rim, Qianlong period, 18in (45.5cm) wide.
£1,500–2,000 *Bon*

A pair of *famille rose* pseudo Tobacco Leaf plates, Qianlong period, 9in (23cm) diam.
£2,000–2,200 *CSK*

A *famille rose* basket, Qianlong period, 10in (25.5cm) wide.
£2,000–2,200 *Bon*

r. A pair of crested plates, painted in *famille rose* enamels with mottoes 'Bonaespei' and 'Brevis estusus', Qianlong period, 6½in (16cm) diam.
£600–800 *Bon*

A *famille rose* dish, Qianlong period,
16½in (42cm) wide.
£1,000–1,500 *Bea*

A *famille rose* dish, painted in
pink, blue, green and brown,
small rim chip, Qianlong period,
20in (49.5cm) diam.
£1,500–2,000 *C*

A pair of *famille rose* armorial
plates, painted with a coat-of-
arms and flower festoons at the
border, one with minor chips,
Qianlong period, 9in (23cm) diam.
£1,700–2,000 *C*

A pair of *famille rose* plates,
painted with 'The Judgement
of Paris', one with rim chips
restored, the other with minute
rim chips, Qianlong period,
9in (23cm) diam.
£1,600–1,800 *C*

A Canton *famille rose*
quatrefoil dish, painted with
European figures in a wooded
landscape, Qianlong period,
11½in (29cm) wide.
£2,000–2,500 *CSK*

A *famille rose* plate, painted with a
pair of quail and flowers below a yellow
spearhead at the well, *bianco-sopra-
bianco* sprays at the borders, early
Qianlong period, 9in (23cm) diam.
£600–800 *C*

A pair of *famille rose* meat
dishes, painted and gilt
within spearhead borders,
both cracked, Qianlong,
12½in (32cm) wide.
£1,000–1,200 *CSK*

A Canton *famille rose*
yellow ground saucer
dish, decorated with
blue *shou* roundels,
surface wear, blue
enamel Qianlong seal
mark and of the period,
9in (23cm) diam.
£1,000–1,200 *C*

Two *famille rose* pseudo
Tobacco Leaf plates, and
2 large saucer dishes,
restored, late Qianlong
period, 9½ and 11in
(24 and 28cm) diam.
£1,200–1,500 *C*

Six *famille rose* plates, each
painted with birds above prunus
and bamboo, with floral borders,
one restored, one cracked,
chipped, Qianlong period,
9in (23cm) diam.
£1,200–1,500 *C*

l. A *famille rose* wavy
rimmed plate, outlined in
gilt against reserves of iron-
red whorls, Qianlong period,
12½in (31.5cm) diam.
£2,000–2,200 *Bon*

A pair of *famille rose* dishes, decorated with 2 peacocks, small rim chips, Qianlong period, 13in (33cm) wide.
£1,500–2,000 *C*

Two *famille rose* dishes, one painted with crabs, the other with flowers, Qianlong period, 15in (38cm) diam.
£1,000–1,200 *CSK*

A *famille rose* saucer dish, painted with flowers issuing from blue pierced rockwork within a gilt spearhead border, Qianlong period, 10in (25.5cm) diam.
£300–350 *CSK*

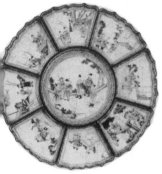

A Canton *famille rose* hors d'oevres set, with pale blue borders reserved with dark brown scrolling foliage, Qianlong period, 17in (43cm) diam.
£700–800 *CSK*

A *famille rose* meat dish, painted with flowers, Qianlong period, 16in (40cm) wide.
£1,200–1,400 *CSK*

A *famille rose* European subject dish, painted at the centre with a naked lady, with *grisaille* and gilt strapwork and cartouches containing doves at the rim, repainted and restored, Qianlong period, 16in (40cm) wide.
£2,000–2,500 *C*

The scene is after an engraving of 1781 by Bonnet entitled 'Le Bain'.

A *famille rose* and underglaze blue dish, with everted foliate rim, painted with a central panel of a river landscape within a whorl pattern, Qianlong period, 15in (38cm) diam.
£800–1,000 *CSK*

Two *famille rose* meat dishes, painted with bouquets of flowers within iron-red and gilt spearhead wells and rims, the borders with flowersprays, Qianlong period, 12in (30.5cm) wide.
£2,000–2,500 *CSK*

A *famille rose* plate, painted with an elderly fisherman and assistants, minor chips, Qianlong period, 9in (23cm) diam.
£700–800 *C*

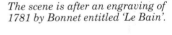

l. A pair of *famille rose* soup plates, painted with gilt monograms within chain pattern wells and borders of flowers and exotic birds, Qianlong period, 9in (23cm) diam.
£600–700 *CS*

The crest and cypher are those of William Braund.

A *famille rose* dish, painted within a pierced iron-red and gilt border, Qianlong period, 14in (35.5cm) diam.
£1,800–2,000 *C*

A *famille rose* dish, painted within an iron-red and gilt spearhead well and rim, fritted, Qianlong period, 14in (35.5cm) diam.
£1,200–1,500 *CSK*

A set of 3 Chinese export *famille rose* plates, Qianlong period, 9in (23cm) diam.
£700–800 *DN*

A pair of Chinese export *famille rose* plates, painted in orange and black, rims within black lines, slight glaze damage, Qianlong period, 13½in (35cm) diam.
£800–1,000 *Bea*

A pair of Chinese export *famille rose* meat dishes, Qianlong period, 15in (38cm) wide.
£1,700–2,000 *DN*

A pair of *famille rose* plates, each painted with a coat-of-arms, small rim chips, Qianlong period, 9in (23cm) diam.
£850–950 *CSK*
The arms are those of Carr, c1765–70.

A set of 7 *famille rose* plates, 4 octagonal and 3 circular, decorated within an underglaze blue border, Qianlong period, 9in (23cm) diam.
£650–850 *S(S)*

A set of 3 *famille rose* plates, the rims with iron-red and gilt bands, one with hairline crack and chip, Qianlong period, 9in (23cm) diam.
£700–800 *CSK*

A pair of *famille rose* plates, painted with sprays of flowers, within iron-red and gilt whorl pattern surrounds, divided by blue enamel clouds and iron-red half flowerheads, one cracked, Qianlong period, 11in (28cm) diam.
£1,200–1,500 *CSK*

A pair of *famille rose* dishes, decorated in bright enamels, the ground enriched with multi-coloured blooms, small chips, Qianlong period, 15in (38cm) diam.
£3,000–3,500 *CAm*

A *famille rose* pseudo Tobacco Leaf meat dish, painted with large serrated leaves and flowerheads, rim chips, Qianlong period, 18½in (47cm) wide.
£2,700–3,200 *CSK*

A *famille rose* meat dish, painted and gilt within a gilt chain border, minute rim frits, Qianlong period, 12½in (30.5cm) wide.
£700–800 *CSK*

A *famille rose* dish, Qianlong period, 14in (35cm) diam.
1,500–2,000 *CAm*

A *famille rose* armorial plate, with gilt spearhead border, the rim with sepia landscape and bird vignettes, Qianlong period, 8½in (21.5cm) diam.
£700–800 *L*

A *famille rose* dish, the centre painted and gilt with a chrysanthemum, within a border of interlacing peonies and further chrysanthemums and bands of flowerheads on geometric grounds, chipped, Qianlong period, 16in (40.5cm) diam.
£500–600 *CSK*

A pair of *famille rose* and underglaze blue meat dishes, painted and gilt, damaged, Qianlong period, 6½in (42cm) wide.
750–1,000 *CSK*

A pair of *famille rose* plates, painted with cockerels in a garden and sprays of flowers, slight damage, Qianlong period, 13in (33cm) diam.
£650–750 *Bea*

l. A *famille rose* armorial plate, painted with the arms of Pigot below a wolf's head crest, gilt bands, small rim chip, Qianlong period, 9in (23cm) diam.
£1,000–1,200 *S*

A pair of *famille rose* plates, each decorated in underglaze blue with a river landscape within spearhead and decorative borders, cracks, Qianlong period, 12¼in (31cm) diam.
£300–350 *DN*

A *famille rose* armorial plate, with the arms of Michel of Kingston Russell, Dorset, above a motto, Qianlong period, 9in (23cm) diam.
1,600–1,800 *S*

A *famille rose* armorial plate, decorated with floral sprays to the rim and with the Bigland arms, Qianlong period, 13¾in (35cm) diam.
£2,100–2,500 *DN*

This plate was made for the second marriage of Ralph Bigland (1711–84).

A *famille rose* dish, enamelled with iron-red, lime green, pink and dark brown feathery leaves and hibiscus blooms, small rim chip, Qianlong period, 15in (38cm) wide.
£1,500–1,800 *C*

A pair of *famille rose* armorial foliate plates, modelled on a European silver shape, painted in iron-red and gilt, with central coat-of-arms, crest and motto, chipped and cracked, Qianlong period, 10in (25.5cm) diam.
£3,000–3,500 *C*

r. A *famille rose* armorial plate, painted with iron-red and gilt arms of Lauder, and a motto, within a border of flowersprays and gilt spearhead bands, rim chips, Qianlong period, c1760, 9in (23cm) diam.
£600–700 *CSK*

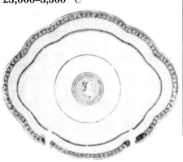

A Chinese export *famille rose* dish, painted with a pink ground portrait medallion, green and gilt rim, late Qianlong period, 6½in (16.5cm) wide.
£350–450 *CSK*

A Chinese export *famille rose* dish, decorated with a seated figure and attendants, floral border heightened in gilt, 18thC, 13½in (34.5cm) diam.
£950–1,100 *CNY*

A *famille rose* saucer dish, 18thC, 10½in (26.5cm) diam.
£250–300 *DN*

l. A pair of Chinese export *famille rose* plates, 18thC, 8½in (21.5cm) diam.
£600–700 *DN*

A pair of *famille rose* dishes, painted and gilt, slightly chipped, c1800, 8½in (21.5cm) long.
£450–500 *CSK*

A pair of *famille rose* dishes, late 18thC, 10in (25.5cm) wide.
£1,200–1,400 *Wai*

A *famille rose* green ground tea tray, the central reserve panel inscribed in iron-red and with a date for 1797, painted on a pale green ground, iron-red Jiaqing six-character seal mark and of the period, 6½in (16cm) wide.
£3,000–3,500 *C*

A *famille rose* European subject dish, painted with a lady wearing a puce dress with green bodice, c1820, 15in (38cm) wide.
£1,500–2,000 *C*

A Canton *famille rose* dish, painted and gilt to the centre, late 18thC, 14½in (37cm) diam.
£1,000–1,200 *CSK*

r. A Canton *famille rose* meat dish, painted in the centre with figures, the border with iron-red and gilt dragons chasing flaming pearls, late 18thC, 14½in (37cm) wide.
£500–600 *CSK*

Garden Seats

A pair of *famille rose* barrel-shaped garden seats, with phoenix, birds, cranes and flower decoration, 19thC, 19in (48.5cm) high.
£2,000–2,200 *EL*

The pierced work on the sides of these seats is based upon the design of Chinese cash (coins).

A pair of Canton *famille rose* garden seats, painted with figure and bird panels around pierced cash between gilt stud borders, late 19thC, 19in (48cm) high.
£2,500–3,000 *S(S)*

A Canton *famille rose* garden seat, painted with panels of figures and birds and pierced with double cash, between bands of moulded bosses on a ground of dense floral meander, late Qing Dynasty, 8½in (47cm) high.
£1,600–2,000 *C*

A pair of Canton *famille rose* hexagonal garden seats, 19thC, 24in (61cm) high.
£2,400–2,700 *GAZE*

Garden Seats

Garden seats can vary in price depending on age, size, quality, decoration and condition. Eighteenth century garden seats are the most expensive, the *famille rose* ones fetching higher prices than the underglaze blue 'Nankin' ones.

Current decorating trends can also affect demand and thus price.

A pair of *famille rose* barrel-shaped garden seats, the panels enamelled with birds on a flower-decorated ground, the top and sides with pierced cash decoration, late Qing Dynasty, 18¼in (46.5cm) high.
£1,000–1,200 *CNY*

A pair of *famille rose* garden seats, decorated with *shou* characters on a yellow ground, late Qing Dynasty, 18½in (47cm) high.
£800–1,000 *CNY*

A pair of *famille rose* and *famille verte* barrel-shaped garden seats, decorated on a closely patterned gilt grounds, 19thC, 18½in (47cm) high.
£3,500–4,000 *GC*

A pair of *famille rose* pink ground barrel-shaped garden seats, with pierced cash and rows of moulded studs, painted and gilt with shaped panels of phoenix and birds among flowers, all between yellow ground formal borders of lappets, 19thC, 18½in (47cm) high.
£2,000–2,500 *CSK*

A Canton *famille rose* garden seat, decorated on a dense gilt floral ground, late Qing Dynasty, 18½in (47cm) high.
£1,600–1,800 *C*

A pair of *famille rose* garden seats, painted with panels reserved on a yellow ground, late Qing Dynasty, 18in (46cm) high.
£3,000–3,500 *C*

Jardinières

A pair of *famille rose* jardinières and stands, brightly decorated with alternate panels of inscriptions and Immortals, Daoguang seal marks, 9½in (24cm) high.
£900–1,200 *DN*

A Canton *famille rose* jardinière and stand, reserved on a gold decorated blue ground, 19thC, 16in (41cm) diam.
£900–1,200 *Bea*

A *famille rose* reticulated jardinière, painted with roundels of flowers and river landscapes, damaged, Yongzheng period, 7½in (19cm) high.
£600–660 *CSK*

A pair of Canton *famille rose* jardinières, with widely flaring sides and stands, 11in (28cm) diam.
£4,000–4,500 *CSK*

A Canton *famille rose* jardinière and stand, painted and gilt with alternating panels of dignitaries on terraces and birds and butterflies among flowers, minor restoration, 19thC, 11in (28cm) wide.
£850–950 *CSK*

l. A *famille rose* jardinière, painted with flowers in coloured enamels within blue and iron red borders, 19thC, 13in (33cm) diam.
£2,000–2,400 *P(N)*

A *famille rose* jardinière, decorated *en grisaille* with barbed panels, each enclosing a scene of a palace in a lake landscape, ring handles missing, damaged, Yongzheng period, 22½in (57cm) diam, on wood stand.
£25,000–30,000 *S*

Jars

A *famille rose* armorial jar, painted in black, gilt and iron-red, foot restored, c1720, 8in (20.5cm) high.
£3,000–4,000 *C*

A *famille rose* jar, painted with phoenix among flowering shrubs issuing from pierced blue rockwork, Qianlong period, 8in (20.5cm) high.
£700–800 *CSK*

An ormolu-mounted *famille rose* jar and cover, the decoration on a pink ground, the porcelain c1800, 22in (56cm) high.
£2,200–2,400 *C*

A *famille rose* pale blue ground oviform jar and cover, painted with gilt *shou* characters below yellow lappets to the shoulder, star crack, cover chipped, iron-red Daoguang seal mark, 9½in (24cm) high.
£800–900 *CSK*

Services

r. A *famille rose* Tobacco Leaf supper set, comprising a central octagonal box and cover and 8 fan-shaped boxes and covers, all in an octafoil dish, damaged, Qianlong period, 15½in (39.5cm) diam.
£6,500–7,500 *C*

This is a desirable pattern, particularly in the USA.

famille rose part service, comprising dishes, 11 plates, 5 bowls and Spode pottery matching plates, namelled with exotic birds and owers, Qianlong period.
5,000–5,500 *GSP*

The remainder of a Canton *famille rose* dinner service, comprising an oval dish, oval vegetable dish and cover, 4 rectangular vegetable dishes and 2 covers, a pair of oval dishes, 4 liners and 2 covers, each piece with a panel of figures meeting by a veranda framed by a border of butterflies among scattered flowers, some damage, early 19thC.
£2,000–2,200 *S(S)*

A *famille rose* part dinner service, comprising 71 pieces, made for the Swedish market, decorated with sprays of flowers below an iron-red and gold stylised florette and C-curl border, Qianlong period.
16,500–17,500 *S*

Tea & Coffee Wares

A Chinese export *famille rose* miniature part tea service, comprising: a teapot and cover, 2 teabowls, 2 cups and 8 saucers, slight glaze chipping, Qianlong period.
£1,200–1,400 *Bea*

A *famille rose* globular teapot and cover, chip to cover, Qianlong period, 4½in (11.5cm) high.
£400–500 *CSK*

A *famille rose* Mandarin pattern part tea service, comprising a silver-mounted teapot and domed cover, a milk jug and domed cover, baluster tea caddy and domed cover, an octagonal lobed spoon tray, a hexagonal lobed spoon tray, a large teabowl and saucer and 6 teabowls and saucers, enamelled with a dignitary seated in a chair being attended by his wife, a child and a female servant, with floral panels reserved on gilt and *grisaille* borders, Qianlong period.
£3,400–3,800 *CAm*

A *famille rose* teapot, c1770, 4in (10cm) high.
£300–400 *Wai*

A *famille rose* teapot and cover, the sides, handle and spout moulded as bamboo, the flat cover applied with a twig finial, fritting, handle cracked, Qianlong period, 5in (12.5cm) high.
£550–650 *CAm*

A *famille rose* coffee pot and cover, painted with figures below bird and cell cartouches, Qianlong period, 9in (23cm) high.
£1,000–1,200 *C*

A *famille rose* teapot and cover the cover with a knop finial enamelled in yellow, Qianlong period, 4½in (11.5cm) high.
£400–450 *Bon*

A *famille rose* Tobacco Leaf pattern teapot and cover, restored, c1760, 6in (15cm) high.
£3,000–3,500 *C*

The Tobacco Leaf pattern is particularly popular in the USA.

A *famille rose* part tea and coffee service, comprising a coffee pot and cover, 3 cups and 6 saucers, 6 smaller cups and 7 saucers, and 3 tea cups, all painted and gilt with scattered flowersprays within diaper borders, damaged, Qianlong period, pot 7½in (19cm) high.
£400–500 *CSK*

A Canton *famille rose* enamelled tea kettle and stand, with a swing handle, covered in plaited cane, fitted with a lamp, some damage, Qianlong period, 11½in (29cm) high.
£900–1,200 *CSK*

r. A Chinese export miniature tea service, comprising 30 pieces, painted in *rouge de fer* and gilt with butterflies among peonies and lotus, 18thC, teapot 4in (10cm) wide.
£2,000–2,400 *CSK*

A Chinese export *famille rose* child's tea service, comprising a teapot and cover, milk jug and cover, tea caddy, sugar bowl, spoon tray, 2 teabowls, 2 coffee cups and 2 saucers, each piece painted with figures in conversation by a table, Qianlong period.
£1,200–1,400 *Bea*

Miniature Tea Services

From the Queen Anne period (1702–14) onwards it was fashionable in Europe to collect miniatures. Export 'toy' services were not necessarily made as children's toys but were looked upon as collectable curiosities. There was an enormous variety in quality, with the best being very expensive, both then and now. The more complete the service the greater the value will be.

A Chinese export *famille rose* toy tea service, comprising: a teapot, cover and stand, milk jug and cover, tea caddy, spoon tray and 6 cups and 4 saucers, each painted with flowersprays and a puce scale border, some damage, Qianlong period.
£800–1,000 *S(S)*

Tureens

A *famille rose* tureen and cover, the double rabbit head handles in iron-red, Qianlong period, 13in (33cm) wide.
£4,200–4,800 S

A Chinese export *famille rose* tureen and cover, with animals' head handles and pomegranate knop, with matching dish, minor chips and some glaze rubbing, Qianlong period, dish 17in (43cm) wide.
£4,500–5,500 Bea

A *famille rose* tureen and domed cover, with boars' head handles and pomegranate finial, painted and gilt, damaged, Qianlong period, 13in (33cm) wide.
£3,000–3,500 CSK

A *famille rose* tureen and cover, modelled after a European silver original, supported on 4 claw feet, with rococo scroll finial, chipped, Qianlong period, 12½in (32cm) wide.
£2,500–3,000 C

A *famille rose* tureen, cover and stand, with iron-red hares' head handles and knop finial, enamelled with mixed floral sprays, Qianlong period, 14½in (37cm) wide.
£4,200–4,700 C

A *famille rose* armorial tureen and cover, the tureen with iron-red handles, body cracks, enamel slightly worn, Qianlong period, 16in (40.5cm) diam.
£2,000–3,000 C

A *famille rose* and blue and white tureen and domed cover, chipped, Qianlong period, 11½in (29cm) wide.
£4,500–5,000 C

A *famille rose* soup tureen and cover, and a similar meat dish, 18thC, 18in (45.5cm) wide.
£2,500–3,000 GM

A *famille rose* hen tureen and cover, with brightly enamelled wing and tail feathers, restored, Qianlong period, 8in (20.5cm) wide.
£3,000–4,000 C

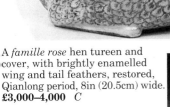

A *famille rose* tureen and cover, damaged, 18thC, 11in (28cm) wide.
£1,200–1,700 CSK

A Chinese export *famille rose* tureen, cover and stand, some damage, 18thC, stand 16in (40.5cm) wide.
£3,000–3,500 HSS

A Cantonese vegetable tureen and domed cover, painted on a green scroll gold ground, 19thC, 9½in (24cm) wide.
£400–500 C

Vases

A pair of Transitional *wucai* baluster vases and covers, slight damage, c1640, 15in (38cm) high.
£3,000–3,500 *C*

A pair of vases and covers, painted with exotic birds, iron-red flowers, green foliage and insects, the necks with barbed decoration in green and red, one with hair crack, 13½in (34.5cm) high.
£3,200–3,500 *GSP*

A *famille rose* vase, painted in bright enamels, Yongzheng period, 8in (20.5cm) high
£1,000–1,200 *C*

A *famille rose* relief-moulded square baluster vase, some damage, Yongzheng/Qianlong period, 20in (51cm) high, with lamp fitting.
£1,800–2,500 *C*

A garniture of Mandarin pattern vases, some damage, Qianlong period, tallest 12½in (32cm) high.
£800–1,000 *Bon*

A *famille rose* baluster vase, Qianlong period, 11½in (29cm) high.
£350–400 *CSK*

A *famille rose café-au-lait* ground garniture, comprising 3 baluster vases and covers and 2 beaker vases and covers, fritted, Qianlong period, tallest 11in (23cm) high.
£3,000–3,400 *C*

A pair of *famille rose* vases and one beaker vase, each painted with a duck swimming amongst lotus and iris, covers restored, Qianlong period, tallest 11in (28cm) high.
£2,000–2,500 *C*

A pair of *famille rose* square baluster vases, painted with a landscape within iron-red and gilt rococo borders, chipped, gilt rubbed, Qianlong period, 10½in (26.5cm) high.
£1,500–2,000 *C*

A *famille rose* baluster vase, reserved on a rich ruby ground between bands of cell pattern and flower cartouches at the foot and shoulder, Qianlong period, 13½in (34.5cm) high.
£2,000–2,200 *C*

l. A *famille rose* beaker vase, decorated on a ground of gilt scrolling foliage, rim fritted, base chip, Qianlong period, 16½in (42cm) high.
£1,500–2,000 *C*

A *famille rose* vase of quatrefoil cross-section, with underglaze blue floral surrounds, Qianlong period, 11in (28cm) high.
£400–500 *CSK*

A *famille rose* Mandarin pattern three-piece garniture, all reserved on a white raised-dot ground embellished with flowersprays and iron-red and gilt bats, one foot rim chipped, one small rim chip re-stuck, Qianlong period, 10in (25.5cm) high.
£2,200–2,800 *C*

A pair of *famille rose* vases and covers, each painted beneath a band of turquoise lappets embellished with flowers at the shoulder, some damage, Qianlong period, 14in (35.5cm) high.
£1,500–2,000 *C*

A *famille rose* mallet-shaped vase, with pierced handles, iron-red Qianlong seal mark, early 20thC, 8½in (21.5cm) high.
£600–700 *CSK*

A *famille rose* bottle vase, painted with 2 iron-red bats in flight beside fruiting and flowering peach branches, iron-red six-character Qianlong mark, 21in (53.5cm) high.
£2,400–2,600 *CSK*

A pair of *famille rose* Mandarin pattern vases, with dragon handles and domed covers, painted and gilt with panels of figures on terraces overlooking river landscapes, damaged, 18thC, 14in (35.5cm) high, and a matching beaker.
£1,500–2,000 *CSK*

A Chinese export *famille rose* baluster vase, the interior fitted with a brass liner, restored, 18thC, 22in (56cm) high.
£8,000–9,000 *S(NY)*

A Chinese *famille rose* vase, 18thC, 6in (15cm) high.
£350–400 *Wai*

A pair of *famille rose* baluster enamelled vases and covers, with 2 lion mask handles and Buddhistic lion finial, cracked and restored, Qianlong/Jiaqing period, 24in (61cm) high.
£5,000–5,500 *CAm*

A Canton *famille rose* vase, cracked, early 19thC, 28in (71cm) high.
£1,200–1,500 *C*

A Canton *famille rose* celadon ground vase, the neck applied with *chilong* handles, Daoguang period, 18in (45.5cm) high.
£650–800 *Bon*

A pair of Canton *famille rose* vases, with applied dragons, 19thC, 22½in (57cm) high.
£3,000–4,000 *C*

A *famille rose* vase, painted with a peach spray and a peony, underglaze blue Qianlong seal mark, 19thC, 21½in (54.5cm) high.
£2,500–3,000 *C*

A pair of Canton *famille rose* vases, with reserved panels of warriors and other figures in interiors and alternate panels with vases of flowers and insects, restored, 19thC, 10in (25.5cm) high.
£400–500 *GAK*

A Canton *famille rose* vase, with embossed butterfl handles, 19thC, 23in (58.5cm) high
£700–800 *CDC*

A pair of Canton *famille rose* vases, decorated with peacocks and other exotic birds in flowering branches, 19thC, 24in (61cm) high.
£1,200–1,500 *P(Ch)*

A *famille rose* pear-shaped vase, painted with deer, Qianlong seal mark, 19thC, 18in (45.5cm) high.
£6,000–8,000 *C*

A pair of Canton *famille rose* vases, moulded with *shishi*, decorated in brightly coloured enamels, the grounds with birds and flowers, slight damage, 19thC, 18in (45.5cm) high.
£800–1,000 *P(S)*

l. A pair of *famille rose* yellow ground beaker vases, 19thC, 10½in (26.5cm) high.
£300–400 *Bon*

A Canton *famille rose* vase, decorated in enamels and gilt, the shoulders applied with pairs of *chilong*, the neck with confronting *shishi*, 19thC, 32in (81.5cm) high.
£2,000–2,500 *Bon*

A *famille rose* baluster vase, painted with a pheasant on rock-work among peonies and prunus, 19thC, 20½in (52cm) high.
£2,500–3,000 *C*

r. A pair of Canton *famille rose* vases, the shoulders with lions' mask ring handles, 19thC, 14in (35.5cm) high.
£1,000–1,200 *LAY*

A pair of Canton *famille rose* flaring vases, with pierced covers, each painted with figure panels, divided by gilt squirrels and vines, with gilt handles, the covers similarly decorated, 19thC, 9in (23cm) high.
£2,500–3,000 *CAm*

A pair of Canton *famille rose* baluster vases and domed covers with Guanyin finials, reserved on a ground of scrolling flowers, fruit, exotic birds and butterflies, slight damage, 19thC, 21½in (55cm) high.
£4,000–4,500 *C*

A *famille rose* oviform enamelled vase, the interior and base with a turquoise glaze, Qianlong seal mark, 19thC, 9in (22.5cm) high.
£1,800–2,200 *C*

A *famille rose* vase, with flaring neck, the base unglazed, 19thC, 17in (43cm) high.
£800–1,000 *C*

A pair of Canton *famille rose* baluster vases, each with swan-neck handles, restored, 19thC, 25in (63.5cm) high.
£2,500–3,000 *C*

A *famille rose* vase, with tall flaring neck, painted and gilt with *shou* medallions surrounded by flowerheads and scrolling leaves, underglaze blue Guangxu six-character mark and of the period, 15½in (39.5cm) high.
£2,000–2,400 *CSK*

A pair of Canton *famille rose* vases, decorated with bright colours, late 19thC, 13in (33cm) high.
£800–1,000 *DDM*

A pair of *famille rose* vases, with birds and flowers on a yellow ground, c1920, now mounted as lamps, 17in (43cm) high.
£480–530 *RIT*

A *famille rose* vase, moulded with vases of flowers on a white ground, Qing Dynasty, 23in (58.5cm) high.
£280–330 *SLN*

A pair of *famille rose* baluster vases and covers, with crouching lion cub finials and blue enamel lions' mask fixed ring handles, late Qing Dynasty, 19in (48.5cm) high.
£2,500–3,500 *C*

Miscellaneous

A pair of *famille rose* Mandarin bough pots, repaired, 19thC, 8½in (21.5cm) high.
£3,000–4,000 *SK(B)*

An ormolu-mounted *famille rose* brush pot, porcelain Yongzheng period, mounts stamped 'E. F. Caldwell Co, New York', 7½in (19cm) high
£5,000–5,500 *CNY*

A Canton *famille rose* bough pot and cover, reserved on a relief-decorated ground, with gilt rope-twist handles, 19thC, 8½in (21.5cm) high.
£1,700–2,000 *C*

A *famille rose* covered box, the cover enamelled with a fruiting peach tree with *lingzhi* and flowers, the base with flowers, late 19thC, 10¼in (26cm) diam.
£600–660 *RIT*

A pair of *famille rose* elephant candlesticks, each with 'jewelle and painted trappings, Qing Dynasty, 7in (18cm) high.
£1,500–1,750 *S(S)*

A *famille rose* Mandarin pattern chocolate pot, with cartouches of figures on terraces on a Y-pattern ground, the domed cover with a peach spray finial, painted and gilt, restored, Qianlong period, 7in (17.5cm) high.
£350–450 *CSK*

A *famille rose* kendi, painted with a band of peonies, the neck and spout with entwined lotus and peonies, 18thC, 8in (20.5cm) high.
£640–700 *CSK*

A *famille rose* wine cooler, painted with sprays of flowers, Qianlong period, 8in (20.5cm) high.
£1,850–2,200 *S(S)*

A *famille rose* brush pot, painted around the exterior in bright enamels, the base and interior glazed turquoise and the rim gilded, Jiaqing seal mark and of the period, 5½in (14cm) high.
£4,000–4,500 *S*

A pair of *famille rose* candle-holders, each modelled as a lady wearing long pleated robes, restored, Qianlong period, 16in (40.5cm) high.
£15,000–16,000 *C*

These candleholders are of exceptionally good quality.

A *famille rose* Meissen-style stand, minor damage, c1775, 12in (30.5cm) high, mounted in gilt-metal as a table lamp.
£1,500–1,800 *CNY*

A *famille rose* stupa reliquary, painted on a deep blue ground, the top with a lapis lazuli sphere slight damage, mid-Qing Dynasty, 12in (30.5cm) high.
£1,200–1,500 *C*

FAMILLE VERTE
Bowls & Dishes

A *famille verte* bowl and cover, damaged, Kangxi period, 5½in (14cm) diam, wooden stand.
£800–900 *C*

A *famille verte* bowl, decorated with panels of beasts on a plain ground, slight damage, Chenghua mark, Kangxi period, 6½in (16.5cm) diam.
£350–400 *DN*

A *famille verte* dish, painted on a dense green cracked ice pattern ground scattered with iron-red and blue daisy heads, small rim chips, Kangxi period, 20in (51cm) diam.
£7,000–8,000 *C*

Kangxi porcelain

Much Kangxi porcelain bears the retrospective six-character mark of the Chenghua period (1465–87). The Kangxi mark often appears on late 19th and early 20thC export wares, especially ginger jars.

A pair of *famille verte* dishes, enamelled within an iron-red diapered border, one with minor rim restoration, Kangxi period, 7in (18cm) square.
£1,200–1,400 *CNY*

An aubergine ground Brinjal bowl, incised and painted in green, yellow and cream enamels, square seal mark, Kangxi period, 4½in (11.5cm) diam.
£1,800–2,200 *C*

A *famille verte* shallow bowl and domed cover, with animal head handles, painted in blue and green, Kangxi period, 7½in (19cm) diam.
£800–1,000 *CSK*

l. A *famille verte* fish bowl, enamelled in bright colours, the interior with iron-red fish swimming among seaweed, late Qing Dynasty, 22in (56cm) diam.
£2,500–2,800 *CNY*

r. A *famille verte* fish bowl, painted in Kangxi style on a seeded ground, 19thC, 17in (43cm) diam.
£1,000–1,200 *CNY*

Ewers

A pair of *famille verte* lobed globular ewers, one spout restored, pierced, Kangxi period, 9in (23cm) high.
£4,000–5,000 *CSK*

> **Miller's is a price GUIDE not a price LIST**

A *famille verte* ewer, modelled as a standing Buddhistic lion, decorated in iron-red and green with a yellow character *wang* below an aubergine horn, chipped, spout damaged, Kangxi period, 8in (20.5cm) high.
£3,500–4,000 *C*

A *famille verte* biscuit ewer, the 3 moulded bands enamelled with horses leaping over waves, restored, Kangxi period, 17½in (45cm) high.
£2,000–2,400 *C*

A *famille verte* ewer and cover enamelled with phoenix and pheasants, damaged, Kangxi period, 14in (35.5cm) high.
£25,000–30,000 *C*

Figures

Five *famille verte* figures of Daoist Immortals, wearing coloured robes and seated with one knee raised, 4 with their attributes missing, damaged and restored, Kangxi period, 6in (15cm) high.
£5,000–6,000 *C*

A pair of *famille verte* figures of boys, painted with precious objects and *ruyi* head collars, their hair tied in a bow at the front, minor damage, Kangxi period, 11in (28cm) high.
£3,000–3,400 *CSK*

A *famille verte* group of 2 ladies both wearing coats decorated with roundels of flowerheads, damaged and repaired, Kangxi period, 8½in (21.5cm) high.
£3,300–3,600 *C*

A *famille verte* biscuit figure of a warrior, restored, Kangxi period, 8in (20.5cm) high.
£2,300–2,800 *C*

A *famille verte* figure of Li Tie guai, and a *famille rose* figure of an Immortal on a mound base, both damaged, early 19thC, 8in (20.5cm) high.
£650–700 *C(S)*

A *famille verte* figure of an official, some fritting, Kangxi period, 8½in (22cm) high.
£2,000–2,200 *C*

Flatware

A pair of *famille verte* dishes, painted in strong enamels, one damaged, Kangxi period, 14in (35.5cm) diam.
£4,500–5,000 *C*

A *famille verte* dish, with a green seeded floral border and gadrooned rim, Kangxi period, 13in (33cm) diam.
£2,600–3,000 *C*

A *famille verte* saucer dish, with an iron-red cell pattern ground at the well, the reverse with simple flowersprays, damaged, encircled lotus mark, Kangxi period, 10½in (26.5cm) diam.
£1,200–1,500 *C*

A pair of *famille verte* plates, the borders with floral green ground, the white exteriors incised with leafy sprays, one chipped, Kangxi period, 9½in (24cm) diam.
£2,000–2,200 *C*

A *famille verte* plate, painted within an elaborate green floral border, Kangxi period, 9in (23cm) diam.
£2,500–3,000 *C*

An 'egg-and-spinach' glazed plate, with mottled glaze of yellow, green and aubergine, the base glazed white, damaged, Kangxi period, 8in (20.5cm) diam.
£1,000–1,200 *C*

A set of 6 *famille verte* plates, each painted with an equestrian dignitary and a foot attendant, rim chips, restored, Kangxi period, 9in (23cm) diam.
£3,500–4,000 *C*

A set of 6 *famille verte* plates, each painted with 5 lotus heads in iron-red, yellow, black, blue and aubergine, damaged and restored, Kangxi period, 8½in (21.5cm) diam.
£3,500–4,000 *C*

A *famille verte* saucer dish, painted in vivid colours, restored, encircled Kangxi six-character mark and of the period, 9½in (24cm) diam.
£5,000–5,500 *C*

A pair of *famille verte* plates, each painted with an equestrian figure and a boy attendant, Kangxi period, 9in (23cm) diam.
£2,000–2,200 *CSK*

A pair of *doucai famille verte* plates, the borders with the Eight Daoist Immortals, each riding a fish among green waves, one slightly cracked, Kangxi period, 9in (23cm) diam.
£1,600–1,800 *CSK*

A *famille verte* dish, with a rich blue translucent enamel, the centre with a Buddhistic lion playing with a ball, damaged, Kangxi period, 20½in (52cm) diam.
£3,000–3,500 *C*

l. A pair of *famille verte* deep plates, minor frits, Kangxi period, 8½in (21.5cm) diam. **£1,000–1,200** *CSK*

Pronunciation

For information on the pronunciation of Chinese words, please refer to page 12.

A *famille verte* dish, painted with chrysanthemums issuing from green rockwork within a cell pattern border, small cracks, Kangxi period, 14½in (37cm) diam. **£2,000–2,200** *CSK*

A *famille verte* plate, Kangxi period, 9in (23cm) diam. **£700–800** *Wai*

A *famille verte* dish, painted in pencil underglaze blue to the centre an iron-red and gilt band at the well and flowersprays at the border, Kangxi period, 15in (38cm) diam. **£3,200–3,500** *C*

A pair of *famille verte* plates, painted with auspicious emblems and scholars' objects, the exterior with 6 ribboned emblems, restored, rim chips, Kangxi period, 8½in (21.5cm) diam. **£1,400–1,600** *C*

A pair of *famille verte* plates, each painted at the centre with a boy on a terrace, the borders with scholars' utensils beneath cash emblems at the rim, Kangxi period, 9in (23cm) diam. **£2,400–2,700** *C*

A *famille verte* dish, painted within a seeded green border, rim frit, Kangxi period, 14in (35.5cm) diam. **£1,600–1,800** *C*

l. A pair of *famille verte* plates, each painted at the centre with a bird perched above dense prunus and tree chrysanthemums, the seeded border reserved with bird and butterfly cartouches, one cracked, Kangxi period, 8½in (22cm) diam. **£1,400–1,600** *C*

A *famille verte* dish, the border decorated with panels of sea creatures, restored, Kangxi period, 15in (38cm) diam. **£650–800** *CSK*

A *famille verte* dish, painted at the centre, the piecrust rim decorated in iron-red and gilt, fritted, slight damage, Kangxi period, 14in (35.5cm) diam.
1,500–2,000 *S*

A pair of *famille verte* deep dishes, painted with scrolling peony flowerheads and foliage, slight rim frits, Kangxi period, 11in (28cm) diam.
£650–800 *CSK*

A *famille verte* plate, decorated with a garden scene, the rim with flower and foliage border, Kangxi period, 9in (23cm) diam.
£800–1,000 *WW*

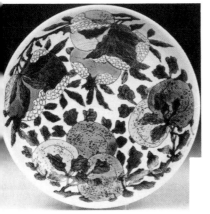

A *famille verte* pomegranate saucer dish, painted in aubergine, yellow and shades of green with fruiting peaches and pomegranates, with an incised design of five-clawed dragons, riveted, cracked, encircled Kangxi six-character mark and of the period, 10in (25.5cm) diam.
3,000–3,500 *C*

A pair of Chinese export monogrammed *famille verte* plates, painted and gilt with foliage below coronets within borders of spearhead and floral sprays, rims repaired, early 18thC, 12½in (32cm) diam.
£1,000–1,200 *CSK*

Jardinières

A *rose verte* charger, enamelled with coat-of-arms and inscribed 'Uytrecht', restored, Yongzheng period, 19in (48.5cm) diam.
£5,000–5,500 *S*

A *famille verte* charger, 19thC, 21in (53.5cm) diam.
£350–400 *MJB*

A *famille verte* jardinière, painted with 4 panels of warriors, reserved on a dense scrolling foliage ground, 19thC, 21½in (54.5cm) diam.
£3,000–4,000 *C*

r. A *famille verte* jardinière, with Buddhistic lions' mask and ring handles, with flowers and birds below iron-red scrolling foliage, Kangxi six-character mark below the rim, 19thC, 21½in (54.5cm) diam.
£2,600–3,000 *CSK*

A *famille verte* jardinière, decorated in iron-red with a band of leafy stems, slight damage, Kangxi period, 20in (51cm) diam.
£3,200–3,500 *CNY*

Jars & Vases

A pair of *famille verte* jars, painted
in reserve with 2 vertical panels of
bajixiang, drilled bases, one chipped,
one cracked, Kangxi period,
12⅛in (32cm) high, with wooden
covers and stands.
£4,500–5,000 *C*

r. A pair of *famille verte*
jars and domed covers,
with knop finials,
decorated with a defeated
soldier kneeling before
his conqueror, 2 *chilong*
forming a roundel at the
base in underglaze blue,
19thC, 20in (51cm) high.
£3,000–3,500 *CAm*

A *famille verte yen
yen* vase, painted
with a dense scrolling
ground of peonies and
foliage, and phoenix,
slight damage,
Kangxi period,
18in (46cm) high.
£3,000–3,500 *C*

A *famille verte* vase,
painted with 2 panels of
equestrian figures before
buildings and among
clouds divided by panels
of scrolling leaves,
restored, Kangxi period,
20in (51cm) high.
£1,400–1,600 *CSK*

A *famille verte* rouleau vase,
base repaired, Kangxi
period, 17½in (44.5cm) high.
£3,600–4,000 *C*

> **Miller's is a price
> GUIDE not a
> price LIST**

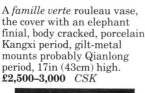

A *famille verte* rouleau vase,
the cover with an elephant
finial, body cracked, porcelain
Kangxi period, gilt-metal
mounts probably Qianlong
period, 17in (43cm) high.
£2,500–3,000 *CSK*

A *famille verte* rouleau
vase, painted in bright
enamels, Kangxi period,
17½in (44.5cm) high.
£5,000–6,000 *S(NY)*

r. A *famille verte*
rouleau vase, encircled
Xuande six-character
mark, Kangxi period,
7in (18cm) high.
£1,400–1,600 *C*

A *famille verte* vase
and stand, with pierced
bamboo-style handles,
painted with panels of
lotus flowers on a
trellis pattern ground,
damaged and repaired,
Kangxi period,
9in (23cm) high.
£800–1,000 *CSK*

A *famille verte* vase, painted
with flowers issuing from
rockwork, the shoulder with
a band of half flowerheads
on a green ground, Kangxi
period, 9in (23cm) high,
with a wooden cover.
£1,600–1,800 *C*

... famille verte yen yen ...se, decorated with ...ndscape scenes and ...scriptions, restored, ...angxi period, ...8in (71cm) high. ...5,000–6,000 S(NY)

A famille verte vase, decorated with battle scenes with brown borders, 19thC, 24in (61cm) high.
£320–400 MJB

A pair of famille verte square tapering vases, with waisted cylindrical necks, decorated with exotic birds, flowers and foliage, one rim damaged, Kangxi marks, 19thC, 16in (40.5cm) high.
£1,200–1,400 GAK

A pair of famille verte vases, with lions' mask and ring handles, painted with warriors, 19thC, 24in (61cm) high.
£3,000–3,500 CSK

...pair of famille verte vases, the necks ...pplied with iron-red Buddhistic lions, ...airline cracks, 19thC, 24in (61cm) high, ...n wood stands.
...1,400–1,600 S(S)

A pair of famille verte squat vases and covers, the cylindrical necks with cloud scrolls and the pierced domed covers with fruit and foliage beneath the iron-red scroll finial, slightly chipped, 19thC, 19in (48.5cm) high.
£5,000–5,500 C

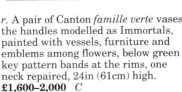

A pair of famille verte vases, painted on each side with a warrior Immortal above yellow ground bands of scrolling foliage, 19thC, 25in (63.5cm) high.
£2,400–2,600 CSK

Sets/Pairs

Unless otherwise stated, any description which refers to 'a set' or 'a pair' includes a guide price for the entire set or the pair, even though the illustration may show only a single item.

... famille verte vase, ...ritted, Kangxi ...ix-character mark, ...9thC, 20½in ...52cm) high.
...2,000–2,400 C

A pair of famille verte vases, one with hairline crack at rim, 19thC, 18in (45.5cm) high.
£1,000–1,200 Bon

r. A pair of Canton famille verte vases, the handles modelled as Immortals, painted with vessels, furniture and emblems among flowers, below green key pattern bands at the rims, one neck repaired, 24in (61cm) high.
£1,600–2,000 C

Miscellaneous

A *famille verte* brush pot, painted in black enamel with an inscription from Su Tongpo's *Ode to the Red Cliff*, Kangxi period, 5½in (14cm) high.
£5,000–6,000 *CNY*

A pair of *famille verte* pear-shaped bottles, rims restored, Kangxi period, 7in (18cm) high.
£1,000–1,200 *C*

A *famille verte* wall cistern, cover and basin, the cistern decorated with dragons pursuing a flaming pearl, repaired, Kangxi period, 16in (40.5cm) high.
£14,000–18,000 *S*

A *famille verte* cistern and cover, the rim applied with 2 dragon carp flanking a shell, restored, Kangxi period, 16½in (42cm) high.
£3,500–4,000 *C*

A *famille verte* wine cup, painted in underglaze blue and enamels with a blossoming peach tree, the reverse with a couplet, Yongzheng mark and of the period, 2½in (6.5cm) diam.
£6,500–7,500 *S(HK)*

A *famille verte* cup, painted with an erotic scene, Kangxi period, 4in (10cm) high.
£1,200–1,400 *C*

A pair of *famille verte* models of dogs Fo, Kangxi period, 18in (45.5cm) high.
£15,500–18,000 *S*

A pair of *famille verte* Buddhistic lions, one with a cub, the other with a ball, slight damage, 19thC, 17in (43cm) high.
£2,300–2,800 *C*

A pair of *famille verte* moon flasks, each painted with flowers on a pale yellow ground, the neck decorated with scrolling peonies on a pale green ground, 18th/19thC, 11in (28cm) high.
£5,000–6,000 *C*

A *famille verte* joss stick holder, Kangxi period, c1720, 2½in (6.5cm) high.
£600–800 *Wai*

A *famille verte* barrel-shaped teapot and cover, with Buddhistic lion finials, painted and gilt with a phoenix among peonies and rockwork, metal handle, Kangxi period, 4½in (11.5cm) high.
£200–250 *CSK*

r. A *famille verte* tureen and cover, modelled as a cockerel, moulded and enamelled with green, blue, iron-red and grey feathers, the head with iron-red serrated comb, rim chip restored, cover cracked, probably Kangxi period, 9¾in (25cm) high.
£32,500–35,000 *C*

Chinese Transitional
wucai enamelled and painted
baluster jar, small crack,
1650, 18in (46cm) high.
£2,800–3,500 *C*

A Chinese *wucai* wine jar,
painted with a continuous frieze
of carp, neck restored, Jiajing
six-character mark and of the
period, 13½in (34.5cm) high.
£450,000–500,000 *S*

A Canton bowl, c1870,
15½in (39.5cm) diam.
£1,000–1,200 *CAI*

Japanese porcelain bowl,
1880, 16in (40.5cm) diam.
£1,200–1,500 *CAI*

A Chinese polychrome
box and cover, some wear,
Wanli mark and of the
period, 9½in (24cm) diam.
£35,000–40,000 *S*

A Shonzui-style serving
dish, the base with
a *fu* mark in a double
square, Chongzhen
period, 6in (15cm) diam.
£3,500–4,000 *C*

A Chinese *famille verte* enamelled dish,
the reverse with a band of formal lotus
scrolls, rim slightly chipped, Kangxi
period, 17½in (44.5cm) diam.
£5,000–6,000 *C*

A Chinese *famille verte*
incised jar, decorated
with pomegranates,
possibly Kangxi period,
7in (18cm) high.
£3,000–3,500 *C*

A Chinese *famille rose* dish,
slight damage, Yongzheng
six-character mark and of the
period, 8in (20.5cm) diam.
£2,500–3,000 *C*

A Chinese export punchbowl, the centre
painted with 2 long-tailed birds, damaged,
Qianlong period, 15in (38cm) diam.
£4,000–4,800 *C*

A Chinese armorial dish, with the
full arms of Hohenzollern encircled
by the collar and badge of the Order
of the Black Eagle, monogrammed
and inscribed 'Gott Mit Uns',
Qianlong period, 13in (33cm) diam.
£24,000–26,000 *S*

A Chinese *sancai*
phoenix-head ewer, slight
damage, Tang Dynasty,
11in (28cm) high.
£14,000–16,000 *S*

A Japanese Imari jardinière, decorated in enamels and gilt on underglaze blue, late 19thC, 18in (45.5cm) high.
£4,000–4,500 *C*

A Japanese Arita teapot and cover, damaged and repaired, early 18thC, 10½in (26.5cm) wide.
£1,200–1,500 *C*

A Japanese Kakiemon teapot and cover, c1680, 6in (15cm) wide.
£6,000–7,000 *C*

A Chinese bottle vase, Qianlong period, 12in (30.5cm) high.
£30,000–35,000 *CN*

A Japanese Imari tureen and domed cover, repaired, Genroku period, 12in (30cm) diam.
£3,000–3,500 *C*

A Chinese *famille rose* fish bowl, minor damage, Qianlong period, 26½in (67cm) diam.
£12,000–15,000 *CNY*

Three Imari jars and covers, damage and restoration, Genroku period, 24in (61cm) high.
£6,500–8,000 *C*

A Chinese jar, with the Three Friends, Yongzheng six-character mark and of the period, 3in (8cm) high.
£10,000–12,000 *CHK*

A pair of Chinese jardinières, Yongzheng marks, 3in (7.5cm) high.
£2,500–3,000 *C*

A pair of Chinese *famille rose* tureens, covers and stands, Qianlong period, stands 11in (28cm) wide.
£7,500–9,000 *C*

A pair of Chinese Imari tureens, covers and stands, restored, early 18thC, stands 14½in (37cm) high.
£10,000–12,000 *C*

A Japanese Imari tureen and cover, slight damage, Genroku period, 9½in (24cm) high.
£1,200–1,500 *C*

r. A pair of Régence ormolu-mounted Chinese porcelain jardinières, the porcelain c1650, 8in (21cm) high.
£17,000–20,000 *C*

A Chinese *famille rose* vase, decorated with The Doctor's Visit after the design by Cornelis Pronk, neck restored, c1738, 9in (23cm) high.
£6,500–7,500 *C*

A Chinese vase and cover, decorated in enamels, cracked, 18thC, 17in (43cm) high.
£1,200–1,500 *DN*

A Chinese *famille noire* three-piece garniture, comprising a pair of hexagonal baluster vases with covers and a *zun*-shaped vase, restored, Kangxi period, tallest 12½in (32cm) high.
£4,600–5,000 *S(NY)*

A Chinese *doucai* jar and cover, with underglaze blue Qianlong four-character seal mark and of the period, 5in (12.5cm) high.
£16,000–18,000 *S(NY)*

A Canton *famille rose* storage jar and cover, restored, Qing Dynasty, 26in (66cm) high.
£3,500–4,000 *S*

A Chinese *famille verte* rouleau vase, restored, Kangxi period, 18in (45.5cm) high.
£7,000–8,000 *C*

A Chinese *doucai* dragon and phoenix *meiping*, decorated with a scaly dragon and a soaring phoenix amid scrolling vines, multi-coloured blooms and serrated leaves, Yongzheng period, 17¼in (44cm) high.
£24,000–28,000 *S(HK)*

A pair of Chinese *famille rose* jardinières, enamelled with butterflies in flight between bands of bat roundels and scrolling hibiscus, *ruyi* heads and lappets, restored, Jiaqing period, 18in (45.5cm) diam.
£7,000–8,000 *C*

A pair of Chinese *famille rose* jars and covers, enamels retouched, 19thC, 16½in (42cm) high.
£9,200–10,000 *C*

A Chinese *famille rose* vase and cover, decorated with a lake, Yongzheng period, 24¾in (63cm) high.
£7,000–8,000 *C*

A Chinese Fahua jardinière, decorated with birds, flowers and insects, cracked, c1600, 11¾in (30cm) high.
£3,500–4,000 *S*

A Chinese jar, with 4 mask handles, restored, Wanli period, 12in (30.5cm) high.
£1,800–2,200 *C*

A Japanese Nabeshima dish, with a design of jars over a ground of stylised waves, the footrim with comb pattern, hair crack, c1690, 7¾in (20cm) diam.
£55,000–60,000 *S*

A Japanese Arita blue and white dish, in *kraak porselein* style, late 17thC, 15⅝in (40cm) diam.
£3,500–4,000 *S*

A pair of Japanese Satsuma earthenware vases, signed 'Kinkozan zo', Meiji period, 11¾in (30cm) diam.
£3,300–4,000 *S*

A Japanese Satsuma earthenware vase, signed 'Yabu Meizan', impressed 'Meizan', gilt rubbed, Meiji period, 4½in (11.5cm) high.
£4,200–4,600 *S*

A Japanese Satsuma jar and cover, signed 'Dai Nihon Ryozan Zukuri', finial restored, Meiji period, 7¼in (18.5cm) high.
£3,800–4,200 *DN*

A Japanese Kakiemon *tokuri*, painted in enamels, neck replaced, c1690, 7⅜in (20cm) high.
£6,000–7,000 *S*

A Korean *punch'ong* bottle, decorated in sgraffito, covered in celadon glaze, Choson Dynasty, 15th/16thC, 12¼in (31.5cm) high.
£11,500–12,500 *S(NY)*

A Korean blue and white dish, with a central roundel enclosing a stylised character *bok*, Choson Dynasty, 19thC, 10¼in (26cm) diam.
£4,200–4,800 *S(NY)*

A Japanese Imari vase, decorated with a band of *kiku*, c1690, 16¼in (41.5cm) high.
£6,500–8,000 *S*

A Korean blue and white water dropper, Choson Dynasty, 17thC, 3¼in (8cm) wide.
£165,000–175,000 *S(NY)*

A Korean blue and white dish, painted with a bird perched on pomegranates, Choson Dynasty, 19thC, 6¼in (16cm) diam.
£35,000–38,000 *S(NY)*

A Korean bowl, painted with a carp, Choson Dynasty, 19thC, 7¼in (18.5cm) diam.
£12,000–15,000 *S(NY)*

A pair of Chinese iron-red dragon bowls, each painted with 2 scaly five-clawed dragons, Kangxi marks and of the period, 6in (15cm) diam.
£24,000–28,000 *S(HK)*

A Chinese *famille rose* lotus punchbowl, restored, Yongzheng period, 15in (38cm) diam.
£2,000–2,500 *C*

A Chinese *doucai* ogee bowl, mark of Chenghua, Kangxi/Yongzheng period, 8½in (21.5cm) diam.
£5,000–5,500 *S(HK)*

A Chinese *famille rose* lotus bowl, Qianlong seal mark and of the period, 6in (15cm) diam.
£7,800–8,600 *S(HK)*

A Chinese *famille rose* punchbowl, rim chipped, Yongzheng period, 15½in (39.5cm) diam.
£5,000–5,500 *C*

A pair of Chinese glazed dishes, with underglaze cobalt blue six-character Yongzheng marks within double lines, 3in (7.5cm) diam.
£19,000–20,000 *S(NY)*

A Chinese *famille rose* bowl, Qianlong period, 9in (23cm) diam.
£400–450 *ORI*

A *famille rose* bowl and cover, the mounts and handles in the form of a bearded face, Qianlong period, 10in (25.5cm) diam.
£4,200–4,800 *S*

A Chinese enamelled lotus bowl, with gilt knop, Daoguang period, 4in (10cm) diam.
£2,000–2,500 *S(NY)*

A Chinese *famille rose* bowl, Qianlong seal mark and of the period, 6in (15cm) diam.
£5,200–6,000 *S(HK)*

A Chinese *famille rose* bough pot, in the form of a European bombé commode, chipped, Qianlong period, 8½in (21.5cm) wide.
£5,800–6,400 *C*

A Chinese dragon bowl, painted and enamelled with a green and a red dragon, Kangxi mark and of the period, 5½in (14cm) diam.
£9,250–10,000 *S(HK)*

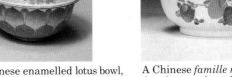

A marbled bowl, with a clear yellow glaze, encircled by a narrow filet, on a slightly splayed low cut foot, Tang Dynasty, 4in (10cm) high.
£9,200–10,000 *S(HK)*

A *famille verte* stem bowl, the interior painted with parrots on a tree peony above rockwork, Kangxi period, 6¼in (16cm) diam.
£4,200–5,000 *C(HK)*

A *famille verte* enamelled bowl and cover, with floral knop finial, minor damage, Kangxi period, 9in (23cm) diam.
£3,500–3,800 *C*

A *famille verte* deep bowl and cover, enamelled with flowers, minor enamel flakes, Kangxi period, 9¼in (23.5cm) diam.
£2,000–2,200 *C*

A *wucai* bowl, decorated with a dragon and phoenix, the interior with a dragon roundel, chips to rim, Yongzheng mark and of the period, 5in (15cm) diam.
£3,000–3,500 *S*

A *doucai* bowl, the interior decorated with a flower, rim ground, six-character Yongzheng mark, 4½in (11.5cm) diam.
£2,100–2,500 *S(NY)*

A Chinese export bowl, painted in the Tobacco Leaf palette with peonies, chrysanthemums and other flowers in a fenced garden, Qianlong period, 16in (40.5cm) diam.
£2,000–2,500 *Bea*

An underglaze blue and copper-red bowl, the exterior decorated with the Eight Immortals, Qing Dynasty, 5in (12.5cm) high.
£1,800–2,200 *S(HK)*

A *famille rose* bowl, painted with a butterfly, bamboo and fruit on flowering vines, Qianlong seal mark and of the period, 4½in (11.5cm) diam.
£5,500–6,500 *S(HK)*

A poem tea bowl, with iron-red decoration, the exterior enamelled with an Imperial poem, Qianlong seal mark and of the period, 4¼in (11cm) diam, boxed.
£3,500–4,000 *C(HK)*

A *sanduo* stem bowl, decorated in underglaze copper-red, minor restoration, Xuande six-character mark, 5¼in (14.5cm) diam.
£3,600–4,000 *C(HK)*

A *wucai* bowl, painted with a dragon pursuing flaming pearls, the interior with a red dragon roundel, Daoguang seal mark and of the period, 6¼in (16cm) diam.
£2,800–3,500 *S*

A yellow-ground *famille rose* bowl, the interior painted with 5 iron-red bats, Daoguang seal mark and of the period, 7¼in (18.5cm) diam.
£6,400–7,000 *S(NY)*

A turquoise-ground bowl, with iron-red seal of the Empress Dowager, Guangxu mark and of the period, 5in (12.5cm) diam.
£2,800–3,400 *S(HK)*

A Chinese *famille rose* ormolu-mounted five-piece garniture, restored, Qianlong period.
£10,500–12,000 *C*

A pair of Canton enamel vases, mid-19thC, 24in (61cm) high.
£1,800–2,200 *Wai*

A Chinese beaker vase, restored rim, 19thC, 17½in (44.5cm) high.
£800–900 *Wai*

A Chinese bottle vase, damaged, Daoguang mark, Qing Dynasty, 12in (30.5cm) high.
£500–600 *N(A)*

A pair of Japanese Imari flasks, marked 'Shin', c1710, 9in (23cm) high.
£5,000–6,000 *WW*

A Chinese Transitional *wucai* baluster vase, c1640, 11⅜in (29cm) high.
£4,500–5,000 *C*

A Chinese *famille verte* rouleau vase, Kangxi period, 18½in (47cm) high.
£16,500–18,000 *C*

A pair of gilt-decorated mirror black vases, Kangxi period, 14in (35.5cm) high.
£16,500–18,000 *S*

A Chinese *famille rose* garniture, damaged and repaired, one cover matched, Qianlong period, vases 10½in (26.5cm) high.
£4,500–6,000 *S*

l. A Chinese five-piece garniture, decorated in *famille rose* Mandarin pattern, Qianlong period, largest 13½in (34.5cm) high.
£9,000–10,000 *C*

A pair of Japanese porcelain vases, one with interior firing crack, 19thC.
£1,200–1,400 *Bea*

A Chinese moon flask, firing cracks, Qianlong six-character seal mark, 19½in (49.5cm) high.
£45,000–50,000 *CNY*

A Chinese moon flask, painted in iron-red with peonies and leaves, Kangxi period, 9in (23cm) high.
£15,000–18,000 *CNY*

A Chinese *sancai* pottery flask, moulded with a dense floral scroll beneath foliate loop handles, the glaze stopping irregularly at the spreading foot, enamel added to unglazed spots, Tang Dynasty, 6in (15cm) high.
£16,000–18,000 *C*

A Chinese *famille rose* jardinière, Yongzheng/early Qianlong period, 14½in (37cm) wide.
£8,000–10,000 *C*

l. A cloisonné enamel moon flask, 15th/16thC, 10½in (26.5cm) high.
£8,000–10,000 *C*

A *doucai* jardinière, restored, Qianlong seal mark and of the period, 13in (33cm) diam.
£15,000–18,000 *C*

A pair of Chinese *verte-Imari* cachepots, with lions' masks applied to the sides, fritting, mid-18thC, 8in (20.5cm) diam.
£9,000–11,000 *CNY*

A green glazed pottery *lian*, restored, Han Dynasty, 12in (30.5cm) diam.
£5,000–6,000 *CNY*

A Chinese jardinière, with gilt lacquer biscuit lions' masks, chipped, Qianlong period, 24½in (62cm) diam.
£12,000–15,000 *CNY*

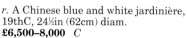

A Chinese *famille rose* jardinière, cracked, fritting, Yongzheng/Qianlong period, 25½in (65cm) diam.
£12,000–15,000 *CNY*

r. A Chinese blue and white jardinière, 19thC, 24½in (62cm) diam.
£6,500–8,000 *C*

An Imari charger, with a fan-shaped panel, late 19thC, 24in (61cm) diam.
£1,200–1,500 *Bea*

A Chinese underglaze blue dish, slight damage and wear, Hongzhi mark and of the period, 10¼in (26cm) diam.
£37,000–40,000 *S(HK)*

A pair of Japanese Imari dishes, each painted and enamelled on a black ground, the reverse with flowering branches, slight damage, early 18thC, 21¼in (54cm) diam.
£12,000–15,000 *C*

A pair of Chinese *rose/verte* dishes, each enamelled with a lady and a boy offering a lotus spray to a second lady seated at a table, Yongzheng period, 14in (35.5cm) diam.
£7,000–8,000 *C*

A Chinese *famille rose* platter, decorated with Don Quixote, Qianlong period, 18½in (47cm) diam.
£3,800–4,200 *S*

A pair of Chinese export *famille rose* meat dishes, Qianlong period, 17½in (44.5cm) diam.
£6,400–7,000 *DN*

A pair of Chinese *famille verte* chargers, one decorated with lovers being watched by attendants, the other with the lovers being watched by a woman, Kangxi period, 15¼in (39cm) diam.
£28,000–30,000 *S*

A Chinese *famille rose* tobacco leaf tureen, cover and stand, Qianlong period, stand 15in (38cm) wide.
£5,000–6,000 *C*

A Chinese enamelled 51-piece part tea service, depicting *Le Pêcheur*, after an engraving by C. J. Vissher, from a drawing by Abraham Blomaert, Yongzheng/early Qianlong period.
£4,000–4,500 *C*

A Chinese dragon dish, painted with a dragon pursuing a flaming pearl, restored, Yongzheng mark and of the period, 18½in (47cm) diam.
£11,000–13,000 *S*

A Chinese *famille rose* Mandarin palette tankard, Qianlong period, 4in (10cm) high.
£350–400 *AnE*

A Chinese *famille verte* armorial ewer, made for the Portuguese market, restored, Kangxi period, 12½in (32cm) high.
£9,000–10,000 *S*

A Chinese enamelled *doucai* bowl, the sides with slightly flaring rim, restored, Yongzheng six-character mark and of the period, 9½in (24cm) diam.
£6,500–8,000 *C*

A Japanese Ko-Imari ewer, decorated with a wide band of plum blossom, slight chips and restoration, late 17thC, 9in (23cm) high.
£12,000–15,000 *C*

A Chinese Fahua garden seat with a central band of lions grasping ribbons, Ming Dynasty, 16thC, 12½in (32cm) diam.
£3,000–3,600 *S*

A Dutch beaker and saucer, painted with flowerheads, Qianlong period, saucer 5½in (14cm) diam.
£200–245 *AnE*

A Chinese *famille rose* tea service, comprising 13 pieces, decorated with floral panels on a gold diaper ground, gilding rubbed, some restoration, Qianlong period.
£2,500–3,000 *S*

A pair of assembled gilt-metal and Chinese porcelain candlesticks, painted in *famille verte* and *famille rose*, on 2 inverted Arita saucer dishes, 19thC, 10½in (26.5cm) high.
£4,500–5,500 *C*

A pair of Chinese dragon bowls, the interior decorated with a *shou* medallion, Kangxi marks and of the period, 4in (10cm) high, on wooden stands.
£13,500–15,000 *S*

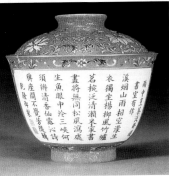

A Chinese *famille rose* bowl and cover, the interior and cover each painted in iron-red, damaged and repaired, Qianlong seal marks and of the period, 4½in (11.5cm) diam.
£24,000–26,000 *S*

A Chinese dragon dish, restored, Jiaqing seal mark and of the period, 10in (25.5cm) diam.
£2,000–2,500 *C*

A teapot stand, painted with figures, Qianlong period, 5in (13cm) diam.
£200–240 *AnE*

A Chinese *doucai* bowl, painted and enamelled with an Immortal drifting on a branch, Kangxi six-character mark and of the period, 3½in (9cm) diam.
£40,000–44,000 *C*

A *doucai* painted and enamelled bowl, Daoguang seal mark and of the period, 6½in (16.5cm) diam.
£8,000–10,000 *C*

A pair of Chinese saucers, painted in underglaze blue and enamels, slight damage, Wanli marks and of the period, 4in (10cm) diam.
£3,000–3,500 *S*

A Chinese dragon vase and cover, damaged, Daoguang seal mark and of the period, 8in (20.5cm) diam.
£2,500–3,000 *S*

A pair of Chinese *doucai* dishes and a pair of blue and white dishes, Guangxu six-character marks and of the period, 8in (20.5cm) diam.
£1,800–2,200 *C*

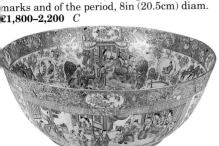

A Canton *famille rose* punchbowl, enamelled with dignitaries, 19thC, 21in (53.5cm) diam.
£7,000–8,000 *C*

A pair of Chinese dragon dishes, painted in underglaze blue and yellow enamels, some damage, one rim polished, Qianlong seal marks and of the period, 10in (25.5cm) diam.
£3,500–4,000 *C*

Five Chinese saucer dishes, painted and enamelled, one with Qianlong seal mark and 4 with Daoguang seal marks and of the period, 7½in (19cm) diam.
£6,500–7,000 *C*

A pair of Chinese *famille rose* yellow ground butterfly bowls, with flaring rims, cracked, iron-red Tongzhi four-character marks and of the period, 10in (25.5cm) diam.
£2,000–2,500 *C*

A Chinese *famille verte* tureen and cover, surmounted by a cockerel finial, Kangxi period, 10½in (26.5cm) diam.
£9,000–10,000 *C*

A Japanese Imari dish, decorated in iron red enamel and gilt on underglaze blue, late 17th/18thC, 12½in (32cm) diam.
£4,500–5,000 *C*

A Japanese Imari jar, damaged, c1700, 23½in (59.5cm) high.
£4,000–4,500 *C*

A Japanese Arita blue and white jar, slight damage, cover missing, late 17thC, 24½in (62cm) high.
£3,500–4,000 *C*

An Imari dish, signed 'Dai Nihon Hichozan Shinpo zo', 19thC.
£12,000–14,000 *C*

A Japanese Kakiemon-style blue and white tureen and cover, decorated with a continuous band of pavilions beneath pine trees, the domed cover with later gilt-metal finial, c1680, 10½in (26.5cm) high.
£5,000–6,000 *C*

A Japanese Arita blue and white ship's tureen, decorated with peony and prunus blossom, late 17thC, 11½in (29cm) diam.
£4,000–5,000 *C*

A set of 5 Chinese graduated sepia Fitzhugh pattern armorial dishes, painted with a crest, slight damage, c1800.
£5,000–6,000 *C*

A Japanese Arita blue and white jar, decorated in the Kakiemon manner, c1680, 16in (40.5cm) high.
£25,000–30,000 *C*

A Chinese *famille rose* Masonic armorial dish, with initials 'MJD', Qianlong period, 15½in (39.5cm) wide.
£4,000–5,000 *C*

A Chinese *famille rose* eggshell dish, the reverse painted with 3 flowersprays, slight damage, early Qianlong period, 8½in (21.5cm) diam, with fitted box.
£4,000–5,000 *C*

Japanese E-Shino dish,
mall repair, slight damage,
omoyama period,
½in (16cm) wide.
£1,600–5,000 C

A Japanese Nabeshima porcelain dish,
decorated in underglaze blue with flowers on
a celadon ground, the exterior with scrolling
peony sprays, early 18thC, 8in (20cm) diam.
£50,000–55,000 S(NY)

A Japanese flask, Dutch-
decorated with European
scenes, slight damage,
c1720, 6½in (16.5cm) high.
£2,000–2,200 S

Japanese Arita ewer, in
utani style, decorated in
loured enamels and gilt,
8thC, 5½in (14.5cm) high.
£2,200–2,500 C

A Japanese Satsuma
earthenware vase, by Kinkozan,
painted by Matsuyama, Meiji
period, 14in (36cm) high.
£2,200–2,500 S

A Korean celadon lobed cup and stand,
the petals inlaid with chrysanthemum
heads, small chips, Koryo Dynasty,
12thC, stand 5¼in (13cm) diam.
£7,800–8,500 S(NY)

Japanese Satsuma carved
d inlaid vase, Kinkozan
udio, black seal mark,
890, 4in (10cm) high.
£2,500–2,800 MER

A pair of Japanese Satsuma earthenware covered
vases, decorated in imitation brocade cloth with
folds moulded in relief, one restored, impressed
mark, 19thC, 13½in (34cm) high.
£10,500–11,500 S

A Korean iron-brown
decorated celadon vase,
Koryo Dynasty, 13thC,
10½in (26.5cm) high.
£27,000–30,000 CNY

Korean inlaid celadon bowl,
corated with a central
rysanthemum, Koryo Dynasty,
thC, 5½in (13cm) diam.
£1,400–1,700 CNY

A Korean white porcelain water
dropper, slight chips, Choson
Dynasty, 18th/early 19thC,
4½in (11.5cm) long.
£10,500–11,500 CNY

A Korean blue and white bowl,
inscribed on base in underglaze blue, Choson Dynasty,
19thC, 3½in (9cm) high.
£2,500–3,000 CNY

A Chinese Transitional brush pot, *bidong*, painted with scholars and travellers, marked, c1645, 8in (20.5cm) high.
£5,000–5,500 *C*

A pair of Chinese *famille verte* baluster vases, slight damage, Kangxi period, 23in (58.5cm) high.
£7,500–9,000 *C*

A Japanese garden lantern restored, signed 'Nihon Se Kato Keisa sei', late 19thC 69in (175.5cm) high.
£8,000–10,000 *C*

A pair of Chinese *famille rose* garden seats, slight damage, 19thC, 19in (48.5cm) high.
£3,400–4,000 *C*

A Chinese blue and white bottle vase, *yuhuchunping*, Yongle period, 10½in 25.5cm) high.
£380,000–400,000 *C*

A pair of Chinese *famille rose* vases, restored, Qianlong period, 18½in (47cm) high.
£8,000–10,000 *C*

A Japanese Imari tureen, decorated in enamels and gilt on underglaze blue, a peony spray on the interior and cover, c1700, 10in (25.5cm) wide.
£4,500–5,000 *CAm*

An Imari vase, decorated in coloured enamels, 19thC 34½in (87.5cm) high.
£5,000–6,000 *C*

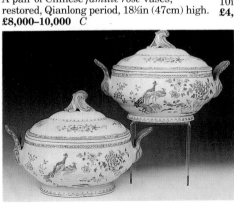

A pair of Chinese *famille rose* tureens and covers, one finial restored, Qianlong period, 14in (35.5cm) wide.
£8,000–10,000 *C*

A Japanese Imari tureen and cover, with knop finial, restored, c1700, 15½in (39.5cm) high.
£3,500–4,000 *C*

A Korean *punch'ong* war vase, decorated in *hakeme* style, restored, 15th/16thC 11in (28cm) high.
£90,000–95,000 *C*

set of 3 Chinese *doucai*
shes, slight damage, 18thC,
in (38cm) diam.
,000–4,500   *C*

A Chinese foliate charger,
painted in Yuan-style, Kangxi
period, 26½in (67.5cm) diam.
£2,000–2,500   *C*

A Ming-style dish, restored,
Qianlong seal mark and of
the period, 7in (18cm) diam.
£5,000–6,000   *C*

Chinese Ming-style dish,
ianlong seal mark and of
e period, 9in (23cm) diam.
0,000–33,000   *C*

A Japanese Imari shaped dish,
17th/18thC, 18in (45.5cm) diam.
£4,000–4,500   *C*

A Chinese celadon saucer
dish, Song Dynasty,
7in (18cm) diam.
£6,500–7,000   *C*

Chinese *kraak porselein* dish
Delft style, frits, Wanli period,
4in (35.5cm) diam.
2,000–2,500   *S*

A Chinese *kraak porselein*
dish, Chongzhen period,
14in (35.5cm) diam.
£2,500–3,000   *C*

A Chinese Ming dish, minor damage,
encircled Hongzhi six-character mark
and of the period, 10½in (26.5cm) diam.
£90,000–95,000   *C*

A pair of Chinese dragon dishes, with Qianlong seal
marks and of the period, 7in (18cm) diam.
£10,000–12,000   *C*

l. A Chinese Junyao barbed rim dish,
Song Dynasty, 7in (18cm) diam.
£22,000–24,000   *C*

A Chinese Canton hand-painted
sandalwood and paper fan, c1860,
9in (23cm) wide.
£120–130 *AVA*

A Chinese *famille rose*
tankard, the panel decorated
with mandarins, c1760,
4¼in (11cm) high.
£350–400 *GeW*

A Chinese Yixing red-coloured
clay teapot, some damage,
18thC, 6¾in (17cm) high.
£175–200 *GVA*

A Chinese *famille rose* plate,
18thC, 9in (23cm) diam.
£180–200 *AVA*

A Chinese Canton enamel bowl,
small chip to base, c1800,
5in (12.5cm) diam.
£50–60 *AVA*

A Chinese Canton hand-painted
lacquered wood and paper fan,
c1860, 9in (23cm) wide.
£120–130 *AVA*

A pair of Chinese gouache
paintings, damaged, 19thC,
8¾ x 13in (22 x 33cm).
£150–160 *AVA*

A Japanese lacquered dish,
depicting Mount Fuji with
a temple in the foreground,
Meiji period, 3½in (9cm) diam.
£80–100 *AVA*

A set of 4 Chinese jade wine
cups, c1900, 2in (5cm) diam.
£180–200 *AVA*

A Chinese Yixing teapot,
19thC, 4in (10cm) high.
£55–65 *GVA*

A Chinese embroidered silk jacket
c1880–1900, 39in (99cm) long.
£300–350 *ATo*

A Chinese Republic saucer dish,
decorated on a blue sgraffito ground,
early 20thC, 7¼in (18.5cm) diam.
£80–100 *AVA*

A Japanese hand-painted vase,
decorated with birds and flowers
on a yellow ground, hair crack,
1920–30s, 7in (18cm) high.
£40–50 *POR*

r. A Japanese Fukagawa vase,
depicting Mount Fuji, c1935,
6½in (16.5cm) high.
£40–50 *POR*

FAMILLE NOIRE

famille noire ewer, damaged, Kangxi period, 6⅝in (17cm) wide.
700–800 *C*

A pair of ormolu-mounted *famille noire* figures of boys, one mounted as a lamp, damaged, the porcelain 19thC, 13in (33cm) high.
£4,500–5,500 *CAm*

A pair of *famille noire* vases, decorated and heavily gilt with scrolling lotus and *shou* symbols between bands of lappets, underglaze blue Kangxi marks, 19thC, 18in (45.5cm) high.
£900–1,000 *CSK*

r. A pair of *famille noire* rouleau vases, enamels chipped, small glaze crack to mouth of one vase, 19thC, 23⅝in (60cm) high.
£2,000–2,500 *C*

l. A *famille noire* broad pear-shaped vase, incised Kangxi six-character mark, 19thC, 18½in (47cm) high.
£550–650 *CSK*

Famille noire

Famille noire was introduced during the Kangxi period. The enamel was applied directly to the biscuit porcelain then a translucent green enamel was added, resulting in an extremely dense black. It is quite rare and differs from the thick opaque black enamel of the 19thC, also referred to as *famille noire*.

FAMILLE JAUNE

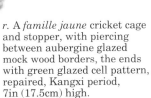

l. A *famille jaune* fish bowl, early 20thC, 18in (45.5cm) diam.
£700–800 *SAg*

A pair of Empress Dowager *famille jaune* bottle vases, with yellow ground, turquoise interiors, the undersides inscribed 'Eternal Prosperity' and 'Enduring Spring', 1900, 12½in (31.5cm) high.
£3,000–3,500 *CNY*

r. A *famille jaune* cricket cage and stopper, with piercing between aubergine glazed mock wood borders, the ends with green glazed cell pattern, repaired, Kangxi period, 7in (17.5cm) high.
£800–1,000 *C*

A pair of *famille jaune* vases, with upright cylindrical handles, one restored, one chipped, 19thC, 15in (38cm) high, mounted as lamps.
£1,800–2,000 *C*

l. A *famille jaune* incense ball and cover, painted in green and iron-red to the sides and base, the top with small aperture with cover, all suspended on a cord with 2 jade beads from an elaborately carved ivory stand, 18thC, 10in (25.5cm) high, including stand.
£4,500–5,000 *C*

CHINESE IMARI

A Chinese Imari gilt-metal-mounted bowl, the porcelain 18thC, the mounts and cover later, 9½in (24cm) wide.
£1,400–1,600 *C*

A Chinese Imari barber's bowl, painted with peony and lotus, below cartouches reserved on a band of scrolling lotus at the border, the reverse with iron-red flowersprays, fritted, early 18thC, 11in (28cm) diam.
£1,400–1,600 *C*

A Chinese Imari bowl, painted and gilt, cracked, rim chips, glaze scratches, 18thC, 16in (40.5cm) diam.
£1,400–1,700 *CSK*

A Chinese Imari mug, with loop handle and lotus flower terminal, painted and gilt, 18thC, 6in (15cm) high.
£600–700 *CSK*

A pair of Chinese Imari ewers and covers, painted with lotus and chrysanthemum clusters, one restored, early 18thC, 7½in (19cm) high.
£2,000–2,500 *C*

A pair of Chinese Imari dishes, painted within a border of birds and flowersprays, early 18thC, 11in (28cm) diam.
£600–700 *CSK*

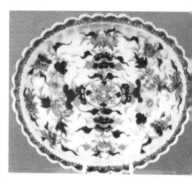

A Chinese Imari shallow bowl, painte[d] within a border of blue and gilt tightl[y] scrolling foliage, early 18thC, 10½in (26.5cm) wide.
£1,300–1,500 *CSK*

Chinese Imari

Chinese Imari wares were copies or pastiches of Japanese Imari, made largely for export from the early 18thC. The decoration involved Japanese brocade designs and the typical Imari palette of dark underglaze blue, iron-red and gilt.

A Chinese Imari jar and cover, painted with a pheasant among flowering shrubs and pierced rockwork, Qianlong period, 9in (23cm) high.
£1,800–2,000 *CSK*

l. A pair of Chinese Imari tankards, with loop handles, domed covers and interior drainers, painted and gilt with alternating panels of lotus flowers and leaves and quatrefoil panels of daisies on stylised foliage grounds, 18thC, 8½in (21.5cm) high.
£2,000–2,500 *CSK*

A Chinese Imari mug, painted with flowers, earl[y] 18thC, 6½in (16.5cm) high.
£700–800 *C*

ADDITIONAL COLOURS
Bowls

A *doucai* bowl, painted with scrolling branches within bands of *ruyi* heads, slight damage, Chenghua six-character mark, 18thC, 7½in (19cm) diam.
£450–550 *CSK*

An aubergine and green glazed bowl, cracked, encircled Kangxi six-character mark and of the period, 4in (10cm) diam.
£1,000–1,200 *C*

An iron-red dragon bowl, painted in bright enamels, repaired, Kangxi six-character mark and of the period, 6in (15cm) diam.
£1,000–1,200 *C*

An underglaze blue and copper-red bowl, slight fritting, Qianlong seal mark and of the period, 8in (20.5cm) diam.
£850–1,000 *CSK*

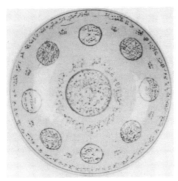

A Swatow bowl, the interior with Arabic script in turquoise and black enamels, iron-red border, cracked and restored, early 17thC, 15½in (40cm) diam.
£950–1,100 *CAm*

Swatow wares
Made at kilns close to Swatow in the north of Guangdong province, these wares were made mainly for the export trade to south-east Asia, Indonesia and Japan. These items were often highly original in design and include slip-painted wares. They were made from the late 16th century to the middle of the 17th century.

A *wucai* bowl, painted with *ruyi* cartouches of flowers, underglaze blue six-character mark, 17thC, 7in (18cm) diam.
£550–650 *CSK*

A pale-green rice bowl and cream-coloured spoon, Kangxi period, bowl 4¼in (11cm) diam.
£80–90 *SPU*

These items were rescued c1990 from the Chinese trading vessel Vung Tau, *wrecked off the coast of Vietnam in about 1696. The ship was on its way to the Dutch trading post of Jakarta with a cargo of Chinese items bound for the great houses of Europe.*

A *wucai* bowl, painted with dragons in green enamel and iron-red, slight damage, Qianlong mark and of the period, 5⅛in (13cm) diam.
£350–400 *Bea*

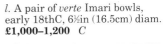

r. A Chinese export bowl, the exterior with 4 reserves, small edge chip, hairline crack, 18thC, 9in (23cm) diam.
£200–250 *EL*

l. A Chinese export bowl, with floral decoration, hairline crack, 18thC, 9in (23cm) diam.
£220–240 *EL*

l. A pair of *verte* Imari bowls, early 18thC, 6½in (16.5cm) diam.
£1,000–1,200 *C*

A *kinrande* bowl, the interior decorated with a fisherman, Jiajing period, 5in (12.5cm) diam.
£1,400–1,600 *Wai*

Kinrande, named after the Japanese word for gilding, has an iron-red wash on the outside with added gilded decoration.

A *doucai* bowl, damaged, Chenghua six-character mark, Yongzheng period, 3in (7.5cm) diam.
£350–450 *CSK*

A Chinese export reticulated armorial bowl and domed cover, with pierced handles, painted in coloured enamels and gilt, slight damage, Qianlong period, 8in (20.5cm) diam.
£1,000–1,200 *CSK*

A coral glazed bowl, reserve-decorated with scrolling lotus, the interior glazed white, Qianlong seal mark and of the period, 5in (12.5cm) diam.
£5,500–6,500 *S(HK)*

Miller's is a price GUIDE not a price LIST

An *anhua*-decorated white-glazed stem bowl, the interior decorated in low slip relief with a lotus scroll, Jiajing period, 4½in (11.5cm) diam.
£3,500–4,000 *S*

A glazed bowl, covered overall with a thick glaze of bright turquoise and copper imitating peacock feathers, restored, inscribed Yongzheng four-character seal mark and of the period, 8in (20.5cm) diam.
£1,000–1,200 *S(NY)*

A saucer dish, the exterior under a liver-red glaze, the interior plain, encircled Yongzheng six-character mark and of the period, 6in (15cm) diam.
£2,000–2,200 *C*

An underglaze copper-red and white bowl, the copper-red of soft rich cherry tones firing green in places, Qianlong six-character mark and of the period, 6in (15cm) diam.
£2,500–3,000 *C*

A yellow glazed bowl, with slightly everted rim under a glaze of even tones thinning slightly at the rim, glaze rubbed, rim chipped, encircled Jiajing six-character mark and early in the period, 8in (20.5cm) diam.
£5,500–6,500 *C*

A *doucai* bowl, painted in yellow, purple, green and iron-red enamel with 5 clusters of flowers forming medallions, underglaze blue around the rim of the plain interior, damaged, Yongzheng six-character mark within a double square, 4½in (11.5cm) diam.
£11,000–12,000 *S(NY)*

An export porcelain *rouge de fer* punchbowl, Qianlong period, 11in (28cm) diam.
£1,300–1,500 *RIT*

A liver-red glazed bowl, with widely flaring sides, the interior plain, rim rubbed, underglaze blue Qianlong seal mark and of the period, 7in (17.5cm) diam, on a wood stand.
£800–1,000 *CSK*

A pair of *wucai* dragon and phoenix bowls, Daoguang seal marks and of the period, 6in (15cm) diam.
£4,000–4,500 *C*

A yellow-ground porcelain bowl, Daoguang seal mark, 6in (15cm) diam, with wood stand.
£2,500–3,000 *HCH*

A blue-ground porcelain bowl, Daoguang seal mark, 6in (15cm) diam, on hardwood stand.
£800–900 *HCH*

A *doucai* bowl, painted with ducks among lotus beneath bands of dragons chasing pearls, cracked, underglaze blue Daoguang seal mark and of the period, 6½in (16.5cm) diam.
£1,300–1,500 *CSK*

A bowl, on short foot, painted in aubergine with 2 dragons chasing flaming pearls among clouds, above a band of stylised rocks and breaking waves, on a green ground, plain interior, underglaze black Daoguang seal mark and of the period, 6in (15cm) diam.
£3,200–3,700 *CSK*

A pair of yellow-glazed bowls, incised and decorated with dragons chasing flaming pearls among cloud scrolls and above foaming waves and rockwork, both cracked, underglaze blue Guangxu marks and of the period, 6in (15cm) diam.
£700–800 *CSK*

Imperial yellow

Traditionally, only the Imperial household was allowed to use the colour yellow.

An Imperial yellow-ground dragon bowl, with overglaze green enamel decoration, Guangxu mark and of the period, 6in (15cm) diam.
£700–800 *RIT*

A green enamelled yellow-ground bowl, incised with dragons, Guangxu six-character mark and of the period, 5¾in (14.5cm) diam.
£1,100–1,300 *C(HK)*

A pair of copper-red bowls, with 5 roundels of phoenix, small chip to one, Daoguang seal marks and of the period, 6in (15cm) diam.
£1,600–1,800 *S*

A pair of bowls, decorated with incised dragons under yellow glaze, the interior turquoise, Guangxu mark and of the period, 8in (20.5cm) diam.
£1,600–1,800 *Wai*

A Canton blue-ground bowl, made for the Persian market, painted with panels of figures on terraces and gold-ground panels of birds and flowers below a trellis pattern border, 19thC, 8in (20.5cm) diam.
£450–550 *CSK*

Dragons

The dragon is one of the oldest mythical creatures in China. Considered just and benevolent, dragons have come to symbolise Imperial authority and are associated with all aspects of the ruling Emperor. They are therefore used on court costume and as a decorative motif on artefacts made specifically for Imperial use. To a Chan Buddhist, a dragon appearing from the clouds is a cosmic event, symbolising the elusive vision of the truth.

Boxes

A seal paste box, painted with roses, c1930, 2in (5cm) diam.
£350–400 *Wai*

A blue and white and underglaze copper-red box and cover, painted in a strong blue on a moulded panel, four-character mark, Qing Dynasty, 3⅓in (9cm) wide.
£2,500–3,000 *C*

An armorial triple spice box and cover, from a French royal service, painted in underglaze blue, enamelled and gilt, on 3 coral-glazed paw feet, the top joined to the bottom by a rotating metal fitting, repaired, small frits, c1720, 5¾in (14.5cm) wide.
£14,000–16,000 *C*

Brush Pots

A brush pot, with fluted corners and flattened rim, painted in iron-red and gilt, slight damage, Qianlong seal mark, 6½in (16.5cm) high.
£750–900 *CSK*

A biscuit brush pot, by Chen Guozhi, with carved and moulded chickens gazing at a butterfly, slight chip, 19thC, 5½in (14cm) high.
£1,300–1,500 *S*

A brush pot, painted in iron-red and black with groups of men, gilt highlights, wear to pigments, Kangxi period, 6¾in (17cm) diam.
£3,200–3,500 *CNY*

Cups, Mugs & Beakers

An Imperial yellow wine cup, with white interior, encircled Kangxi six-character mark and of the period, 3in (7cm) diam.
£4,500–5,000 *C*

A yellow-glazed wine cup, with white-glazed interior, the handles in the form of dragons, Kangxi mark and of the period, 1¾in (4.5cm) high.
£2,500–3,000 *S(NY)*

A pair of beakers, painted on the exterior in iron-red and gold with carp, later mounted in silver, with pewter covers to fit, with a silver spoon, fitted into a covered wooden box as tea caddies, together with key, Kangxi period, mounted cups 4¾in (12cm) high.
£6,000–7,000 *S(HK)*

r. A pair of *doucai* wine cups, painted on the exterior with phoenix among scrolling lotus, the interiors plain, Jiajing six-character marks, Kangxi/Yongzheng period, 3in (7cm) diam.
£2,000–2,500 *CSK*

l. A Chinese export porcelain mug, with underglaze blue and polychrome figural decoration, repairs, 18thC, 5½in (14cm) high.
£150–170 *EL*

tea bowl and saucer, decorated
ith a marriage cypher, hairline crack,
8thC, saucer 4¼in (11cm) diam.
250–300 *DAN*

*hese are probably part of a service
dered specifically for use at a wedding.*

Two London-decorated
Chinese porcelain
coffee cups, painted
with bouquets,
flowersprays and
a butterfly, showing
2 distinct styles of
painting, c1760,
4in (10cm) high.
£200–250 *C*

A tea bowl and saucer,
decorated in orange and
blue with a country house
scene, c1790, saucer
5½in (14cm) diam.
£180–200 *DAN*

l. A tea bowl and
saucer, Qianlong
period, saucer
4in (10cm) diam.
£100–120 *AnE*

Tea

When tea was first imported
from China in the mid-17thC,
it sold for as much as £10 a
pound – the equivalent of
around £800 today.

A gilt-decorated cup, decorated
vith scrolls and peony sprays,
ats and *shou* characters, on
blue ground, the interior and
ase glazed turquoise, iron-red
iaqing seal mark and of the
eriod, 3¼in (8.5cm) diam.
12,500–14,000 *S(HK)*

A Chinese export Jesuit
ware coffee cup, c1770,
2½in (6.5cm) high.
£150–180 *DAN*

A Chinese export tankard,
painted in sepia and gilt,
Qianlong period,
4½in (11.5cm) high.
£350–400 *CSK*

Ewers & Kendi

A monk's cap white glazed ewer,
Yongle mark and of the period,
7¾in (19.5cm) high.
£170,000–200,000 *S(HK)*

*The monk's cap form, taken from
an original bronze form, has been
used throughout all periods of
Chinese ceramics.*

A ewer, carved with peony
blossoms above a lotus petal
border, covered with a green
glaze with dark brown
splashes, the glaze burning
to a rusty orange around
the foot, Ming Dynasty,
6¼in (16cm) high.
£4,200–5,000 *S(HK)*

A *kinrande* green glazed and gilt
fluted *kendi*, decorated with bands
of scrolling foliage, gilt rubbed,
Ming Dynasty, 8in (20.5cm) high.
£1,000–1,200 *CSK*

Figures – Animals

A pair of figures on horseback, old wear and damaged, Ming Dynasty, 15¾in (40cm) high.
£1,600–1,800 *CSK*

A *sancai*-glazed tilemaker's figure of a carp, with gaping mouth and flaring nostrils, chipped, 16thC, 16in (40.5cm) long.
£650–750 *C*

A green glazed horse and groom, Ming Dynasty, groom 16in (40.5cm) high.
£1,400–1,600 *CSK*

A pair of ormolu-mounted green glazed figures of parrots, each standing astride a pierced brown glazed rockwork base, the beaks and feet unglazed, on gilt-bronze bases, the porcelain Kangxi period, ormolu 19thC, 9¾in (24.5cm) high.
£5,000–5,500 *C*

A pair of tilemaker's figures, Ming/Qing Dynasty, 14in (35.5cm) high.
£1,000–1,200 *CSK*

A pair of white glazed cockerels, modelled in mirror image, decorated in black, their combs and wattles red, restored, 18thC, 14½in (36.5cm) high.
£3,700–4,200 *CAm*

A white glazed dog, with deep blue eyes, Qianlong period, 9½in (24cm) long.
£2,500–2,800 *C*

A Compagnies des Indes figure of a pug dog, Qianlong period, 9½in (24cm) high.
£5,200–5,800 *S*

Two Chinese export models of hounds, Qianlong period, 3in (7.5cm) high.
£850–1,000 *Wai*

A flambé glazed model of a parrot, decorated in tones of pale lavender, purple and deep burgundy, 18th/19thC, 12in (30.5cm) high.
£700–800 *CNY*

A pair of turquoise glazed parrots, naturalistically moulded, chipped, c1850, 14½in (36.5cm) high.
£2,000–2,500 *C*

A turquoise glazed figure of a water buffalo, c1800, 14in (35.5cm) long.
£700–850 *C*

A pair of polychrome pheasants, each standing on an outcrop of aubergine with green splashes, their feathers brightly enamelled, 19thC, 13½in (34.5cm) high. £4,000–4,500 *C*

A pair of green glazed parrots, biscuit feet and beaks, Qing Dynasty, 8½in (21.5cm) high. £1,000–1,200 *C*

A pair of Chinese export white-glazed models of cranes, with sgraffito and moulded wing feathers, seal mark, Qing Dynasty, 24in (61cm) high. £1,600–1,800 *C*

A pair of pale green glazed hawks, on brown rockwork bases, late Qing Dynasty, 11in (27.5cm) high. £650–800 *C*

A pair of green parrots, the beaks and feet painted in iron-red, on brown glazed rockwork, one beak chipped, Qing Dynasty, 7in (17.5cm) high. £800–1,000 *C*

A pair of white-glazed models of cockerels, with deep scarlet combs and eyes heightened in cobalt blue, one comb with restoration, 19thC, 16in (40cm) high. £3,000–3,500 *Bon*

A pair of Chinese export coral-glazed models of hounds, seated on their haunches, each with a green-glazed collar and bell, glaze rubbed, 6½in (16.5cm) high. £500–600 *CSK*

A pair of ochre-glazed pottery models of recumbent dogs, early 19thC, 5in (12.5cm) long. £1,500–2,000 *CSK*

A Sichuan red pottery model of a dog, damage to tail, Sichuan nine-character mark in relief, late Qing Dynasty, 16in (40cm) long. £4,500–5,000 *C*

A pair of Canton models of Buddhistic lions, supporting candle holders, painted in iron-red with gilt markings, damaged, early 19thC, 6in (15cm) long. £2,500–3,000 *CSK*

A Chinese export white glazed goat, impressed seal mark, Qing Dynasty, 15in (38cm) high. £2,500–3,000 *C*

Figures – People

A green, turquoise and ochre glazed pottery figure of a seated Buddha, Ming Dynasty, 22½in (57cm) high.
£1,700–2,000 *CSK*

A black, green and mustard glazed roof tile, modelled as an official on a horse with an elaborate saddlecloth, Ming Dynasty or later, 13in (33cm) high.
£1,400–1,700 *C*

A pair of *wucai* figures of boys, each wearing a short robe, decorated with *shou* character panels reserved on a cell-pattern ground below a *ruyi*-shaped collar, on rectangular bases, restored, 17thC, 13in (33cm) high.
£3,800–4,200 *C*

A tilemaker's figure of Guandi, with detachable head, dressed in elaborate armour, with turquoise and amber glazes, the hands unglazed, chipped, 16th/17thC, 19½in (49.5cm) high.
£1,000–1,200 *C*

r. A *wucai* figure of a laughing boy, holding a lotus bud, hand chipped, fritted, 17thC, 9in (23cm) high.
£1,700–2,000 *C*

A tilemaker's figure, modelled as a heavily armoured mounted warrior, with green and yellow glazes, some restoration, Ming/Qing Dynasty, 15½in (39cm) high.
£850–1,000 *C*

An aubergine and turquoise glazed official, holding a plaque and wearing flowing robes, seated on a low seat, Kangxi period, 4in (10cm) high.
£1,800–2,000 *C*

A pair of green and ochre glazed pottery groups, each of a deity seated on the back of a recumbent horse, the deities' features left unglazed, late Ming/Qing Dynasty, 12in (30.5cm) high.
£1,000–1,200 *CSK*

A pair of nodding-head figures, depicting an official and his wife, he wearing a black hat, a chestnut-brown blue collared jacket over robes, she wearing a blue floral robe, restored, 18thC, 24½in (62cm) high.
£23,000–27,000 *C*

A pair of tilemaker's figures, in ceremonial robes, glazed in blue, turquoise and brown, late Ming/Qing Dynasty, 13in (33cm) high
£700–800 *CAm*

atware

saucer dish, the interior incised
d painted in bright green enamel
biscuit, old damage, encircled
ngzhi six-character mark and
he period, 8in (20.5cm) diam.
00–1,000 C

A *wucai* five-lobed saucer,
Longqing mark and of the period,
4in (10cm) wide.
£12,000–15,000 S(HK)

A Swatow polychrome dish,
painted to the centre in green
and turquoise with 2 Daoist
figures, cracked, 17thC,
15½in (39cm) diam.
£750–900 C

yellow-ground underglaze
e-decorated saucer dish,
enghua six-character mark,
ngxi period, 6in (15cm) diam.
00–700 CSK

A *doucai* iron-red enamel dish,
small chips, encircled Kangxi
six-character mark and of the
period, 8½in (21.5cm) diam.
£1,800–2,000 C

An iron-red European subject baptism
plate, small rim chip, Qianlong period,
10½in (26.5cm) diam.
£1,700–2,000 C

polychrome basin, painted
an iron-red Y-pattern ground
low iron-red lotus on a blue
ashed ground at the border,
acked and chipped, Kangxi
riod, 15in (38cm) diam.
50–1,000 C

A *doucai* dish, underglaze blue
Chenghua mark, Yongzheng
period, 6in (15cm) diam.
£700–800 CSK

A pair of silver-shaped dishes,
each painted in iron-red and gilt
with peonies, chrysanthemum
and scrolling foliage, chipped,
18thC, 12in (30.5cm) diam.
£1,000–1,200 C(S)

armorial soup plate, painted
th a double-headed eagle and
motto, Qianlong period,
in (22cm) diam.
,000–1,200 S

A *grisaille* and gilt armorial
plate, inscribed with the gilded
initials, Qianlong period,
9in (23cm) diam.
£1,200–1,500 S

A fluted teapot stand,
decorated in the Mandarin
palette, Qianlong period,
5in (12.5cm) diam.
£200–240 AnE

A Chinese export plate, painted in sepia and gilt with a castle before a bridge and a hilly landscape, Qianlong period, 9½in (24cm) diam.
£450–550 *CSK*

A dragon dish, later enamelled in green and iron-red and underglaze blue, Qianlong seal mark and of the period, 17½in (44.5cm) diam.
£7,000–8,000 *S*

A pair of liver-red saucer dishes, Qianlong mark and of the period, 6in (15cm) diam.
£1,200–1,400 *C*

A Chinese export armorial plate, hair crack, c1760, 9in (23cm) diam.
£250–300 *DAN*

A Fitzhugh pattern dish, painted in orange with Daoist emblems, c1800, 19in (48cm) wide.
£2,400–2,600 *C*

A dish from the *Diana* cargo, decorated with Starburst pattern, c1816, 11in (28cm) diam.
£120–150 *DAN*

A Chinese export plate armorial plate

l. A pair of pink 'camaieu' Judgement of Paris plates, painted at the centre with Juno, Minerva and Venus, below thin *grisaille* and gilt rings at the well, some chips, Qianlong period, 9in (23cm) diam.
£1,400–1,700 *C*

Six dessert plates, with pierced borders, painted in green and white on iron-red bands, all damaged, c1795, 7½in (19cm) diam.
£500–600 *C*

An iron-red and gilt dragon dish, the centre enamelled with 2 five-clawed dragons pursuing a flaming pearl, rim crack, Guangxu six-character mark and of the period, 20½in (52cm) diam.
£1,500–1,800 *C*

A Canton plaque, the centre painted with a basket of flowers reserved on a ground of insects, fruit and foliage, mid-19thC, 14½in (37cm) diam.
£700–800 *Bea*

A Canton meat dish, painted and gilt with alternating figures of warriors and ladies, mid-19thC, 19in (48cm) wide.
£900–1,000 *CSK*

‍ardinières

Transitional *wucai* jardinière, ‍inted with yellow Buddhistic ‍ns, fritted, 9½in (24cm) diam. ‍,500–1,800 *CSK*

A blue and white jardinière, with brown and gilt lion mask handles, rim chip, 18thC, 25½in (65cm) diam, with wood stand.
£3,500–4,000 *C*

A *rose/verte* jardinière, the interior painted with iron-red fish among water plants, 19thC, 19in (48cm) diam.
£2,000–2,200 *CSK*

‍ars

Fahua baluster jar, moulded ‍ a cloisonné technique, painted ‍ yellow and turquoise on a deep ‍ue ground, the interior green ‍azed, neck restored, foot ‍placed, c1500, 13in (33cm) high.
‍,000–4,500 *C*

A *wucai* jar, painted with boys at play, some surface fritting, base star crack and short neck crack, encircled Wanli six-character mark and of the period, 5in (12.5cm) high.
£8,500–10,000 *C*

An olive glazed storage jar, the broad shoulder fitted with lug handles, applied with dragons chasing flaming pearls, all under a brownish-green glaze, late Ming Dynasty, 21in (53cm) high.
£2,500–3,000 *C*

A Transitional *wucai* broad baluster jar, painted with iron-red scale pattern and floral lappets, rim restored, 10½in (26cm) high.
£600–700 *CSK*

Transitional *wucai* baluster ‍r, painted with dragons and ‍hoenix among cloud scrolls ‍nd above waves, the neck ‍ith stiff leaves, damaged, ‍2½in (31cm) high.
‍,000–1,200 *CSK*

r. An underglaze copper-red and blue celadon-ground jar, painted with peach sprays, the glaze pooling in places, Kangxi period, 6½in (16.5cm) high.
£1,300–1,500 *C*

A *wucai* baluster jar and domed cover with knop finial, cover rim chip and finial restored, mid-17thC, 16in (40.5cm) high.
£3,000–3,500 *C*

CHINESE MONOCHROME CERAMICS

Low-fired coloured glazes had been used to great effect during the Tang Dynasty (618–907) and many high-fired coloured stonewares such as Yue, Henan, oil-spot, hare's fur, celadon and Jun ware were produced during the Song (960–1279) and Yuan (1279–1368) Dynasties. Perhaps the most famous of these were the celadons, made at kilns in Yaozhou, Shaanxi Province, and at Longquan in Zhejiang Province.

Monochrome glazes were a major innovation of the early Ming period: copper-red was introduced first, then blue and, in the 15th century, a yellow glaze made from antimony. Monochromes were further developed during the early Qing Dynasty, the peach bloom of the Kangxi period being the most famous. The 18th-century *flambé* and *sang-de-boeuf* glazes proved very popular with the Europea export market. A small, good quality monochrome vase or saucer dish can be bought for £1,000, whereas a fine Imperial piece can cost as much as £30,000–40,000.

The kilns of Dehua, Fujian Province, produced a very fine white porcelain with a glassy, ivory glaze. Known as *blanc de Chine* in the West, this porcelain reached its peak the mid-17th century, producing wonderful figures of Guanyin and Buddha as well as small objects. For its age and quality *blanc d Chine* is still moderately priced, and may be worth considering by the potential collector.

BLANC DE CHINE
Figures & Animals

A *blanc de Chine* figure of Guanyin, the even glaze with a green tinge, chipped, the back impressed 'He Chao Cong', 17thC, 15in (37.5cm) high, on wood stand.
£9,500–11,000 *C*

A *blanc de Chine* figure of Guanyin, wearing flowing robes and a high cowl and seated beside rockwork, damaged, 17th/18thC, 7½in (19cm) high.
£750–850 *CSK*

A *blanc de Chine* figure of Guanyin, holding a *ruyi* sceptre, a boy attendant at her side, slight damage, Qing Dynasty, 10½in (26.5cm) high.
£350–400 *S(S)*

A Dehua *bla de Chine* fig of Damo, sm chips, early 18thC, 15in (38cm) high.
£3,500–4,0

A *blanc de Chine* figure of Buddha Heshang, holding prayer beads in his left hand and laughing, a flask in his right hand, small chip, 18th/19thC, 6½in (16.5cm) high.
£1,800–2,000 *CNY*

l. Two *blanc de Chine* figures of Guanyin, chipped, 18thC, 9½in (24cm) high.
£1,600–1,800 *C*

r. A *blanc de Chine* figure of Guanyin, standing on a swirling base, marked, 18thC, 16in (40.5cm) high.
£3,400–3,800 *S(NY)*

A *blanc de Chine* figure of Guanyin and a child, on a rocky base, chipped, 18thC, 11in (28cm) high.
£1,800–2,000 *C*

A *blanc de Chine* figure of Guanyin, standing beside a deer on a rockwork base, slight restoration, 18thC, 8in (20.5cm) high.
£1,300–1,500 *CSK*

A *blanc de Chine* figure of the Virgin Mary, 18thC, 14¼in (36cm) high.
£1,600–1,800 *CSK*

A *blanc de Chine* figure of Wenshu, seated on the back of a Buddhistic lion, restored, marked, 18th/19thC, 15½in (39.5cm) high.
£3,200–3,500 *CNY*

Two *blanc de Chine* figures, one modelled as Guanyin seated cross-legged, the other as an emaciated Immortal, damaged, 18th/19thC, 13in (33cm) high.
£3,200–3,500 *CSK*

Blanc de Chine

Blanc de Chine (white china) refers to the ivory-white porcelain from the Dehua kilns in Fujian Province, and not the white undecorated porcelain from the rest of China.

l. A *blanc de Chine* figure of Buddha, surrounded by 5 boys, restored, 19thC, 10¼in (26cm) high.
£2,800–3,200 *C(HK)*

A pair of *blanc de Chine* models of cockerels, 19thC, 16in (40cm) high.
£1,400–1,600 *S*

Vases & Ewers

l. A Dehua *blanc de Chine* vase, chipped, 17thC, 14in (35.5cm) high.
£850–1,000 *C*

A Dehua *blanc de Chine* *gu*-shaped beaker vase, 17th/18thC, 15½in (39.5cm) high.
£5,000–5,500 *C*

A Dehua *blanc de Chine* Montgolfier balloon-shaped ewer, supported on a pierced wave base, Qing Dynasty, 9½in (24cm) high.
£1,600–1,800 *C*

l. A Dehua *blanc de Chine* sleeve vase, with pale creamy ivory glaze, incised and applied with lion masks, the broad foot unglazed, Kangxi period, 9½in (24cm) high.
£1,700–2,000 *C*

CELADON
Bowls & Dishes

A Longquan celadon tripod vessel, moulded with a frieze, under a rich olive-green glaze, Song/Yuan Dynasty, 5in (12.5cm) diam.
£1,000–1,200 *C*

A Longquan heavily potted celadon dish, the exterior undecorated, covered with an olive-green glaze, 14thC, 14in (35.6cm) diam.
£1,800–2,000 *C*

A moulded ribbed celadon bowl, with a florette in the centre below chrysanthemums, on a short foot, Northern Song Dynasty, 7in (18cm) diam.
£4,000–4,500 *S(NY)*

A Longquan celadon dish, carved to the centre, all under an even glaze of bright olive tones, 14th/15thC, 13in (33cm) diam.
£1,400–1,600 *C*

A celadon dish, incised under a pale olive-green glaze, with traces of gilt to rim, 14th/15thC, 15½in (40cm) diam.
£1,300–1,500 *C*

A Longquan celadon dish, with thickly potted sides, the underside moulded with petals, 14thC, 13½in (34.5cm) diam.
£1,000–1,200 *C*

l. A Longquan celadon dish, carved with a peony spray below petals, the unglazed ring burnt orange in the firing, rim crack, 14th/15thC, 17in (43cm) diam.
£1,500–1,800 *C*

A celadon saucer, carved with a recumbent ox gazing at the moon, under and olive green-glaze, Jin Dynasty, 7in (18cm) diam.
£5,300–5,800 *S(NY)*

A Longquan celadon barbed dish, carved with numerous flutes radiating from and encircling the centre, early Ming Dynasty, 24½in (62cm) diam.
£40,000–45,000 *S(HK)*

A pale celadon dish, carved and moulded with a peony spray, the exterior lightly carved with leaves, slight wear, Ming Dynasty, 13½in (34.5cm) diam.
£3,200–3,500 *S(HK)*

l. A celadon shaped and fluted dish, moulded with a central flowerspray, Ming Dynasty, 14in (35cm) diam.
£800–1,000 *CSK*

Did You Know?

Because no two pieces of celadon ware ever fired in the same way, the quality can vary enormously. Two similar pieces from the same kiln and with the same date of manufacture can vary in price by up to 20 times, depending upon the even depth and colour of the glaze.

Vases

A Zhejiang Province celadon vase, trim left biscuit, Song Dynasty, 8in (20.5cm) high.
£900–1,100 C

A celadon glazed baluster vase, incised and decorated with scrolling flowering stems, 16thC, 18in (45.5cm) high.
£1,200–1,400 CSK

A blue and white celadon ground vase, lightly moulded and painted with Immortals, including Shoulao, minor glaze crack, Kangxi period, 15½in (39.5cm) high.
£2,400–2,800 C

l. A celadon glazed zhadou vase, covered with a soft bluish-green glaze, Yongzheng six-character seal mark and of the period, 5¼in (13.5cm) high.
£40,000–50,000 S(NY)

A pair of Cantonese celadon ground oviform vases, with gilt Buddhistic lion handles, painted in underglaze blue, iron-red and gilt, moulded in low relief, 19thC, 24½in (62cm) high.
£2,000–2,500 CSK

Miscellaneous

A celadon glazed tripod censer, incised to the exterior with clouds in trellis pattern, c1500, 14in (35.5cm) diam.
£750–850 CSK

A celadon glazed bottle, Qianlong seal mark and of the period, 11in (28cm) high.
£2,400–2,600 CNY

A celadon glazed water pot, applied with 6 figures of boys surrounding a tank, 2 moulded fish to the interior, damaged, Ming Dynasty, 4in (10cm) high.
£250–300 CSK

A Longquan celadon jardinière, the sides moulded with flowerheads, covered in a rich green glaze thinning around the edges, cracked, Yuan/Ming Dynasty, 9½in (24cm) diam, wood stand and fitted box.
£1,200–1,400 C

A celadon glazed moon flask, some surface crackle, Yongzheng seal mark and of the period, 21½in (54cm) high.
£6,500–8,000 C

Celadon

Celadon is said to be named after the hero of Honoré d'Urfé's pastoral romance L'Astrée (1610), who wore a green costume. In Chinese it is known as qingei, 'greenish porcelain'.

A pale celadon glazed flattened globular teapot, Ming Dynasty, 5in (12.5cm) high.
£500–600 CSK

JAPANESE CERAMICS

The first known ceramics were produced in Japan by the Jomon culture from as early as 5000–4000 BC, and a strong Japanese ceramics tradition has continued through to the present day. Early Japanese potters were often influenced by techniques brought from China, such as the *sancai* (three colour) wares of the 8th century AD.

The first porcelains were blue and white, and produced in Arita about 1600 AD. During the first half of the 17th century the industry developed, both in terms of technique and artistry, and the early underglaze painting showed great spirit and simplicity of style, often using a 'rapid ink' technique. From 1659 the Dutch East India Company (VOC: Vereenigde Oostindische Compagnie) ordered porcelain to be made for export. Potters were given Chinese wares to copy and further develop into a distinctive style, known as Imari after the port from which it was shipped. The typical Imari palette consisted of dark underglaze blue, red and gold.

Kakiemon

Some of the finest polychrome wares were those from the Kakiemon kiln in Arita. This porcelain has a fine milky-white body and is delicately painted with leaf green, light yellow and flat iron-red enamels. First exported around 1684, production reached its peak about 1690, diminishing in quality over the next 130 years. A small piece of early Kakiemon porcelain may be bought for £1,500–2,000, whereas a large early piece can cost up to £100,000.

Nabeshima

One of the best Japanese porcelains was the Nabeshima ware made in the Arita area from around 1675 to 1868 specifically for the ruling Shogun and lords. A very fine clay was used to produce a perfect body, which was decorated with subdued underglaze blue combined with a few overglaze enamels and the occasional use of a celadon glaze. A late 18th-/early 19th-century small saucer dish can still be found for about £1,200, whereas an early large dish can cost up to £100,000.

Kutani

Kutani is a much sought-after Japanese porcelain that was produced in the village of Kutani in Kaga Province. The kiln was established by 1656 and became famous for its artistic wares, known as Ao-Kutani (green Kutani) because of the predominance of a dark green enamel, particularly on large dishes. These pieces rarely appear on the open market. After a lull in the 18th century, there was a revival in the early 19th century, when copies of earlier wares were made. These were nearly always marked under the base with a *fuku* (happiness) mark. Towards the end of the 19th century, a large number of wares were made for the export market. These have a predominance of finely painted overglaze iron-red decoration and are often marked 'Kutani'.

Satsuma

Satsuma wares were produced in the town of Satsuma, where a good white clay was found. The first brocade-style wares were made at the Chosa kiln in Osumi Province. After the Meiji Restoration of 1868, Satsuma style wares were made in large quantities for export to the West, where Satsuma became the generic term for a light porous pottery with a crackled cream glaze and intricate enamelled designs. These wares have little connection with the town of Satsuma and were more likely to have been made in large commercial ventures in Tokyo, Kobe or Kyoto. The worst excesses included ceramics with raised human figures or large writhing dragons. These pieces are summarily dismissed by the Japanese as 'export' ware.

Satsuma ware is currently enjoying a collecting boom in the West. The fine quality and painstakingly detailed decoration are easily appreciated, and because vast quantities were exported to the West at the turn of the century a ready supply is available. Small pieces of reasonable quality can be obtained for as little as £100. The very best pieces, from famous studios, can fetch up to £20,000.

Later Ceramics

During the 20th century many fine and famous studio ceramic masters have produced work of outstanding quality. Famous and sought-after artists such as Shoji Hamada (1894–1978), Kanjiro Kawai (1890–1966) and Kenkichi Tomimoto (1886–1963) produced pieces based upon classic pottery forms, notably tea ceremony wares.

Artistic painting on porcelain wares also flourished, and the fine paintings of irises by Shozan Komamitsu (circa 1900), geese by Kanjoen Tamon (circa 1890) and white overglaze painting by Seifu Yohei (1850–1922) are all eagerly sought-after. The traditions of Nabeshima were continued by Imaizumi Imaemon XII (1897–1975) and the Kakiemon tradition by Sakaida Kakiemon XII (1888–1963). These beautiful works, although relatively late in the history of Japanese ceramic production, are yet another field for the discerning collector. It is important, where possible, to retain the original fitted wooden boxes in which the items left the studio. These boxes are signed by the artist and help to confirm the provenance of the piece.

Bottles

A pair of Arita apothecary bottles, with silver-mounted rims, painted in underglaze blue with song birds perched on trailing flowering and fruiting branches, late 17thC, 7in (18cm) high.
£2,200–2,500 *CAm*

A Japanese celadon-glazed bottle, carved with sprays of leaves below a band of key-pattern at the shoulder, slight damage, 17thC, 13in (33cm) high.
£1,500–2,000 *CSK*

l. An Imari blue and white sake bottle, painted with chrysanthemums and peony sprays, restored, early 18thC, 8¾in (22cm) high.
£800–900 *CSK*

An Imari bottle, painted in underglaze blue, the neck with iron-red and gilt scrolling foliage, c1700, 9in (23cm) high.
£650–800 *C*

r. An earthenware bottle, in the form of a pilgrim flask, decorated in enamels and gilt, gilt rubbed, late 19thC, 5in (12.5cm) high.
£1,400–1,600 *S(NY)*

An Arita bottle, painted in inky-blue with a bird and the reverse with fruit, Edo period, 10in (25.5cm) high.
£1,500–1,650 *S(S)*

Sets/Pairs

Unless otherwise stated, any description which refers to 'a set' or 'a pair' includes a guide price for the entire set or the pair, even though the illustration may show only a single item.

A Satsuma bottle vase, decorated in various coloured enamels and gilt, rim gilt, signed 'Tozan sei', 19thC, 4½in (11.5cm) high.
£1,400–1,700 *C*

l. A pair of Imari double-gourd bottles, the upper sections with oval panels of *ho-o* birds, all on a ground of large stylised flowerheads and dense flowering shrubs, late 19thC, 17½in (44.5cm) high.
£2,000–2,500 *CSK*

l. A Satsuma bottle, painted with a gold ground roundel of children with cranes wading in water below gilt clouds, late 19thC, 3½in (9cm) high.
£500–600 *CSK*

r. A pair of Hirado blue and white oviform bottles, painted with wooded landscapes and flowers, 19thC, 6½in (16.5cm) high.
£1,200–1,400 *C*

Bowls

A pair of Arita bowls, late 17thC,
6½in (16.5cm) diam.
£500–600 *Wai*

A Kakiemon two-handled bowl
and domed cover, with lion finial,
painted in blue and green enamels
and iron-red above underglaze
blue rockwork, repaired, late
17thC, 6in (15cm) wide.
£3,000–3,400 *CSK*

A Kamiemon bowl, decorated in
enamels and gilt with pine and
prunus, the everted rim with
peonies within a brown edge,
late 17thC, 5½in (14cm) diam.
£1,400–1,700 *S*

An Imari saucer dish, with gilt-metal stand, cracked,
the porcelain 17thC, 15½in (39.5cm) wide.
£850–950 *CSK*

An Imari bowl, painted in typical
palette, late 17thC, 14in (35.5cm) diam
£2,500–3,000 *Bon*

l. A Kakiemon bowl,
decorated in iron-red,
green, yellow, black and
blue enamels and gilt,
rim restored, late 17thC,
10½in (26.5cm) wide.
£5,000–6,000 *C*

Imari

The Imari palette
usually includes
underglaze blue, iron-
red and gilding, but
can also contain green,
brown, yellow and
sometimes turquoise.
The term Ko Imari
refers to the blue and
white porcelain made
in Arita.

An Imari barber's bowl, painted with a
large central vase of flowers on a table,
the everted rim with buildings and flowers
restored, late 17thC, 11in (28cm) diam.
£500–600 *CSK*

An Arita deep bowl,
painted in underglaze blue,
coloured enamels and gilt,
cracked, 17th/18thC,
14½in (37cm) diam.
£1,200–1,400 *CSK*

r. An Imari barber's bowl,
painted in underglaze
blue, yellow, green and
iron-red enamels and gilt,
late 17th/early 18thC,
11in (28cm) diam.
£1,500–2,000 *Bon*

A Kakiemon bowl, painted in iron-
red, enamels and gilding with floral
sprays, the everted rim with florets
on a red ground, all within a brown
edged rim, slight cracks, late 17thC
4½in (11.5cm) diam.
£1,000–1,200 *S*

An Imari barber's bowl, painted and gilt, with a central vase of peonies on a fenced terrace, within a border of further flowerheads, chipped and rubbed, c1700, 11in (28cm) wide.
£500–600 *CSK*

An Arita polychrome ogee-shaped bowl and domed cover, painted in iron-red, yellow, green and aubergine enamels, minor flaking, c1700, 7½in (19cm) diam.
£1,400–1,800 *CSK*

An Imari barber's bowl, painted and gilt within a border of panels of trees, rockwork and buildings, chipped, c1700, 11in (28cm) diam.
£620–720 *CSK*

An Imari bowl and cover, painted in typical palette with landscapes in scrolling panels reserved on a ground of peonies and other flowers, knop restored, c1700, 10in (25.5cm) diam.
£1,600–1,800 *S*

A pair of Imari reticulated bowls, decorated in colours with flowers, the interlocking circles forming the rim, painted with wisteria, c1700, 8½in (21.5cm) diam.
£2,400–2,600 *CAm*

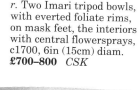

r. Two Imari tripod bowls, with everted foliate rims, on mask feet, the interiors with central flowersprays, c1700, 6in (15cm) diam.
£700–800 *CSK*

An Imari bowl, painted and gilt to the interior, the exterior with panels of chrysanthemum sprays and stylised heads on geometric grounds, damaged, c1700, 10in (25.5cm) diam.
£800–1,000 *CSK*

l. An Imari deep bowl, enamelled in iron-red, yellow and aubergine, underglaze blue and gilt, base cracked, c1700, 6in (15cm) diam.
£500–550 *CSK*

Three Kakiemon foliate rimmed bowls, decorated in iron-red, green and black enamels and gilt on underglaze blue, restored, minor chips, c1700, 6in (15cm) diam.
£1,200–1,500 *C*

A pair of Imari bowls and covers, painted and gilt with *shishi* lions, the interiors with flowersprays, the covers similarly decorated, minute chips, c1700, 6½in (16.5cm) diam.
£700–800 *CSK*

An Imari barber's bowl, early 18thC, 11in (28cm) diam.
£1,200–1,400 *Bea*

A spittoon, Genroku period, late 18thC, 5in (12.5cm) diam.
£800–1,000 *Wai*

An Imari fluted bowl, decorated in typical coloured enamels and gilt on underglaze blue, early 18thC, 8½in (21.5cm) diam.
£2,000–2,500 *CAm*

An Arita moulded bowl, with foliate rim, decorated in coloured enamels and gilt, the exterior with a band of *hanabishi* roundels, minor chip, 18thC, 7in (18cm) diam.
£800–1,000 *C*

A Nabeshima blue and white bowl, with flared rim, decorated in underglaze blue with foliate designs, footrim chipped, cracked, early 18thC, 4½in (11.5cm) diam.
£2,500–3,000 *S*

An Imari bowl, painted on the interior with branches of fruit, the exterior with flowers and scrolling foliage in underglaze blue, red, yellow and green enamels, Edo period, 7in (18cm) diam.
£550–650 *S(S)*

A Kakiemon bowl, painted in blue, turquoise, iron-red, green and gilt with bamboo, pine and prunus, the base with wheel-engraved Dresden Palace collection mark, 18thC, 4in (10cm) diam.
£2,200–2,500 *CAm*

An Imari bowl, painted with a central floral panel within radiating panels, Meiji mark and of the period, 14in (35.5cm) diam.
£700–770 *S(S)*

A Kenjo Imari-style bowl, *kiku* signature, mid-18thC, 12½in (32cm) diam.
£1,600–1,800 *S(S)*

An Imari bowl, decorated in iron-red, green, aubergine and black enamels and gilt, base with *ju* character, Meiji period, 10in (25.5cm) diam.
£800–1,000 *C*

A Satsuma earthenware bowl, richly painted and moulded with Buddha and deities, a dragon in a landscape, signed 'Choshuzan saku', Meiji period, 13½in (34.5cm) diam.
£1,700–2,200 *S*

A Satsuma bowl, the exterior enamelled with a dragon, the inside filled with the 18 *Rakkan*, signed, Meiji period, 5in (13cm) diam.
£400–500 *S(S)*

An Imari bowl, painted on an iron-red ground between brocade borders, *ho-o mon* within, Meiji period, 15in (38cm) diam.
£700–800 *S(S)*

An earthenware bowl, by Kizan, painted in enamels and gilt with 2 panels showing a formal and an informal picnic, marked 'Dai Nihon Kizan tsukuru', Meiji period, 5in (12.5cm) diam.
£2,500–3,000 *S*

A Satsuma bowl, the interior decorated with flowers, the exterior with a panel of a cockerel and a quail, and adults and children, signed 'Dai Nihon, Kyoto, Tojiki Goshigaisha, Ryozan Sho', Meiji period, 16in (40.5cm) diam.
£11,500–13,500 *SK*

A Satsuma bowl, decorated with butterflies, *mon* and good luck symbols, marked in iron-red 'Dai Nihon Satsuma Yaki Koseki Ga', Meiji peirod, 3¼in (8.5cm) high.
£400–500 *WW*

A bowl, by Zengoro Hozen, his son Wazen, or grandson Tokizen, finely painted in underglaze blue in late Ming-style with 2 Immortals on a raft, the exterior with dragons and Buddhist objects, the rim with brown edge, signed 'Dai Nihon Eiraku tsukuru', 19thC, 7½in (19cm) wide.
£1,400–1,600 *S*

A fish bowl, decorated with a hawk and a tiger, and blue and white floral landscape motif, late 19thC, 24in (61cm) diam.
£650–800 *LHA*

An Imari deep bowl, decorated with Buddhistic emblems and peonies, late 19thC, 10in (25.5cm) diam.
£1,200–1,400 *C*

A Satsuma bowl and cover, decorated in relief with flora, c1860, 4½in (11.5cm) diam.
£1,400–1,600 *MER*

A Satsuma bowl, decorated in coloured enamels and gilt, with Yamato Takeru no Mikoto and his retainers, gilt rim, slight damage, signed 'Choshuzan', late 19thC, 9½in (24cm) diam.
£2,000–2,200 *C*

A Kaga ware deep bowl, decorated in iron-red and green enamels and gilt, late Kutani period, 12in (30.5cm) diam.
£1,400–1,600 *C*

r. An Imari monteith, decorated in typical coloured enamels and gilt on underglaze blue, late 19thC, 12½in (32cm) diam.
£1,200–1,400 *C*

Three Imari graduated fluted bowls, painted and gilt, all slightly damaged, underglaze blue running *fuku* marks, 19thC, largest 13⅝in (34.5cm) wide.
£1,500–1,800 *CSK*

A Satsuma bowl, painted with pheasants and other birds beneath wisteria and bamboo, Mount Fuji beyond, character marks, 19thC, 9⅜in (24cm) diam.
£350–400 *L*

A Fukagawa bowl, painted and gilt with panels of carp and fan-shaped cartouches of bamboo on an iron-red ground, Mount Fuji mark, 19thC, 12in (30.5cm) diam.
£550–700 *CSK*

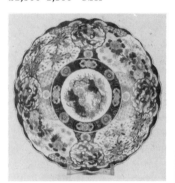

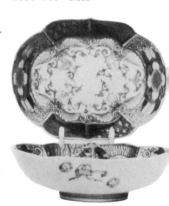

A Fukagawa fluted shallow bowl, with foliate rim, painted and gilt with panels of chrysanthemums and orchids, blue bird mark, 19thC, 10in (25.5cm) diam.
£300–400 *CSK*

An Imari monteith-style deep bowl, with panels of chrysanthemums and lotus, 19thC, 16½in (42cm) diam.
£1,600–2,000 *CSK*

Firing
Japanese porcelain was thickly potted and sometimes warped during firing. Kiln supports were used under the bases of even small wares to prevent them from sagging.

An Imari bowl, painted and gilt with a design of *bijin* holding parasols, 10in (25.5cm) diam, and 6 quatrefoil bowls painted and gilt with flowersprays and geometric patterns, 19thC, 7in (18cm) diam.
£250–300 *CSK*

A pottery deep dish, the pale grey body burnt to a brick-red and glazed in *Ki-Seto*-style, patches unglazed and pooling in the well, gold lacquer *naoshi* in the rim, signed 'to', 19thC, 12in (30.5cm) diam.
£1,000–1,200 *C*

A Satsuma fluted bowl, painted in blue enamel, iron-red, colours and gilt with 5 seated figures, the interior with chrysanthemums growing on a fence, rim cracked, late 19thC, 7in (18cm) diam.
£800–1,000 *CSK*

l. A Satsuma bowl, the interior decorated with a scene of a man and 3 ladies on a river bank, late 19thC, 10in (25.5cm) diam.
£300–350 *HCH*

r. A Satsuma egg-shaped tripod bowl and cover, painted and heavily gilt, late 19thC, 7½in (19cm) wide.
£450–600 *CSK*

A set of 20 Arita blue and white bowls, enriched with gilding, 19thC, 3½in (9cm) diam, in an inscribed two-tier wood box.
£1,200–1,500 *CSK*

An Imari fluted oviform bowl, with flared rim, painted on an underglaze blue ground reserved with iron-red and gilt scrolling flowers and leaves, 19thC, 18in (46cm) diam.
£1,000–1,200 *CSK*

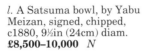

A Satsuma bowl, painted on the interior with ducks beneath prunus blossom and bamboo, the exterior with flowersprays on a dark blue ground, signed, late 19thC, 5in (12.5cm) diam.
£500–600 *CSK*

l. A Satsuma bowl, by Yabu Meizan, signed, chipped, c1880, 9½in (24cm) diam.
£8,500–10,000 *N*

r. A Satsuma fluted bowl, painted in colours and richly gilt with shaped panels of seated Immortals and ladies, late 19thC, 5in (12.5cm) diam.
£800–900 *CSK*

A Satsuma thickly-potted foliate-rimmed bowl, painted in colours and richly gilt, late 19thC, 12in (30.5cm) diam.
£2,000–2,500 *CSK*

A Satsuma shallow bowl, painted in colours and gilt, the interior with sprays of flowers on a fine gilt dot ground, late 19thC, 5in (12.5cm) diam.
£2,000–2,500 *CSK*

r. An earthenware bowl, decorated with figures and floral medallions, the interior with a chrysanthemum among butterflies, signed 'Yabu Meizan', c1905, 3¼in (8.5cm) diam.
£2,200–2,500 *S(NY)*

A Satsuma bowl, the interior painted in colours and richly gilt, the exterior with a dark-blue ground enriched with gilt flowers and *ho-o*, late 19thC, 5½in (14cm) diam.
£700–800 *CSK*

Boxes

A Satsuma lozenge-shaped box and cover, decorated on one side with a panel containing birds amid blossoming foliage, the reverse with a panel of figures, probably by Kinkozan, Meiji period, 3¼in (8.5cm) wide.
£1,750–2,000 *HDS*

r. An Imari lozenge-shaped box and wood cover, painted and gilt with panels of Europeans aboard ships, alternating with vases of flowers, on a floral trellis pattern ground, late 19thC, 6in (15cm) wide.
£1,000–1,200 *CSK*

A late Kutani box and cover, decorated in various coloured enamels and gilt, damage to fingers, signed 'Takayama ga', late 19thC, 10in (20.5cm) high.
£3,000–3,500 *C*

An Imari box and domed cover, with *shishi* lion finial, painted and gilt with floral and geometric designs, 19thC, 8in (20.5cm) high.
£450–500 *CSK*

> **Japanese Chronology Chart**
> Please refer to page 11 for Japanese periods and dates.

Censers

A Kakiemon-style censer, with ormolu mounts, late Meiji period, 4in (10cm) diam.
£850–1,000 *Wai*

A Satsuma earthenware censer, decorated in iron-red, blue and turquoise enamels and gilt with a *ho-o* bird among flowers, with a silver pierced cover, signed 'Ippo Zo', 19thC, 5½in (14cm) diam.
£1,900–2,000 *S(NY)*

A Satsuma earthenware censer, decorated in iron-red, blue, turquoise and black enamels and gilt, with a silver metal wire-form cover, signed 'Satsuma Yaki', 19thC, 5in (12.5cm) diam.
£2,000–2,200 *S(NY)*

Drinking Vessels

A Kakiemon cup and an Arita saucer, the cup decorated in iron-red, green, blue and black enamels, damaged, late 17thC, cup 2½in (6.5cm) high.
£800–1,200 *S*

l. An Imari tankard, decorated in coloured enamels, damaged, late 17thC, 8in (20.5cm) high.
£1,400–1,700 *C*

An Arita blue and white tankard with loop handle, late 17thC, 8½in (21.5cm) high.
£1,000–1,200 *C*

A pair of Arita blue and white teabowls, decorated in Van Frytom style, c1700, 3in (7.5cm) diam.
£900–1,000 *C*

A pair of Imari tankards, painted and gilt with shaped panels of peony sprays, on a ground of lotus heads and trellis pattern, early 18thC, 5in (12.5cm) high.
£1,000–1,200 *CSK*

n Imari mug, with loop andle, decorated in nderglaze blue, iron-red d gilt, on a blue ground ith flowerheads, rim ipped, late 17thC, ½in (21.5cm) high.
,400–1,700 *C*

A Hirado cup stand, decorated in underglaze blue with 3 *aoi-mon*, with a tall foot with lappet design, damaged, 19thC, 7in (18cm) high.
£550–650 *S*

An earthenware teabowl, decorated in enamels and gilt, decorated with chrysanthemums and scattered butterflies, the exterior with a ground of gilt lattice, signed 'Shizan', late 19thC, 5¼in 13.5cm) diam.
£3,800–4,200 *S(NY)*

Ninsei teabowl, decorated ith panels imitating cloth, te 18th/early 19thC, ¾in (12cm) diam.
,700–9,500 *C*

Satsuma mug, early 20thC, in (10cm) high.
90–120 *JHW*

A Satsuma pottery gilt-bronze mounted oil lamp base, finely enamelled and gilded, lacking oil lamp receiver, late 19thC, 12in (30.5cm) high.
£650–800 *P(Re)*

A teabowl, with blue decoration, Genroku period, 17th/18thC, 4in (10cm) diam.
£650–800 *Wai*

Hirado

Hirado porcelain was produced at Mikawachi, close to the Arita kilns. Started c1770, the kiln became famous for its fine quality underglaze blue decorated porcelain. Made to the highest technical standard, with a white glassy body and fine painting, it became very popular in the West. The body was often cut with fine openwork or applied in high relief. At the beginning of the 20th century the Hirado factory was taken over by the Fukagawa Company.

l. An Imari beaker, decorated in iron-red, green and black enamels and gilt on underglaze blue, chipped, Genroku period, late 17thC, 3½in (9cm) high.
£700–800 *C*

A blue and white beaker, painted with bands of flowers on a ground of lappet borders and *tama*, 19thC, 7½in (19cm) high.
£200–250 *CSK*

Ewers & Kendi

A pair of Arita ewers, decorated in underglaze blue with figures in a garden, damaged, c1670, 10in (25.5cm) high.
£800–1,000 *S*

An Arita ewer, decorated in blue and iron-red, late 17thC, and a Chinese copy, 18thC, 3½in (9cm) high.
£550–600 *DN*

l. An Imari ewer, decorated in iron-red enamel and gilt on underglaze blue with sprays of chrysanthemum and wild pinks surrounding a roundel with 'O', for olieum, loop handle, slight chips to neck, c1700, 7in (18cm) high.
£700–800 *C*

A set of 3 Imari pear-shaped ewers, covers and stand, painted with flowering shrubs, one handle repaired, one spout missing, late 17thC, 5in (12.5cm) high.
£1,500–1,650 *CSK*

Two Arita blue and white ewers and covers, one decorated with tree peonies, the cover with a phoenix, a flowerhead and scrolling foliage, the other similarly decorated with a mountainous water landscape, damaged, late 17thC, largest 8½in (21.5cm) wide.
£2,800–3,200 *C*

An Arita blue and white Kakiemon-type *kendi*, the neck and spout restored, c1700, 8in (20.5cm) high.
£500–600 *CSK*

An Arita ewer, decorated in underglaze blue with peonies between floral and geometric bands, drilled towards the foot, c1670, 11in (28cm) high.
£1,000–1,200 *S*

An Arita blue and white moulded *kendi*, late 17thC, 8in (20.5cm) high.
£1,200–1,400 *CAm*

An earthenware miniature ewer, decorated in coloured enamels and gilt with cherry blossoms encircling the shoulder, panels of flowers surrounding the waist, restored, signed 'Yabu Meizan', c1905, 3½in (9cm) high.
£3,500–4,000 *S(NY)*

Figures – Animals

l. An Arita celadon cockerel censer, covered overall with a green glaze, the feet applied to the separate base, beak and tail with restored chip, late 17th/early 18thC, 8½in (21.5cm) high.
£1,000–1,200 *S*

An Arita polychrome group a cockerel, hen and chick, rched on rockwork, hole unched in base, c1700, n (15cm) high.
00–1,000 *CSK*

An Arita model of a cockerel, perched on a rockwork base applied with flowers and fungus, painted in underglaze blue, iron-red, enamels and gilt, restored, early 18thC, 9¾in (25cm) high.
£2,500–3,000 *S*

A Japanese model of a piebald rabbit, with ears pricked, slight damage, 18thC, 3½in (9cm) high.
£750–850 *CSK*

Kutani jar and cover, odelled in the form of a own and white cat wearing brocade collar, with a kitten, gned 'Kanzan', Meiji period, n (23cm) high.
,000–2,200 *S(S)*

An earthenware model of a crane, painted in black, brown and red enamels, impressed seal mark 'Tozan', Meiji period, 5in (12.5cm) high.
£1,400–1,600 *S*

Kutani Ware

Wares made in the region of Kutani from the 17th to the early 20th centuries include the following:
• thin eggshell porcelain tea and coffee services, mostly painted in shades of grey and gold, often marked 'Kutani'
• large dishes, vases and figures of the Meiji period, decorated predominantely in iron-red enamel with grey, black and gilding
• Kaga ware, oatmeal-coloured earthenware, often with 'Kutani' mark, decorated in brocade designs
• Ko (old) Kutani wares, often painted with panels outlined in black and in-filled with dark colours such as green, dark yellow, blue, aubergine and iron-red.

Hirado white-glazed odel of a cockerel, 19thC, n (20.5cm) high.
00–1,000 *C*

A pair of Kutani models of eagles, each decorated in iron-red, black enamels and gilt, 19thC, 7in (18cm) high.
£1,000–1,200 *C*

A Hirado *hanaike*, modelled as a hawk, its feathers detailed in underglaze blue and brown enamels, slight crazing, late 19thC, 8½in (21.5cm) high.
£1,200–1,500 *C*

An Imari model of 2 ducks, decorated in iron-red, green, brown and black enamels and gilt, one beak restored, 19thC, 9½in (24cm) high.
£1,400–1,600 *C*

A porcelain model of a cat, late 19thC, 6½in (16.5cm) high.
£250–300 *Bea*

A Hirado white-glazed model of a tiger, late 19thC, 6in (15cm) high.
£650–800 *CSK*

l. A pair of Arita models of recumben goats, 19thC, 5½in (14cm) long.
£650–800 *Wai*

l. A stoneware eagle, modelled on a rockwork base, slight touches of ash glaze, chipped, engraved mark, Bizen Province, 19thC, 15½in (39.5cm) high.
£900–1,200 *S*

Bizen Ware

Since the 12th century, Bizen has been known for its dark red-brown stoneware made from iron-rich clay with a deliberate ash glaze. Fired with pinewood, the ash flies up in the kiln and is deposited on the pottery. Famous for its tea ceremony wares, Bizen also produces sculptures and finely turned export wares.

A late Kutani moulded model of a pug dog, decorated in iron-red, green, blue, yellow and aubergine enamels and gilt, chips to front paws, slight crack to tail, mid-19thC, 10in (25.5cm) long.
£1,600–1,800 *C*

A Hirado model of goat, horns restuck, late 19thC, 7½in (19cm) long.
£550–650 *CSK*

A Kutani group of cats, modelled as a mother and 4 kittens, each asleep with their paws tucked beneath them, with gilt fur markings and orange bows, Taisho period, mother 11in (28cm) long.
£800–1,000 *S(S)*

A Hirado white-glazed model of a rabbit, with red eyes, damaged c1900, 6in (15cm) long.
£700–800 *CSK*

igures – People

Two Imari figures, each wearing a kimono, decorated in underglaze blue, iron-red, enamels and gilding, the man with a *kiri* and *ju* characters, the woman with thistles, some damaged and repaired, late 17th/early 18thC, largest 14in (35.5cm) high.
£3,200–4,000 S

An Imari figure of a *bijin*, decorated in iron-red, green and black enamels and gilt on underglaze blue, damaged, c1700, 15in (38cm) high.
£3,000–3,400 C

Imari figure of a *bijin*, corated in iron-red, een, aubergine and ack enamels and gilt underglaze blue, late thC, 20in (51cm) high.
,500–4,000 C

A pair of Arita figures of Kintaro astride a carp, decorated in iron-red, green and black enamels and gilt, c1700, 10in (25.5cm) long.
£2,200–2,500 C

l. A Satsuma figure of Kannon, signed on the back 'Seto Seizan' with Shimazu *mon*, late 19thC, 15in (38cm) high.
£2,000–2,400 CNY

pair of Imari gures of *bijins*, corated in coloured amels and gilt on nderglaze blue, ight damage, c1700,)in (25.5cm) high.
,700–2,200 C

An Imari figure of a *bijin*, hair damaged, c1700, 6½in (16.5cm) high.
£450–500 CSK

A Satsuma earthenware figure of a boy, holding a glove puppet of a dog, his robe painted in enamels and gilt with scattered clouds and formal designs, early Meiji period, 9½in (24cm) high.
£1,800–2,000 S

l. A Satsuma earthenware figure of Fugen Bosatsu seated on an elephant, by Kizan, decorated in enamels and gilt, restored, marked 'Dai Nihon Satsuma yaki Kizan', Meiji period, 13in (33cm) high.
£3,200–3,500 S

r. An Imari figure of a woman, her kimono painted with small birds in flight among wisteria and fences, chipped, 19thC, 11in (28cm) high.
£450–500 CSK

Two Imari figures, one repaired, early 19thC, 11in (28cm) high.
£750–850 *PCh*

A Satsuma figure of a temple servant, decorated in coloured enamels, late 19thC, 6½in (16.5cm) high.
£1,100–1,300 *C*

A pair of Satsuma figures, each holding a fan and a fir cone, slight damage, late 19thC, 6½in (16.5cm) high.
£350–400 *Bea*

A Satsuma figure of Buddha, during his period of fasting, restored, late 19thC, 12½ (32cm) high.
£600–700 *C*

Two Imari figures of *bijins*, late 19thC, largest 10⅓in (26.5cm) high.
£450–500 *JH*

Two Satsuma figures, both decorated in red enamel, Meiji period, largest 7in (18cm) high.
£1,700–2,000 *JH*

r. A Kutani model of Kannon, holding a scroll, her clothes painted and gilt with lotus flowers and leaves, hole in base, late 19thC, 24½in (62cm) high.
£1,200–1,700 *CSK*

Flatware

An Arita blue and white *kraak-*style deep dish, painted with flowers, butterflies, birds and emblems, cracked and chipped, late 17thC, 24in (61cm) diam, and a wood frame.
£1,800–2,000 *CSK*

A set of 5 Kakiemon foliate dishes, each painted in enamels with a bird perched in a prunus tree above blue and green rockwork, damaged, late 17thC, 4½in (11.5cm) diam.
£2,600–3,000 *CSK*

An Arita Imari plate, late 17thC, 9in (23cm) diam.
£220–250 *Wai*

r. An Arita blue and white Kakiemon-type dish, painted within a border of flowers and leaves, rim chips, late 17thC, 8⅓in (21.5cm) diam.
£700–800 *CSK*

A Chinese bronze rain drum, with pale green patination and azurite blue, Shang Dynasty, circa 1st century AD, 28in (71cm) high, on a wood stand.
£35,000–40,000 S

A Chinese mottled grey jade model of a horse, 17thC, 10in (25.5cm) long.
£5,000–5,500 S

A Chinese carved spinach jade dragon, Qing Dynasty, 3in (7.5cm) wide.
£2,000–2,500 S

A Chinese bronze vase, with a twelve-character inscription in the neck, 9th–8th century BC, 12in (30.5cm) high.
£15,000–16,000 S

A Chinese bronze tripod food vessel, with malachite, azurite and earth encrustation, 9th–8th century BC, 21½in (54.5cm) wide.
£8,500–9,500 S

A Chinese gold-decorated bronze *hu* and cover, slight damage, 3rd–2nd century BC, 11½in (29cm) high.
£12,500–13,500 S

A Chinese bronze mirror, with green patination, impressed with traces of fabric wrapping, 770–476 century BC, 3½in (9cm) diam.
£7,200–8,200 S

A Chinese celadon jade plaque, mounted as a table screen, Qianlong period, 9½in (24cm) wide.
£10,000–12,000 C

A Chinese carved stone pouring bowl and handle, 12th–14th century AD, 10½in (26.5cm) high.
£3,500–4,000 S

A Chinese black inlaid bronze tripod food vessel, with three-character inscription, 9th–8th century BC, 15½in (39.5cm) wide.
£8,500–10,000 S

A white jade incense burner and cover, 5½in (14cm) wide, and a spinach jade bowl, Qianlong/Jiaqing period.
£3,500–4,500 C

A Chinese pierced celadon green jade magnolia cup, 17thC, 10in (25.5cm) high, on a wood stand.
£1,200–1,500 S

A Chinese celadon jade *ruyi* sceptre, carved with figures, cranes, a deer and a figure on an elephant, late Qing Dynasty, 15½in (39.5cm) long.
£4,500–5,000 C

A silver and *shibayama koro* and cover, decorated with cloisonné enamel, mother-of-pearl and horn, damaged, signed 'Yoshietsu', Meiji period, 9in (23cm) high.
£4,000–5,000 *S*

A pair of Japanese painted bronze vases, decorated with a cockerel and other exotic birds, insects and bamboo, mid-19thC, 41in (104cm) high.
£7,500–9,000 *S*

A Japanese repoussé iron *kabuto*, in the form of a coiled dragon, the horns added as well as the *mabezashi* with a silver *fukurin*, in the style of Miochin Ryoei, 18thC.
£5,000–6,000 *C*

A Japanese repoussé iron *kabuto*, in the form of a conch shell, with diagonal striations, the large *mabezashi* without decoration, the *shikoro* lacking, 18thC.
£5,500–6,500 *C*

A pair of Japanese cloisonné enamel vases, each decorated in gold and silver wire with sprays of chrysanthemums, by Namikawa Sosuke, slight damage, Meiji period, 5in (15cm) high.
£20,000–22,000 *S*

A Chinese or Japanese lacquer and wicker picnic basket, the lid with removable trays, decorated with figures and flowers with loop handle, mid-19thC, 28in (71cm) high.
£650–800 *S*

A pair of Japanese silver candlesticks, chased and worked in repoussé, impressed on base 'Arthur & Bond, Yokohama' and 'yogin', Meiji period, 11in (28cm) high.
£2,000–2,500 *C*

A Japanese bronze incense burner, inlaid with gilt, depicting a god figure seated on a carp, 19thC, 9½in (24cm) high.
£160–180 *PCh*

A Japanese inlaid *shibuichi* and silver tripod *koro* and cover, by Ozeki and others, the body carved in *shishiaibori* and inlaid with silver, copper and gold, slight damage, c1896, 7in (18cm) wide.
£26,000–28,000 *S*

A Japanese model of 2 wrestlers, by Chokichi Suzuki, Kawazu no Saburo Sukeyasu lifting up Matano no Goro Kagehis by his belt, on a carved wood base, unsigned, Meiji period.
£26,000–28,000 *C*

日本の古美術

M.C.N. ANTIQUES (UMEZAWA)

Japanese Porcelain & Works of Art

183 Westbourne Grove, London W11 2SB
Tel: 0171-727 3796 Fax: 0171-229 8839
OPEN: 9.30-5.30 (Sat 11.00-3.00)

l. A *roironuri* box and cover, Meiji period, 3½in (9cm) high.
£3,000–3,500 *C*

A Japanese *roironuri suzuribako* and *bundai*, minor chips to *bundai*, Meiji period, 23in (58.5cm) wide.
£4,000–5,000 *C*

l. A Chinese ormolu-mounted crackle-glazed celadon vase, with lions' mask handles, 14in (35.5cm) wide.
£7,000–8,000 *C*

A Chinese gold openwork plaque, Five Dynasties, 3½in (9cm) high.
£16,000–18,000 *C*

A pair of Japanese gold *kobako*, n the form of male and female Mandarin ducks, both damaged, late 19thC, 7½in (19cm) long.
£4,500–5,500 *C*

A pair of Japanese iron stirrups, 19thC, 11½in (29cm) long.
£3,500–4,000 *C*

A Japanese enamelled silver teapot and cover, the body worked in gold and silver wire, minor restoration, triangular mark with 'SM', Meiji period, 7in (18cm) high.
£4,000–5,000 *C*

A Chinese archaistic silver and gold-inlaid bronze wine pot, central finial missing, Song Dynasty, 9½in (24cm) high.
£9,500–10,500 *CNY*

r. A Japanese ostrich egg, decorated in *hiramakie*, Meiji period, 6in (15cm) long.
£4,000–4,500 *C*

A Chinese flat inkstone, with a bamboo box and lid, 17th/18thC, 4in (10cm) long.
£11,000–12,000 *CNY*

A Japanese lacquered *tonkotsu*, unsigned, with an ivory *netsuke* and *ojime*, signed 'Shogyoku', late 19thC.
£2,500–3,500 *C*

r. A Japanese model of a boat carrying a family, signed 'Shoun', Meiji period, 18in (45.5cm) long.
£6,000–7,000 *C*

A gilt-bronze figure of *lohan*, dated 'Da Ming hengtong', 4th Year, rd month, AD 1439.
14,000–18,000 *C*

A Chinese carved wood figure of a *lohan*, Song Dynasty.
£10,500–12,000 *S*

A Japanese bronze sculpture of Benten, on a high stepped stand, supported by 4 demon head legs, signed 'Joun' with *kao*, Meiji period, 38½in (98cm) high.
£8,000–9,000 *S*

A Chinese carved limestone figure of a Bodhisattva, Northern Qi/Sui Dynasty.
£58,000–60,000 *S*

A Japanese iron charger, cast in relief with *rakkan*, inlaid in gold and silver, by Komai, Meiji period, 19in (48cm) diam.
14,000–16,000 *S*

A Japanese gold lacquer and *shibayama koro* and cover, with mother-of-pearl, ivory and horn, slight damage, signed 'Kaneko', Meiji period, 11in (29cm) high.
£10,000–12,000 *S*

A cloisonné *yenyen* vase, Ming Dynasty.
£10,000–12,000 *S*

A Japanese Namban export inlaid lacquer escritoire, damaged and restored, early Edo period, 17½in (44.5cm) wide.
7,000–8,000 *S*

A Chinese Longmen relief limestone carving of Maitreya, a pair of recumbent lions flanking his knees, damaged and repaired, Northern Wei Dynasty, 13½in (34cm) high.
£8,500–9,500 *S*

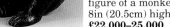

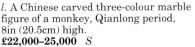

l. A Chinese carved three-colour marble figure of a monkey, Qianlong period, 8in (20.5cm) high.
£22,000–25,000 *S*

A Chinese gilt-lacquered bronze figure of a crowned Buddha, his loose robe with incised floral borders, Ming Dynasty, 29in (74cm) high.
£15,000–18,000 *S*

A stained and inlaid ivory *netsuke*,
Temple Servant, signed 'Yasumasa',
late 19thC, 2in (5cm) high.
£2,500–3,500 *C*

An ivory *netsuke*, Daruma
Doll, signed 'Mitsuhiro'
and 'kao', 1810–75, small
age cracks, 1½in (4cm) high.
£4,000–5,000 *C*

A stained and painted ivory *netsuke*, Fly
on an Octopus Tentacle, signed 'Mitsuh
and 'kao', 1810–75, 2¼in (5.5cm) long.
£3,000–4,000 *C*

Ivory

Both China and Japan
are signatories to the
Cites Convention, which
regulates trade in
substances such as ivory.

An ivory *netsuke*, Ox and Calf, signed
'Mitsuharu', 18thC, 2¼in (5.5cm) long
£7,000–8,000 *C*

An ivory *netsuke*, Crane, signed
'Masatoshi', 20thC, 1¾in (4.5cm).
£4,000–5,000 *C*

An ivory *netsuke*, Dog and Awabi
Shell, signed 'Tomotada', 18thC,
1½in (4.5cm) high.
£7,000–9,000 *C*

An ivory *netsuke*, Wild Duck, signed 'Ohara Mitsuhiro',
1810–75, 2in (5cm) long. **£7,500–9,000** *C*

An ivory *netsuke*, Songoku
the Magical Monkey,
by Ohara Mitsuhiro,
1810–75, 2in (5cm) high.
£10,000–13,000 *C*

An ivory *netsuke*, Ryuji
signed 'Masatoshi',
20thC, 3¾in (9cm) high.
£4,500–6,000 *C*

l. A *netsuke* carved from a stag's
antler, Owl, signed 'Masatoshi',
20thC, 1¾in (4.5cm) high.
£3,500–4,500 *C*

An ivory *netsuke*,
Young Wrestler,
inscribed 'Masanao',
Kyoto, age crack,
18thC, 2in (5cm) high.
£2,000–2,500 *C*

An ivory *netsuke*,
Seated Kirin, signed
'Yoshimasa', c1800,
4in (10.5cm) high.
£27,000–30,000 *C*

An ivory *netsuke*, Karashisl
and Young with a Tama, sign
'Eijusai Masayoshi', 19thC.
£6,000–8,000 *C*

An ivory *netsuke*, Omori Hikoshichi and the
Witch, signed 'Shoko', 20thC, 2in (5cm) high.
£8,000–9,000 *C*

An ivory *netsuke*, Tiger and
Monkey, signed 'Kaigyokusa
with seal Masatsugu, 1813–9
£15,000–20,000 *C*

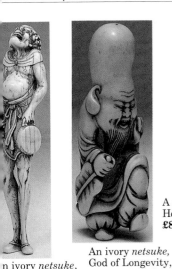

A Japanese *rogin* box and cover, formed as Hotei's treasure bag, late 19thC, 4in (10cm) wide.
£8,000–9,000 *C*

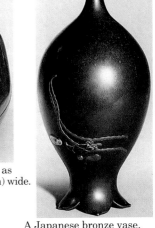

A Japanese bronze vase, signed in seal form 'Yuasa zo', late 19thC, 7in (18cm) high.
£3,500–4,500 *C*

An ivory *netsuke*, God of Longevity, unsigned, 18thC, 3½in (9cm) high.
£18,000–20,000 *C*

n ivory *netsuke*, gned 'Shugetsu', 3thC, 6in 5cm) high.
50,000–55,000 *C*

A Japanese silver box and cover, signed 'Yukiteru', late 19thC, 6½in (16.5cm) wide.
£4,500–5,500 *C*

silver lined *shibuichi* box and cover, signed Kogyokusai', late 19thC, 5½in (14cm) wide.
10,000–12,000 *C*

A Japanese bronze moon flask, signed 'Shoami Katsuyoshizo', c1880, 7in (18cm) high.
£8,000–9,000 *C*

l. A Korean gilt-bronze seal, Yi Dynasty, 15th/16thC.
£5,000–6,000 *C*

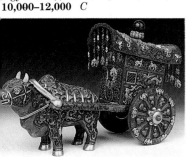

n ox and cart, inlaid with silver, lapis azuli, turquoise, mother-of-pearl and amber, ate Qing Dynasty, 18½in (47cm) long.
4,500–5,500 *C*

A Japanese *shibuichi-ji natsume*, unsigned, 19thC, 4in (10cm) high.
£1,700–2,000 *C*

A Japanese *komai* iron box and cover, signed 'Kyoto ju Komei sei', late 19thC, 7in (18cm) wide.
£2,500–3,000 *C*

A Chinese archaic gold and silver inlaid bronze axe head, some encrustations, Warring States, 5in (12.5cm) wide.
£8,000–9,000 *C*

A Japanese *suzuribako*, decorated in *fundame*, silver *heidatsu*, *aogai okibirame*, the interior similarly decorated, damaged, unsigned, late 17thC, 8½in (21.5cm) high.
£1,500–2,000 *C*

A Chinese glass snuff
bottle, carved in high
relief, Qianlong period,
3in (7.5cm) high.
£280–320 *S*

A Chinese glass snuff bottle,
of flattened form with a waisted
neck, decorated with swirls,
1740–1800, 2¾in (7cm) high.
£850–950 *S(HK)*

A Chinese glass snuff bottle, by Chen
Zhongsan, with figures searching for prunus
and a grasshopper, 1918, 2¼in (6cm) high.
£1,500–1,800 *S*

A Chinese single
overlay snuff bottle,
19thC, 2¾in (7cm) high.
£370–420 *S*

A Japanese gold lacquer three-case
inro and *netsuke*, by Masayuki,
with *shibayama* decoration, 19thC,
inro 4¼in (11cm) high.
£6,500–7,500 *S*

A Chinese decorated
lac burgauté snuff
bottle, early 20thC,
3in (7.5cm) high.
£920–1,000 *S(NY)*

A double overlay glass
snuff bottle, Daoguang
period, 2in (5cm) high.
£2,500–3,000 *S*

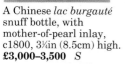

A Chinese *lac burgauté*
snuff bottle, with
mother-of-pearl inlay,
c1800, 3¼in (8.5cm) high.
£3,000–3,500 *S*

A Japanese carved *tsuba*
with gilt edging, 19thC,
2¾in (7cm) high.
£1,900–2,200 *C*

A Japanese inlaid *sentoku tsuba*,
depicting Daikoku, signed
'Inabanosuke Terusugu',
Meiji period, 4in (10cm) wide.
£1,500–1,800 *S(NY)*

A Japanese four-case gold ground
inro, decorated in gold and silver,
minor chips, signed 'Toyo Saku',
19thC, 3¼in (8.5cm) high.
£3,500–4,000 *C*

A Japanese gold and *gyobu*
ground five-case *inro*,
signed 'Toshihide', late
19th, 3¼in (8.5cm) high.
£5,750–6,500 *C*

Chinese coral snuff ottle, carved with bats nd emblems over waves nd rocks, Qianlong eriod, 2¼in (6cm) high. 5,500–6,000 *S*

A Chinese Canton enamel snuff bottle, enamelled with a stylised lotus scroll, mark and period of Qianlong, 2¾in (7cm) high. **£5,000–5,500** *S*

A Chinese three-colour overlay glass snuff bottle, carved with lotus flowers and foliage, 18thC, 2¼in (6cm) high. **£2,000–2,200** *S*

A Chinese red overlay glass snuff bottle, carved with peonies above lotus and symbols, 1780–1860, 2¾in (7cm) high. **£3,200–3,500** *S*

. Chinese glass snuff ottle, carved with lotus eaves, on a foot in the rm of a leaf, 1750–1860, ½in (3.5cm) high. 4,600–5,000 *S*

A Chinese overlay glass snuff bottle, carved with fish on a snowstorm ground, 19thC, 2¾in (7cm) high. **£650–700** *CNY*

A Chinese overlay glass snuff bottle, with fixed ring handles, 19thC, 2¾in (7cm) high. **£1,800–2,000** *CNY*

A Japanese two-case *inro*, by Kanshosai Toyo, with a stained ivory bowl and iron plate, carved and inlaid with a court musician, 19thC, inro 2½in (6.5cm) high. **£3,500–3,850** *S*

Chinese glass snuff bottle, he snowflake body overlaid with he image of a watch, small chips, Daoguang period, 1¾in (4.5cm) high. 2,500–2,750 *S(NY)*

A Chinese single overlay snuff bottle, carved with a stag under a pine tree and a crane, Qianlong period, 2½in (6.5cm) high. **£3,000–3,300** *S(NY)*

Japanese four-case ggshell ground *inro*, ecorated with a group f fish, eyes inlaid with orn, and a *netsuke*, 1800, 3½in (8cm) long. 7,200–8,000 *C*

A Chinese gilt-silver mounted white jade snuff bottle, embellished with precious stones, 19thC, 2¼in (6cm) high. **£600–660** *S(NY)*

A Japanese Somada-style four-case *inro*, decorated with a Chinese sage and attendants, with gold and silver details, early 19thC, 3in (7.5cm) high. **£2,300–2,500** *S*

A Japanese lacquered three-case inro, decorated in gold, signed 'Shoho Saku' at the age of 80, with seal, and an agate *ojime*, unsigned, 19thC, 3½in (8cm) high. **£6,000–6,600** *S(NY)*

A Chinese agate snuff bottle, carved with a silhouette of a bird on a tree, c1800–80, 2in (5cm) high.
£7,000–8,000 *S(NY)*

A Chinese inside-painted glass snuff bottle, depicting rabbits beneath a soaring bat, the base carved as a basket stand, c1800–80, 2in (5cm) high.
£1,200–1,400 *S(NY)*

A Japanese four-case *inro*, by Koma Kansai, signed, 19thC, 3½in (9cm) high.
£18,500–20,000 *S*

A Japanese five-case *inro*, by Shunsho, decorated with a scene of Sojobo, the reverse with 2 *tengu* fighting, signed, 19thC, 3½in (9cm) high.
£26,000–28,000 *S*

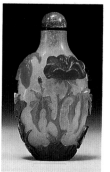

l. A Japanese four-case *inro*, by Koma Kyui, the sharkskin decorated in gold with a dragonfly, possibly 17thC, 2½in (6.5cm) high.
£4,800–5,200 *S*

A Chinese nine-colour overlay glass snuff bottle, depicting a bat, butterfly and peony, c1760–1820, 2in (5cm) high.
£15,000–16,500 *S(NY)*

A Chinese two-colour jade snuff bottle, carved as a recumbent water buffalo, 18thC, 2½in (6.5cm) long.
£5,500–6,000 *S(NY)*

A Japanese four-case black lacquer *inro*, with metal inlay, by Hara Yoyusai and Haruaki Hogen, signed, 19thC, 3½in (9cm) high.
£52,500–57,000 *S*

A Japanese four-case gold lacquer *inro*, by Shojosai, decorated with a mandarin duck, slight damage, signed, early 20thC, 3½in (9cm) high.
£13,000–14,000 *S*

A collection of 10 Chinese miniature snuff bottles, including a flask-form ruby bottle, 2 chalcedony bottles, and a metal bottle in the form of an eggplant.
£3,000–4,000 *S(NY)*

Chinese glass snuff
ttle, dappled with
ight blue, 18thC,
in (4.5cm) high.
00–600 *S(NY)*

A Chinese enamelled glass
snuff bottle, by Ye Bengqi,
with four-character
Qianlong mark on base.
£20,000–25,000 *S(NY)*

A Chinese carved glass
overlay snuff bottle,
decorated with an egret
in flight, c1800.
£7,000–8,000 *S(NY)*

A Japanese ivory *okimono*
of a fisherman, on a carved
wood base, c1900,
16½in (42cm) high.
£1,300–1,800 *AAV*

Chinese glass overlay snuff
ottle, decorated with a grass-
pper, c1810, 2in (5cm) high.
,400–2,600 *S(NY)*

A pair of Japanese carved ivory groups,
depicting a toy vendor and a fruit seller,
signed, late 19thC, 12in (30.5cm) high.
£260–300 *PCh*

A Japanese ivory *netsuke* of
a hare, signed 'Yoshinaga',
early 19thC.
£1,600–2,000 *DN*

gold-ground moulded
rcelain double snuff bottle,
owing ladies with lanterns,
ith gold stoppers, c1825.
,000–2,500 *S(NY)*

A Chinese amethystine
glass snuff bottle, c1830,
2in (5cm) high.
£1,800–2,400 *S(NY)*

A Chinese amber snuff
bottle, carved with a bear
and eagle in combat, the
reverse with an eagle on
a flowering prunus,
c1850, 2¼in (5.5cm) high.
£2,500–3,000 *S(NY)*

A Japanese coloured
and carved ivory
figure of a sage,
late 19thC,
6½in (16.5cm) high.
£1,000–1,200 *PCh*

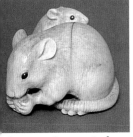

Japanese ivory *netsuke*
f a rat and her young, the
other holding a candle,
igned 'Okatomo', 19thC.
5,500–6,000 *DN*

l. A Chinese *lac burgauté*
and mother-of-pearl snuff
bottle, 2in (5cm) high.
£2,200–2,600 *S(NY)*

A Chinese porcelain
famille rose snuff bottle,
Qianlong Nianzhi mark,
19thC, 2½in (6.5cm) high.
£1,400–1,600 *RHa*

Three Chinese snuff bottles:
l. A gourd grown into a mould,
c1780–1850, 2½in (6.5cm) high.
c. Yixing enamelled pottery, 19thC,
2in (5cm) high.
r. Imperial yellow glass, c1780–1850,
2½in (6.5cm) high.
£2,000–3,500 each *RHa*

A Chinese quartz jasper
snuff bottle, c1750–1830,
2½in (6.5cm) high.
£10,000–12,000 *RHa*

A Chinese glass snuff
bottle, c1730–1800,
2in (5cm) high.
£1,000–1,100 *RHa*

Three Chinese jade snuff bottles, c1720–1850,
2½in (6.5cm) high.
l. **£3,500–4,500** *c.* **£7,000–8,000** *r.* **£5,000–6,000** *RHa*

A Chinese porcelain snuff
bottle, the base inscribed
with four-character mark,
c1796–1850, 2in (5cm) high.
£1,000–1,200 *RHa*

A Chinese snuff bottle, the
glass imitating tortoiseshell,
c1730–1800, 2in (5cm) high.
£500–600 *RHa*

A Chinese snuff bottle, with overlay of
bats, c1780–1850, 2½in (6.5cm) high.
£1,500–1,600 *RHa*

A Chinese wooden snuff bottle,
c1780–1850, 2in (5cm) high.
£2,000–2,800 *RHa*

A Chinese pudding stone
snuff bottle, c1780–1850,
2in (5cm) high.
£2,000–2,800 *RHa*

A Chinese peach stone snuff
bottle, carved with horses,
19thC, 1½in (4cm) high.
£2,000–2,400 *RHa*

A Chinese porcelain snuff bottle,
moulded and enamelled with
dragons, 19thC, 2½in (6.5cm) high.
£2,000–3,000 *RHa*

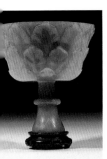

Chinese celadon jade
us-head stem cup,
rved with 3 layers of
tals, Ming Dynasty,
n (10cm) high.
,600–5,000 C

Chinese jade dragon
d vase group, the cover
th a phoenix knop,
thC, 5in (12.5cm) high.
,600–1,800 S(NY)

A pair of Chinese archaistic jadeite ewers and covers,
the tongue-form spouts extending from the mouths of
mythical beasts, the covers set with 2 loops and
stylised phoenix knops, 19thC, 6½in (16.5cm) wide.
£13,500–15,000 S(NY)

A Chinese white jade hanging
pendant, with 3 rows of Eight
Daoist Emblems, 17thC,
13½in (34.5cm) long.
£1,400–1,600 S(NY)

A Chinese jade
group, one fish in
grey stone, one in
celadon stone, 18thC,
5½in (14cm) high.
£3,500–4,000 S

A Chinese white and
brown jade carving of
an old man and a boy,
on pierced rockwork,
c1700, 4in (10cm) high.
£3,000–3,300 C

Chinese woman's
nbroidered silk jacket,
orked in gold threads,
te Qing Dynasty.
,000–1,200 CNY

A rank badge, probably
from a Chinese army
general's robe, late 19thC.
£500–600 Wai

A Chinese jadeite
figure of Guanyin,
wearing a beaded
necklace, 19thC,
16in (40.5cm) high.
£5,300–5,800 S(NY)

A Chinese woven panel,
depicting boys at play,
on a fine metallic ground,
17thC, 27 x 12½in
(68.5 x 32cm).
£7,500–8,250 S(NY)

ne back of a Chinese Daoist priest's robe, woven
ith dragons and a pagoda, flanked by the moon
re and sun bird interspersed with cranes, c1600,
" x 69in (119.5 x 175cm).
350–450 S(NY)

A Chinese lady's
embroidered silk jacket,
the cuffs worked with gold
and silver threads, late
19thC, 34½in (90cm) long.
£1,100–1,200 CNY

A Chinese embroidered
silk coat, with Daoist
and Buddhistic
Emblems, late 19thC,
45½in (115.5cm) long.
£1,800–2,200 CNY

A Chinese cloisonné enamel and gilt-bronze censer, supported on 4 gilt-bronze legs with 3 talons, Ming Dynasty, 17in (43cm) wide.
£14,000–15,000 *S*

A Chinese woven belt, Han Dynasty, 2½in (6.5cm) wide.
£3,500–4,000 *MA*

A pair of lacquered wooden tigers, Han Dynasty, 9½in (24cm) long.
£7,000–8,000 *MA*

A Japanese *hoshi bachi kabuto*, with raised rivets, covered with printed leath signed 'Nagamichi', early Edo period.
£8,500–9,500 *C*

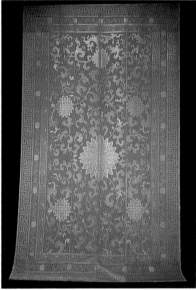

A Chinese stone figure of a judge, Ming Dynasty, 19in (48.5cm) high.
£1,200–1,500 *MA*

A Chinese velvet carpet, with gilt-metal threads and eau-de-nil silk floral design, 18thC, 117 x 72in (297 x 183cm).
£3,500–4,500 *CSK*

A Japanese red silk damask resist-dyed *furisode*, 19thC.
£600–700 *CSK*

A Japanese russet iron *mempo*, with detachable nose, 18thC, 8in (20.5cm) wide.
£2,200–2,700 *C*

A Japanese bronze elephant, with ivory tusks, 19thC, 9½in (24cm) high.
£650–700 *SWO*

A Japanese embroidered blu silk *furisode*, lined in red sil with padded hem, mid-19th
£1,000–1,400 *CSK*

Chinese poster, 'Forward
ith our Great Leader', c1969,
0¼ x 20¾in (77 x 53cm).
180–200 *Wai*

*ome posters were ready-
rinted with a general
lustration, leaving a white
rip across the bottom of the
oster for up-to-date messages
) be added.*

. Chinese poster,
Iero of the People', c1970,
0¼ x 20¾in (77 x 53cm).
180–200 *Wai*

. Chinese poster, 'The Red
.antern Girl is my Heroine',
1974, 30¼ x 20¾in (77 x 53cm).
:180–200 *Wai*

A Chinese poster, 'Chairman
Iao Instructs the Young People',
1978, 30¼ x 20¾in (77 x 53cm).
200–240 *Wai*

A pre-printed 'message' poster, 'The People's Voice', c1970, 30¼ x 20¾in (77 x 53cm).
£180–200 *Wai*

A Chinese poster, 'Off To School With Grandad', c1970, 30¼ x 20¾in (77 x 53cm).
£180–200 *Wai*

It is the traditional role of grandparents to look after the children, thus allowing the parents to go to work.

A Chinese poster, 'Raise the Red Lantern', c1970, 30 x 20¾in (76 x 53cm).
£180–200 *Wai*

The Red Lantern *was one of the revolutionary operas performed by the Peking National Opera during the Cultural Revolution.*

A Chinese poster, 'Working Together to Bring in the Harvest', c1976, 30¼ x 20¾in (77 x 53cm).
£180–200 *Wai*

A Chinese poster, 'The Barefoot Doctors', c1970, 20½ x 14½in (52 x 37cm).
£120–140 *Wai*

After the retraining of many professionals, including doctors, young undergraduates from the medical colleges were sent to the country to take their places. Known as 'the barefoot doctors', they performed elementary first aid until such time as patients could be taken into town to hospital.

A Chinese poster, 'Singing the Praises of the Nation', c1972, 20¾ x 15in (53 x 38cm).
£120–140 *Wai*

A Chinese poster, 'Defending the Coastline', c1975, 30¼ x 20¾in (77 x 53cm).
£180–200 *Wai*

A Chinese Imperial dragon robe, with 8 dragons in gilt thread and 12 symbols, over a sea-wave, probably re-lined, altered, 19thC.
£6,200–6,800 *CSK*

A Chinese summer dragon robe, with 4 Imperial symbols and 9 dragons, 19thC.
£7,500–8,500 *CSK*

A Chinese fine gauze dragon robe, with couched gold dragon and *shou* medallions, late 19th
£2,000–2,500 *S(NY)*

A Chinese informal coat, the peonies worked in Peking knots, 19thC.
£400–450 *CSK*

A pair of Chinese reverse mirror painting depicting female deities riding Buddhist lions, in giltwood frames, one mirror cracked, 18thC, 22 x 16in (56 x 41cm).
£4,000–4,500 *P*

A Korean embroidered court official rank apron, the top with original gilt rings, Choson Dynasty, 19thC, 23½ x 10½in (59.5 x 26.5cm).
£3,000–3,500 *S(NY)*

Dragon Robes

Dragon robes, known as *longpao* in Chinese, were dragon-decorated robes worn by the Emperor, the Imperial family and senior officials of the court.

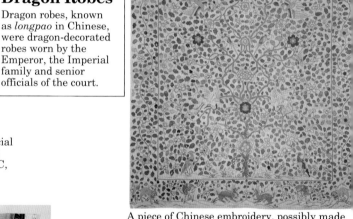

A piece of Chinese embroidery, possibly made for the Portuguese market, depicting blossoms, birds, mythical beasts and deer, within a floral border, now backed, c1700, 63in (160cm) squar
£1,500–1,800 *S(NY)*

A Chinese New Year's robe, with narcissus roundels, black borders and flowering prunus, late 19thC, 55½in (141cm) long.
£3,000–3,500 *S(NY)*

A Chinese mirror painting, painted with figures, a hors and deer, probably depicting the estuary of the Pearl River, mid-18thC, in gilt frame, 29 x 49in (74 x 124cm).
£8,700–9,500 *S*

Kakiemon-type underglaze blue dish, decorated with 2 herons, 1680, 7in (18cm) diam.
£1,400–1,600 *C*

A pair of Kakiemon dishes, with foliate rims, decorated in iron-red, green, yellow, blue and black enamels with a dragon coiled beneath sheets of stylised lightning, ring feet, one with slight chip to rim, late 17thC, 3½in (9cm) wide.
£1,400–1,600 *C*

An Arita blue and white *kraak*-style charger, the central roundel containing branches of pomegranates surrounded by alternate panels of Buddhistic emblems of stylised flowerheads and foliage, late 17thC, 16½in (42cm) diam.
£1,800–2,000 *C*

An Imari deep dish, the centre painted with a jardinière of pine and prunus, cracked, late 17thC, 19in (48.5cm) diam.
£2,400–2,600 *CSK*

A pair of Arita blue and white Kakiemon-style saucer dishes, *fuku* marks, late 17thC, 6in (15cm) diam.
£1,400–1,600 *C*

An Arita blue and white Kakiemon-style dish, decorated in the centre with cranes, the border with prunus, pine and bamboo, the exterior with scrolling foliage, late 17thC, 8in (20.5cm) diam.
£1,400–1,600 *C*

l. An Arita blue and white painted dish, small rim chip, *fuku* mark, late 17thC, 8in (20.5cm) diam.
£500–600 *CSK*

An Arita blue and white deep dish, painted with a jardinière on a terrace, within foliate panels, stained, late 17thC, 12½in (32cm) diam.
£700–800 *CSK*

An Arita blue and white dish, with a border of scrolling foliate, cracked, late 17thC, 24in (61cm) diam.
£2,000–2,400 *CSK*

A Kakiemon blue and white foliate-rimmed dish, decorated with a lakeside scene, the reverse with scrolling *karakusa*, repaired, late 17thC, 7½in (19cm) diam.
£700–800 *C*

A Kakiemon-type shallow dish, decorated in iron-red, green, blue and black enamels on underglaze blue, late 17thC, 9in (23cm) diam.
£1,200–1,400 *C*

A pair of Arita foliate-rimmed blue and white dishes, minor chip, late 17thC, 11in (28cm) diam.
£1,400–1,600 *C*

An Arita dish, decorated in underglaze blue with floral designs, late 17thC, 12½in (31.5cm) diam.
£800–1,000 *S*

A Kakiemon dish, decorated in iron-red, enamels and gilding, with a tiger beside bamboo and prunus, chipped and cracked, late 17thC, 9½in (24cm) diam.
£1,200–1,400 *S*

An Arita blue and white charger, painted with a roundel enclosing the letters 'VOC', surrounded by *ho-o* birds, one perched on a rock, the other in flight among pomegranate and peony sprays, within a border of 6 alternate panels of peony and *shochikuba* sprays divided by vertical bands of stylised flowerheads and foliage, late 17thC, 14½in (37cm) diam.
£5,000–6,000 *C(S)*

A blue and white Kakiemon-style foliate-rimmed dish, with chocolate rim, marked, late 17thC, 9½in (24cm) diam.
£800–1,000 *C*

An Arita blue and white charger, late 17thC, 23in (58cm) diam.
£2,400–2,600 *CAm*

Japanese Chronology Chart

For Japanese periods and dates please refer to page 11

An Arita blue and white plate, late 17thC, 8½in (21cm) diam.
£350–400 *Wai*

l. A set of 8 Imari dishes, each with a pierced border picked out in green within 2 underglaze blue bands, centrally decorated with a courtesan smoking a pipe and reading a scroll before a screen, some damage, late 17thC, 10½in (26.5cm) diam.
£8,000–9,000 *DN*

A set of 4 Arita blue and white *kraak*-style dishes, painted to the centre with a deer below pines and overhanging rockwork within panels of flowersprays, the everted rims with masks, c1700, 7in (17.5cm) diam.
£1,200–1,400 *CSK*

An Arita blue and white charger, the wide everted rim with flowerheads and scrolling foliage, star cracks to base, c1700, 25in (63.5cm) diam.
£1,800–2,000 *C*

An Imari saucer dish, decorated in iron-red and gilt on underglaze blue, c1700, 21in (53.5cm) diam.
£2,400–2,700 *CAm*

A pair of Arita blue and white dishes, painted with coiled dragons within broad bands of *shishi* lions and foliage, Chenghua six-character marks, 18thC, 6½in (16.5cm) diam.
£350–400 *CSK*

An Imari foliate-rimmed dish, decorated in iron-red, yellow, green, aubergine and black enamels and gilt on underglaze blue, the reverse with scrolling *karakusa*, c1700, 11in (28cm) diam.
£1,200–1,400 *C*

r. A pair of Kakiemon dishes, decorated in iron-red, green, yellow and black enamels, on underglaze blue, with sprays of wild pinks and other flowers and foliage, 18thC, 6in (15cm) diam.
£2,000–2,400 *C*

A pair of Arita dishes, the centre of each painted in underglaze blue in the manner of Van Frytom, Ming/Chenghua mark, c1700, 5in (12.5cm) diam.
£800–900 *C*

A pair of Arita moulded dishes, decorated in iron-red, blue, green and black enamels and gilt, with panels each depicting the character 'ju', c1700, 8½in (21.5cm) diam.
£1,600–1,800 *C*

l. Four Arita moulded dishes, decorated in iron-red enamels and gilt on underglaze blue, Chenghua six-character mark, early 18thC, 8½in (22cm) diam.
£1,800–2,000 *C*

An Imari charger, painted and gilt within a border of *ho-o* roundels and pavilions, damaged and restored, c1700, 21in (53cm) diam.
£2,000–2,200 *CSK*

A pair of Arita fluted leaf-shaped dishes, painted and gilt with leafy sprays of prunus, early 18thC, 9in (23cm) wide.
£1,200–1,400 *CSK*

An Imari dish, painted and gilt, slight damage, 18thC, 15½in (39.5cm) diam.
£450–500 *CSK*

An Arita dish, modelled in the form of an *uchiwa*, decorated in coloured enamels and gilt on underglaze blue, the reverse with scrolling foliage, Chenghua six-character mark, early 18thC, 7½in (19cm) wide.
£1,200–1,500 *C*

An Arita blue and white shallow dish, with the design of the Hall of One Hundred Boys, the centre painted with the characters *Hyakushido*, 18thC, 8in (20.5cm) diam.
£1,000–1,200 *C*

An Imari saucer dish, painted with figures and dogs in a garden within a border of radiating panels of birds and foliage, gilding slightly rubbed, 18thC, 13½in (35cm) diam.
£1,200–1,400 *S*

l. A Kakiemon foliate-rimmed saucer dish, decorated in typical coloured enamels and gilt, c1700, 5in (13cm) diam.
£900–1,000 *C*

r. A blue and white porcelain charger, the interior decorated with a mountainous landscape, the exterior with insects among flowers, 18thC, 17¾in (45cm) diam.
£2,000–2,200 *S(NY)*

An Imari shallow basin, with flattened rim, painted and gilt with alternating panels of boats below pine and stylised peony, surrounding a central basket of flowers, damaged, c1700, 18½in (47cm) diam.
£550–700 *CSK*

A pair of Imari lobed saucer dishes, painted within bands of trailing pine, the borders with red and green ground panels, rim chip, early 18thC, 10in (25.5cm) diam.
£1,200–1,400 *CSK*

An Imari dish, painted and gilt, with a central brocade ball surrounded by flowering lotus and peony stems, slight fritting to rim, 18thC, 18½in (47cm) diam.
£1,500–1,700 *CSK*

A set of 9 Arita foliate dishes, each painted with the Hall of One Hundred Boys, 3 with rim repairs, 18thC, 4in (10cm) diam.
£1,600–1,800 *CSK*

An Arita blue and white dish, boldly decorated with sprays of tree peony issuing from swirling waters beneath cumulus clouds, late 18thC, 9in (23cm) diam.
£800–1,000 *C*

An Arita dish, with foliate chocolate rim, painted in underglaze blue, Kakiemon enamels and gilt, damaged, 18thC, 11in (28cm) diam.
£750–850 *CSK*

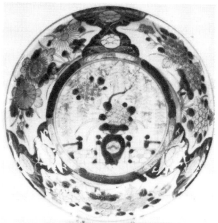

A pair of Imari dishes, centrally painted with baskets of flowers on fenced terraces, within borders of flowers, mid-18thC, 10in (25.5cm) diam.
£500–600 *CSK*

A Kinkozan dish, decorated in various coloured enamels and gilt on a deep-blue ground, signed and impressed 'Kinkozan zo', painter's mark 'Hosui', late 19thC, 8½in (21cm) diam.
£1,600–1,800 *C*

A pair of Imari dishes, decorated in underglaze blue, ochre and gilt, c1800, 14in (35.5cm) diam.
£1,200–1,400 *P(S)*

r. A Kakiemon dish, with blue and white floral and bamboo decoration, Edo period, 8in (20.5cm) diam.
£800–1,000 *Wai*

A pair of Imari dishes, decorated in underglaze blue, iron-red and gilt, some pitting from firing, marked 'Fuku cho shun', 19thC, 18in (45.5cm) diam.
£1,800–2,000 *S*

A Nabeshima-style dish, decorated overall in underglaze blue with finely scrolling foliage, the exterior with larger scrolls, the tall tapering foot with 'comb' design, 19thC, 19in (48cm) diam.
1,700–2,000 *S*

Wear & Tear

Arita porcelain, particularly blue and white and Imari, is usually resilient and not easily cracked. However, its glaze is quite soft and can be stratched. Some Arita export wares have crackled glazes, and must be examined carefully to ensure that the body itself is not damaged.

r. An Imari charger, with radial flower decoration in blue and iron-red with gilt, 19thC, 24½in (62cm) wide.
£500–600 *AH*

An Imari charger, decorated
in underglaze blue, iron-red,
enamels and gilding, 19thC,
17½in (44.5cm) diam.
£1,400–1,600 *S*

A Satsuma earthenware dish,
by Kozan, painted with a *bijin*
and attendants beside a vase
filled with peonies and
wisteria, surrounded by a
flower and textile-decorated
border, six-character mark,
Meiji period, 8½in (22cm) diam.
£800–900 *S(S)*

A Satsuma earthenware dish,
by Kyoto Shoun, painted with
figures near the temple at Nikko
in the autumn, the angled rim
with flowers, Meiji period,
9in (23cm) long.
£2,300–2,800 *S*

A Nabeshima saucer-dish,
decorated with the Narcissus
pattern, Meiji period,
8in (20.5cm) diam.
£1,200–1,500 *Wai*

Nabeshima

Nabeshima porcelain was
made at Okawachi, north of
Arita, and was named after
the prince who founded the
kilns at the end of the
17thC. The porcelain was of
higher quality than that
made for export, and was
originally made as
presentation ware for the
local nobility. The decoration
on these wares was usually
outlined in underglaze blue
and infilled with overglaze
enamels in iron-red,
turquoise, pale manganese,
yellow and, rarely, black
detailing. Nabeshima wares
are never marked.

An Imari charger, decorated
with peony sprays and scrolling
karakusa, 19thC, 22½in (56cm) diam.
£1,400–1,600 *C*

An Imari porcelain saucer dish,
decorated with central wheel
motif and flanked with floral
panels, c1880, 12in (30.5cm) diam.
£170–200 *BRU*

l. An Imari dish, the lobed rim
with carefully drawn decoration,
late 19thC, 8½in (21.5cm) diam.
£100–120 *ORI*

An Imari charger, brightly
decorated with figures by a garden
pavilion, within a panelled border
of scrolling flowerheads, reserved
with shaped panels of lotus, c1800,
18in (46cm) diam.
£900–1,200 *DN*

An Imari dish, decorated in
iron-red enamel and gilt on
underglaze blue, with gilt rims,
late 19thC, 22½in (57cm) diam.
£1,400–1,600 *C*

n Imari salver, decorated in
ue, rust and green palette,
)thC, 17in (43cm) diam.
500–600 *GAK*

An Imari porcelain charger,
painted with 4 reserves of figures
and birds in 4 colours and gilt,
19thC, 18½in (47cm) diam.
£500–600 *RBB*

An Imari charger, decorated
with a dragon on a blue ground,
the central plaque with a lady
holding a fan, blue and white
decoration on the reverse, 19thC,
18½in (47cm) diam.
£500–600 *WeH*

Satsuma dish, decorated in
arious coloured enamels and gilt
ith a *ho-o* bird among clouds
nd foliage, the rim with a
epeating foliate motif, signed,
ate 19thC, 12¾in (32.5cm) diam.
1,500–1,650 *C*

A Satsuma dish, decorated in
various coloured enamels and
gilt, with a winding *daimyo*
procession, within a key pattern
border, signed 'Fuzan', late 19thC,
7½in (19cm) diam.
£1,000–1,200 *C*

An Imari foliate-
rimmed charger,
decorated in iron-red
and gilt on underglaze
blue, late 19thC,
25in (63.5cm) diam.
£1,400–1,600 *CAm*

Satsuma earthenware charger,
ecorated with panels of figures
nd lakeland landscapes, Satsuma
on and mark in gilt, late 19thC,
0¼in (26cm) diam.
500–600 *P(HSS)*

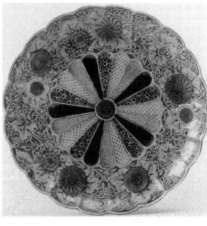

l. An Imari foliate-
rimmed shallow dish,
decorated in coloured
enamels and gilt,
signed in underglaze
blue 'Dai Nihon Bizen
Arita...sei', late 19thC,
12in (30.5cm) diam.
£1,700–2,000 *C*

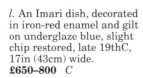

l. An Imari dish, decorated
in iron-red enamel and gilt
on underglaze blue, slight
chip restored, late 19thC,
17in (43cm) wide.
£650–800 *C*

r. An Imari plate,
with foliate rim, c1890,
14in (35.5cm) diam.
£350–400 *AnE*

A Satsuma dish, painted with figures, on a brocade ground, late 19thC, 10in (25.5cm) diam.
£450–500 *Bea*

A Satsuma shallow dish, late 19thC, 12in (30.5cm) diam.
£750–850 *Bea*

An Imari deep dish, painted with *bijins* among pine in a landscape beside dense flowering shrubs reserved with panels of *ho-o* and foliage, 19thC, 20½in (52cm) diam.
£1,400–1,600 *CSK*

A set of 6 Imari fluted dishes, painted with central iron-red and gilt floral medallions, late 19thC, 8½in (22cm) diam.
£750–900 *CSK*

A pair of chargers, with scalloped edges, decorated in Imari-style with a central panel of a ginger tree, 19thC, 18in (45.5cm) diam.
£1,000–1,200 *P(M)*

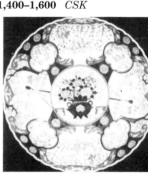

A pair of Imari fluted dishes, printed and painted with central roundels of jardinières of flowers on terraces, within panels of *ho-o* among flowers, 19thC, 18½in (47cm) diam.
£950–1,200 *CSK*

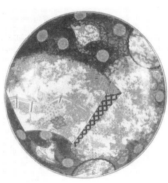

An Imari dish, painted on a blue gilt ground, reserved with scrolling foliage, 19thC, 24in (61cm) diam.
£1,200–1,500 *CSK*

l. An Imari charger, decorated in underglaze blue, iron-red and coloured enamels, 19thC, 22in (56cm) diam.
£1,500–1,800 *LT*

A Satsuma dish, painted and heavily gilt, late 19thC, 12in (30.5cm) diam.
£800–1,000 *CSK*

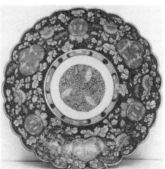

An Imari dish, painted with a central blue floral medallion, 19thC, 25in (63.5cm) diam.
£1,200–1,500 *CSK*

A Komai dish, signed 'Kyoto ju Komai sei', 19thC, 19in (48cm) diam.
£10,000–12,000 *CSK*

satsuma dish, painted
d gilt with a multitude
chrysanthemums, signed,
te 19thC, 7½in (19cm) diam.
250–300 *CSK*

An earthenware dish, decorated
with irises, birds and leaves, within
a gilt-ground flower and diaper
border, 19thC, 13½in (34.5cm) diam.
£170–220 *DN*

An Imari charger, painted and
gilt, underglaze blue Chenghua
six-character mark, 19thC,
18in (45.5cm) diam.
£650–750 *CSK*

n Imari charger, decorated with
alloping fabulous animals with a
hoenix overhead, the floral lattice
order with groups of pendant
exagons painted with flowering
ranches and formal designs,
te 19thC, 24in (61cm) diam.
800–900 *P(S)*

An Imari charger, painted with
panels of mountain landscapes and
kara shishi on gilt and blue ground,
cranes amid clouds, and gilt and red
phoenix, 19thC, 21½in (54.5cm) diam.
£400–450 *ALL*

Two Imari chargers, painted
and gilt with shaped and
scrolled panels, late 19thC,
18in (45.5cm) diam.
£400–500 *CSK*

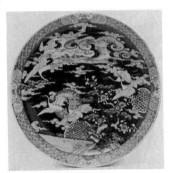

An Arita dish, painted in colours
on an iron-red ground, with a
turquoise and blue 'cracked ice'
border, reserved with gilt foliate
motifs, 19thC, 18in (45.5cm) diam.
£250–300 *L*

An Imari plaque painted with
panels, 19thC, 18in (45.5cm) diam.
£350–400 *Bea*

Kutani dish, painted and gilt
ith a lady, attendant, screen
nd cranes on a terrace,
te 19thC, 9½in (24cm) diam.
350–450 *CSK*

Chinese marks on Japanese porcelain

In the race to capture the
export market, it was common
practice for both the Chinese
and Japanese to copy each
other's work. The Japanese
often applied spurious Chinese
reign-marks, particularly
the Chenghua mark.

l. Two Imari dishes, decorated
in underglaze blue, iron-red,
black enamel and gilding,
with a *bijin* and attendants,
both restored, 19thC, largest
19in (48cm) diam.
£2,000–2,500 *S*

A Satsuma thickly potted fluted
saucer dish, enamelled and gilt,
late 19thC, 13in (33cm) diam.
£800–1,000 *CSK*

Jardinières

A Satsuma jardinière, Meiji period, 17in (43cm) diam.
£650–800 *Nam*

An Arita jardinière, decoration in underglaze blue with *kirin*, *ho-o* and Buddhistic emblems, damaged, mid-19thC, 29½in (75.5cm) diam.
£1,800–2,200 *C*

A Fukagawa jardinière, painted to the interior with a *ho-o* among pawlonia, the exterior with prunus on an iron-red ground, Mount Fuji mark, c1900, 15½in (39.5cm) diam.
£450–550 *CSK*

An Imari jardinière, with flattened rim, painted and gilt with shaped panels of birds above baskets of flowers on a ground of *kiku* heads and foliate stems, slight stems, slight damage, 19thC, 15in (38cm) diam.
£550–700 *CSK*

A Satsuma pot globular jardin and stand, pai in colours and with moulded leaves around foot rim, late 1 39½in (100cm)
£1,500–1,700

Koros

decorated and enamelled lozenge-shaped *koro*, with pierced cover, signed 'tsuseki', c1890, 5in (12.5cm) high.
£1,800–2,000 *MER*

A Satsuma *koro* and cover, decorated in enamels and gilt, on 3 elephant head feet, Meiji period, 36½in (92.5cm) high.
£3,500–3,800 *S*

A Satsuma earthenware *koro* and cover, the sides painted with a border of flowers, slight damage, signed 'Dai Nihon, Tojiki Goshigaisha, Ryozan', below the Yasuda company trademark, Meiji period, 5½in (14cm) wide.
£4,500–5,000 *S(S)*

Satsuma earthenware *koro* and cover, painted with chrysanthemums, peonies and dianthus among clouds, on 3 bracket feet, cover pierced and with bud finial, 19thC, 7in (18cm) high, with wood stand.
£3,500–4,000 *S(S)*

A Satsuma earthenware *koro*, with metal cover, damaged and repaired, Meiji period, 6in (15cm) high.
£1,300–1,500 *S(S)*

A *koro* and cover, painted and gilt with a coiled dragon above foaming waves, the sides with floral medallions, signed 'Kinkozan zo', late 19thC, 2in (5cm) high.
£200–220 *CSK*

Tea & Coffee Ware

> ### Tea & Coffee Ware
> During the Momoyama period (1568–1600) the tea ceremony was consolidated and refined, and tea wares were produced at such pottery centres as Bizen, Seto, Kyoto, Hagi, Karatsu and Satsuma. Extant tea wares from this period are rare and among the most prized Japanese ceramics; they must be accompanied by a full and accurate provenance if they are not to be confused with numerous later copies.

A Kyoto earthenware kettle, painted in enamels and gilding, on a seeded gilt ground, spout repaired, painted mark, Meiji period, 5in (12.5cm) high.
£500–600 *Bon*

An Arita blue and white silver-mounted coffee pot and cover, the loop handle decorated with scrolling foliage, porcelain late 17thC, mounts 19thC, 13in (33cm) high.
£2,000–2,500 *CAm*

r. A blue and white teapot and cover, decorated with *ho-o* birds, by Makuzu Kozan, late 19thC, 8in (20.5cm) wide.
£1,600–1,800 *C*

An Imari teapot and cover, decorated in underglaze blue, iron-red, green and yellow, slight damage, Edo period, c1700, 4¾in (12cm) high.
£2,600–3,000 *S(S)*

A Hirado teapot, late 19thC,
8in (20.5cm) high.
£500–600 *Wai*

A Satsuma kettle, decorated with
a design of figures and flowers,
small floral borders above and
below, the lid with floral design,
late 19thC, 6in (15cm) diam.
£1,250–1,500 *SK*

A Satsuma teapot, decorated
with panels of figures,
signed 'Kichizan', c1890,
7in (18cm) high.
£1,000–1,250 *MER*

l. A Satsuma pottery tea service,
reserved on a gold-decorated deep-
blue ground, comprising teapot and
cover, sugar basin and cover, milk
jug and 6 cups and saucers, c1900.
£700–800 *Bea*

Tokkuri

l. An Arita *tokkuri*,
enamelled and gilt
on underglaze blue,
chip to neck, c1700,
7½in (19cm) high.
£1,000–1,200 *C*

Tokkuri

Tokkuri were
used for sake,
and were made in
many different
shapes and sizes.

An Imari *tokkuri*, in the form
of a barrel, the handle formed
as a gnarled pine branch, late
19thC, 12in (30.5cm) high.
£1,500–1,800 *C*

An Imari *tokkuri*,
decorated in iron-red,
green and brown
enamels and gilt on
underglaze blue, 19thC,
8½in (21.5cm) high,
with wood stopper.
£1,700–2,000 *C*

Tureens

An Imari tureen and cover, on a
a moulded foliate-rimmed dish,
restored, Genroku period,
11in (28cm) diam.
£1,700–2,000 *C*

An Imari tureen and cover, decorated
in typical coloured enamels and gilt on
underglaze blue, the cover similarly
decorated with a finial modelled as
cherry blossoms scattered on a piece of
poem paper, Genroku period, c1700,
13½in (34.5cm) diam.
£1,700–2,000 *C*

An Imari tureen and cover, gilt
on underglaze blue, Genroku
period, 13½in (34.5cm) diam.
£1,700–2,000 *C*

ases & Jars

Three Arita blue and white jars and covers, damaged and covers repaired, late 17thC, 18½in (47cm) high.
£3,500–4,000 *CAm*

Arita vase, decorated blue, some damage, thC, 19in (48cm) high.
,000–1,200 *DN*

Arita jar, painted in derglaze blue with panels chrysanthemums and onies, the shoulder with oral medallions on a brocade ound, late 17thC, slight mage, 14in (35.5cm) high.
,000–3,500 *S*

multi-faceted Kakiemonpe vase, decorated in on-red enamel on derglaze blue, the oulder with a band of erry blossoms among rolling *karakusa* enamels d glaze rubbed, neck duced, chip to rim, late thC, 7½in (19.5cm) high.
,000–8,000 *C*

A Shoki Imari underlaze blue bottle vase, ith everted rim, decorated ith a hatched design elow double lines, late 7thC, 7in (18cm) high.
,000–1,200 *C*

An Arita vase, painted in greyish-blue underglaze, on a floral ground, the shoulder and neck with formal motifs, late 17thC, 15½in (39.5cm) high.
£1,800–2,200 *S*

An Arita blue and white vase, with 3 panels, restored, late 17thC, 19in (48cm) high.
£1,500–2,000 *C*

An Arita blue and white jar, painted in underglaze blue with panels of *ho-o* and peonies, reserved on a foliate ground, the shoulders with leaf-shaped panels of stylised flowers, late 17thC, 12in (30.5cm) high.
£1,200–1,400 *S*

A pair of Arita blue and white baluster vases and covers, with *shishi* lion finials, painted with *ho-o* among flowering trees and grasses issuing from pierced rockwork, both damaged, 12in (30.5cm) high.
£600–700 *CSK*

r. An Arita blue and white jar and cover, painted all over, body crack, rim chip, cover repaired and with chips, late 17thC, 25in (63.5cm) high.
£2,000–2,500 *CAm*

Arita

The majority of early Japanese porcelain was produced at factories founded near Arita at the beginning of the 17thC. By the middle of the 17thC white wares decorated with underglaze blue were being exported to Europe by the Dutch. Later in the 17thC polychrome enamelled Kakiemon and Imari wares were made, and by the 18thC much of the best Japanese porcelain was being made at Arita.

An Imari polychrome bottle vase, painted in typical enamel colours and gold, minor glaze chip to rim, late 17thC, 12in (30.5cm) high.
£1,500–2,000 *Bea*

A pair of Imari vases and covers, painted in underglaze blue, iron-red and gilt with 3 panels depicting hydrangeas, weeping cherries and peonies, one vase dented and with glaze defect in firing, foot chipped and hair cracks, the other and both covers restored, late 17th/early 18thC, 28in (71cm) high.
£3,500–4,000 *S*

An Arita blue and white baluster jar and cover, restored, late 17th/early 18thC, 27½in (70cm) high.
£1,500–2,000 *C(S)*

A pair of Imari baluster vases, painted and gilt, crack to rim of one, no covers, gilt rubbing 17th/18thC, 13in (33cm) high.
£1,800–2,000 *CSK*

A pair of Imari jars, painted on an inky-blue ground, one cover damaged, early 18thC, 10½in (26cm) high.
£800–1,000 *Bea*

An Imari vase, decorated in iron-red and black enamels and gilt on underglaze blue, the neck with *ho-o* birds, restored, Genroku period 24½in (62cm) high.
£3,500–4,000 *C*

An Arita vase, enamelled and gilt on underglaze blue with *ho-o* birds among peonies and rockwork, slight cracks, Genroku period, 12in (30.5cm) high.
£2,000–2,500 *C*

An Imari oviform vase, decorated in various coloured enamels and gilt on underglaze blue, with a wide panel of *ho-o* birds among pawlonia and peonies, the neck with iris sprays, restored, Genroku period, 16½in (42cm) high.
£2,000–2,500 *C*

l. A pair of Imari vases and covers, each decorated in coloured enamels and gilt on underglaze blue, the covers with large knob finials and similiarly decorated to the vases, both covers damaged, Genroku period, 18in (46cm) high.
£4,500–5,500 *C*

An Imari vase and cover, decorated in iron-red and black enamels and gilt on underglaze blue, the rim with flowerheads, pierced for electricity, *kara shishi* finial missing, Genroku period, 23½in (60cm) high.
£5,500–6,500 *C*

Imari baluster jar and domed cover, th *shishi* lion finial, painted and gilt, acked, c1700, 25½in (65cm) high.
00–900 *CSK*

An Arita blue and white bottle vase, with slightly everted rim, painted with flowering prunus branches, crack to base, c1700, 11½in (29cm) high.
£850–950 *CSK*

An Imari beaker vase, painted and gilt with peonies and oxen before a retreat, restored, c1700, 26in (66cm) high.
£550–650 *CSK*

Arita baluster vase, painted underglaze blue, coloured amels and gilt, minute chip foot, slight gilt rubbing, 700, 18in (46cm) high.
,200–2,700 *CSK*

An Imari bottle vase, with lobed body, painted and gilt with trailing peony and chrysanthemum sprays, the neck with bands of geometric design and scrolling foliage, gilt rubbed, c1700, 9in (23cm) high.
£1,300–1,700 *CSK*

An Arita clobbered jar, the shouldered sides painted with peonies and rocks beneath a band of shell and flowerhead motifs, the neck with foliate scrolls, overpainted and gilt in iron-red, green, pink and yellow, Edo period, 19in (48cm) high.
£1,500–1,700 *S(S)*

Imari fluted jar, painted d gilt in coloured enamels d underglaze blue with wers and branches, a band flowers around the base, 700, 16in (40.5cm) high.
,500–4,000 *CSK*

A pair of Imari vases and covers, painted with panels of flowering plants, the covers with *shishi* knops, early 18thC, 10in (25.5cm) high.
£1,200–1,400 *L*

A Bizen *ikebana* vase, reddish brown to one side, the other with a yellow and light brown glaze, with 2 lug handles, marked, mid-Edo period, 9½in (24cm) high.
£1,400–1,600 *C*

An Imari garniture, comprising 3 jars and covers and
2 trumpet-shaped vases, decorated in iron-red enamel and
gilt on underglaze blue, some restoration and one cover
cracked, Genroku period, jars and covers, 15in (38cm) high.
£3,000–3,500 *C*

A pair of Imari baluster vases and covers, ea
painted on a blue foliate ground, the shoulde
with lappet panels of plants the domed cover
each with a *bijin* figure finial, covers matche
damaged, early 18thC, 20in (51cm) high.
£2,000–2,500 *L*

A pair of Imari beaker vases,
with splayed rims, each
painted with coloured
enamels and panels of flowers
on a blue foliate ground, early
18thC, 12in (30.5cm) high.
£1,800–2,000 *Bea*

An Imari vase, painted
with a phoenix in flight
above flowering plants,
small hair crack, 18thC,
15½in (29.5cm) high.
£450–550 *L*

A pair of Kutani vases,
each decorated with a
continuous landscape
with figures and
buildings, Meiji period,
18in (46cm) high.
£2,500–3,000 *N*

An Imari beaker vase,
painted and gilt on a
ground of chrysanthemu
heads below a border of
floral lappet heads, ormo
mounted with fruiting
grape vines, the porcelai
18thC, 15in (38cm) high
£600–700 *CSK*

An Arita blue and white
baluster vase, neck chipped
and possibly reduced, 18thC,
10in (25.5cm) high.
£500–650 *CSK*

A pair of Imari vases, painted
against an iron-red ground,
damaged and repaired, Meiji period,
36in (92cm) high, on wood stands.
£500–650 *S(S)*

l. A Satsuma vase, decorated with 4 fan-
shaped panels, one of a *shishi*, 2 with vases
of flowers and another with a phoenix, on a
diaper ground, slight damage, Meiji period,
9¾in (25cm) high.
£1,000–1,100 *WW*

A porcelain vase, decorate
on an iron-red ground, Me
period, 11½in (29cm) high
£600–750 *P(S)*

A pair of Imari vases, decorated with birds, pine trees and peonies, both restored, Meiji period, 18in (46cm) high. **£700–850** *Bon*

An Arita polychrome oviform jar and cover, with *shishi* and ball finial, painted with scenes above black and iron-red ground panels of scrolling foliage, body cracks, 19thC, 37in (94cm) high. **£2,600–3,000** *CSK*

A large Imari vase, decorated in typical palette, some damage, Meiji period, 42½in (108) high. **£1,700–2,000** *Bon*

A Satsuma vase and stand, with long cylindrical neck, decorated in enamels and gilt, raised on a stand with 5 mask-head feet, stand chipped and tassel chipped, Meiji period, 34½in (87.5cm) high. **£1,000–1,200** *Bon*

A Satsuma earthenware trumpet vase, painted with panels of figures and mountain temples, reserved on a midnight-blue ground densely covered in wisteria and cherry blossom, signed and with impressed seal 'Kinkozan', each panel signed, one 'Senzan', the other 'Seizan', Meiji period, 6in (15cm) high. **£5,200–5,800** *S*

An Oribe-type vase, with *lingzhi*-shaped handles, green glaze extending from rim, patterned design on a grey ground below, mark on base, Meiji period, 16in (40.5cm) high. **£350–450** *SK*

An Arita blue and white vase, painted with floral medallions on a 'cracked ice' and prunus ground, applied with 2 confronting dragons in high relief, Meiji period, 17in (44cm) high. **£1,000–1,200** *Bon*

l. A pair of Imari vases and covers, decorated in bright green, orange, blue and burnished gilt, the domed covers similarly decorated, Meiji period, 24in (61cm) high. **£4,500–5,000** *N*

A Satsuma vase, painted with a landscape and figural panels, marked, Meiji period, 12in (30.5cm) high. **£2,800–3,200** *GOR*

A pair of Kutani vases, decorated with figures on a fern ground, iron-red marks, Meiji period, 14½in (37cm) high. **£1,800–2,200** *S(S)*

A porcelain vase, by Makuzu Kozan, painted with pale maroon irises outlined in white on a shaded leaf green ground, underglaze blue six-character mark, slight damage, Meiji period, 7in (18cm) high.
£750–850 *(S(S)*

A Satsuma earthenware vase, decorated in enamels and gilt, reserved on a midnight-blue ground, signed 'Yasuda zo' beneath a Satsuma *mon*, Meiji period, 10in (25.5cm) high.
£1,000–1,200 *S*

A vase and cover, decorated in Imari style, in underglaze blue, iron-red and gilt, the cover with *shishi* knop, star crack on base, marked 'Fukagawa sei' with *rebu* Meiji period, 21in (53cm) high.
£1,700–2,000 *S*

An earthenware vase, decorated in enamels and gilt with 2 heart-shaped panels over a midnight-blue ground, signed 'Kinkozan zo', Meiji period, 15½in (40cm) high.
£2,800–3,200 *S*

A pair of late Kutani vases, painted in pink, grey and blue enamels, within gilt and polychrome borders, signed 'Nihon Yokohama Imura sei zo', Meiji period, 18in (46cm) high.
£2,300–2,700 *S*

An earthenware vase, enamelled and gilt with figures on a *rinzu* and *kiku* ground, slightly rubbed, signed 'Kinkozan zo kore', Meiji period, 4in (10cm) hig
£1,300–1,700 *S*

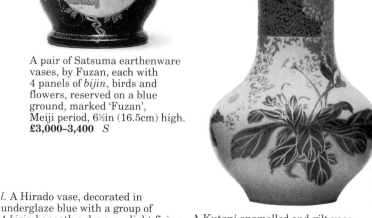

A pair of Satsuma earthenware vases, by Fuzan, each with 4 panels of *bijin*, birds and flowers, reserved on a blue ground, marked 'Fuzan', Meiji period, 6½in (16.5cm) high.
£3,000–3,400 *S*

l. A Hirado vase, decorated in underglaze blue with a group of 4 *kirin* beneath a dragon, slight firing fault, Meiji period, 15½in (39cm) high.
£5,000–5,500 *S*

A Kutani enamelled and gilt vase, marked, Meiji period, 14in (36cm) hig
£2,200–2,500 *S*

A pair of Kutani vases, each painted in brilliant enamels and gilding with figures in a landscape, *fuku* (happiness) mark, Meiji period, 11½in (29.5cm) high.
£1,800–2,200 *S*

Satsuma vase, decorated in enamels nd gilding with sages amid bamboo nd geese by a stream, mounted with lt-bronze handles and base, Meiji eriod, 21½in (54.5cm) high.
,200–1,500 *S*

An Imari vase and cover, decorated in underglaze blue, iron-red, enamels and gilding, with panels of *bijin* and attendants, Meiji period, 25in (64cm) high, with a wood stand.
£1,800–2,000 *S*

An Imari bottle vase, decorated in underglaze blue, iron-red and gilding, with shaped panels of *kiku* and peonies reserved on birds and trees, c1800, 10½in (26.5cm) high.
£1,200–1,500 *S*

An Imari garniture, decorated in underglaze blue, iron-red, black enamel and gilding, beaker vases restored, c1800, jar and cover 19in (48cm) high.
£2,800–3,200 *S*

Satsuma vase, of butterfly utline, one side filled with a panel f *bijin*, the other with *samurai* n a shore, signed, Meiji period, in (10cm) high.
450–550 *S(S)*

pair of Imari vases, each in the orm of Benkei clinging to a giant eaping carp, decorated in underglaze lue, iron-red, enamels and gilding, amaged, c1800, 9in (23cm) high.
2,600–3,000 *S*

Benkei, a hero of the 12thC, as a boy as nicknamed Oniwaka (young lemon), and is often depicted xhibiting great feats of strength.

An Imari vase, decorated in underglaze blue, iron-red and gilding with *ho-o* among flowering trees, c1800, 13in (33cm) high.
£1,200–1,500 *S*

An Imari vase, traditionally decorated with blue, rust and gilt floral designs, early 19thC, 18in (46cm) high.
£450–550 *GAK*

A pair of Imari vases, decorated in blue, red, green and gilt, 19thC, 18in (45.5cm) high.
£1,300–1,500 *MN*

A pair of lacquered ceramic vases, c1820, 24in (61cm) high.
£1,000–1,200 *SSW*

An Imari vase, painted in underglaze blue, iron-red green enamel and gilt, below a dense *kiku* ground surrounded by flowerhea[...] 19thC, 30in (76cm) high.
£2,500–3,000 *Bon*

An Imari baluster jar, painted and gilt with panels of confronting dragons chasing flaming pearls above foaming waves, and *ho-o* on a ground of peonies, brocade balls and quatrefoil panels of pawlonia, slight damage, 19thC, 24in (61cm) high.
£1,300–1,500 *CSK*

A pair of Imari vases and covers, 19thC, 20in (51cm) high.
£3,000–3,500 *S*

A pair of Arita blue and white baluster vases, both cracked, 19thC, 19in (48cm) high.
£600–700 *C(S)*

Satsuma

Satsuma was an important centre of ceramic production from the 16thC, and the town has now become synonymous with the decorative export wares made from the mid-19thC. The cream-coloured earthenware vases, bowls, ewers, jars and figures have finely crackled glazes, and brightly-coloured enamel and gilt decoration.

A Satsuma bud vase, with 5 cylindrical spouts, encircled with pointed lappet collars, decorated in iron-red, blue, turquoise and white enamels and gilt with chrysanthemums, signed 'Satsuma Yaki', 19thC, 6½in (16.5cm) high.
£3,200–3,500 *S(NY)*

A Hirado reticulated and double-skinned vase, Mikawachi kiln, c1860, 6in (15cm) high.
£1,400–1,600 *Wai*

An earthenware vase, decorated with scenes of geisha and samurai in a garden, between brocade borders, the neck with landscape border, signed and marked 'Kinkozan', 19thC, 12½in (31cm) high.
£5,000–6,500 S(Am)

An Imari vase, decorated in iron-red enamel and gilt on underglaze blue, Fukagawa device, 19thC, 29½in (75cm) high.
£3,000–3,500 C

A Satsuma vase, decorated in coloured enamels and gilt with egrets, irises and stylised clouds, signed 'Satsuma Hosai', with large Satsuma *mon*, late 19thC, 21in (53.5cm) high.
£5,000–5,500 C

An Arita polychrome vase, decorated in Ming style, horizontal Wanli six-character mark at the rim, 19thC, 24in (61cm) high.
£4,000–4,500 C

A pair of Imari vases, decorated in iron-red, green and black enamels and gilt on underglaze blue, late 19thC, 18½in (47cm) high.
£1,400–1,600 C

A pair of porcelain polychrome vases, late 19thC, 11in (28cm) high.
£350–400 Bea

A pair of Kutani style vases, the white ground decorated with figures in burnt orange and charcoal grey, richly gilded, 19thC, 14in (35.5cm) high.
£1,200–1,500 GH

A pair of late Kutani vases, decorated in iron-red and gilt with black enamel detail, some damage, signed 'Nihon Kutani sei Setsu do', late 19thC, 14½in (37cm) high.
£2,500–3,000 C

A pair of Satsuma vases, decorated in enamels and gilt, damaged, signed 'Satsuma yaki Hotoda', late 19thC, 9½in (24cm) high.
£1,400–1,600 C

A Satsuma faceted vase, painted with panels containing vases of flowers, with lappet foot and shoulder, 19thC, 9½in (24cm) high.
£3,600–4,000 Bea

A pair of Imari vases, each painted with cockerels, bats, flowers and blossom, within moulded hexagonal panels, late 19thC, 18in (46cm) high.
£3,000–3,500 C(S)

r. A pair of Imari moulded trumpet-necked vases, decorated in iron-red and gilt on underglaze blue with panels of flowers and foliage, late 19thC, 22½in (58cm) high.
£5,000–5,500 CAm

A Louis XVI-style Imari potpourri vase, the domed lid above a pierced gilt-bronze rim, the body flanked by ram's head handles, late 19thC, 19in (48.5cm) high.
£4,000–4,500 *S(NY)*

A pair of Satsuma vases, with ring handles, decorated in coloured enamels and gilt, slight damage, late 19thC, 37in (94cm) high.
£7,000–8,000 *C*

A Satsuma baluster vase, decorated in various coloured enamels and gilt, with peacocks against a yellow sky, gilt rim, signed on base 'Kinkozan sei', late 19thC, 7in (17cm) high.
£1,000–1,200 *C*

A Satsuma vase, decorated in enamels and gilt, the body with a design of swimming carp, gilt rim, signed 'Kinkozan zo' on base and sealed 'Kisui' on foot, late 19thC, 11½in (30cm) high.
£3,000–3,400 *C*

A Kinkozan vase, decorated in coloured enamels on a glazed blue ground, gilding slightly rubbed, signed 'Ryuzan', late 19thC, 18½in (46.5cm) high.
£2,200–2,500 *C*

l. A moulded Satsuma vase, decorated in coloured enamels and gilt, neck restored, signed 'Dai Nihon Satsuma yaki Meigyokudo', late 19thC, 10in (25.5cm) high.
£1,700–2,200 *C*

An Imari vase, decorated in iron-red enamel and gilt on underglaze blue, late 19thC, 22½in (57cm) high.
£700–800 *C*

A pair of Imari jars and covers, each painted with a figure standing outside a house by a river, reserved on a foliate-decorated orange and blue ground, one cover chipped, 19thC, 13in (33cm) high.
£800–1,000 *Bea*

A pair of Satsuma vases, seal mark, late 19thC, 19in (48cm) high, each with a wood stand.
£1,800–2,000 *DN*

r. A large Satsuma vase, decorated in various coloured underglaze enamels and gilt, base restored, unsigned, late 19thC, 19½in (49cm) high.
£3,000–3,500 *C*

pair of Satsuma iform vases, corated in various loured enamels and lt, with gilt rims, gned 'Dai Nihon izon sei', late 19thC, in (30cm) high.
,600–2,000 *C*

A pair of Satsuma heart-shaped vases, decorated within shaped cartouches with floral borders, square necks and pedestal bases, late 19thC, 13½in (34.5cm) high.
£1,700–2,000 *WW*

A Satsuma vase with everted rim, the blue ground finely gilded, chip to rim, late 19thC, 8in (21cm) high.
£300–350 *MN*

A pair of Kutani vases, decorated with female figures and flowers, c1880, 18in (45.5cm) high.
£450–500 *BRU*

n Arita jar, decorated in nderglaze blue with a ntinuous landscape of temples nd trees, diapering and eywork, slight chipping to neck, te 19thC, 10½in (26cm) high.
,500–1,800 *HSS*

A pair of Arita blue and white vases, decorated with landscapes, c1880, 16in (40.5cm) high.
£260–300 *BRU*

A Satsuma double-gourd vase, decorated with figures and gilt, c1890, 4in (10cm) high.
£1,000–1,200 *MER*

A pair of Imari oviform jars and domed covers, with *shishi* finials, painted in gold ground panels, repaired, 19thC, 21in (53cm) high.
£1,800–2,000 *CSK*

Kinkozan

The Kinkozan workshop was based in Awata, Kyoto. It was led by Kinkozan Sobei VII, and specialised in Satsuma wares for export.

A Kinkozan pottery vase of lobular form, painted with n encircling band of women n conversation under sprays f wisteria, the foot and neck ainted with flowers, late 19thC, in (12.5cm) high.
1,200–1,400 *Bea*

A pair of Imari jars, each with inner and outer covers, each facet painted with a jardinière of chrysanthemums or peonies within a gold-decorated deep blue border, 19thC, 10in (25.5cm) high.
£1,000–1,200 *Bea*

A pair of Satsuma vases, painted in colours and richly gilt, late 19thC, 7½in (18.5cm) high.
£850–950 *CSK*

A Satsuma vase, with flared rim, gilt dragon handles and polychrome figure decoration on patterned gilt ground, late 19thC, 10in (25.5cm) high.
£750–850 *AH*

A pair of Satsuma vases, painted in colours and richly gilt, late 19thC, 12in (30.5cm) high.
£1,700–2,000 *CSK*

A Fukagawa vase, decorated in various coloured enamels and gilt on underglaze blue and brown, signed in underglaze blue 'Dai Nihon Arita-cho Fukagawa sei', late 19thC, 15in (38cm) high.
£3,000–3,500 *C*

A pair of Satsuma vases, painted in colours and rich raised gilt with panels of warriors and Immortals, neck restored, late 19thC 35½in (90cm) high.
£5,000–6,000 *CSK*

A pair of Satsuma vases, painted in colours and gilt on crackled cream grounds, c1900, 17in (43cm) high.
£2,500–3,000 *CSK*

A pair of Kutani beaker vases, painted and heavily gilt with the Eight Immortals, one with star crack base, signed, 18in (45.5cm) high.
£1,700–2,000 *CSK*

A Satsuma vase, painted with figures reserved within a narrow decorative band, the neck and foot painted with flowers and geometric designs, c1900, 4½in (11.5cm) high.
£550–650 *Bea*

A pair of Kutani vases, painted with figures and birds, reserved on a gold-decorated orange ground, c1900, 14in (35.5cm) high.
£600–700 *Bea*

l. A pair of Satsuma vases, painted with figures on a brocade ground, in typical enamel colours and gold, late 19thC, 11in (28cm) high.
£1,400–1,600 *Bea*

pair of Satsuma moulded ses, heavily gilt, signed, e 19thC, 9in (23cm) high.
00–600 *CSK*

A Satsuma pottery vase, enamelled and gilt with panels of figures, geometric designs and flowers, late 19thC, 28in (71cm) high.
£600–700 *CSK*

A Satsuma vase, painted on a dark blue gilt flowerhead ground and between bands of lappets, signed 'Kinkozan', c1900, 10½in (26cm) high.
£1,000–1,200 *CSK*

A pair of Kaga vases, painted in iron-red, black and gilt with birds and flowers by a river, c1900, 15in (38cm) high.
£700–800 *CSK*

Satsuma vase, painted in lours and gilt on a ground geometric designs, late thC, 4in (10cm) high.
70–200 *CSK*

A pair of Satsuma vases, painted in colours and gilt on one side with panels of ladies and children below bamboo in gardens, cracked, signed 'Shozan', late 19thC, 7½in (19cm) high.
£1,500–1,700 *CSK*

A Kutani jar and domed cover with a rat and nut finial, damaged, late 19thC, damaged, 16½in (42cm) high.
£1,000–1,200 *CSK*

pair of Satsuma ases, painted in lours and gilt with anels of *bijin* and *kan* on dark blue rounds, late 19thC, ½in (24cm) high.
1,200–1,500 *CSK*

A Satsuma jar and cover with a mythical dragon finial, c1880, 23in (58.5cm) high.
£700–800 *ALB*

A Satsuma moulded jar and cover, decorated in coloured enamels and gilt on a brocade ground, signed 'Nihon Bijitsuto Satsuma yaki Shuko', late 19thC, 8in (20.5cm) high, and a wood stand.
£4,000–4,500 *C*

An Imari jar, enamelled and gilt on underglaze blue, gold lacquer repaired, late 19thC, wooden cover, 25in (63.5cm) high.
£900–1,000 *C*

An earthenware jar and cover, decorated in coloured enamels and gilt, reserved on a cobalt blue ground with scattered flying geese, gilt rubbed, signed 'Kyoto Kinkozan zo Sozan' late 19thC, 5in (12.5cm) high.
£2,100–2,300 *S(NY)*

An earthenware jar and cover, decorated on a brown glaze in gilt and oxidised silver with still life, landscape and birds, signed 'Kinkozan zo', Meiji period, late 19thC, 4in (10cm) high.
£1,000–1,300 *S*

A Satsuma vase, painted with groups of geishas, pagodas, bridges and a mountain, four-character mark, late 19thC, 14⅜in (36.5cm) high.
£700–800 *CDC*

A pair of Imari lobec vases and domed cove painted with shaped panels of *ho-o*, bats a objects before fenced landscapes, late 19th 18½in (46cm) high.
£1,200–1,400 *CSK*

A pair of Satsuma vases, signed, late 19thC, 10in (25.5cm) high.
£700–800 *DN*

A Satsuma conical two-handled tripod miniature vase, painted in colours and gilt with figures in a continuous mountainous wooded landscape, late 19thC, 3½in (9cm) high.
£300–350 *CSK*

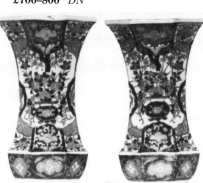

A pair of Imari beaker vases, painted with jardinières of flowers, divided by *ho-o* roundels, with flowering shrubs above and below, late 19thC, 8½in (22cm) high.
£500–600 *CSK*

A pair of Kutani pear-shape jars and covers, painted in coloured enamels and iron-red, repaired, c1900, 11½in (29.5cm) high.
£450–550 *CSK*

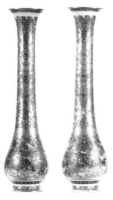

A pair of Satsuma vases, painted in colours and heavily gilt, one cracked and chipped, late 19thC, 18in (46cm) high.
£1,500–1,700 *CSK*

l. A pair of Japanese vases, with foliate rims, decorated in coloured enamels and gilt, on a ground of *ho-o* on rockwork and flowers, late 19thC, 49in (124.5cm) high, wooden stand.
£2,500–3,000 *CSK*

A pair of Imari vases, painted, gilt and enamell in typical palette with bir of paradise, prunus and dragons, late 19thC, 18in (45.5cm) high.
£1,700–2,000 *P(Re)*

l. An Imari vase and cove with dog of Fo finial, late 19thC, 22in (56cm) high.
£700–800 *MGM*

A Kutani double-gourd vase, painted with bands of scrolling peony and chrysanthemum flowers between floral and geometric lappets, signed, late 19thC, 13½in (34cm) high.
£700–850 *CSK*

A pair of Kutani vases and covers, of double-gourd form, each painted with figures and flowers, on an iron-red ground, with gilt decoration, damaged, late 19thC, 18in (46cm) high.
£1,300–1,600 *L*

A pair of Satsuma vases, painted and gilt with Immortals and boys at leisure, signed, late 19thC, 14in (35.5cm) high.
£550–600 *CSK*

A pair of Kutani vases, with pierced handles and reticulated necks, painted and heavily gilt with panels of legendary scenes, signed, late 19thC, 10in (25.5cm) high.
£2,000–2,500 *CSK*

A Kutani vase, painted with *shishi* among flowers and foliage between bands of lappets, damaged, late 19thC, 17½in (44.5cm) high.
£300–350 *CSK*

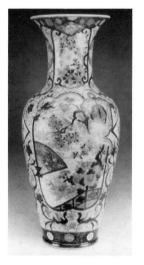

An Imari baluster vase, painted and gilt with birds among flowers, on a ground of confronting *ho-o* and scattered ferns and foliate, restored, late 19thC, 30in (76cm) high.
£800–900 *CSK*

A pair of Imari bottle-shaped vases, late 19thC, 11½in (29cm) high.
£600–700 *CSK*

A pair of Satsuma vases, with mask loop handles, painted and heavily gilt with panels of dignitaries and attendants before river landscapes, late 19thC, 30in (76cm) high.
£2,000–2,500 *CSK*

A pair of Imari double-gourd vases, with narrow necks, painted and gilt with boys at play among flowerheads and foliage, some gilt rubbing, late 19thC, 12in (30.5cm) high.
£800–1,000 *CSK*

A pair of Imari bottle vases, one with body crack, late 19thC, 12in (30.5cm) high.
£200–250 *CSK*

A pair of Imari vases, each painted and gilt with stylised flowerheads and hexagonal panels on a ground of foliage above a band of leaves to the foot, late 19thC, 24in (61cm) high.
£800–1,000 *CSK*

A porcelain vase, decorated beneath the glaze with red scrolling *karakusa* on a celadon green ground, signed 'Kozan sei', late 19thC, 10in (25.5cm) high.
£2,500–2,700 *S*

A pair of Satsuma earthenware vases, decorated in coloured enamels and gilt, one neck restored, late 19thC, 7½in (19cm) high.
£1,800–2,000 *HSS*

A Sota ware blue and white vase, cover and liner, decorated with birds and flowers, late 19thC, 11½in (29cm) high.
£350–450 *P(M)*

A pair of Imari vases, of baluster form, with frilled rims, late 19thC, 18in (45.5cm) high.
£800–900 *S(S)*

An Imari trumpet-shaped vase, decorated with panels of flowers on a floral ground in rust, blue and gilt, late 19thC, 16½in (42cm) high.
£1,000–1,200 *RID*

A Satsuma vase, the slim ovoid body painted with figures in conversation in a garden and on a verandah, reserved on a brocade ground, late 19thC, 15½in (40cm) high.
£400–500 *Bea*

A pair of Satsuma earthenware vases, decorated in typical palette, late 19thC, 17½in (44cm) high.
£5,800–6,500 *HSS*

A pair of Satsuma vases, damaged, signed in gold within the pattern, late 19thC, 6in (15cm) high.
£500–600 *MJB*

A Satsuma quatrefoil vase, painted and gilt with panels of figures before buildings in mountainous landscapes, lat 19thC, 19½in (49.5cm) high.
£1,700–2,000 *CSK*

pair of Satsuma vases, painted and
lt with continuous scenes, signed
enji', late 19thC, 7in (17.5cm) high.
,000–1,200 *CSK*

A Satsuma pottery vase, with
foliate neck, gilt and decorated
with peonies, Meiji period,
19in (48.5cm) high.
£8,000–9,000 *LHA*

An Imari bottle vase, painted
on a ground of flowering shrubs
and *ho-o*, the neck with 2 dragon
roundels on a ground of dense
flowers, Fukagawa mark, c1900,
16in (40cm) high.
£1,200–1,500 *CSK*

pair of Satsuma
rthenware vases,
Gyokushu, each
corated in enamels
d gilt, decorated with
ndscapes and still life,
gned, one rim chip
paired, late 19thC,
n (10cm) high.
,500–2,000 *S*

A Satsuma miniature vase,
decorated with figures,
black seal mark, c1900,
3¾in (9.5cm) high.
£900–1,100 *MER*

A pair of Satsuma vases, decorated with panels
of figures, c1900, 9½in (24cm) high.
£140–160 *PCh*

Fukagawa

Chuji Fukagawa founded the
Fukagawa Manufacturing Co in
Arita in 1894, and was renowned
for painting finely detailed bird
and floral subjects. He often
marked his wares with a leaf
spray and an image of Mount Fuji.

pair of Satsuma
rthenware vases,
e pale yellow shaded
round decorated with
rtridges, foliage, flowers
d butterflies in coloured
amels, painted and
pressed marks, c1900,
in (56cm) high.
80–320 *P(HSS)*

A pair of earthenware vases, one
damaged, c1900, 31in (79cm) high.
£1,200–1,500 *DN*

A pair of Satsuma vases,
painted in colours and gilt,
on dense floral and geometric
grounds, c1900, 9½in (24cm) high.
£700–800 *CSK*

An Imari bottle vase, painted and gilt with shaped panels of trees and flowers, bordered by *ho-o* birds on a geometric and floral ground, c1900, 16½in (42cm) high.
£500–600 *CSK*

A Fukagawa vase, painted and gilt with a scroll style dragon below a neck of scrolling flowers, Mount Fuji mark, c1900, 12in (30.5cm) high.
£250–300 *CSK*

A Satsuma vase, painted and gilt with a panel of ladies and children at leisure before trees and beside a lake, the reverse with pigeons in a landscape, a between formal borders, signe c1900, 10½in (26.5cm) high.
£2,400–2,700 *CSK*

A pair of Satsuma vases, with rich embossed gilding and text, small gilt *kylin* handles, signed on base, c1900, 12in (30.5cm) high.
£1,400–1,600 *CDC*

A porcelain vase, by Makuzu Kozan, painted in underglaze blue, highlighted in transparent enamels and gilt, c1930, 11¼in (28.5cm) high.
£2,300–2,800 *S*

A Satsuma vase, painted with opposing panels depicting a furious battle and a tranquil garden scene on a gilt and black brocade ground, impressed and painted signatures, c1900, 5½in (14cm) high.
£2,500–3,000 *P(EA)*

A pair of Satsuma vases, enamelled and gilt with Manchurian cranes in flight, 20thC, 31½in (80cm) high.
£3,000–3,500 *Bon*

A Satsuma slender oviform vase, painted in colours and gilt on one side, the shoulder within iron-red ground band of emblems, c1900, 6½in (16.5cm) high.
£3,500–4,000 *CSK*

A pair of Satsuma earthenware vases, the bodies decorated with panels of figures, with Mount Fu in the background, marked in a square 'Paris and Kobe 1915', 25in (63cm) high.
£2,500–3,000 *CAm*

KOREAN CERAMICS

Korean ceramics are normally studied in three groups named after the dynasties in which they were made: Silla (57 BC–AD 936), Koryo (AD 936–1392), and Yi (1392–1910) sometimes known as Choson. The best Korean ceramics were produced in the Koryo Dynasty, particularly during the period 1050–1170. These were mostly fine celadons with a soft wax-like glaze. Towards the end of the Koryo period the unique and beautiful inlaid design technique began to be used. This technique involved incising a design and filling the lines with black or white slip (liquid clay) prior to glazing. Some of the best wares of the later Yi Dynasty are the underglaze blue and white wares made between the mid-17th century and mid-19th century. Very little Korean ware found its way to the East as there was no export trade with the East Indies companies. It is now illegal to export antique ceramics from Korea so the market consists of those pieces discovered in Japan or brought out of Korea in the 1950s. The downfall in the Far Eastern economy has recently led to the postponement of specialist Korean sales. However, as with all works of art, there is still a demand for the rarest and highest quality pieces.

Bowls

l. A blue and white bowl, decorated with flowerheads within a double line medallion in the centre, Yi Dynasty, 19thC, 10in (25.5cm) diam.
£40,000–45,000 *S*

A fragment with similar cobalt blue design, excavated from the Punwonli kiln site, is in the National Museum of Korea, Seoul.

A parrot bowl, covered in a crackled translucent celadon glaze, warped, slight damage, early 12thC, 7in (18cm) diam.
£1,800–2,000 *S*

r. A celadon bowl, the centre moulded with a floral spray, the foot with 3 spur marks, Koryo Dynasty, 12thC, 7¼in (18.5cm) diam.
£2,400–2,600 *S(NY)*

Cups & Cup Stands

A celadon foliate cup stand, with floral decoration, Koryo Dynasty, 12thC, 6in (15cm) diam.
£4,500–5,000 *S(NY)*

A celadon foliate cupstand, the everted tray of eight-petalled outline, decorated with floral spray clusters, Koryo Dynasty, 12thC, 5½in (14cm) diam.
£6,500–7,000 *S(NY)*

A white glazed cup with saucer, moulded with cranes, Choson Dynasty, 19thC, saucer 5¾in (14.5cm) wide.
£9,500–10,500 *S(NY)*

Dishes

A blue and white dish, painted with a catfish, carp, waves and rockwork, on a high foot, Choson Dynasty, 19thC, 6in (15cm) diam.
£57,000–63,000 *S(NY)*

A blue and white dish, the centre decorated with a stylised *su* character roundel, encircled by a band of chrysanthemums on leafy stalks, the exterior decorated with bamboo stalks, on a glazed foot, Choson Dynasty, 19thC, 12½in (32cm) diam.
£12,000–13,000 *S(NY)*

A blue and white dish, painted with a landscape of rockwork and mountains beneath a half-visible sun, the underside with ribboned florettes between line borders, Choson Dynasty, 19thC, 6in (15cm) diam.
£8,500–9,000 *S(NY)*

Jars, Bottles & Vases

A celadon *maeby'ong* vase, painted in iron-brown with leaves, Koryo Dynasty, 12thC, 10¾in (27.5cm) high.
£10,500–11,500 *S(NY)*

A baluster vase, covered overall with a deep brown glaze, Yi Dynasty, 12in (30.5cm) high.
£3,500–4,000 *SK*

A celadon mallet-shaped bottle the glazed underside with 5 sp marks, Koryo Dynasty, 11thC, 9½in (24cm) high.
£65,000–75,000 *S(NY)*

A celadon *maeby'ong* vase, painted in iron-brown with a stylised leafy spray, Koryo Dynasty, 12thC, 10¾in (27.5cm) high.
£4,000–4,500 *S(NY)*

A blue and white bottle, painted with butterflies and grass, restored, Choson Dynasty, 19thC, 14½in (37cm) high.
£8,000–9,000 *S(NY)*

A *punch'ong* flask, carved in sgraffito with a leafy arabesque, covered with a celadon glaze, on a glazed foot, Choson Dynasty 15th/16thC, 8¾in (22cm) high.
£40,000–45,000 *S(NY)*

An underglaze blue and white jar, cracked and chipped, Yi Dynasty, 19thC, 5in (12.5cm) high.
£1,200–1,500 *S*

A bamboo brush pot, decorated with engraved vertical lines, Choson Dynasty, 19thC, 6in (15cm) high.
£3,000–3,500 *S(NY)*

A blue and white faceted jar, decorated in underglaze blue, small chip, Yi Dynasty, 19thC, 5in (12.5cm) high.
£1,700–2,000 *S*

l. A pale blue glazed *koro* and pierced domed cover, with knop finial and upright handles, cover damaged, Koryo Dynasty, 6in (15cm) high.
£700–800 *CSK*

Miller's is a price GUIDE not a price LIST

Chinese *sancai* glazed pottery head
a horse, ear restored, Tang Dynasty,
½in (24cm) long.
4,000–5,000 *CNY*

A Chinese painted pottery
model of a horse, Six
Dynasties/early Tang
Dynasty, 18in (46cm) high.
£6,000–7,000 *CNY*

A pair of Chinese spaniels,
each modelled in mirror
image, one repaired, Qianlong
period, 9in (23cm) high.
£15,000–16,000 *CNY*

Chinese group of painted pottery musicians
nd dancers, restored, Tang Dynasty. £13,000–15,000 *CNY*

Chinese Dynasties and Marks

For a full
description of
Chinese Dynasties
and marks, please
refer to pages 10
and 11 at the front
of this book.

A Chinese painted pottery model
of a horse, damaged and repaired,
Tang Dynasty, 18in (46cm) high.
£12,000–14,000 *CNY*

Chinese painted red pottery
model of a horse, Tang Dynasty.
4,000–5,000 *CNY*

A Chinese *famille rose*
model of a pheasant
chipped, late
18th/early 19thC,
14in (36cm) high.
£5,000–6,000 *CNY*

A painted grey pottery model of a tricorn, late
Eastern Han/Six Dynasties, 17in (44cm) long.
£7,500–8,500 *CNY*

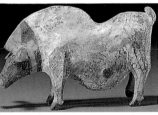

l. A Chinese painted
pottery figure of a boar,
restored, Northern Wei
Dynasty, 6in (15cm) long.
£10,000–12,000 *CNY*

pair of Japanese Imari models of cockerels,
ight damage, late 17thC, 6½in (16.5cm) long.
8,000–10,000 *C*

A pair of Chinese
famille rose models of
pheasants, repaired,
Qianlong period,
13in (33cm) high.
£25,000–30,000 *CNY*

A Chinese pottery
figure of a flautist
astride on a horse,
Sui Dynasty,
11½in (29cm) high.
£6,000–7,000 *CNY*

A Chinese tureen and cover, modelled as a crouching
hawk, the feathers detailed in sepia with gilding,
restored, Qianlong period, 8½in (21.5cm) wide.
£6,000–7,000 *S*

A pair of Chinese models of hawk
each perched on a jagged pierced
rock with one claw raised and
clenched, the feathers heightened
with gilding, restored, Qianlong
period, 11in (30cm) high.
£48,000–52,000 *S*

A pair of Chinese ormolu-mounted glazed
parrots, each perched on pierced rockwork
bases, Kangxi period, 8½in (21.5cm) high.
£10,000–12,000 *S*

A Chinese model of a horse,
tail restuck, Tang Dynasty,
14in (35.5cm) high.
£8,000–9,000 *S*

A Chinese *sancai* glazed pottery
horse, with an unglazed saddle,
on a wooden stand, restoration t
legs, neck, saddle and ears, Tan;
Dynasty, 19½in (49.5cm) high.
£8,000–9,000 *S*

A *sancai* model of a horse, restored,
Tang Dynasty, 12½in (32cm) high.
£4,500–5,500 *C*

A Chinese glazed model of a
horse, c1600, 11½in (29cm) high.
£600–675 *AnE*

A Chinese glazed pottery model of a horse,
the rump with aperture for the tail,
restored, Tang Dynasty, 25½in (65cm) high.
£65,000–70,000 *C*

A pair of Japanese Kakiemon models of cockerels,
standing on rockwork bases, slight restoration,
late 17thC, largest 9½in (24cm) high.
£40,000–45,000 *C*

pair of Chinese pottery
igures of guardians,
anding on rock plinths,
restored, Tang Dynasty,
3½in (85cm) high.
2,500–3,000 *S*

A pair of Chinese warriors,
Northern Song Dynasty,
22½in (57cm) high.
£3,500–4,000 *MA*

A pair of Chinese green
and amber-glazed court
attendants, Ming Dynasty,
18in (45.5cm) high.
£750–900 *GHa*

pair of Chinese pottery
nmortals, Song Dynasty,
18½in (47cm) high.
2,500–3,000 *MA*

A Chinese *famille rose*
cistern, Qianlong period,
restored, 13in (33cm) high.
£25,000–35,000 *S*

A Chinese *famille rose*
cistern, Qianlong
period, hat re-gilded,
13in (33cm) high.
£25,000–30,000 *S*

A large Chinese *famille
rose* figure of a boy,
late Yongzheng period,
mounted on a painted
wooden stand.
£64,000–68,000 *S*

A Chinese Fahua
figure of a *lohan*, reign
and date mark and of
the period, c1577,
18in (45.5cm) high.
£7,000–8,000 *C*

Chinese matched pair of *sancai* pottery
igures of *lokapala*, each standing on a
ecumbent bull, the heads unglazed, restored,
Tang Dynasty, 36in (91.5cm) high.
18,500–22,000 *C*

A Chinese *famille rose* figure
of a courtier, holding a sceptre,
body cracked, Qianlong period,
24in (61cm) high.
£25,000–28,000 *S*

A Chinese painted pottery
figure of a *lokapala*,
Tang Dynasty, restored,
30in (76cm) high.
£4,000–6,000 *S*

A Japanese Kakiemon model
of a seated tiger, restorations,
late 17thC, 7½in (18.5cm) high.
£18,000–20,000 *C*

A pair of Chinese
sancai Buddhistic
lions, some chips,
42½in (107cm) high.
£4,000–5,000 *C*

A pair of Japanese Imari *bijins*,
old damage and restoration,
Genroku period, 12½in (31.5cm) high.
£4,000–5,000 *C*

A pair of Japanese Arita puppies,
restored, late 17thC, 9½in (24cm) long.
£25,000–30,000 *C*

A painted figure of a woman, Han Dynasty.
£5,000–6,000 *CNY*

A Japanese Arita model of a seated dog, some
restoration, late 17thC, 16in (40cm) high.
£35,000–40,000 *C*

A Japanese Arita model of a seated puppy,
late 17thC, 7in (17.5cm) high.
£14,000–15,000 *C*

Japanese Figures

Japanese polychrome
ceramic figures were
very popular in
Europe at the end
of the 17thC. Purely
ornamental, the most
popular were *bijin*,
(beautiful women),
small boys, dogs, cats,
eagles, horses, deer
and cockerels.

A pair of Chinese export ormolu-
mounted figures, porcelain Qing
Dynasty, 16in (40.5cm) high.
£4,000–5,000 *C*

r. A Dehua *blanc-de-Chine*
figure, mid-Qing Dynasty,
18½in (46cm) high.
£10,000–12,000 *C*

l. A painted and *sancai*-glazed
pottery equestrian figure, restored,
Tang Dynasty, 15in (38cm) long.
£100,000–120,000 *CNY*

pair of Chinese models
warthogs, green
onochrome, restored,
820, 6½in (16.5cm) high.
00–600 *Wai*

r. A Japanese Imari model
of a cockerel, painted in
underglaze blue, iron-red,
black, green enamel and gilt,
restored, Genroku period,
10in (25.5cm) high.
£4,000–5,000 *Bon*

A Chinese export model of a
recumbent hound with iron-red
decoration, 9⅓in (24cm) long.
£3,000–4,000 *Wai*

A Chinese amber-glazed red pottery model of a
dog, restored, Han Dynasty, 12½in (32cm) long.
£5,500–7,000 *CNY*

A Chinese red-painted pottery
model of a dog, Han Dynasty,
10½in (26.5cm) high.
£4,000–5,000 *CNY*

l. A pair of Chinese pottery
mythical beasts, Six
Dynasties, 11in (28cm) wide
£10,000–12,000 *C*

A Chinese pottery model of a dog,
the green glaze with iridescent
areas, restored, Han Dynasty,
13in (33cm) long.
£6,500–8,000 *C*

l. A Chinese green-glazed cockerel,
c1820, 8½in (21.5cm) high.
£650–800 *Wai*

pair of *famille verte* enamelled models of Buddhistic
ons, restored, Kangxi period, 17in (43cm) high.
12,000–15,000 *CNY*

r. An Arita model of a seated horse, after a Dutch
Delft original, damaged, c1700, 7in (18cm) long.
£8,000–10,000 *C*

A pair of Chinese Fahua Buddhistic lion dogs, small chips and minor restoration, 16thC, 19in (48cm) high.
£7,000–8,000 *C*

A Chinese *sancai* glazed flask, Tang Dynasty, 6in (15cm) high.
£55,000–60,000 *S*

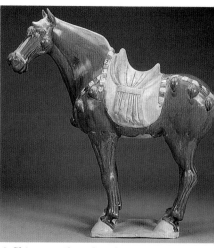

A Chinese amber-glazed pottery figure of a caparisoned horse, restored, Tang Dynasty, 19½in (50cm) high.
£14,000–15,000 *S*

A pair of Chinese *famille rose* boar's head tureens and covers, Qianlong period, 8½in (21.5cm) long.
£18,000–20,000 *C*

A Japanese Ko-Imari figure of Hotei, restored, c1700, 9½in (24cm) high.
£7,000–8,000 *S*

Two Japanese Kakiemon figures of boys, seated on *Go* boards, with later European ormolu caps, late 17thC, 10in (25.5cm) high.
£90,000–95,000 *S*

A Chinese *famille rose* group of a lady and a seated child, restored, Qianlong period, 9in (23cm) high.
£3,500–4,000 *C*

A pair of Chinese models of spaniels, one slightly damaged, one restored, Qianlong period, 9½in (23.5cm) long.
£7,000–8,000 *C*

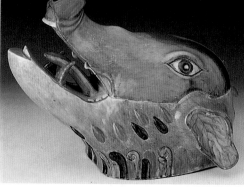

A Chinese *famille rose* boar's head tureen and cover, restored, Qianlong period, 16in (40.5cm) long.
£17,000–18,500 *C*

A pair of Chinese *sancai* glazed pottery figures of Earth spirits, restored, Tang Dynasty, 26in (66cm) high.
£4,000–5,000 *S*

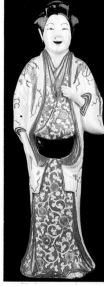

A Japanese Kakiemon figure of a *bijin*, damaged and restored, late 17thC, 14½in (36.5cm) high.
£10,000–12,000 *C*

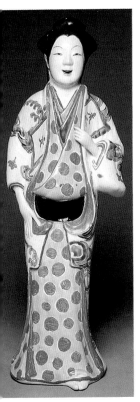

A pair of Chinese *famille rose* pheasants, perched on rockwork, cracked and restored, Qianlong period, 13in (33cm) high.
£28,000–30,000 *C*

A Japanese Kakiemon figure of a lady, head replaced, restored, late 17thC.
£10,000–12,000 *S*

Japanese Kakiemon figure f a *bijin*, restored, late 7thC, 15in (38cm) high.
10,000–12,000 *S*

A Chinese glazed *sancai* horse, saddle unglazed, restored, Tang Dynasty, 12in (30.5cm) high.
£3,800–4,500 *C*

A pair of Chinese ormolu-mounted *famille verte* biscuit Buddhistic lions, restored, Kangxi period, 15in (38cm) high. **£24,500–26,000** *C*

Japanese Kakiemon model of a *shishi*, ecorated in enamels, cracked and estored, late 17thC, 6in (15cm) high.
6,500–8,000 *S*

A pair of *famille rose* parrots, c1820, 20½in (52cm) high.
£3,500–4,500 *C*

A Kakiemon model of a boy, damaged, c1680, 5½in (14cm) high.
£6,500–8,000 *S*

A Kakiemon figure of a *bijin*, c1680, 15½in (39.5cm) high.
£8,500–10,000 *S*

A Chinese *famille rose* model of a recumbent tag, rubbed in places, Qianlong period, in (15cm) long, with wood stand and box.
9,000–11,000 *C*

A pair of Chinese export dragon-headed carp tureens and covers, restored, early 19thC, largest 9in (23cm) long.
£7,500–10,000 *S(NY)*

A pair of grey-painted pottery figures of horses, the riders seated with hands pierced for reins, their faces with flesh-coloured pigment and detailed moustaches and eyebrows, Han Dynasty, 11¼in (28.5cm) high.
£6,000–6,500 *S(NY)*

A Chinese brown-glazed pottery horse, head and legs restored, tail missing, Tang Dynasty, 14in (35.5cm) high.
£3,500–4,000 *C*

A Chinese *sancai*-glazed pottery figure of an offici restored, Tang Dynasty, 36in (91cm) high.
£2,300–2,800 *C*

A painted stucco bust of a woman, her patterned robes over a white undergarment, pigment flaking, Tang Dynasty, 15⅝in (40cm) high.
£10,500–11,500 *CNY*

Two Chinese painted stucco heads of female attendants, some pigment loss, late Song/early Ming Dynasty, 13½in (34.5cm) high.
£12,000–14,000 *CNY*

A Chinese export *famille rose* group of 4 boys at play, 18thC, 3in (7.5cm) high.
£600–700 *Wai*

A Chinese blue and white figure of a crane, standing astride rockwork, beak restored, 19thC, 10in (25.5cm) high.
£5,500–6,000 *C*

A Chinese *sancai*-glazed figure of a seated monk, restored, late Tang/Liao Dynasty, 15in (38cm) high.
£2,300–2,800 *C*

A Chinese Shiwan ware flambé-glazed figure of Guanyin, seated with her left hand on her knee, Guangdong Province, 18th/19thC, 9½in (24cm) high.
£2,000–2,200 *CNY*

A *sancai* figure of an attendant Tang Dynasty, 23in (59cm) hig
£3,000–3,500

A pair of Chinese *famille verte* models of *kylins*, late 19thC, 7½in (19cm) high.
£175–250 *DAN*

A pair of Chinese turquoise-glazed models of *kylins*, c1900, 14in (35.5cm) high.
£300–400 *DAN*

A Chinese water dropper, modelled as a carp, from the *Diana* cargo, c1816, 4in (10cm) high.
£500–550 *DAN*

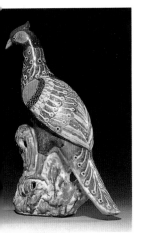

Chinese *famille rose* model
a peacock, standing on pierced
ckwork, damaged, restored,
te Qianlong/Jiaqing period,
in (38cm) high.
,800–2,200 *C*

A pair of Chinese *famille rose* models of elephants, wearing saddlecloths
enamelled on each side with *lingzhi*, a musical stone and a bat above
breaking waves, below floral saddles supporting 2 detachable *gu*-shaped
cylinders, restored, 19thC, 11in (28cm) high.
£4,200–4,800 *C*

pair of Chinese *wucai* figures
boys, wearing robes decorated
ith moulded feather markings
th phoenix reserves on cell
ttern ground, below a *ruyi*-
aped collar, restored, 17thC,
½in (26.5cm) high.
,000–3,500 *C*

A Neolithic painted pottery
funerary jar, surmounted
by a cover in human head
form with 2 different faces,
one pierced with eyes and
mouth, the other with a
wide smile, Banshan type,
Yangshao culture,
11in (28cm) high.
£2,500–3,000 *S(NY)*

A Chinese gold-
enamelled porcelain
snuff bottle,
set on a footrim
and recessed base,
c1820–80,
3in (7.5cm) high.
£1,500–1,800 *S(NY)*

A Chinese *famille
rose* porcelain
snuff bottle,
inscribed 'Yong
xing chang chun'
on the base,
c1820–80,
3in (7.5cm) high.
£800–1,000 *S(NY)*

Chinese export model of a crane,
d black plumage, standing on
base beside a gnarled tree trunk,
ipped and restored, Qianlong
riod, 6½in (16.5cm) high.
,200–2,500 *C*

A Chinese biscuit porcelain group
of a man carrying a boy on his
back, some damage, Kangxi
period, 8½in (21.5cm) high.
£4,200–4,700 *S*

A Chinese *sancai* glazed
figure of a lady, standing on
a plinth, Tang Dynasty,
12in (30.5cm) high.
£4,600–5,000 *S(NY)*

A pair of Chinese black lacquer horseshoe-back armchairs, each upper panel with a beaded cloud medallion, 17th/18thC.
£3,000–3,500 *S(NY)*

A pair of Chinese elm horseshoe-back chairs, with cane seats, c1860.
£1,800–2,000 *ORI*

Lacquered Furniture

Lacquer is the natural sap of the tree *Rhus vernicifera*, which is often used in Chinese and Japanese furniture as an impermeable and decorative coating.
As many as one hundred thin layers of lacquer are built-up on the wood base and then carved through to create patterns or landscapes.

A Chinese carved walnut floor-standing cabinet, c1870, 42in (106.5cm) wide.
£2,000–2,250 *ORI*

A pair of Chinese carved elm square-backed chairs, with hardwood seats, c1870.
£1,800–2,000 *ORI*

A Chinese coffer, the top with everted ends, the frieze with 3 drawers, above 2 doors flanked by removable panels, 18thC, 71½in (181.5cm) wide.
£6,200–7,000 *S(NY)*

A Chinese tall stand, with carved apron, 18thC, 48in (122cm) high.
£7,600–8,200 *S(NY)*

A Japanese gilt-decorated lacquered rosewood table, 19thC, 14in (35.5cm) wide.
£3,000–3,500 *S(NY)*

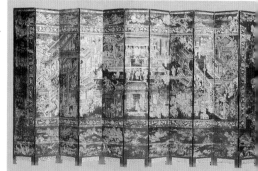

A Chinese black lacquer and gilt eleven-fold screen, decorated with figures, pagodas and foliage, dated '1782', 104in (264cm) high.
£30,000–35,000 *CSK*

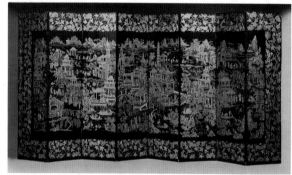

A Chinese export lacquer eight-leaf screen, decorated with a scene of palace life and a foliate border with birds and insects perched in trees, 19thC, 85in (216cm) high.
£8,000–9,000 *C*

A Japanese lacquered wood *norimono*, with sliding doors, hinged flap in roof, interior with padded back support and armrests, lined with gold paper, 18th/19thC, 33in (84cm) wide.
£55,000–60,000 *S*

At TANSU you will discover Europe's largest collection of antique Japanese furniture, where each piece, sourced in Japan, has been painstakingly restored by skilled craftsmen and is unique in every way. Our fine Japanese collection is regularly supplemented with shipments from Japan, so call in and witness for yourself a whole new world of antique furniture.

The TANSU collectors club

Free customer pick up service, train or plane

News and information, special events

Interest free credit, subject to status

Free furniture trial in your home

Exchange furniture service

New arrivals of furniture

Quarterly newsletter

Advice service

TANSU

ANTIQUE JAPANESE FURNITURE

SKOPOS MILLS, Bradford Road, Batley,
West Yorkshire WF17 6LZ
Tel:01924 422391 Fax:01924 443856
www.tansu.co.uk.
email:tansu@tansu.co.uk

A Chinese export black and gilt lacquer decorated cabinet-on-stand, on a Charles II giltwood stand, with naturalistic legs headed by putti, stand regilded and previously ebonised, 66in (167.5cm) high.
£8,500–9,500 *C*

A Chinese cinnabar lacquer stand, with bowed and incurved legs carved with foliage, Yuan Dynasty, c1300, 8½in (21.5cm) wide.
£12,000–15,000 *S*

A Japanese decorated gold lacquer *kodansu*, or perfume cabinet, the doors opening to reveal 4 drawers, carved with scrolling foliage, Meiji period, 10in (26cm) wide, with 2 storage boxes.
£12,000–14,000 *S*

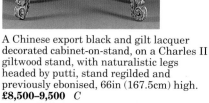

A Chinese pine storage cabinet, with gilt decoration, mid-19thC, 49in (124.5cm) high.
£1,500–2,000 *ORI*

A Japanese gold lacquer *shodon* the central compartment with hinged doors, the others with sliding doors, 19thC, 34½in (86.5cm) wide.
£31,500–35,000 *S*

A Japanese *roironuri* decorated ground tobacco set, with 4 drawers, brazier and ashtray, 19thC, 10½in (26.5cm) high.
£4,500–5,000 *C*

A Japanese coffer, with copper mounts, 17thC, on later stand, 35in (89cm) high
£3,750–4,250 *S*

A Christian folding missal stand, decorated with a sunburst halo with monogram of the Society of Jesus, restored, late 16th/early 17thC, 13⅜in (34cm) high.
£32,500–36,000 *C*

A Japanese cabinet-on-stand, with pierced apron and square shaped legs, c1720, 70in (178cm) high.
£5,500–6,500 *S(S)*

A Japanese picnic box, with copper carrying handle, early Meiji period, 12in (30.5cm) high.
£4,750–5,250 *S*

Chinese export red and
t lacquer armoire, with
shelves and 2 drawers,
thC, 46in (117cm) wide.
,500–4,000 *C*

A Chinese coromandel lacquer ten-leaf screen,
with an extensive scene of court life, the reverse
with Chinese characters, restored, early 18thC,
108½in (275.5cm) high.
£8,000–10,000 *C*

A Chinese padouk wood
chair, with a marble panel,
20thC, 24in (61cm) wide.
£350–400 *SIG*

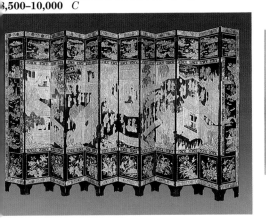

Chinese export black and gilt lacquer eight-leaf screen,
th a scene of buildings and boats, the reverse with
ees and birds, 19thC, 81in (205.5cm) high.
,500–10,000 *C*

A Chinese coromandel lacquer eight-leaf
screen, with a scene of court life, 19thC,
97½in (247.5cm) high.
£6,500–7,500 *C*

Chinese coromandel lacquer twelve-leaf screen,
ith a scene of palace life, the reverse with birds
nd animals, 18thC, 113½in (287cm) high.
0,000–22,000 *C*

A Japanese carved
polychrome decorated
table cabinet and
stand, 19thC,
17½in (44.5cm) wide.
£500–600 *C*

A Chinese export red
and gilt lacquer armoire,
18thC, 62½in (159cm) wide.
£2,500–3,500 *C*

Korean mother-of-pearl inlaid lacquer table,
me damage, 16th/17thC, 18½in (47cm) wide,
a Japanese fitted wooden box.
,000–8,000 *C*

A Chinese incised red lacquer altar
table, damaged, Wanli period,
73½in (186.5cm) long.
£34,000–38,000 *C*

A Chinese canopy bed, with latticework back
and sides, on incurved legs with hoof feet,
18thC, 86in (218.5cm) wide.
£6,500–7,500 *S(NY)*

A Chinese horseshoe-
back armchair, the
splat carved with a
cloud medallion, 17thC.
£3,500–4,200 *S(NY)*

A Korean red-lacquered wood
storage chest, with openwork
iron hinges, Choson Dynasty
35½in (90cm) wide.
£1,600–1,800 *S(NY)*

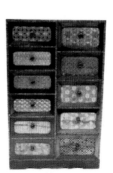

A Japanese parquetry
chest of 11 drawers, with
geometric patterns, late
19thC, 32in (81cm) wide.
£720–800 *E*

A Chinese carved padouk
wood table, with marble top
c1870, 22in (56cm) diam.
£600–700 *GBr*

A pair of Chinese tapered cabinets, with panelled
doors, each interior with 2 shelves and a pair of
short drawers, restored, 17thC, 28in (71cm) wide.
£20,000–22,000 *S(NY)*

A Chinese bamboo table, with black lacquer
top and everted ends above a latticework
apron, c1800, 84in (213cm) long.
£4,000–5,000 *S(NY)*

A Chinese coromandel and black lacquer screen
one side with a palace garden scene, the reverse
with flowers and birds, 19thC, 136in (345cm) wide
£3,500–4,200 *S(NY)*

A Chinese table, the top
inset with a cloisonné panel
depicting a pheasant, 19thC,
37½in (95.5cm) wide.
£7,000–7,700 *HOLL*

A Chinese bamboo screen,
the upper panels open
above latticework, c1800,
84in (213cm) wide.
£4,000–5,000 *S(NY)*

A Chinese elm table, with everted ends above
pierced foliate carved cloud spandrels, recessed
beaded legs joined by *ruyi* and cloud-decorated
pierced panels, c1800, 82in (208cm) long.
£2,700–3,000 *S(NY)*

A Chinese lacquered wood lady's chair, damaged and restored, Kangxi period.
£4,000–5,000 *CNY*

A Chinese scarlet and gold lacquered low table, with foliate ormolu frame, 44in (112cm) wide.
£5,000–6,000 *C*

A Chinese *huanghuali* altar table, 17th/18thC, 57in (145cm) wide.
£5,500–7,000 *CNY*

A pair of Chinese lacquer chairs, Mieguishi, Jiaqing period.
£5,000–6,000 *CNY*

A pair of Chinese *huanghuali* armchairs, the legs joined by stretchers, minor repair, 17thC.
£8,000–10,000 *CNY*

A Chinese export gilt-decorated black lacquer cabinet-on-stand, restored, early 19thC, 35½in (90cm) wide.
£8,000–10,000 *S(NY)*

A Japanese lacquer domed chest, latch replaced, Momoyama period.
£3,500–4,000 *C*

A Chinese six-leaf screen 19thC, 80in (203cm) hi
£80,000–90,000 *C*

A Chinese painted four-leaf screen, the reverse painted with waterfront scenes and domestic utensils, 19thC, 74in (188cm) high.
£4,000–5,000 *C*

Japanese Gold Lacquer

The application of gold dust onto the surface of a thin layer of lacquer gives the appearance of flat gold (*hiramakie*). If the surface is then burnished it looks like a lustred metallic gold (*togidashi makie*).

A Chinese six-leaf screen 19thC, 81½in (207cm) hi
£15,000–18,000 *C*

A Chinese export black and gold lacquer coffer, mid-18thC. **£17,000–20,000** *C*

A Japanese lacquer storage coffer, 18th/19th 69in (175.5cm) long. **£80,000–100,000** *CNY*

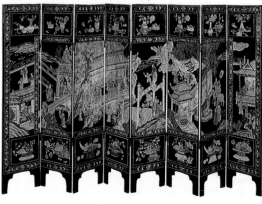

A Chinese eight-leaf black lacquer hardwood screen, painted with a continuous scene, the reverse with landscape, 19thC, 72in (183cm) high.
£5,000–6,000 *C*

A black lacquer *tsuitate*, 19thC, 51in (129.5cm) high.
£10,000–12,000 *C*

CHINESE ANTIQUITIES

Antiquities are works of art or utilitarian objects from ancient times, which have normally been excavated from tombs or historical sites. The huge worldwide demand for these ancient and often beautiful pieces causes major problems. The irresponsible and wanton destruction of historical sites and the excavation and smuggling of antiquities has been illegal in China, Japan and Korea for many years. Major museums in the West will now only access antiquities that are known to have been exported before 1939. The recent flood of tomb pieces onto the market can therefore have come only from illegal sources, and responsible collectors and dealers will question the source of such pieces.

The demand for antiquities has also led to a flourishing market in fakes. Collectors are advised to purchase only from recognised expert dealers belonging to a national association which offers guarantees, or from one of the major auction rooms offering similar security. Where possible, a thermoluminescence (TL) dating certificate should be requested.

Bowls

A red earthenware single-handled bowl, with green glaze, Eastern Han Dynasty, 8in (20.5cm) wide.
£450–500 *GRG*

A *sancai* moulded pottery bowl, the exterior decorated in relief with flowers on a granular ground, coloured in green, cream and chestnut glazes, restored, Tang Dynasty, 4in (10cm) high.
£850–950 *S*

A green and straw-glazed water pot, glaze irregular towards foot, Tang Dynasty, 5in (12.5cm) diam.
£1,500–1,800 *C*

l. A *sancai* water pot, the glaze stopping irregularly above the flattened base revealing the buff-coloured body, Tang Dynasty, 2½in (6.5cm) high.
£2,000–2,500 *C*

An amber-glazed dish, the interior moulded with foliage, the centre with 3 spur marks, Liao Dynasty, 5½in (14cm) diam.
£1,300–1,500 *C*

A Fujian ware dark brown stoneware teabowl, with thick brown and blue hare's fur glaze, Southern Song Dynasty, 4in (10cm) diam.
£1,000–1,200 *GRG*

A Junyao bowl, the pale lavender glaze with a purple splash to the interior thinning to a celadon at the rim, Song/Yuan Dynasty, 7½in (19cm) diam.
£1,800–2,000 *C*

A bowl and cover, the body carved with overlapping bands of lotus petals, the cover with carved sgraffito, covered with a greenish-white glaze, Northern Song Dynasty, 3½in (9cm) diam.
£1,000–1,200 *GRG*

l. A Yingqing bowl, with a fine transparent glaze of delicate blue tones pooling heavily around the foot, minute chip, Song Dynasty, 8in (20.5cm) diam, in a fitted box.
£4,000–4,500 *C*

A Junyao stem bowl, heavily potted with shallow rounded sides, crackled pale lavender glaze, purple splash inside and outside, Song/Yuan Dynasty, 5in (12.5cm) diam.
£800–1,000 *C*

Two Junyao bowls, covered in a crackled blue glaze, one with purple splashes to interior, Song Dynasty, 4in (10cm) diam.
£3,000–3,500 *C*

A *shufu* stem bowl, with a line of lotus heads and floral sprays, the bluish-white glaze pooling at the rim, slight damage, Yuan Dynasty, 5in (12.5cm) diam, with a fitted box.
£1,300–1,500 *C*

A Junyao saucer dish, the thick bluish-grey opalescent glaze thinning at the rim, Song Dynasty, 8in (20.5cm) diam.
£2,200–2,500 *C*

A pair of Yingqing shallow bowls, carved at the centre with 2 fish, both bowls fired upside down on the unglazed rims, with pale grey glaze, Southern Song/Yuan Dynasty, 6½in (16.5cm) diam.
£700–800 *C*

A blue and white dish, the base unglazed with a continuous groove, Yuan Dynasty, 11in (28cm) diam.
£6,000–7,000 *C*

l. A Junyao purple-splashed bowl, under a pale lavender glaze thinning to celadon at the rim, on a buff stoneware foot, Song/Yuan Dynasty, 7in (18cm) diam.
£2,000–2,200 *C*

A blue and white bowl, with lotus panels below a *lingzhi* scroll, restored, c1340, 7½in (19cm) diam.
£1,300–1,500 *C*

Dishes

A Yingqing conical dish, with rounded sides and flaring rim, the interior with a flower and leaves under a greenish-blue glaze, Song Dynasty, 7½in (19cm) diam.
£1,400–1,600 *GRG*

A Dingyao hexafoil dish, the centre carved, under a glaze of fine ivory pooling into 'tear drops' near the foot, repaired, Northern Song Dynasty, 7in (18cm) diam.
£1,800–2,000 *C*

A Junyao saucer dish, with shallow sides, under a pale blue glaze, the centre with a crescent-shaped purple splash, Song Dynasty, 7in (18cm) diam.
£3,800–4,200 *C*

Figures – Animals

A pair of red-painted grey pottery horses' heads, traces of ochre and white harnesses, some rubbing, one repaired, Han Dynasty, 5½in (14cm) high.
£750–900 *C*

A grey earthenware horse's head, with some natural pigment, Han Dynasty, 6in (15cm) high.
£450–500 *GRG*

A buff pottery recumbent lion-dog, with traces of pigment, possibly restored, probably Han Dynasty, 19in (48.5cm) long.
£1,700–2,000 *Bon*

A painted grey pottery body of a horse, with traces of red strapwork on a white ground, Han Dynasty, 17½in (44.5cm) long.
£1,800–2,000 *CSK*

A green-glazed red pottery dog, restored, Han Dynasty, 11in (28cm) long.
£1,300–1,500 *C*

A red pottery horse, with an angular neck, the sculpted head held forward with jaw open to reveal clenched teeth, large flared nostrils beneath the protruding eye sockets and spiky ears, restored, Han Dynasty, 19in (48.5cm) high.
£2,600–3,000 *S(NY)*

A pair of painted grey pottery owls, with orange and white plumage and features, the heads pierced, Han Dynasty, 7in (18cm) high.
£800–1,000 *C*

Tomb Figures

The burying of ceramic figures and animals with the dead was common practice among the nobility in China. It was a way of announcing their high status to the spirits, and it was essential to be accompanied in the tomb by the things that had been enjoyed during their lifetime.

A grey pottery horse, with legs slightly turned out, head held downwards, the neck decorated with applied floret trappings, layers of flaring blankets over a wide saddle, restored, Northern Wei Dynasty, 10¼in (26cm) high.
£13,500–15,000 *S(NY)*

This horse has particularly fine detailing.

l. A painted grey pottery mythical beast, with bulging eyes, flaring nostrils and pricked ears, a pair of wings sprouting from its shoulders, remains of a white slip with black overpainting and painted details on the wings, Six Dynasties, 16in (40.5cm) long.
£5,000–6,000 *S(NY)*

A painted pottery camel, with traces of pigment, Wei Dynasty, 9in (23cm) high.
£15,000–17,000 *S*

A pottery horse and rider, old damage and repair, early Tang Dynasty, 12in (30.5cm) high.
£2,600–3,000 *C*

A *sancai* glazed buff pottery horse, damaged and restored, Tang Dynasty, 18½in (47cm) high.
£13,000–15,000 *CNY*

A painted red pottery horse and rider, restored, Tang Dynasty, 14½in (37cm) high.
£3,500–4,000 *C*

A straw-glazed Bactrian camel, traces of red pigment, restored, Sui/Tang Dynasty, 13in (33cm) high.
£1,200–1,500 *C*

A pair of painted red pottery models of earth spirits, restored, Tang Dynasty, 18½in (47cm) high.
£3,000–3,500 *C*

A painted red pottery camel, traces of red, black, white and orange pigment, legs restored, Tang Dynasty, 18in (45.5cm) high.
£2,000–2,200 *C*

A straw-glazed pottery camel, damaged, Tang Dynasty, 12½in (32cm) high.
£800–1,000 *Bea*

A buff pottery camel, with simulated tufted hair, traces of pigment, Tang Dynasty, 17in (43cm) high.
£3,000–3,500 *CSK*

A red pottery horse and rider, traces of painted pigment, restored, Tang Dynasty, 12in (30.5cm) high.
£2,000–2,500 *C*

A painted buff pottery camel, traces of pigment, Tang Dynasty, 14½in (37cm) high.
£5,000–5,500 *C*

> **Miller's is a price GUIDE not a price LIST**

l. A *sancai* pottery horse, with brown, amber and straw glazes, chipped and restored, Tang Dynasty, 13½in (34.5cm) high.
£6,000–7,000 *C*

A buff pottery model of an ox and cart, the detachable wheels with spokes and hubs, Tang Dynasty, 9½in (24cm) long, on a wood stand.
£2,700–3,200 *CAm*

Figures – People

Two grey pottery figures of dancers, the grotesque heads with traces of pigments, Han Dynasty, 5½in (14cm) high.
£2,000–2,200 C

l. A painted grey pottery figure of an attendant wearing a flowing robe, hands clasped, traces of white slip overall and painted details, Han Dynasty, 26½in (67.5cm) high.
£8,000–10,000 CAm

A pottery figure of a lady, with traces of orange and white pigment, head detachable, Han Dynasty, 29½in (75cm) high.
£1,500–1,700 S(Am)

A pair of grey pottery figures of attendants, naturalistically painted, facial features picked out in black on a pink ground, Han Dynasty, 18½in (47cm) high.
£5,800–6,200 S(NY)

A pair of painted pottery figures of ladies, features picked out in black, Han Dynasty, 12in (30.5cm) high.
£3,800–4,500 S

r. A painted pottery figure of an attendant, the robe with brick-red border, Han Dynasty, 16in (40.5cm) high.
£2,500–3,000 CAm

A pair of painted grey pottery figures of male officials, the robes painted in yellow, white and red pigments flaring out sharply below the knees, Han Dynasty, 14in (35.5cm) high.
£2,200–2,500 C

A red-painted pottery figure of a guardian, remains of black, grey and brown pigment over white slip, slight damage, Tang Dynasty, 22¾in (58cm) high.
£7,000–8,000 S(NY)

An unglazed buff pottery figure of an attendant, with orange pigment, Tang Dynasty, 8in (20.5cm) high.
£220–250 CSK

A red pottery grotesque figure of a fat man, some restoration, Six Dynasties/Tang Dynasty, 14in (35.5cm) high.
£1,300–1,500 C

A red-painted pottery figure of a court lady, picked out in black, some restoration, Tang Dynasty, 12¾in (32.5cm) high.
£7,000–7,700 S(NY)

A red pottery figure of a fat man, with white slip glaze, restored, Tang Dynasty, 18¼in (46.5cm) high.
£11,500–13,000 *S(NY)*

A white-painted red pottery figure of a court lady, damaged, Tang Dynasty, 9in (23cm) high.
£125–150 *Bea*

A brown-glazed pottery figure of a groom, with dark amber hues, Tang Dynasty, 10½in (26.5cm) high.
£800–1,000 *C*

A pair of glazed buff pottery figures of warriors, their heads and clothes under an iridescent straw glaze with traces of red and green pigment, Sui/Tang Dynasty, 16in (40.5cm) high.
£2,500–3,000 *C*

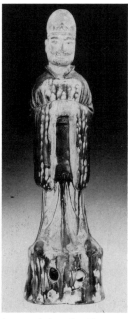

A *sancai* glazed pottery figure of a bearded official, on a rockwork base, glaze rubbed, Tang Dynasty, 26½in (67.5cm) high.
£3,500–4,000 *CSK*

A red pottery model of a winged earth spirit, seated on its haunches, some red pigment remaining, restored, Tang Dynasty, 18in (45.5cm) high.
£350–400 *CSK*

An unglazed pottery figure of a standing attendant, covered in red, pink and black pigments, Tang Dynasty, 10½in (26.5cm) high.
£700–800 *CAm*

A straw-glazed pottery equestrian figure, Sui/Tang Dynasty, 13in (33cm) high.
£3,000–3,500 *CAm*

A pair of Cizhou brown, red and olive painted figures of ladies, Song Dynasty, 5in (12.5cm) high.
£800–1,000 *CNY*

A Qingbai figure of Avalokitesvara, covered in thick grey-white glaze, restored, Yuan Dynasty, 14in (35.5cm) high.
£2,500–3,000 *CNY*

r. A Yingqing glazed standing figure, the arms, eyes and hair unglazed, slight damage, glaze crackled, Song/Yuan Dynasty, 8in (20.5cm) high.
£350–400 *CSK*

ars

Neolithic pottery funerary jar,
ainted with geometric roundels
nd arabesques in black and
eddish-brown pigments,
achang type, Yangshao
ulture, 15¼in (38.5cm) high.
1,200–1,500 *S(NY)*

A green-glazed impressed jar, the
top half covered with an olive-green
glaze stopping above mid-body,
Zhou Dynasty, 15½in (39.5cm) wide.
£3,500–4,000 *C*

A jar and carved cover, Han
Dynasty, 8in (20.5cm) high.
£450–550 *KOT*

A green-glazed jar, some
restoration, Han Dynasty,
7½in (19cm) diam.
£1,200–1,500 *C*

A glazed pottery baluster jar,
decorated in brown and blue
chevrons on an olive-green and
straw streaky ground over a
white slip, some restoration,
Tang Dynasty, 8in (20.5cm) high.
£3,500–4,000 *C*

grey pottery jar, the shoulder
ainted in white and orange
igments with an equestrian among
aves, the reverse with an abstract
iger, Warring States/early Western
Ian Dynasty, 17½in (44.5cm) high.
7,000–8,000 *S(NY)*

A green-glazed pottery jar, the crackled
olive-green glaze revealing buff below,
Tang Dynasty, 6½in (16.5cm) high.
£1,500–1,700 *S*

l. A Longquan
celadon funerary
jar and cover, with
crackled glaze,
damaged, Southern
Song Dynasty,
7in (18cm) high,
with a stand and
fitted box.
£2,000–2,500 *C*

A jar and domed cover, with marbled
chre and brown glaze, restored,
Tang Dynasty, 4in (10cm) high.
£1,700–2,000 *CSK*

A white-glazed jar,
the slightly degraded
whitish-straw glaze
stopping below mid-
body revealing the
fine-grained body,
kiln adhesion to
body, Tang Dynasty,
9½in (24cm) high.
£900–1,000 *C*

l. A phosphatic-splashed
miniature jar, the thick
black glaze extending to
mid-body with suffusions
of pale lavender blue,
Tang Dynasty,
2½in (6.5cm) wide.
£1,800–2,000 *C*

l. A Jizhou jar, covered
with a black glaze and
grey spots, rising to
a wide neck and an
everted lip, chipped,
Southern Song Dynasty,
7½in (19cm) high.
£2,000–2,400 *C*

A Henan jar, with white slip-trailed
ribs to the body, the black glaze
pooling at the buff stoneware foot,
the rim biscuit, chipped,
Song Dynasty, 5in (12.5cm) wide.
£1,800–2,000 *C*

A Chinese export
crackle-glazed jar,
late Song Dynasty,
11in (28cm) high.
£120–150 *GRG*

A dark glazed storage jar,
with applied flame
decoration, Song Dynasty,
9in (23cm) high.
£170–200 *AnE*

A buff pottery jar,
partly glazed in green,
Tang Dynasty,
4½in (11.5cm) high.
£550–600 *ORI*

l. A *sancai* moulded tripod
jar, on cabriole legs with
paw feet, splashed with
straw, chestnut and green
glaze over buff, some
repainting, Tang Dynasty,
5in (12.5cm) high.
£1,500–1,800 *S(NY)*

Marble & Stone Sculpture

A white marble head of a Dvarapa**l**
with buff patina, chipped, Liao/Son**g**
Dynasty, 11in (28cm) high.
£6,000–7,000 *C*

A marble sculpture of a seated
Bodhisattva, in the posture of
contemplation, damaged and
restored, the stand inscribed
with possible date, Northern Wei
Dynasty, 10½in (26.5cm) high.
£4,200–5,000 *S*

A marble sculpture of a standing
Bodhisattva, on a lotus plinth and
inscribed stand, holding attributes,
the head surmounted by a
mandorla, damaged, Northern
Wei Dynasty, 8in (20.5cm) high.
£1,300–1,500 *S*

Antiquities

Most of the earthenware for which
the Tang Dynasty is best known was
excavated at the beginning of the
20th century by railway engineers.
Tomb figures were so keenly
collected by Europeans that the
Chinese produced forgeries that are
hard to spot from the originals.

r. A grey stone head of
Damo, carved bald with a
furrowed brow, pronounced
eyes, moustache, sideburns
and a beard, teeth exposed,
his ears with distended
lobes, Song Dynasty,
10½in (26.5cm) high.
£2,000–2,500 *C(HK)*

Metalware

A pair of gilt-bronze figures of crouching Bodhisattvas, some encrustation, Tang Dynasty, 2in (5cm) high.
£4,700–5,300 *S*

r. An archaic bronze bell, cast with 3 bands of raised knops above scrollwork to one side, earth and malachite encrustation, Western Zhou Dynasty, 15in (38cm) high.
£1,400–1,700 *C*

r. An archaic Ordos bronze dagger, the tapered blade of thin lozenge section, deeply patinated with some malachite encrustation, small losses to blade edges, 4th century BC, 13in (33cm) long.
£3,000–3,500 *C*

Pillows

l. A Cizhou figural-form pillow, painted in *café au lait* and dark brown over a pale ivory slip, with brilliant glaze, Jin Dynasty, 15½in (39.5cm) long.
£3,500–4,000 *CNY*

A *sancai* glazed buff pottery pillow, impressed with a pair of ducks, the sides reserved on an amber ground, the face with a green ground, Tang/Liao Dynasty, 6in (15cm) wide.
£1,000–1,200 *C*

A Cizhou pillow, modelled as a recumbent tiger, with a broad mouth, pierced nostrils and bold eyes, the black stripes on a flame-coloured ground, panel on the back with a bird within a lozenge, Jin Dynasty, 14½in (37cm) wide.
£3,000–3,500 *C*

A Cizhou white-glazed pillow, the top incised to an ochre slip with a young boy holding a lotus spray, under a finely crackled glaze over a white slip pooling at the edges, Song Dynasty, 8in (20.5cm) wide.
£1,400–1,800 *C*

Miller's is a price GUIDE not a price LIST

l. A Cizhou stoneware pillow, the top painted with a striding tiger, the border in chocolate brown on a crackled white slip, the sides with freely drawn stylised foliage, chipped, Song Dynasty, 10in (25.5cm) wide.
£1,800–2,000 *C*

A Cizhou polychrome pillow, carved and combed with a flowerspray, painted in green, yellow and amber, the sides green-glazed, Jin Dynasty, 12in (30.5cm) wide.
£4,500–5,000 *C*

Vases & Bottles

A green-glazed red pottery baluster vase, with a greenish-gold glaze, Han Dynasty, 16in (40.5cm) high.
£1,000–1,200 *C*

A pottery vase, covered overall with an iridescent green glaze, Han Dynasty, 17½in (44.5cm) high.
£4,500–5,000 *S(NY)*

A *sancai* glazed vase, the body splashed overall in chestnut and green on a straw-coloured ground, pale buff showing at the foot, 2 restored chips, Tang Dynasty, 4½in (11.5cm) high.
£1,000–1,200 *S*

A red pottery baluster vase, with green glaze and some iridescence, slightly chipped, Han Dynasty, 18½in (47cm) high.
£1,300–1,500 *C*

A red pottery *hu*-shaped vase, with ring handles and bands of ribbing, under a thin pale greenish-yellow degraded glaze, Han Dynasty, 13½in (34.5cm) high.
£700–800 *CSK*

Two Yingqing funerary vases, the crackled glaze of pale bluish tone, slight damage, Song Dynasty, 13in (33cm) high.
£1,000–1,200 *DN*

A Cizhou *meiping*, carved through a rich dark brown glaze to the buff pottery body with 3 large panels of peony divided by swirling waves, neck restored, Song Dynasty, 13½in (34.5cm) high.
£2,200–2,500 *C*

A Yingqing moulded vase, the integral stand pierced with 'keyhole' design, Yuan Dynasty, 17in (43cm) high.
£750–1,000 *ART*

A bottle, the tall ringed neck with a stylised phoenix head, covered with a buff-coloured glaze, Northern Song Dynasty, 13¾in (35cm) high.
£7,000–8,000 *S(NY)*

This bottle was made in Guangzhou province for the Indonesian market.

A Cizhou vase, covered with a thick brownish-black glaze with a sgraffito design, the shoulder with 2 lugs, Song Dynasty, 13½in (34.5cm) high.
£2,200–2,500 *C*

CHINESE JADE

In Europe and the USA the word jade is used to describe nephrite (a silicate of calcium and magnesium) and jadeite silicate of aluminium and sodium). For collectors of Chinese antiquities, jade – in China a symbol of purity that was often used as a tomb adornment to comfort the soul and confer immortality – is also a symbol of the Chinese culture. Most of the archaic Chinese jades were made of nephrite. There are many different types of nephrite, including 'mutton fat' jade, a pure white jade that has a slightly greasy, lard-like appearance, and 'spinach' jade that comes from Siberia and is characterised by black flecks of graphite. Jadeite was first used in China in the 18th century when it was imported from Burma (now Myanmar). Jadeite is harder than nephrite, often pure green in colour and is used extensively in jewellery.

Jade carving started in the Neolithic culture. Ritual objects, including sacrificial and auspicious utensils, were carved, and the earliest examples often have minimal carving to form representations of animals, birds and fish. Later jades became more ostentatious as the craftsmen's skill and artistry developed. Fine ornaments, small sculptures and items for the scholar's desk became the main output. Jade workshops opened up in almost every main city in China and, as the workmanship became more sophisticated, fine artistry was accepted as the norm. However, the value of a finished object became more dependent on the quality of the stone and, over the last 200 years, a simple bangle of the purest, flawless green jadeite has become more valuable than the finest carving on a flawed piece of nephrite.

The varying colours of nephrite may not fully show themselves until the pebble is partly carved, when skillful artistry can incorporate these colour changes into the overall design. Even flaws can be enhanced and incorporated; thus an insect on a flower or a small squirrel on a tree will make a finished work more desirable.

All Chinese art is subject to international fashion, and jade is no exception. In recent years the later Qing Dynasty (1644–1916) pure white jade carvings have become popular and spectacular prices have been achieved. These prices have currently slowed down, mainly due to the economic ills of the Far East. Unfortunately, the celebrated skills of Chinese workmanship have, of late, been used to make brilliant fakes of archaic jades, some of which can deceive even the most experienced expert. As a result many collectors are now turning away from early jades and today only those archaic jades of impeccable provenance are fetching the high prices of a few years ago.

Bowls, Brush Washers & Cups

A pierced jade *coupe*, the sides carved and pierced with handles, late Ming Dynasty, 5in (12.5cm) diam.
£1,600–1,800 *S*

A carved jade libation vessel, the stone of mottled pale grey colour with extensive areas of darker grey and brown tending to a 'chicken bone' effect on the interior, Song/Ming Dynasty, 6½in (16.5cm) long.
£9,500–10,500 *S*

A dark grey jade bowl, with pale grey inclusions, probably Ming Dynasty, 5in (12.5cm) diam, in a plush box.
£800–900 *CSK*

A mottled grey jade brush washer, carved as an upturned lotus leaf, with incurved edges forming the bowl, the interior carved with a lotus pod and the exterior carved in relief with branches of lotus flowers and leaves, 17thC, 5in (12.5cm) wide.
£2,500–3,000 *C*

A carved jade bowl, the sides decorated in light relief, the interior with a begonia spray in high relief, the stone of pale celadon colour with darker markings and chalky inclusions, rim lightly ground, Kangxi period, 6½in (16.5cm) diam.
£4,400–5,000 *S*

A pierced jade censer and cover, the stone of pale celadon colour, the body and domed cover carved and incised in openwork with scrolling peony flowers and 3 peony stem handles, on a flaring openwork base, 18thC, 5in (12.5cm) wide, with wooden stand.
£5,000–5,500 *C*

A jade brush pot, carved in varying relief with a continuous mountainous scene depicting the Three Star Gods, a crane and a deer, the stone of greenish-white colour with some darker areas, Qianlong period, slight damage, 8½in (21.5cm) diam.
£55,000–60,000 *S*

A white jade marriage bowl, the rim carved on top with a border of *ruyi* heads interrupted at 2 sides with bats flying amid lotus forming a loop below, supporting a ring handle, the stone of fine even white colour with one chalky inclusion, Qianlong period, 9½in (24cm) diam.
£50,000–55,000 *S*

A spinach jade lobed dish, carved in the centre with scrolling peonies and tendrils forming a roundel, Qing Dynasty, 5½in (14cm) diam.
£800–900 *S*

r. A celadon jade bowl and cover, the inner rim with a narrow channel to receive the low domed cover, the stone of even pale greenish white colour, Qianlong period, 5in (12.5cm) diam.
£3,700–4,200 *S*

White Jade

Pure white jade has always been in demand by collectors, particularly pieces finely carved during the 18thC when intricate carving was at its peak. Both the pieces on the left were carved from large, single pieces of white jade. Large stones of white jade are quite rare and values increase dramatically in accordance with size.

A spinach jade bowl, flecked and black inclusions, and streaked with white areas, rim polished, small chips, Jiaqing period, 7in (18cm) diam.
£1,800–2,000 *Bon*

A carved spinach jade bowl, with inscription, late 19thC, 2½in (6.5cm) diam.
£500–550 *LHA*

l. A pair of celadon jade bowls, each decorated in gilding with dragons among scrolling flowers and foliage, the exteriors with lappet bands to the footrims, chipped, Qianlong period, 4½in (11.5cm) diam.
£2,700–3,000 *Bea*

A pierced jade bowl and cover, the sides carved in high relief below the rim with 4 winged beasts, the domed cover pierced with a lotus and bat scroll below the crouching dragon knop, the stone of even pale brown colour, Jiaqing period, 6in (15cm) diam.
£5,700–6,300 *S*

A carved jade brush holder, 19thC, 3½in (9cm) wide.
£550–600 *Bon*

l. A pale celadon jade brush washer modelled as an open lotus, carved to the exterior with a shell and leafy tendrils, 19thC, 5in (12.5cm) long, on a wooden stand, and a green quartz carving of a reclining Buddha.
£450–500 *CSK*

r. A carved spinach jade brush pot, late 19thC, 4in (10cm) high.
£680–750 *LHA*

dark green nephrite jade bowl, of shallow form, e everted rim rising from a short foot, 19thC, n (20.5cm) diam, with box.
800–900 *CSK*

moss agate peach shaped libation up, with *qilong* handle, carved the exterior with leafy tendrils, 9thC, 4½in (11.5cm) wide.
250–300 *CSK*

l. A celadon jade pouring vessel, with dark brown inclusions, carved in archaic style in the form of a three-legged mythological animal, carved to the rear in relief with coiled dragons, 19thC, 6in (15cm) long.
£700–800 *CSK*

Figures – Animals

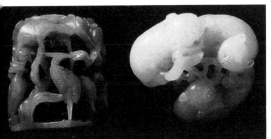

A greyish celadon jade hat finial, carved and pierced with cranes standing among lotus leaves, base chipped, Ming Dynasty, 1½in (4cm) high.
A white jade model of 3 cats, clutching a spray of ungus, 18thC, 2in (5cm) wide.
500–600 *CSK*

A reddish-brown jade model of a horned mythical lion, its tail flicked to one side, with celadon inclusions, small chips, Ming Dynasty, 3in (7.5cm) long, on a wooden stand.
£450–500 *CSK*

yellow jade model of a recumbent unicorn, curled to one side and scratching his right brow with his hoof, Song Dynasty, 3½in (9cm) long.
2,700–3,000 *C*

l. A yellow-green jade lion dog, with teeth bared below thick eyebrows and single short horn, tail curled-up, mid-Qing Dynasty, 4in (10cm) long.
£2,200–2,500 *C*

A celadon jade elephant group, surmounted by a boy holding a crop, the opaque green stone with tan skin highlights, Ming Dynasty, 3½in (9cm) high.
£1,400–1,600 *S(NY)*

Dating Jade

It is sometimes difficult to date jade. Generally, the heavier, more elaborate and intricate pieces are more likely to be of recent date.

A speckled burnt jade model of an elephant, draped with a decorative tasselled *howdah*, surmounted by a boy grasping a lotus stem, another standing holding a vase, the pale cream jade richly speckled with black flecks, repaired, probably Ming Dynasty, 7½in (19cm) long.
£1,500–1,800 *C*

A carved jade mythical beast, Qianlong period, 6in (15cm) long.
£6,000–7,000 *S*

A carved celadon jade group of a buffalo and a boy, 14in (35.5cm) wide.
£2,200–2,500 *C*

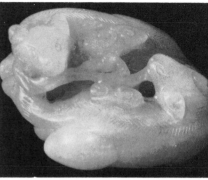

A carved pale celadon jade model of 2 recumbent animal grasping a *lingzhi* fungus, 18thC, 2in (5cm) wide.
£300–350 *CSK*

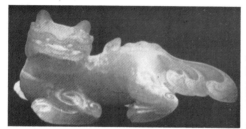

l. A carved jade crouching Buddhistic lion, grasping *lingzhi* in its mouth, its head turned to the left, 18thC, 3in (7.5cm) long.
£600–700 *CSK*

A carved mottled grey jade mythical lion, turning to look behind, with bifurcated tail, russet inclusions, 20thC, 2½in (6.5cm) long.
£350–400 *CSK*

A carved pale celadon jade toad, among pomegranates, 19thC, 4½in (11.5cm) long.
£1,200–1,400 *CSK*

A carved green and russet jade phoenix, seated with its head on its back and holding a lotus spray in its beak, 19thC, 9in (23cm) wide.
£1,600–1,800 *C*

Figures – People

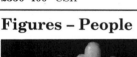

A white jade group of 3 bearded Immortals and boy attendant, on rockwork beside a crane, before a pine tree, 18thC, 5in (12.5cm) wide.
£1,000–1,200 *CSK*

A hardstone mountain, carved on one side with a bearded sage walking along a mountain path, the reverse carved with a monkey carrying another on his back, 19thC, 7in (18cm) high, with wooden stand.
£4,000–4,500 *CNY*

A jadeite figure of Lan Caihe in a coat and skirt, holding a flower basket, her celestial scarf over her shoulders, 19thC, 8½in (21.5cm) high.
£2,000–2,200 *S(NY)*
Lan Caihe was one of the Eight Immortals.

l. A pair of mottled green and brown jadeite carvings of ladies seated on deer, each holding a *ruyi* spray, the animals' heads turned left and right, one broken at the ankles, 10in (25.5cm) high, on pierced wooden stands.
£1,000–1,200 *CSK*

The Eight Immortals

The Eight Immortals were a common subject for jade carvers, the tradition dating back to the Song Dynasty. Considered to be guardian figures representing virtue and the quest for eternity, three of the Eight Immortals were historical figures and five were purely legendary.

A pale celadon jade figure group, 19thC, 12½in (32cm) high.
£1,300–1,500 *HSS*

An emerald green and lavender flecked white jade figure, 19thC, 10in (25.5cm) high.
£2,200–2,500 *C*

A creamy celadon jade Buddhistic figure, carved from a thin section of stone, late Qing Dynasty, 8in (20.5cm) high, with wooden stand.
£1,200–1,400 *C*

A carved jadeite figure of Guanyin, wearing a high headdress, flowing robes and holding her hands before her, with pale green and mauve inclusions, on a double lotus base, 20thC, 4½in (11.5cm) high.
£450–550 *CSK*

A celadon jade figure of Buddha, 9thC, 6in (15cm) high.
650–750 *C*

l. A carved green jade figure, 19thC, 7in (18cm) high.
£450–500 *CDC*

Jewellery

A celadon jade dragon pendant, both sides with a low relief pattern of intertwined swirls, pierced with one hole drilled from both sides, the semi-translucent stone suffused with fine dark and russet flecks, now with areas of opaque white mottling from burial, tail restuck, possibly slightly reduced, Eastern Zhou Dynasty, 4in (10cm) wide.
3,500–4,200 *C*

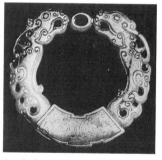

A celadon and brown jade bangle, in the form of confronting dragons above bands of stylised *taotie* masks, Ming Dynasty, 3½in (9cm) wide.
£350–400 *CSK*

A pair of white jade bangles, 17th/18thC, 3in (7.5cm) diam.
£1,800–2,000 *C*

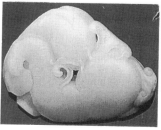

r. A white jade pendant, carved as a pair of catfish, 18th/19thC, 2in (5cm) long.
£1,300–1,500 *C(HK)*

Properties of Jade

- very hard: jadeite is harder than nephrite, jade cannot be scratched by a steel penknife, but jadeite can scratch nephrite
- very brittle: will break if dropped
- cold to the touch
- jadeite is heavier than nephrite

Sceptres

A green jade *ruyi* sceptre, 19thC, 15in (38cm) long.
£700–800 *CSK*

A mother-of-pearl inlaid and jade-s
hardwood sceptre, of 3 celadon jade
plaques carved with Immortals,
repaired, 19thC, 22in (56cm) long.
£700–800 *CNY*

A celadon jade *ruyi* sceptre, the top carved with
an openwork dragon amid clouds, the handle
with a knotted prunus bough and a bat at the
end, Jiaqing period, 17in 43cm) long.
£6,000–7,000 *S*

A jade *ruyi* sceptre, carved with a figure in
a river landscape, 19thC, 19in (48.5cm) long.
£4,500–5,000 *DN*

Ruyi Sceptres

Ruyi sceptres were made in many
materials, including gold, ivory, crystal,
agate, coral, porcelain, wood and jade.
The workmanship was always meticulous
and the designs were either simple or very
elaborate. *Ruyi* invariably carry symbols
of good wishes such as 'pine and crane'
(longevity), 'phoenix and peony' (prosperity
etc. The *ruyi* had its origin in the humble
back-scratcher, a stick about 18in (45.5cm)
long with a bent hand at one end. As the
Imperial scratchers became more fancy and
therefore valuable, so the shape developed
into that which we know today. On court
celebration days *ruyi* sceptres would be
presented to the Emperor who would then
present them to favoured ministers or
subjects. The *ruyi* presentation custom is
relatively modern, and originated in the
Qing Dynasty.

Vases

A pale celadon jade vase
and cover, with animal
mask loose ring handles,
19thC, 7½in (19cm) high,
with wooden stand.
£4,500–5,000 *C*

A polished white jade flattened baluster vase,
with 2 openwork dragon handles, one loose ring
missing, Qianlong period, 5½in (14cm) high.
£1,000–1,200 *C*

l. A pale celadon
jade vase and
cover, 19thC,
6in (15cm) high.
£1,500–1,700 *C*

A celadon jade vase, carved
in relief around the shoulder
with a sinuous dragon in
pursuit of a flaming pearl,
18thC, 10in (25.5cm) high,
with wooden stand.
£2,500–2,800 *C*

l. A dark green jade flattened
vase and cover, with mask ring
handles, carved in deep relief
with confronting dragons,
19thC, 10½in (26.5cm) high.
£450–500 *CSK*

celadon jade double vase, rved as 2 deep magnolia wers issuing from enwork leafy branches with *gzhi*, the jade of even pale ey-green tone, chipped, thC, 8½in (21.5cm) high, a wooden stand.
,500–10,000 *C*

A white jade double gourd vase and cover, with strapwork double handles above a double loop and ring handle, the stone of even white colour, Qianlong period, 8in (20.5cm) high.
£24,000–28,000 *S*

A two-tone jade Three Friends of Winter double vase, carved and undercut using the black and grey colours of the stone, in the shape of 2 slender naturalistic pine and prunus tree trunks with a tall bamboo stalk, Qianlong period, 6in (15cm) high.
£3,600–4,000 *S(NY)*

An embellished pale celadon jade vase and cover, some hardstone loss, mid-Qing Dynasty, 5in (12.5cm) high.
£1,800–2,000 *C*

iscellaneous

carved celadon jade oval plaque, th a phoenix among peonies, ing Dynasty, 3½in (9cm) wide.
,300–1,500 *CSK*

A jade dragon plaque, carved in relief with a dragon amid lotus, mounted as a table screen, on a carved and pierced wood stand, Kangxi period, 12in (30.5cm) high.
£1,200–1,400 *S(S)*

A pair of jade joss-stick holders and gilt-metal stands, pierced with a trellis diaper border, Qing Dynasty, 18thC, 6in (15cm) high.
£2,500–2,750 *S*

A jade carving, on a stand, early 19thC, 5in (12.5cm) long.
£500–600 *Wai*

jade and white metal-ounted mirror, attached a pale celadon jade belt ook handle, carved with enwork, Qing Dynasty, ½in (26.5cm) long, with box.
,800–2,000 *C*

A jade screen, Qing Dynasty, 11 x 9in (28 x 23cm), with wooden frame and stand.
£700–800 *C*

Gifts of Jade

According to Chinese tradition, a family was thought fortunate to bear a son, and in celebration often presented male progeny with a piece of jade. It was therefore common to be congratulated by friends on 'a fine piece of jade', meaning a male child.

JAPANESE INRO & NETSUKE

The market for Japanese art has been through a difficult time during the last two or three years, due to the downturn in the Japanese economy. This has resulted in somewhat lower prices for works of art hitherto purchased by Japanese collectors and dealers, such as 17th-century porcelain, sword fittings and wood-block prints.

One of the areas that has escaped relatively unharmed is that devoted to *inro* and *netsuke* (pronounced 'net-ski'). *Inro* are small compartmentalised boxes used to carry medicines. They were generally made of lacquered wood, hemp or papier mâché, and hung by a cord from the wearer's belt. The cord was tightened by the *ojime*, or bead, and the *netsuke* is the toggle attached to the cord that was slipped through the belt to hold it in place. They were first made in the 17th century and continued through until the Meiji period (1868–1911) when Western dress was introduced to Japan. The Japanese have always thought of *netsuke* as dress accessories, although they have been widely collected in the West from the end of the 19th century. This is still true, although a few collectors in Japan are becoming interested in *netsuke* and *inro* as works of art.

The quality and artistry of *inro*, combined with the names of certain key artists, determine value. Perhaps the most popular artists among collectors are Ogawa Haritsu, known as Ritsuo (1767–1857), and Shibata Zeshin (1812–92). Good examples of their works can command up to £50,000, while pieces by other artists of the 18th and 19th centuries will realise up to £10,000. The same criteria apply to *netsuke*, with the additional factor of subject matter. The major artists from Kyoto, working in the 18th century, are probably the most popular, with the finest examples realising between £5,000 and £50,000, and occasionally more. On the whole, animal subjects are more popular than figural *netsuke*, while *netsuke* of vegetables or copies of Noh masks can be relatively inexpensive.

Neil Davey

Inro

A single-case *inro*, the black lacquer ground carved with *karakusa*, pewter clasps, signed 'Tsuchida Soetsu', damaged, 17thC, 2½in (6.5cm) long.
£1,300–1,500 *S*

A three-case *inro*, inlaid with tortoiseshell, the cord runners of silver and the interior of *nachiji*, slight damage, unsigned, 17thC, 2½in (6.5cm) high.
£650–750 *S*

A wood two-case *inro*, decorated in gold, silver and black, late 19thC, 2½in (6.5cm) high, and a ivory *netsuke*, damaged, 18thC.
£750–900 *CAm*

A gold lacquer four-case *inro*, decorated with huts among pine and wisteria in a rocky landscape, the reverse with a waterfall, restored, 18thC, 3in (7.5cm) high.
£600–700 *CSK*

A four-case *inro*, decorated in gold, pewter and mother-of-pearl, unsigned, slight wear, 18thC, 3in (7.5cm) high.
£1,300–1,500 *S*

A silver ground four-case *inro*, decorated after painting by Hogen Hakugyoku, signed 'Jokasai', early 19thC, 3½in (9cm) high, with silvered metal *ojime*.
£12,000–14,000 *S*

A black lacquered four-case *inro*, by Kajikawa Hidetaka, late 18thC, 3in (7.5cm) high.
£2,500–3,000 *S*

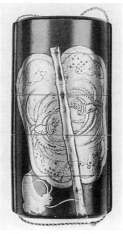

A gold lacquer four-case *inro*, the *fundame* ground decorated in grey, black and gold *takamakie* with a hawk tethered to a perch, signed 'Nikkosai', 19thC, 3½in (9cm) long.
£1,200–1,400 *CSK*

gold lacquer ur-case *inro* and tsuke, both signed ajikawa saku', ith red *koro* seal, rly 19thC, *inro* ½in (9cm) high.
,800–2,000 *S*

A gold lacquer four-case *inro*, decorated with pagodas, pine and willow trees and a mountainous river landscape, early 19thC, 3in (7.5cm) long, and a jadeite *ojime*.
£900–1,100 *CSK*

A *roironuri* ground lacquer four-case *inro*, decorated with fans depicting a coiled dragon, a tiger and confronting *ho-o*, interior in *nashiji*, worn, early 19thC, 3½in (9cm) high.
£550–650 *CSK*

A four-case *inro*, decorated in gold *togidashi, takamakie, kirigane* and gold leaf, with a flight of cranes above a ship, signed 'Kajikawa saku', 19thC, 3.5in (9cm), with a lacquer *hako-netsuke*, showing a ferry boat.
£2,500–3,000 *S*

wood four-case *inro*, ecorated in gold kamakie with peony owers issuing from erced rockwork, the everse with a butterfly, e interior black lacquer, gned 'Gyokushunsai', thC, 3½in (9cm) high.
00–600 *CSK*

A lacquer five-case *inro*, with a *kinji* ground, decorated with a cart filled with flowers, scratched, with coral bead *ojime*, and lacquer *netsuke*, chipped, 19thC, 3½in (9cm) high.
£850–1,000 *S(NY)*

wood three-case *inro*, the form of a turtle, ith inset eyes, nsigned, 19thC, n (10cm) long.
00–800 *CSK*

A wood three-case *inro*, decorated in relief and lacquered with an eagle perched on rocks, damaged, 19thC, 3½in (9cm) high.
£350–400 *S(S)*

A gold lacquer two-case *inro*, decorated with horses, on a *nashiji* ground, restored, 19thC, 2½in (6.5cm) high.
£450–550 *CSK*

A gold and black lacquer four-case *inro*, with a brass *ojime* and wood mask *netsuke*, 19thC, 3½in (9cm) high.
£650–750 *CSK*

A gold lacquer five-case *inro*, decorated with buildings on river banks and in mountainous landscapes, the interior in *nashiji*, rubbed, 19thC, 3½in (9cm) long.
£750–900 *CSK*

A cherry bark three-case inro, inlaid in ivory, horn and mother-of-pearl, 19thC, 3¼in (8.5cm) long.
£1,200–1,400 *C*

An inlaid lacquer two-case inro, 19thC, 5in (12.5cm) high.
£4,500–5,000 *S(NY)*

A gold lacquer five-ca inro, with metal inlay signed 'Kakosai Shoza 19thC, 4in (10cm) hig netsuke in the form of peaches and a ladybir
£8,500–10,000 *S*

A four-case *inro*, with a rich dark brown ground, decorated in gold *takamakie* and inlaid mother-of-pearl, signed 'Koma Kyuhaku saku', 19thC, 3in (8cm) high.
£9,500–11,000 *S*

A six-case *inro*, with bright red ground, signed 'Jokasai', 19thC, 4in (10cm) high, plain *ojime*, signed 'Yoyusai'.
£18,000–20,000 *S*

A lacquer five-case *inro*, decorated in gold with warriors in combat, signed 'Kajikawa saku' with seal, with an ivory *netsuke*, early 19thC, 3½in (8.5cm) high.
£3,500–4,000 *S(NY)*

A *guri* lacquer four-cas inro, the interior of bla lacquer, unsigned, earl 19thC, 4in (11cm) high
£2,500–3,000 *S*

A gold, silver and coloured *takamakie* four-case *inro*, the interior of *nashiji*, signed 'Jukakusai Hisataka', with 'kao', 19thC, 3½in (9cm) high.
£2,500–3,000 *S*

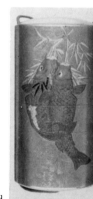

A black lacquer four-case *inro*, in the style of Shibata Zeshin, decorated in relief with Futen carrying his sack of wind, the interior of *kinji* and *nashiji*, unsigned, 19thC, 3in (8cm) high.
£2,200–2,500 *S*

A three-case *inro*, of stitched cherry bark, decorated with a gold and red *takamakie* mask, inlaid with enamelled pottery, slight damage, signed 'Narisoku', 19thC, 3in (7.5cm) high.
£1,700–2,000 *S*

A gold lacquer five-case inro, decorate with bamboo and f signed 'Yasushige saku', 19thC, 4in (10cm) high.
£2,500–3,000 *S*

A four-case *inro*, decorated in gold and coloured *takamakie*, the interior of *nashiji*, damaged, unsigned, 19thC, 3½in (9cm) high, with wood *netsuke*, signed 'Tokoku'.
£1,700–2,000 *S*

A gold lacquer four-case *inro*, decorated with Daikoku and Ebisu as Manzai dancers in gold and coloured *takamakie*, inlaid with silver, the metal *ojime*, signed 'Nikkosai', 19thC, 3½in (9cm) high.
£1,700–2,000 *S*

A gold lacquer five-case *inro*, some wear and losses to *kirigane*, signed 'Kansai ga', 19thC, 3½in (9cm) high.
£2,500–3,000 *S*

A gold lacquer four-case *inro*, with ivory *netsuke* of a *minogame* stalking a crab appearing from inside a clam, damaged, unsigned, 19thC, 4in (10cm) high.
£1,200–1,500 *S*

A gold lacquer five-case *inro*, decorated with prunus, 19thC, 3¾in (9.5cm) long, and a *netsuke* of Hotei.
£1,700–2,000 *S(Am)*

A gold lacquer three-case *inro*, decorated with a wasp on a plant, 19thC, 2½in (6.5cm) long.
£1,200–1,500 *S*

A brown lacquer four-case *inro*, decorated in gold and inlaid with mother-of-pearl, 19thC, 3½in (9cm) long.
£1,700–2,000 *C*

An ivory four-case *inro*, decorated in gold lacquer inlaid in coral, mother-of-pearl and tortoiseshell, Meiji period, 4in (10cm) high.
£1,700–2,000 *S(NY)*

An ivory *inro*, in the form of a jar, inlaid in mother-of-pearl, tortoiseshell and stained ivory, repaired, signed 'Meishun', Meiji period, 4¾in (12cm) high.
£1,800–2,000 *S(NY)*

A single-case *inro*, damaged, 19thC, 3in (7.5cm) wide.
£1,200–1,500 *C*

An *inro*, signed 'Komin', 19thC, 3½in (9cm) high.
£2,500–3,000 *HAM*

A kiriwood two-case *inro*, decorated in gold and black after Shibata Zeshin, late 19thC, 3in (8cm) high.
£3,500–4,000 *S*

Netsuke

A wood *netsuke* of a mythical lion dog, by Nobukatsu, late 18thC, 1¾in (4.5cm) high.
£800–1,000 *S*

An ivory *netsuke* of a *shishi*, its mouth open and containing a loose ball, the ivory is slightly worn and bears a rich patina, unsigned, 18thC, 2in (5cm) high.
£700–800 *S*

A Kurogaki wood *netsuke* figure of a man-faced *kirin*, the eyes of ivory with pupils of dark and light horn, slightly worn, unsigned, 18thC, 4¼in (11cm) high.
£1,200–1,500 *S*

An ivory *netsuke*, carved as a frog wrapped in a lotus leaf with a snail on top, late 18thC, 2in (5cm) wide.
£250–300 *CSK*

An ivory *netsuke* of a *shishi*, one paw supported on a ball, ivory worn, unsigned, late 18thC, 2in (5cm) high.
£1,700–2,000 *S*

The model is recorded as having been carved by Okatomo, Okatori and others of the Kyoto school, during the late 18thC.

An ivory *netsuke* of Kinko on his carp, by Masatsugu of Osaka, seated on the back of the carp, reading a calligraphic scroll, the ivory slightly worn and bearing good colour, signed in an oval reserve, early 19thC, 2½in (6cm) high.
£800–1,000 *S*

A wood *netsuke* of a tiger, the wood slightly worn and the eyes inlaid, signed 'Kokei', early 19thC, 1½in (4cm) high.
£2,200–2,500 *S*

A boxwood *netsuke* of a wolf and a hare caught under the wolf's paw, eyes inlaid in horn, inscribed 'Tomotada', 18thC, 1⅜in (3.5cm) high.
£500–600 *C*

An ivory *netsuke* of a recumbent *karashishi*, 18thC, 2in (5cm) long.
£500–600 *C*

A wood *netsuke* of a cat, seated on a circular mat, the eyes inlaid with pale translucent horn, the wood slightly worn, unsigned, early 19thC, 2in (5cm) high.
£1,700–2,000 *S*

Two lacquered wood mask *netsuke*, one of a Ranryo variant with dragon headdress in red and gold, the other of Shishiguchi, in Negoro style, the eyes and teeth of gold lacquer, the reverse of *roiro*, the first signed 'Koshin', early 19thC, 1½in (4cm) high.
£700–800 *S*

A lacquered wood *netsuke* of a *karashishi* on a pierced brocade ball, 19thC, 1⅝in (4cm) diam.
£200–250 *CSK*

An ivory *netsuke* of 3 figures, signed Tomochika, 19thC, 2in (5cm) high.
£650–750 *C*

An ivory *netsuke* of Momotaro, signed 'Mitsuyuki', 19thC, 2in (5cm) high.
£500–600 *C*

A carved ivory *netsuke* of a man with a kiln, 19thC, 1¾in (4.5cm) high.
£65–75 *PC*

A wood *netsuke*, signed 'Shoraku', 19thC, 1½in (4cm) high.
£700–800 *C*

A buffalo horn *netsuke*, modelled as a standing figure of Hotei lifting a sack containing a boy, old wear, 19thC, 2in (5cm) high.
£450–500 *CSK*

A large ivory *manju netsuke*, carved in deep relief with 2 *tennin* wearing flowing robes and celestial scarves, one holding a lotus and necklace, the other beating a drum with 2 sticks, the reverse with a pine tree, signed 'Insai', 19thC, 3in (7.5cm) diam.
£650–750 *CSK*

An ivory *netsuke* of an ox, with a girl by its side, signed, 19thC, 2in (5cm) wide.
£350–400 *CSK*

An ivory *netsuke* of a spider on a melon, with a vine leaf and bud, 19thC, 1⅝in (4cm) wide.
£450–500 *S(S)*

An ivory *netsuke* of a blind man, straining to lift a large stone, the details in red, signed on a rectangular reserve 'Ryoun', 19thC, 1½in (4cm) high.
£500–600 *CSK*

r. An ivory *netsuke* of Onna Daruma, seated on a removable circular mat, signed 'Mitsutsugu', 19thC, 1½in (4cm) high.
£650–750 *S(S)*

Two ivory *netsuke*, one carved with Konoha Tengu, signed 'Gyokugi', the other of a fishergirl, signed 'Gyokkosai', 19thC, 2in (5cm) high.
£650–750 *S*

A wood mask *netsuke*, carved with a smiling expression, signed, and another mask *netsuke* with grimacing expression and protruding teeth, 19thC, 1½in (4cm) high.
£250–300 *CSK*

A boxwood *netsuke*, carved as a bird emerging from an egg, by Hara Shumin, signed, 19thC, 1½in (4cm) wide.
£1,300–1,500 *HSS*

An ivory *netsuke*, modelled as a reclining *karashishi* and cub, on an oval base, the details well defined and eyes inlaid in horn 19thC, 1½in (4cm) wide.
£350–400 *CSK*

A *kagamibuta* wood netsuke, the bronze disc decorated in *hirazogan, takazogan* and gilt with 2 women with a scroll, signed 'Mitsuharu', 1in (3cm) diam, and an oval bronze flint *netsuke*, the hinged lid opening to reveal a striker, 19thC, 1½in (4cm) wide.
£600–700 *CSK*

Three painted wood *netsuke*, carved in Ittobori technique in the style of Toen, modelled as standing figures of actors wearing long wigs, robes and masks minor wear, all signed, 19thC, 2½in (6.5cm) high.
£350–400 *CSK*

A *kagamibuta,* the horn bowl bearing a gold plate, carved and inlaid with a squirrel leaping towards a hanging grapevine with large leaves in silver, copper and *shakudo takazogan*, signed on reverse 'Jitokusai saku', 19thC, 1½in (4cm) diam.
£1,300–1,500 *S*

Three mask *netsuke*, the first of red lacquer, depicting a smiling man, the second of Negoro style lacquer, depicting Shishiguchi, the eyes of gold lacquer, the third of stoneware, depicting Daikoku, his hat glazed dark green, impressed 'Sekisen', 19thC, 1½in (4.5cm) high.
£650–750 *S*

A *kagamibuta*, the wood bowl bearing a silver plate, carved in relief with a tiger standing on a rock beneath a waterfall, details in gold, signed on a gilt tablet, 'Toju', 19thC, 2in (5cm) high.
£650–750 *S*

A *kagamibuta*, the bowl of walrus ivory, the solid gold plate delicately carved in relief with butterflies among flowering cherry, the bowl signed in relief 'Tomin', 19thC, 1½in (4cm) diam.
£1,300–1,500 *S*

An ivory *netsuke* of a woman, by Ueda Kohosai of Osaka, the ivory slightly stained, one finger damaged, signed, 19thC, 1½in (4cm) high.
£1,300–1,500 *S*

A wood *netsuke* of a puppy, by Masanao of Ise, Yamada, holding the cord of a discarded sandal in its mouth, the wood stained and the eye pupils inlaid, signed, 19thC, 1½in (4cm) high.
£500–600 *S*

Japanese Terms

For a full explanation of the terms used in Japanese works of art, readers are referred to *Netsuke Familiar and Unfamiliar*, and *The Inro Handbook*, both by Raymond Bushell, published by John Weatherhill Inc, both of which are full of valuable information. Please also refer to the Glossary on page 313 of this book.

A wood *netsuke* of a turtle, by Hideharu of Nagoya, the wood stained and the eyes inlaid, signed in a rectangular reserve, 19thC, 2in (5cm) wide.
£1,800–2,000 *S*

A Kyoto school ivory *netsuke* of a dog, the eyes inlaid, slightly worn, unsigned, 19thC, 2in (5cm) high.
£600–700 *S*

A wood *netsuke*, in the form of a *ho-o* bird, by Toyokazu of Tamba, carved and pierced in crisp detail, signed, 19thC, 1½in (4cm) diam.
£850–1,000 *S*

A wood *netsuke* of a woman, by Masanao of Ise, Yamada, the wood slightly worn, good patina, signed, 19thC, 1½in (4cm) high.
£850–1,000 *S*

A carved ivory *netsuke* of a snowman, by Karaku of Osaka, the eyes inlaid, hand prints on the body, slightly worn, signed, 19thC, 2in (5cm) high.
£850–1,000 *S*

An ivory *netsuke* of a mother and child, by Kikugawa family, signed, Edo period, 19thC, 1½in (4cm) high.
£600–700 *S*

A coloured ivory *netsuke* of a *ronin*, by Takamura Koun, the warrior seated on a camp stool, wearing formal dress, partly painted and with inlaid details, signed on a red lacquer tablet, Meiji period, 1½in (4cm) high.
£1,200–1,400 *S*

A coral group *netsuke* of divers, by Ryukosai Jugyoku of Edo, with traces of green pigment, signed on a green stained ivory tablet, 19thC, 1½in (4cm) high.
£1,200–1,400 *S*

A coloured ivory *netsuke* of Hotei, by Yasuaki (Homei), stained red and with inlaid decoration, other details of mother-of-pearl, horn and metal, signed on a pearl tablet, Meiji period, 1½in (4cm) high.
£1,000–1,200 *S*

r. A coloured ivory *netsuke* of a sake seller, by Tomei, with painted details, inlaid with various materials, signed on a red lacquer tablet, Meiji period, 2in (5cm) high.
£700–800 *S*

A stained ivory *netsuke*, carved as a snail crawling over a roof tile, signed, 19thC, 2in (5cm) high.
£500–600 *CSK*

An ivory *netsuke*, modelled as a figure of Daikoku holding a large sack beside him, 19thC, 1½in (4cm) high.
£350–400 *CSK*

A wood *netsuke*, modelled as 2 *hozuki*, 19thC, 1½in (4cm) long.
£450–500 *CSK*

A stag antler *netsuke*, carved as an insect-eaten lotus leaf, an iron and gilt spotted frog perched in the leaf's hollow centre, 19thC, 4in (10cm) diam.
£500–600 *S(NY)*

A lacquered wood *netsuke*, in the form of a filleted fish, decorated with brown lacquer, the flesh in red, 19thC, 4¼in (11cm) long.
£500–600 *P*

A wood *netsuke*, depicting the priest Kensu, gaping at a prawn in one hand, the eyes inlaid in dark horn, chipped, 19thC, 2in (5cm) high.
£850–1,000 *C*

A *kagamibuta,* the ivory bowl carved and pierced, details in gold, silver and *shibuichi*, the bowl signed 'Ikkeisai Hogyoku' with 'kao', 19thC, 2in (5cm) diam.
£500–600 *S*

A wood *netsuke* of a horse, with a blanket tied to its girth, nicks to top of tail and *himotoshi*, unsigned, 19thC, 2in (5cm) high.
£1,000–1,200 *S(NY)*

Cleaning

Netsuke are generally made of wood or ivory, and can be cleaned first with a soft toothbrush. Ivory can then be cleaned with natural lanolin, although this must be wiped off after a short while to avoid the material becoming sticky. *Inro* and other lacquer wares should only be cleaned by an expert.

A wood study of a snail, signed with *ukibori* characters 'Odawara ju Shigeharu', 19thC, 1½in (4cm) high.
£1,800–2,000 *S*

A boxwood *netsuke* of 5 turtles, in the style of Chuichi (Tadakazu), one forming a base for the others to clamber upon, their eyes inlaid, unsigned, 19thC, 2in (5cm) high.
£750–900 *S*

A wooden *netsuke* of Jurojin and a deer, signed 'Shoko', late 19thC, 1¾in (4.5cm) wide.
£650–750 *C*

An ivory *netsuke* group of Oni Nembutsu and son, by Gyokusei of Edo, the ivory stained, signed 19thC, 1½in (4cm) high.
£700–800 *S*

An ivory *netsuke* of a baby boy, by Toshimune, the ivory stained, signed on an oval tablet, Edo period, late 19thC, 2in (5cm) high.
£750–850 *S*

A *kagamibuta,* the *tagasayan* wood bowl bearing a gold plate hammered in relief, signed 'Yoshiteru saku', 19thC, 1½in (4cm) high.
£2,500–3,000 *S*

A *kagamibuta,* the bowl carved in relief in Chinese style, inlaid in silver and gold *takazogan,* signed 'Ichijo saku', 1½in (4cm) high.
£1,800–2,000 *S*

A set of 3 ivory *netsuke*, carved as the Three Mystic Apes, Iwazaru, Kikazaru and Mizaru, 2 signed 'Masatami' (Shomin), late 19thC, 1½in (4cm) high.
£1,700–2,000 *C*

A marine ivory *netsuke*, of a coiled snake resting on a skull, late 19thC, 1½in (4cm) long.
£250–300 *CSK*

A boxwood mask *netsuke* of Bugatu, signed 'Hozan', inscribed 'Shichi ju sai, aged 71', late 19thC, 1½in (4cm) high.
£350–400 *CSK*

A wooden tobacco pouch *ojime* and *netsuke,* the turtles' eyes inlaid in dark horn, signed, late 19thC, pouch 4in (10cm) long.
£1,200–1,400 *CSK*

An ivory *netsuke* of a man holding a bear, the animal's head turned, the details stained black, minor chips, signed, 2in (5cm) high.
£170–200 *CSK*

An ivory *netsuke* of a Pekingese dog, 19thC, 3½in (9cm) long.
£850–1,000 *C*

An ivory *netsuke* of a man and boy, making a model *karashishi* and brocade ball, signed 'Gyokoku', 2in (5cm) long.
£300–350 *CSK*

A carved ivory *netsuke* of a monkey, signed, late 19thC, 1½in (4cm) high.
£500–600 *PC*

A carved ivory *netsuke* of figures on a raft, late 19thC, 1½in (4cm) high.
£80–100 *PC*

CHINESE IVORY

A pair of ivory panels, carved in relief with boys and figures holding flags among flowering lotus branches, 19thC, 7in (18cm) wide.
£1,500–1,700 *CSK*

An ivory mountain group, deeply carved with figures crossing a bridge over a stream below further figures in conversation, and a retreat among scattered pine and crags, 19thC, 8in (20.5cm) high, on a wood stand.
£700–800 *CSK*

An ivory monk's cap-shaped jug and cover, carved with insects among peony and other foliage issuing from rockwork, the handle and body with lines of calligraphy, slight damage, Qianlong four-character mark and of the period, 4in (10cm) high.
£1,200–1,400 *CSK*

An ivory wrist rest, carved in relief with boys playing among pine trees and rockwork, 19thC, 7in (18cm) wide, on a wood stand.
£250–300 *CSK*

An ivory brush pot, carved in relief with a continuous band of figures seated at a table, and figures mounted on an ox and a horse, minor age cracks, 19thC, 4⅛in (11.5cm) high.
£1,000–1,200 *CSK*

r. A carved ivory figure of a sage, with red, blue and gilt decoration, on shaped base, 19thC, 9½in (24cm) high.
£500–600 *BWe*

A Canton ivory hinged box and cover, carved with panels of numerous figures in gardens at various activities, below pine and wisteria, and before further figures in pagodas, slight damage, 19thC, 10in (25.5cm) wide.
£800–1,000 *CSK*

l. A sectional ivory group carving of a battle scene, 19thC, 46in (117.5cm) wide, on wood base with pierced balustrade.
£5,000–6,000 *CSK*

JAPANESE IVORY

An *okimono* of a lady, signed 'Tomochika' and 'Kakihan' late 19thC, 7in (17.5cm) high.
£600–700 *C*

A carving of a man, signed 'Toshimitsu', Meiji period, 7in (18cm) high.
£1,200–1,400 *C*

An ivory group of musicians, 19thC, 3½in (9cm) high.
£450–550 *CSK*

A marine ivory carving of Shoki, the reverse with a lady pouring sake for a skeleton, late 19thC, 4½in (11.5cm) high.
£350–400 *C*

An ivory figure group, depicting warriors in a circle, some damage, signed, c1900, 5in (12.5cm) high.
£700–800 *RBB*

An ivory carving of a figure holding a bird of prey, signed on a red lacquer tablet, late Meiji period, 6in (15cm) high.
£250–300 *CSK*

Japanese Ivory

In 1887 the Tokyo Chokokkai (Tokyo Sculpture Association) was established. This revitalised the ivory-carving industry, setting new standards. Exceptional carvings were created, mainly for the European and North American markets.

A sectional ivory carving of a farmer, with bundles of sticks on his back, a bird in a bird's nest in his left hand, signed 'Gyokushi', late 19thC, 16½in (42cm) high.
£3,500–4,000 *CSK*

An ivory carving of a man, with a tobacco pipe in his left hand and a pouch in his right, signed on a red lacquer tablet, Hideyuki wood stand, late 19thC, 13in (33cm) high.
£2,500–3,000 *CSK*

An ivory *okimono* of Kanyu and Chohi, c1900, 3in (7.5cm) high.
£500–600 *HSS*

An ivory *okimono* of a lady peering into the ear of a grimacing man, signed 'Munehiro', late Meiji period, 2in (5cm) long.
£700–800 *CSK*

A wood and ivory group of a street entertainer and his assistant, signed, Meiji period, 9in (23cm) high.
£1,500–1,700 *WW*

An ivory *okimono* of Kakkio
and his family, late 19thC,
3in (7.5cm) high.
£700–800 *HSS*

l. An ivory *okimono*
of Tenku emerging
from an egg,
late Meiji period,
4in (10cm) wide.
£250–300 *HSS*

A Japanese ivory carving of a
warrior, mounted on a rearing
stallion, the details stained
black, sword missing, old
damage, Meiji period,
5in (12.5cm) long, with stand.
£700–800 *CSK*

An ivory group of a standing
sage holding a staff in one
hand and stroking his
beard, looking at a butterfly
on a palm tree, details
stained black, signed on red
lacquer reserve 'Kogyoku',
late Meiji period,
5⅓in (14cm) high.
£600–700 *CSK*

An ivory vase and cover, carved
in high relief with quail and millet,
the quail with stained plumage,
some cracks, signed on a mother-
of-pearl tablet 'Yoshikazu,
Meiji period, 7in (18cm) high.
£2,500–3,000 *S*

l. An ivory carving
of a kneeling man,
with a woman and
child, Meiji period,
10in (25.5cm) long,
on wood stand.
£800–900 *S(S)*

A pair of ivory vases, carved
in relief with a monkey
trainer, Meiji period,
10½in (26.5cm) high.
£1,800–2,000 *S*

r. An ivory
okimono,
modelled as
a skull, with a
toad and young
crouched on top,
the eyes inlaid
in horn and
details well-
defined, signed,
Meiji period,
2in (5cm) high.
£600–700 *CSK*

r. A Tokyo School carved ivory
figure of a boy, slight damage,
Meiji period, 11½in (29cm)
high, on a wood stand.
£1,600–1,800 *Bea*

An ivory group of bananas, by
Sanshu, the fruit attached to a stem,
signed, Meiji period, 7in (18cm) wide.
£1,500–1,700 *S*

An ivory *okimono* of a
man, with a boy on his
back and another at his
feet holding a rabbit,
signed 'Atsumochi', Meiji
period, 31in (78cm) high.
£4,500–5,000 *S*

An ivory *okimono* of a seated scholar,
the details stained black, signed,
late 19thC, 3in (7.5cm) high.
£700–800 *CSK*

An ivory and lacquer carving
of a leaping carp, flexed upon
its tail, the head ivory, gills
and fins finely rendered,
its body painted to simulate
scales, repaired, Meiji period,
6in (15cm) high.
£1,200–1,400 *S(S)*

A Japanese ivory box and cover,
with flowerhead finial carved
in relief with flowering
chrysanthemums and peony
among foliage, signed, late
Meiji period, 3in (8cm) high.
£450–500 *CSK*

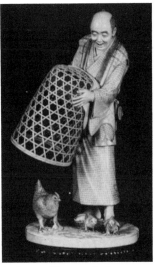

An ivory *okimono* of a farmer,
the details incised and slightly
stained, damaged, signed
'Shomin', Meiji period, 11½in
(29cm) high, with a wood stand.
£4,000–4,500 *S*

An ivory *okimono* of a farmer, with a boy
standing before a basket and boxes, slight
damage, signed on a red lacquer tablet,
late Meiji period, 3in (7.5cm) wide.
£600–700 *CSK*

A Japanese sectional ivory carving of a farmer,
light damage, signed, Meiji period, 15in (38cm) long.
£1,000–1,200 *CSK*

An ivory carving of a
woodcutter, signed,
late Meiji period,
6in (15cm) high.
£250–300 *CSK*

An ivory model of a
Kakemono, by Hidemasa of
Osaka, opening to reveal a
seated Okame, signed, early
19thC, 2½in (6.5cm) high.
£800–1,000 *S*

An ivory *okimono* rat catcher, the details stained black, slight damage, signed, Meiji period, 3in (7.5cm) wide.
£1,000–1,200 *CSK*

An ivory model of a basket seller, his wares slung across his shoulder on a bamboo pole, some old damage, signed 'Hotoda', late 19thC, 14in (36cm) high.
£3,500–4,000 *C*

An ivory group, signed 'Jogyoku', late 19thC, 8½in (21.5cm) wide.
£2,500–3,000 *C*

An ivory sectional group of 2 boys at play, slight damage and minor restoration, signed 'Biho', Meiji period, 6½in (16.5cm) high.
£1,700–2,000 *S*

Ivory Carving

Where possible, ivory figures were carved from a single piece of ivory. Some of the more intricate carvings, however, are made up of separate pieces (sectional ivory). Ivories have greater value if intricately carved from a single piece.

An ivory carving, age cracks and old damage, signed 'Masanobu', c1900, 5in (12.5cm) high.
£400–450 *CSK*

An ivory carving of a fisherman and boy, Meiji period, 8½in (21.5cm) high.
£2,200–2,500 *C*

An ivory figure of a man examining fruit from a basket, a bird at his feet, Meiji period, 11in (28cm) high.
£480–520 *PC*

An ivory carving of a young warrior, signed, late Meiji period, 8in (20.5cm) high.
£2,500–3,000 *CSK*

An ivory model of a peach seller and child, slight damage, signed 'Ikkosai Shizuhide', late 19thC, 10½in (26.5cm) high.
£2,500–3,000 *C*

A *shibayama*-style carving of a caparisoned elephant, Meiji period, 6in (15cm) long.
£3,400–4,000 *C*

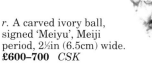

r. A carved ivory ball, signed 'Meiyu', Meiji period, 2½in (6.5cm) wide.
£600–700 *CSK*

A Chinese bronze ritual dish, encircled by 3 raised fillets below the lipped rim, the interior with a 'cartwheel' pictogram, late Shang Dynasty, 14in (35.5cm) diam.
£13,000–14,000 *S*

A Chinese carved grey stone figure of Bodhisattva, slightly polished surface, chipped, Tang Dynasty, 12in (30.5cm) high.
£17,500–18,500 *C*

A Chinese bronze ritual food vessel, with 2 handles, supported on 3 cylindrical legs, late Shang Dynasty, 6in (15cm) diam.
£4,500–5,000 *S*

A Chinese gilt-silver *hu*-shaped cup, the gilt handle comprising a studded ring and thumb flange, the neck gilded, Tang Dynasty, 11in (28cm) high.
£18,000–20,000 *C*

A Chinese bronze ritual wine vessel, the handles with *taotie* masks, a third *taotie* mask and loop handle set just above the base, Shang Dynasty, 13in (33cm) high.
£37,000–40,000 *S*

A Chinese bronze ritual vessel, cast with pairs of stylised dragons, the interior with a pictogram, late Shang/early Western Zhou Dynasty, 10in (25.5cm) high.
£34,000–38,000 *S*

A Chinese bronze covered vessel, with a figure pictogram on the interior of the lid, early Western Zhou Dynasty.
£3,500–4,500 *S*

A Chinese bronze ritual vessel and cover, damaged, inscribed on the interior and cover 'Gou zi', early Western Zhou Dynasty, 9½in (24cm) diam.
£26,000–28,000 *S*

l. A Chinese cast bronze ritual vessel, with stylised horned dragons against a *leiwen* ground, pictogram on the interior, late Shang/early Western Zhou Dynasty, 9in (23cm) high.
£20,000–25,000 *S*

A Chinese bronze wine vessel, the mid-section cast in shallow relief on a *leiwen* ground with *taotie* masks, Shang Dynasty, 11in (28cm) high.
£10,000–11,000 *C*

A Chinese cloisonné enamel archaistic bowl, the C-scroll handles issuing from gilt dragons' heads, 16thC, 10¼in (26cm) wide.
£2,750–3,000 *C*

A Chinese painted Canton enamel censer, with double upright gilt loop handles, on tripod feet, Yongzheng seal mark and of the period, 2¾in (7cm) high.
£5,700–6,300 *S(NY)*

A Chinese cloisonné enamel and gilt-bronze figure-form support, Kangxi period, 11½in (29cm) high.
£4,500–5,500 *S(NY)*

A Chinese enamel stem cup, the yellow ground decorated with flowers and butterflies, c1880, 8¼in (21cm) high.
£350–400 *DAN*

A Chinese cloisonné enamel censer, Qianlong period, 16in (40.5cm) high.
£2,000–2,200 *Wai*

A Chinese enamel hexagonal vase, decorated with flowers and birds on a blue ground, 19thC, 10¼in (26cm) high.
£350–400 *DAN*

A Chinese Canton enamel *zhadou,* with white enamelled interior, 18thC, 4in (10cm) high.
£1,600–1,800 *S(NY)*

A Chinese painted enamel sweetmeat tray and cover, the interior with a central dish surrounded by 8 small dishes, c1800, 14½in (37cm) diam.
£1,400–1,600 *CNY*

A Japanese flask, decorated in lacquer and pottery, with a seed *ojiime* and flask-form *netsuke,* 19thC, 4¾in (12cm) high.
£1,400–1,600 *S(NY)*

A Chinese pink and white overlay Peking glass lotus-form vase, with overlapping graduated finely veined petals, the base carved as a curling leaf and stem, 18thC, 4¼in (11cm) high.
£4,200–5,000 *S(NY)*

A Chinese reverse-painted and gilt glass picture, depicting an interior and 3 ladies with an old man, 19thC, in a later giltwood frame, 34¼ x 25½in (87 x 65cm).
£3,500–4,200 *C*

A Chinese cast gilt-bronze feline seal, with an eight-seal character inscription, slight damage, Eastern Han/Six Dynasties period, 3½in (9cm) long.
£11,000–13,000 S

A Chinese cloisonné enamel incense burner, damaged, Qianlong mark and of the period, 13½in (34.5cm) high.
£7,000–8,000 S

A Chinese Canton enamel clock, the French twin going barrel movement with anchor escapement and strike on bell, restored, mid-Qing Dynasty, 22in (56cm) high.
£8,500–11,000 C

A Chinese cloisonné enamel and gilt-bronze moon flask, with elaborate dragon handles, Qianlong period, 21in (53.5cm) high.
£4,700–5,200 C

A Chinese cloisonné enamel jardinière, with a copper liner and on a stand, Qing Dynasty, 20in (51cm) high.
£4,000–4,500 S

A Chinese cloisonné tripod *koro* and cover, with everted handles, gilt-metal interior, late 19thC, 10½in (26.5cm) high.
£6,500–7,000 C

A Chinese cloisonné tripod incense burner, on cabriole legs, 18thC, 15in (38cm) high.
£2,500–3,000 C

A Chinese gilt-bronze Buddha, wearing an open *dohti* and an openwork tiara, the hair with traces of blue pigment, 16thC, 9in (23cm) high.
£5,000–6,000 C

A Chinese cloisonné enamel five-piece altar garniture, comprising a tripod incense burner, 2 pricket candlesticks and 2 *gu* vases, Qianlong/Jiaqing period, tallest 22½in (57cm) high.
£6,000–7,000 C

A pair of Chinese gilt-bronze and cloisonné enamel incense burners and covers, 18thC, 18in (45.5cm) high.
£8,500–10,000 C

A Chinese lacquered and gilt-bronze Bodhisattva, 18½in (47cm) high.
£3,500–4,000 CSK

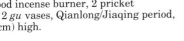

A Chinese censer and cover, painted in *famille rose* enamels with stylised lotus, detachable handles, damaged and restored, Qianlong mark and of the period, 22⅜in (57cm) high.
£8,500–10,000 *S*

A Chinese gilt-bronze-mounted cloisonné enamel bowl, decorated with flowers, Ming Dynasty, 16th/17thC, 7in (18cm) diam.
£5,000–6,000 *S*

A Chinese polychrome stone figure of a *lohan*, traces of pigmentation overall, Song Dynasty, 15in (38cm) high.
£5,000–6,000 *S*

A Chinese cast-bronze censer, decorated around the exterior with mythical sea creatures, traces of gilding, 17thC, 9in (23cm) diam.
£3,000–3,500 *S*

A Japanese gilt-bronze model of a cockerel, with gilt plumage, on wood rockwork base, signed 'Masatsune', Meiji period, 17½in (44.5cm) high.
£5,000–6,000 *S*

A Chinese cast-bronze tripod censer, with loop handles, Xuande mark within a recessed cartouche, 17thC, 10in (25.5cm) diam.
£5,000–6,000 *S*

A Chinese cloisonné censer and cover, Ming Dynasty, 21⅖in (54.5cm) high.
£5,000–6,000 *S*

A Chinese cloisonné enamel mythical beast, with a horn and beard, the rump overlaid with an armour-like shell, multi-cloven feet, slight damage and restoration, Qianlong four-character mark, 10in (25.5cm) long.
£16,500–18,000 *C*

A Chinese seated gilt-bronze figure of Buddha, wearing a gilded loose robe with engraved floral borders, Ming Dynasty, 11in (28cm) high.
£2,500–3,000 *S*

A Chinese carved stone head of Guanyin, with large long-lobed ears, on fitted stand, repaired Tang Dynasty, 11½in (29cm) high.
£11,000–15,000 *S*

A Japanese ormolu-mounted lacquer casket, with paw feet, lacquer 18thC, assembled early 19thC, 17in (43cm) wide.
£16,000–18,000 C

A Tibetan gilt-bronze figure of a deity, holding a *dhorje*, 17thC, 6in (15cm) high.
£2,500–3,000 DN

A Chinese wooden figure of Buddha, with traces of gilt and coloured floral decoration, early Ming Dynasty, repaired 38½in (98cm) high.
£4,500–6,000 C

A Chinese polychromed giltwood figure of Guanyin, traces of pigment and gesso, some damage, Song Dynasty, 37½in (95cm) high.
£100,000–120,000 C

A *kojubako*, with red *tsuba* seal, signed 'Kajikawa', 19thC, 5in (12.5cm) high.
£6,000–7,000 C

A Ryukyu Islands lacquer box, decorated with a Chinese court procession and pavilion, some restoration, 17thC, 29in (74cm) wide.
£5,000–6,000 C

A Japanese lacquer *kodansu*, with silver mounts, mid-19thC.
£2,000–2,500 DN

Two Japanese bronze and gilt censers, one of a seated Temple Guardian, signed 'Miyao zo', late 19thC, 28½in (72cm) high.
£11,500–12,500 C

A Japanese *Kon-ito-shia odishi domaru*, probably Myochin, 18th/19thC.
£9,000–10,000 C

A Canton enamel temple tripod incense burner and cover, with a Buddhistic lion finial, on monster mask legs, small restorations, Qianlong seal mark and of the period, 43½in (110cm) high.
£14,000–15,000 C

A group of 4 Chinese gilt-bronze figures of Daoist warrior Immortals, each standing on rockwork bases, wearing armour and robes, traces of lacquer and gilt on each, minor casting faults, Ming Dynasty, 7¼in (18.5cm) high.
£2,700–3,000 *CNY*

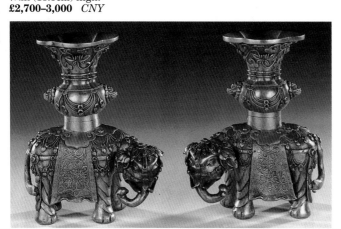

A pair of Chinese gilt-bronze candle holders, in the form of elephants wearing elaborate bridles and straps, the saddle blankets incised with scrolling lotus, restored and regilded, 18thC, 7in (18cm) high.
£3,000–3,300 *C*

A Japanese silver vase, carved with flowers highlighted in gilt, with flowerspray handles, Taisho period, 10in (25.5cm) high.
£7,000–7,700 *S(NY)*

A Japanese bronze figure of an elephant, on a hardwood stand, signed, 19thC, 13in (33cm) wide.
£700–800 *SPU*

A Japanese lacquered wood and ivory *okimono*, signed 'Saneaki', late 19thC, 11in (28cm) high.
£3,000–3,300 *S(NY)*

A Chinese export lacquered tea caddy, the top and sides decorated with panels depicting landscape scenes, c1830, 10in (25.5cm) wide.
£520–580 *SSW*

A Japanese gilt-bronze group, signed 'Miyao', late 19thC, 14½in (37cm) high.
£13,500–15,000 *S(NY)*

A Chinese bronze censer, with stylised beast handles, marked, 17thC, 5in (12.5cm) high.
£4,200–4,600 *C(HK)*

A Chinese export lacquered box, c1820, 4in (10cm) long.
£75–85 *SSW*

A Japanese bronze censer, decorated with archaistic motifs, signed 'Miyao', late 19thC, 54½in (138cm) high.
£16,500–18,000 *S(NY)*

A Chinese celadon jade *champion* vase and cover, Qianlong period.
£17,000–20,000 *C*

A Chinese jadeite figure of a maiden, wearing a robe, 8½in (21.5cm) high.
£2,500–3,500 *C*

A bronze figure of Guanyin, Song Dynasty, 9in (23cm) high.
£4,000–5,000 *C*

A Chinese pottery cocoon jar, the oviform body with waisted neck, Han Dynasty, 18½in (47cm) wide.
£3,000–3,500 *C*

A bronze wine vessel, Western Zhou Dynasty.
£33,000–40,000 *C*

A Chinese bronze group of Zhenwu, Ming Dynasty, 43in (109cm) high, with wooden stand.
£12,000–15,000 *C*

Two painted pottery Zodiac figures, slight damage, Six Dynasties, 9½in (24cm) high.
£4,000–5,000 *C*

A Chinese celadon and russet jade boulder, carved with 2 deer on a river bank, 18thC, 7½in (19cm) long, with wooden stand.
£4,500–5,000 *C*

A *sancai* pottery model of a horse, 20in (51cm) high. £11,000–13,000 *C*

A Dingyao floral dish incised with a single lotus stem, slight damage, Song Dynasty, 5½in (14cm) diam, with box.
£7,000–8,000 *C*

l. A Chinese jade recumbent bull, the mottled grey stone with scattered deep russet inclusions, minor damage, Ming Dynasty, 51½in (131cm) long, with wooden box and stand.
£6,500–8,000 *C*

A Yaozhou celadon bowl, the exterior incised with petal ribs, under a translucent celadon glaze suffused with bubbles, Song Dynasty, 8in (20.5cm) diam.
£10,000–12,000 *C*

A Chinese carved jade marriage bowl, the interior carved with butterflies, one ring restuck, Qianlong mark and of the period, 10½in (26.5cm) diam.
£10,000–12,000 *S*

A Chinese white jade table screen, carved with 3 scholars, a stream, fruiting peach and a pavilion in the distance, Qianlong period, on wood stand, 9½in (24cm) high.
£14,000–15,000 *S*

An ivory *okimono* of an umbrella seller, damaged, unsigned, Meiji period, 9in (23cm) high.
£1,000–1,500 *S*

A Chinese carved jade teapot and cover, with 2 Daoist Immortal figures, dragon mask and phoenix head handle, Ming Dynasty, 7in (18cm) high.
£3,000–4,000 *S*

A Japanese ivory *okimono* of a fisherman, tryng to prevent his catch falling from a broken basket, by Ryuho, Meiji period, signed, 8in (20.5cm) high.
£2,000–2,500 *S*

A Chinese carved ivory model of a barge, with a clinker hull and pierced panelled cabins, painted ivory figures playing cards, with crew members, flags and lanterns, minor damage, c1820, 16½in (42cm) long.
£12,000–13,000 *C*

A Chinese white jade *koro* and cover, carved and pierced with flowering peony on intertwining leafy stems, the footrim with 4 *ruyi* feet, slight damage, Qianlong period, 7in (18cm) diam.
£16,000–18,000 *S*

A set of 8 Chinese ivory figures of *lohans*, Xin Fingdeng, Wu Daxiang, Futuomiduo, Yi Xianchang, Bu Dong, You Boju Duo, Jiao Xingjie, and Yinianjiegong, 19thC, 16½in (42cm) high.
£5,500–6,000 *C*

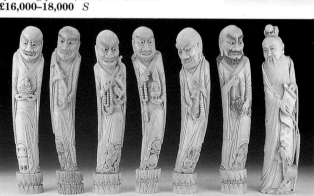

l. A set of 6 Chinese ivory figures of *lohans*, and La Zu, including Bao Jian, De Guang, Yinianjiegong, A Naxi and 2 others, 19thC, 22in (56cm) high.
£8,500–9,500 *C*

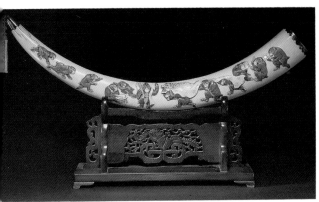

ivory tusk, carved in relief with monkeys dressed as *shishimai* and *nbaso* dancers, the reverse with lions and tigers fighting, on carved od stand, signed 'Kizawa', Meiji period, 36½in (92.5cm) wide. **,500–5,000** *S*

An ivory monkey, holding a fruit, signed in relief seal 'Ishikawa', Meiji period, 4½in (11.5cm) high. **£6,500–7,000** *S*

A Japanese lacquer and gold *tobako-bon*, minor chips, 19thC, 10in (25.5cm) high. **£3,500–4,500** *S*

A Japanese silver-mounted ivory and *shibayama* tankard, Meiji period. **£2,500–3,000** *S*

Chinese embellished gilt-bronze vase, st as 2 phoenix, Qianlong period, ½in (49.5cm) high. **,000–14,000** *C*

A gold lacquer two-case *inro*, by Shiomi Masanari, 19thC. **£12,000–14,000** *S*

A *suzuribako*, decorated in gold and silver, minor damage, 18th/19thC. **£3,500–4,500** *S*

pair of enamelled silver and *shibayama* ses, Meiji period, 13in (33cm) high. **,000–6,000** *S*

Below. A lacquer *kogo*, 19thC, 3in (7.5cm) wide. **£950–1,200** *S*

l. A Japanese gold lacquer box and cover, 19thC, 4in (10cm) wide. **£11,000–12,000** *S*

A Chinese Imperial gilt-bronze mirror, Qianlong period. **£2,600–3,000** *S*

A Japanese *komai*-style gilt-bronze and gold shrine, base marked 'Kusa', Meiji period. **£5,000–6,000** *S*

A Chinese speckled jadeite boulder, carved
with scholars in a garden, 4in (10cm) wide.
£1,200–1,500 *C*

r. A Chinese celadon jade mountain group,
flecked with russet, Kangxi period,
11in (28cm) high.
£8,000–10,000 *C*

A Chinese jade ewer
and cover, the stone
very even tones, 18th
8in (20.5cm) high.
£4,000–5,000 *C*

A Japanese *ikebana* vessel, in the form
of a glazed celadon boat, signed 'Makuzu
Kozan', Meiji period, 17in (43cm) long.
£4,000–5,000 *C*

A pair of black stone water buffalos,
with partially hollowed undersides,
late 17thC, 11½in (29cm) long.
£5,500–7,500 *CNY*

A silver and gilt-inlaid
bronze vase, minor dents,
17thC, 30in (76cm) high.
£4,000–5,000 *C*

A pair of bronze
vases, 19thC,
23in (58.5cm) high
£7,000–8,000 *C*

Two Chinese gilt-splashed bronze censers,
mid-Qing Dynasty, largest 12½in (32cm) high.
£2,500–3,500 *C*

l. A Japanese bronze vase,
marked, 9½in (24cm) high.
£3,500–4,000 *Bea*

r. A Chinese
bronze wine vessel,
Shang Dynasty,
8in (20.5cm) high.
£11,000–13,000 *C*

l. A Chinese archaic bronze two-
handled vessel, some damage and
malachite encrustation, Shang
Dynasty, 10in (25.5cm) wide.
£3,000–4,000 *C*

r. A Chinese archaic bronze food
vessel, worn in places, Shang
Dynasty, 14in (35.5cm) diam.
£13,000–14,000 *CNY*

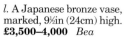

A Japanese silver and *shibuichi* box
and cover, decorated in gold wire
and translucent enamels, signed,
late 19thC, 5in (12.5cm) long.
£1,800–2,200 *C*

A Chinese gilt-bronze figure of
Wei To, 17thC, 9in (23cm) high.
£5,000–6,000 *C*

A Chinese Ming-style gilt copper
seated figure of Buddha,
with inscriptions, incised
Qianlong seven-character
mark, 12½in (32cm) high.
£3,500–4,500 *C*

A Japanese silver *kogo*, decorated in
takabori and gilt *takazogan*, signed
'Tetsuho sei', late 19thC, 3in (7.5cm) diam.
£7,500–9,000 *C*

A pair of archaic Ordos bronze openwork plaques, extensive
malachite encrustation, Warring States, 5in (12.5cm) long.
£4,500–5,500 *C*

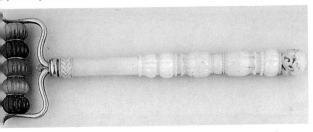

A Chinese celadon jade back massager, with
revolving beads of lapis lazuli, coral and jade,
mid-Qing Dynasty, 10½in (26.5cm) long.
£4,500–5,500 *C*

A pair of inscribed beaten gold lotus
cups, Tang Dynasty, 4in (10cm) diam.
£22,000–25,000 *C*

A Japanese *shibuichi migaki-ji kogo*
and cover, signed 'Isshuhoru',
late 19thC, 2½in (6.5cm) square.
£2,000–3,000 *C*

A Japanese iron box, decorated in *uchidashi*,
takabori and silver *takazogan*, late 19thC,
5in (12.5cm) wide.
£900–1,200 *C*

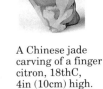

A Chinese jade
carving of a finger
citron, 18thC,
4in (10cm) high.
£1,500–1,800 *C*

A Chinese celadon jade sceptre, 18thC, 14in (35.5cm) long.
£3,500–4,500 *C*

A cloisonné enamel censer and
cover, 19thC. **£3,000–4,000** *C*

A Sino-Tibetan cloisonné
enamel *qilin*, Qianlong
period, 24in (61cm) high.
£9,000–10,000 *C*

A carved marbled lacquer stand,
minor damage, 17th/18thC,
9in (23cm) wide. **£4,000–5,000** *C*

A Chinese lacquer tray, some damage, late
19thC, 28½in (72.5cm) wide. **£25,000–28,000** *C*

A Chinese cloisonné enamel
bronze-mounted vase, early
19thC, 33⅓in (85cm) high.
£4,000–5,000 *C*

An enamelled silver *koro* and cover
minor damage, signed 'Hiratsuka',
late 19thC, 5½in (14cm) high.
£4,500–6,000 *C*

A lady's leather card case, with ivory spine and
covers, leather torn, unsigned, Meiji period.
£2,500–3,500 *C*

l. A Chinese
carved marbled
lacquer bowl,
15th/16thC,
7½in (19cm) wide.
£5,500–6,500 *C*

A lacquer dish, mid-Ming Dynasty.
£8,000–9,000 *C*

A Japanese
leather laced
armour, c1860.
£15,000–18,000 *C*

A pair of Japanese wooden sculptures, some
damage, Kamakura period, 19½in (49.5cm) high.
£55,000–60,000 *C*

A Chinese mirror painting, in George III-
style giltwood carved frame, mid-18thC.
£8,000–9,000 *C*

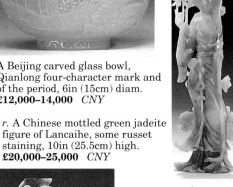

Chinese dragon dish,
aoguang seal mark and
the period, 6in (15cm)
am, in a fitted cloth box.
1,500–1,800 *CNY*

A Chinese *café-au-lait* glazed bowl,
Guangxu mark and
of the period, 4½in
(11.5cm) diam.
£800–950 *CNY*

A Beijing carved glass bowl,
Qianlong four-character mark and
of the period, 6in (15cm) diam.
£12,000–14,000 *CNY*

r. A Chinese mottled green jadeite
figure of Lancaihe, some russet
staining, 10in (25.5cm) high.
£20,000–25,000 *CNY*

pair of Chinese
rey-green jade
uyi sceptres,
7½in (44.5cm) long.
12,000–15,000 *CNY*

r. A Chinese
carved jadeite
group, damaged,
8in (20.5cm) high.
£8,000–9,500 *CNY*

A pair of Chinese jade bowls,
19thC, 8in (20.5cm) diam.
£4,000–4,500 *CNY*

far l. A Chinese gilt-
decorated jade vase, c1800,
8in (20.5cm) high.
£3,500–4,500
l. A Chinese jade beaker
vase, c1700, 9in (23cm) high.
£9,500–11,000 *CNY*

A Chinese jade vase
and cover, carved with
a tree and rocks, c1800,
11in (28cm) high.
£12,000–15,000 *CNY*

r. A Chinese jade
horse, Tang
Dynasty or later,
2in (5cm) long.
£5,000–6,500 *CNY*

Chinese two-colour jadeite group, depicting goats,
½in (16.5cm) long.
1,000–1,200 *CNY*

A Chinese jade model of a camel,
Song Dynasty, 3in (7.5cm) long,
with a wooden stand and a box.
£6,000–7,000 *CNY*

l & r. Two Chinese jade figures
of a man and a woman, 19thC,
largest 3in (7.5cm) high.
£1,500–2,000
c. A jade model of a horse, 3½in (9cm) long.
£2,500–3,000 *CNY*

A pale celadon jade censer, some natural flaws,
17th/18thC, 5in (12cm) square, wood stand.
£2,000–2,500 *C*

A vase and cover,
mid-Qing Dynasty,
9½in (24cm) high.
£12,000–15,000 *CHK*

A celadon jade double cylinder va
and cover, 18thC, 8in (20cm) hig
£25,000–30,000 *C*

A white jade tripod censer and cover, natural
flaw, Qianlong period, 7½in (19cm) wide.
£20,000–22,000 *C*

A celadon vase and cover, Qianlong
period, 14in (35.5cm) high.
£15,000–20,000 *CHK*

A jadeite ding and cover, incised Qianlon
four-character mark, 10½in (27cm) high.
£25,000–30,000 *CNY*

A celadon jade vase, Qing
Dynasty, 8in (21cm) high.
£3,500–4,000 *CHK*

A celadon and jade boulder
mountain, 17thC, 6in (15cm) high,
wooden stand and box.
£8,500–10,000 *C*

A pair of jade vases and covers,
19thC, 9in (23cm) high
£10,000–12,000 *CNY*

A celadon jade vase
and cover, 19thC,
10½in (26.5cm) high.
£2,500–3,000 *CHK*

An Imperial jade box and cover,
signed scroll dated '1821 AD',
Qianlong period.
£25,000–30,000 *CHK*

r. A jade pebble form mountain,
19thC, 5in (12.5cm) long.
£4,500–5,000 *CNY*

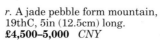

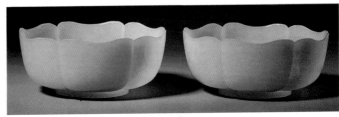

A pair of Chinese white jade flower-shaped bowls, with lobed sides and undulating rims, incised Qianlong four-character marks and of the period, 6in (15cm) diam.
£37,000–40,000 C

Canton enamel dish, restored, Qianlong period, n (20.5cm) diam.
80–450 S(NY)

Chinese cloisonné amel *meiping*, damaged, ing Dynasty, 16th/17thC, in (30.5cm) high.
,000–3,500 S

A cloisonné enamel beaker vase, the sides set with 4 vertical flanges, some damage, Ming Dynasty, 16in (40.5cm) high.
£3,200–3,600 S

A Ginbari cloisonné enamel vase, with silver rims, Meiji period, 12in (30.5cm) high.
£700–800 S(NY)

A jadeite two-handled vase and cover, late Qing Dynasty, 10¼in (26cm) high, on wooden stand.
£8,000–9,000 C

Chinese imitation gilt-bronze nser, the mark carved in relief ithin a countersunk square, ianlong period, 4¼in (11cm) diam.
2,000–13,500 S(HK)

A pair of Canton enamel dishes, decorated with European scenes, the rim with 5 shaped panels, Qing Dynasty, 13⅜in (34cm) diam.
£9,000–10,000 S

Japanese cloisonné namel vase, signed amura', Meiji period, 2¼in (31cm) high.
900–1,000 S(NY)

A pair of Japanese bronze vases, with *ho-o* bird handles, decorated in relief with raised panels of *kirin* and dragons, raised seal marks to base, c1900, 14in (35.5cm) high.
£1,200–1,500 CSK

A Japanese silver bowl, with everted rim, signed, late 19thC, 10½in (26.5cm) diam., on a carved hardwood stand.
£2,700–3,000 DN

A Japanese *roironuri* ground *inro-dansu*, old damage, unsigned, 19thC.
£35,000–40,000 *C*

A Japanese composite lacquer *sage-jubako*, some damage, 18thC, 12in (30.5cm) high.
£5,000–6,000 *C*

A Chinese export cabinet-on-stand, elaborately decorated, 17thC, 32in (81.5cm) high.
£35,000–40,000 *C*

A *Shibayama*-style *kodansu*, the silver ground carved in relief, minor restorations, signed on the *nashiji* ground base 'Masayoshi', late 19thC, 12in (30.5cm) high.
£25,000–30,000 *C*

A Japanese lacquered *palanquin*, the gold *hiramakie* on a *roironuri* ground, with gilt fittings, 19thC, the case 41½in (105.5cm) long.
£30,000–35,000 *C*

A Japanese composite lacquer *sage-jubako*, c1800, 9½in (24cm) high.
£3,500–4,500 *C*

l. A Japanese vase, signed 'Keishu ga', blue Satsuma *mon*, late 19thC, 24in (61cm) high.
£22,000–25,000 *C*

A Japanese lacquer vase and cover minor old damage, signed 'Sadatoshi', late 19thC, 10½in (26.5cm) high.
£12,000–15,000 *C*

CHINESE LACQUER WARE

... red lacquer box and cover, ...rved with 2 parakeets in ...ght among peonies and ...rysanthemums, chipped ...d cracked, Ming Dynasty, ...n (15cm) diam.
1,200–1,400 *CSK*

A red lacquer lobed box and cover, carved with a chrysanthemum medallion within circles of stylised petals enclosing lotus flowerheads, slight chips to rim, 18thC, 7in (18cm) diam.
£900–1,100 *C*

A red, green and cream three-tiered box with canted corners, containing smaller boxes and covers, within a red lacquer pierced container modelled as a table, the cover carved in relief with figures in pavilion gardens in a mountainous river landscape, within a band of key and cell pattern, old damage and restoration, Qianlong period, 7in (18cm) high.
£1,200–1,400 *CSK*

... cinnabar lacquer box and ...ver, the cover carved with ...gentlemen standing beneath a ...ne tree, the sides with a band ...f scrolling chrysanthemums, ...ianlong mark and of the ...eriod, 2½in (6.5cm) diam.
3,200–3,600 *C(HK)*

A red lacquer box and domed cover, slight damage, 18thC, 6½in (16.5cm) wide.
£750–850 *CSK*

A red lacquer box and related cover, slight crack to rim, 18thC, 3in (7.5cm) diam.
£450–500 *CSK*

Miller's is a price GUIDE not a price LIST

A red lacquer sewing box and cover, incised with figures in a landscape of trees, 19thC, 13in (33cm) diam.
£450–500 *RBB*

... pair of red lacquer boxes ...nd domed covers, decorated ...ith a panel of children at ...lay in a landscape on a ...ense diaper ground, 3in ...7.5cm) diam, and a shaped ...riangular red lacquer box ...nd cover, decorated with a ...ardinière of flowers, the ...ides with 'T' pattern, ...8th/19thC, 3½in (9cm) wide.
300–350 *CSK*

A black and gilt lacquered tea chest and hinged cover, cover repaired, 19thC, 13in (33cm) wide.
£1,600–1,800 *CNY*

A Chinese export gilt-decorated black lacquer needlework box, the interior fitted with lidded compartments and containing various ivory accoutrements, drawer to the base, early 19thC, 14in (35.5cm) wide.
£800–900 *P(S)*

A red lacquer bowl, the exterior carved with 2 striding dragons chasing a flaming pearl amid cloud swirls, the interior of dark brown lacquer, damaged, incised six-character Qianlong mark on the base, the footring added later, 11in (28cm) diam.
£4,000–4,500 *S(NY)*

A red lacquer foliate rimmed dish, carved with an Immortal and an attendant in a building among pine and bamboo issuing from rockwork, within a border of floral bands, damaged, 18thC, 8½in (21.5cm) wide.
£1,000–1,200 *CSK*

A lacquer dish, inlaid with mother-of-pearl and decorated with a pair of birds amid flowering peony branches issuing from rockwork, enclosed by a trellis pattern, the exterior decorated with a band of floral scrolls, Ming Dynasty, 8½in (21.5cm) diam.
£3,000–3,500 *C*

Chinese Lacquer Ware

Carved scenes in polychrome lacquer and mother-of-pearl inlay were popular in the Ming Dynasty, and red lacquer became popular later during the Qianlong period (1736–95). From the 16th century, Chinese lacquer was among the many luxury items exported to the West.

A red lacquer *ruyi* sceptre, carved in relief with the Eight Buddhist emblems among lotus and floral designs, the reverse with a 'T' pattern ground, 18th/19thC, 15½in (38cm) long.
£650–750 *CSK*

A set of 3 Chinese export lacquered trays, with crimson grounds, c1870, largest 22in (56cm) long.
£1,200–1,400 *CAT*

CHINESE WOOD

A Sino-Tibetan carved wood figure depicting Nahakala, with lacquer and gilt highlights, 17thC, 20½in (52cm) high.
£1,100–1,300 *LHA*

A wood figure of a seated official, wearing long robes, on a scrolling base, the head painted and gilt, damaged, Ming Dynasty, 27in (68.5cm) high.
£700–800 *CSK*

A pair of wood figures of standing Immortals, both on carved bases, damaged, late Ming Dynasty, 12in (30.5cm) high.
£500–600 *CSK*

r. A hardwood carving of Liu Hai, the jovial Immortal standing with his left leg resting on the back of his three-legged toad, base cracks, 19thC, 15in (38cm) high.
£450–550 *CNY*

A bamboo carving of a group of Buddhistic lions, damage, 18thC, 12½in (32cm) high.
£650–750 *CNY*

A wood carving of a standing figure, wearing long flowing robes, 18thC, 9½in (24cm) high, on a wooden stand.
£250–300 *CSK*

l. A bamboo carving of a mythical tree trunk raft, with an openwork fruiting and flowering branch growing from the gunwales of the hull, and small figures standing on the deck, small loss, 18thC, 8½in (21.5cm) long.
r. A bamboo carving of 2 happy figures holding auspicious attributes including a double-gourd, a turtle and a lotus stem, small chip, 18th/19thC, 7½in (19cm) high.
£1,700–1,900 *C*

A carved wood figure of a seated official, wearing a loosely draped gown and a hat, pigment on gesso, traces of gilt, damaged, Ming Dynasty, 33in (84cm) high.
£600–700 *SK*

A bamboo carving of a seated bearded Immortal, carrying a *ruyi* sceptre, on a pierced rockwork base, 19thC, 3in (7.5cm) wide.
£350–400 *CSK*

A pair of bamboo carvings of Buddhistic lions, playing with numerous cubs beside brocade balls and pierced rockwork, chipped, 19thC, 11in (28cm) high.
£500–550 *CSK*

A bamboo brush pot, carved with a panel of sages and musicians, the reverse with birds in prunus and bamboo, cracked, Daoguang mark and of the period, 3in (7.5cm) diam.
£650–750 *CSK*

An inscribed hardwood brush pot, carved in high relief with a topical, long prose inscription, the wood with a dark lacquered surface simulating *zitan*, and a small illegibly inscribed seal, 18th/19thC, 9in (23cm) high.
£1,500–1,800 *S(NY)*

A Chinese export painted wood tea box, c1830, 12in (30.5cm) wide.
£250–300 *Wai*

r. A hardwood box and cover, in the form of archaic jade, the cover carved with a central *shou* symbol within stylised scrolls and pomegranate, within shaped handles, 18th/19thC, 7in (18cm) wide.
£450–500 *CSK*

JAPANESE LACQUER WARE

A lacquer long document box, damaged, late 18th/early 19thC.
£450–550 *C*

r. A gold-lacquered *kodansu*, decorated in raised gilt with mother-of-pearl inlay, with silver coloured metal hinges and clasp, enclosing 3 drawers with tea dust lacquer interiors, with a signed mother-of-pearl plaque, damaged, 3in (7.5cm) wide.
£3,500–4,000 *HSS*

A black lacquer *zushi*, the 2 doors opening to reveal a giltwood throne with flame mandorla, with a Chinese soapstone seated figure of Guanyin wearing robes and holding a scroll and necklace, the details in black and red, damaged, 19thC, the *zushi* 18in (45.5cm) high.
£700–800 *CSK*

A black lacquer *zushi*, with brass mounts, the 2 doors opening to reveal a gilt interior fitted with a wooden standing Buddha on a lotus petal and rockwork base, slight damage, 19thC, 10in (25.5cm) high.
£250–300 *CSK*

A red, black and gold lacquer box and cover, with pewter rims, decorated in *hiramakie* with fan-shaped panels of bamboo, pine and mountainous landscapes, on a *nashiji* ground, 17thC, 3½in (9cm) long.
£800–950 *CSK*

A black and gold lacquer four-sided *kodansu*, with silver handles modelled as butterflies, each side fitted with sliding drawers decorated in *hiramakie* and scattered *nashiji*, one small door missing, some wear, 19thC, 4½in (11.5cm) square.
£350–400 *CSK*

A lacquered table box, Edo period, 12in (30.5cm) long.
£650–750 *WLi*

A lacquer tea cabinet, the fall-front door opening to 2 deep drawers beneath a pair of sliding grid-framed panels, Meiji period, 16½in (42cm) wide, with a black lacquered storage box.
£2,500–3,000 *S(NY)*

A rounded rectangular *Shibayama* box and cover, with silver rims, signed, Meiji period, 3in (7.5cm) wide.
£1,500–1,800 *P*

A lacquer writing box, decorated in gold and silver, with the original wood box bearing the seal of the Daimyo of Maeda, 19thC, 9½in (24cm) wide.
£10,000–12,000 *S(NY)*

A lacquer desk box, raised on 4 bracket feet, decorated with gold *hiramakie* on a black ground, 18thC, 10½in (26.5cm) wide.
£400–450 *SK*

A lacquer and burr elm calligraphy box, the cover decorated with a mountainous landscape, the underside of the lid with a design of flowering branches, the base fitted with compartments, an ink slate and gilt-bronze scroll paperweight, with a bamboo brush, some damage, 18th/19thC, 9 x 8½in (23 x 21.5cm).
£650–750 *Bea(E)*

A lacquer box and cover, decorated with Tokugawa *mon*, scrolling foliage and diaper panels on a red ground, the sides on a raised and textured ground, the interior fitted with one tray, late 19thC, 11in (28cm) wide.
£650–750 *DN*

A lacquer *shodana* with stand, with asymmetrical shelves, 2 sliding and 5 hinged doors, one curved, 3 drawers, decorated in gold *hiramakie*, *takamakie*, *togidashi* and *kirigane*, 19thC, 24in (61cm) wide, on a later stand.
£5,500–6,500 *S*

A black lacquer table cabinet, on conforming stand with 2 drawers, 19thC, 19½in (49.5cm) wide.
£1,000–1,200 *DN*

A Japanese export lacquer chest, the cover decorated in gold and inlaid in mother-of-pearl with birds and flowers, the sides and front with decorated panels, 2 drawers, damaged and restored, mid-17thC, 17½in (44.5cm) wide.
£2,500–3,000 *C*

A lacquer covered bowl, decorated with symbols, restored, 18th/19thC, 8½in (21.5cm) diam.
£450–500 *SK*

A lacquer *bundai*, minor scratches, 19thC, 9in (23cm) wide.
£1,800–2,200 *C*

A carved red lacquer study of a *shishi*, unsigned, late 18th/early 19thC, 1½in (4cm) wide.
£1,000–1,200 *S*

A lacquer comb and hairpin, signed 'Ryushin Sei', late 19thC, the pin 6½in (16.5cm) long.
£250–300 *CNY*

l. A gold lacquer figure of Hotei, seated on his sack holding a peach in one hand, his robes decorated in *hiramakie* and black, on a gilt-metal base, damaged, 8in (20.5cm) high.
£650–750 *CSK*

A lacquer charger, decorated with carp, octopus, squid, lobster and other fish, with embedded glass eyes, on a black ground, Meiji period, 27in (68.5cm) diam.
£1,800–2,000 *SK*

A lacquered and giltwood Noh mask of Tengu, the nose damaged, 19thC, 8in (20.5cm) high.
£550–650 *CSK*

A lacquered helmet, of Tobigashira form, decorated on the *roiro* ground in gold *takamakie* and mother-of-pearl, damaged, 18thC, 11½in (29cm) wide.
£3,500–4,000 *S*

A pair of black lacquer quatrefoil stands, damaged 19thC, 8in (20.5cm) high.
£450–500 *CSK*

A group of 7 lacquer masks, including Ko-beshimi, Asakura-jo, a young woman and a villain, the second signed 'Omi-uchi', and a Kakihan, all with some damage, 18th and 19thC, the largest 9½in (24cm) long.
£2,500–3,500 each *C*

l. A gold, red and black lacquer group of a clump of lotus in bud, issuing from a jardinière, 15in (38cm) high. *r.* A similar issuing from a hexagonal jardinière decorated with foliate cartouches, slight damage, 19thC, 14½in (37cm) high.
£550–650 *CSK*

A gold lacquer saddle, decorated on the *nashiji* ground in gold *takamakie*, *hiramakie* and foil with *ho-o*, chipped, 18th/19thC, 15in (38cm) long.
£3,500–4,000 *S*

An inlaid lacquer panel, lacquered in *takamakie* and *hiramakie* on a *roiro* ground, surrounded by a natural gnarled wood frame, lacquer cracked, Meiji period, 38½in (98cm) wide.
£1,300–1,500 *S(S)*

A lacquer picnic set, comprising 3 flat square boxes and covers and 4 triangular trays, each decorated to simulate different wood samples, in a fitted lacquer casket with open side panels, early 20thC, 10in (25.5cm) high.
£220–250 *HSS*

A Namban lacquer coffer, decorated in gold, black and mother-of-pearl flaked, c1600, 9in (23cm) wide.
£1,200–1,400 *S*

Namban lacquer items were made for export, principally to Portugal.

Japanese Lacquer

Derived from trees, lacquer is mostly applied in numerous layers to wood or paper to render it waterproof and durable. With time it suffers abrasion from use, and fades from exposure to sunlight. It should not be subjected to pressure or sharp blows. Connoisseurs are fastidious about condition.

JAPANESE WOOD

A boxwood carving of an eagle attacking a monkey, damaged, signed 'Jisen', late 19thC, 6½in (16.5cm) high.
£1,500–1,700 *C*

A boxwood *okimono* of a snake and turtle, the wood lightly stained and the eyes inlaid, signed in an oval reserve 'Shomin', late 19thC, 2½in (6.5cm) wide.
£1,300–1,500 *S*

wood and *Shibayama* style caparisoned elephant, Meiji period, 8in (20.5cm) long.
2,500–3,000 *C*

l. A wood *okimono* of Shibunkin, by Chikuju, the group of long tailed goldfish naturalistically carved, the eyes inlaid in horn, signed on a horn tablet, Meiji period, 10in (25.5cm) wide.
£1,500–1,800 *S*

A wood figure of an *oni* carrying a bell, 19thC, 14in (35.5cm) high.
£1,000–1,200 *OT*

A lacquered wood and ivory *okimono*, modelled as a courtesan and a servant, late 19thC, 11½in (29cm) high.
£2,500–3,000 *S(NY)*

boxwood carving of a ferocious *oni* holding a mortar between his feet, into which he grinds his club, signed 'Gyominchi', Meiji period, in (7.5cm) high.
500–600 *WW*

A painted and gessoed wood mask of Uba, lower jaw missing, 18thC, 7in (18cm) high.
£200–250 *CSK*

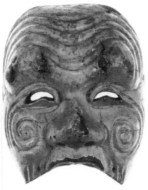

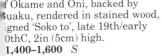

wood *netsuke* of three masks, f Okame and Oni, backed by uaku, rendered in stained wood, gned 'Soko to', late 19th/early 0thC, 2in (5cm) high.
1,400–1,600 *S*

A painted and gessoed wood Noh mask, of a male head with grimacing expression, old wear, 19thC, 8in (20.5cm) long.
£450–500 *CSK*

A painted and gessoed wood mask, modelled as the head of an old man, with inlaid glass eyes, wear to lip, late 19thC, 3½in (9cm) long.
£75–100 *CSK*

CHINESE FURNITURE

Classic Chinese furniture of the Ming (1368–1644) and Qing (1644–1916) Dynasties is much admired in the West for its simplicity of form combined with strong but elegant construction. Most pieces of classical Chinese furniture are made from *huanghuali* wood. This hard, dense wood has a beautiful grain, which is quite distinct and varied and polishes to a light red with darker grain. Other woods used include *zitan*, a purplish-black hardwood with a grain so dense as to be virtually invisible, *tichi*, known as 'chicken wood' because the grain resembles feathers, and *tielimu*, (*mu* meaning wood), an inexpensive hardwood used for the backs of furniture and drawer bottoms.

Chinese furniture is made up with intricate and exact joinery. No nails are used and the minimal amount of glue is secondary to the accurate joinery. The joints are so exact that nothing can be inserted between them. Where boards are joined together they are jointed with a dovetailed tongue-and-groove, which is held so tightly that the join cannot be felt. Different decorative techniques add to the attraction of the furniture. The grain is carefully selected so as to suggest images of clouds etc, and the simple lines are enhanced with complete mouldings, latticework, carving and inlay.

Classic *huanghuali* furniture is now quite rare as it disappears into museums and private collections. As a result, the price continues to rise. However, it is still very good value considering its age, quality and workmanship and in particular when compared to the values of western furniture. With the scarcity of *huanghuali* furniture, attention is being given to pieces made from other woods. Good-quality bamboo furniture from the 18th and early 19th centuries is hard to find and is also in great demand. There has been a recent influx of southern Chinese provincial furniture to the western market, most of which is quite decorative but may not be a good investment. Beware of furniture that has been 'made up' from old bamboo in order to suit western styles and demand. This includes four-poster beds, babies' cots and cradles, clothing and towel stands and magazine racks.

Cabinets

A lacquer robe chest, damaged, late 18thC, 25in (63.5cm) wide.
£2,200–2,500 *C*

A Chinese export black and polychrome cabinet-on-stand, decorated with flowers, on an English black and polychrome japanned stand, doors and stand 18thC, 61½in (156cm) high.
£2,200–2,500 *C*

A table cosmetic cabinet, the hinged cover opening to an arrangement of short drawers, the exterior with bright metal mounts, 18thC, 14¼in (36cm) wide.
£2,800–3,200 *S(NY)*

Table cosmetic cabinets generally have a flat or domed hinged cover, which opens to a recessed area designed to accommodate a hinged mirror stand. The front contains a pair of doors which open to an arrangement of short drawers.

A Chinese export black and gilt lacquer cabinet, on an ebonised stand with plain frieze, damaged, early 18thC, 67in (170cm) high.
£2,500–3,000 *C*

> **Miller's is a price GUIDE not a price LIST**

l. A decorated red lacquer cabine with engraved and chased brass mounts, the doors enclosing an arrangement of 10 drawers, on a stand with cabriole legs and pad feet, late 18th/early 19thC, 41in (104cm) wide.
£3,000–3,500 *MEA*

A black lacquer and chinoiserie decorated cabinet, 18th/19thC, 43in (109cm) wide.
£3,000–3,500 *MEA*

A Chinese export black lacquer and *lac burgauté* brass cabinet, enclosing shelves and a pair of drawers, c1800, 40in (102cm) wide.
£1,500–1,700 *CSK*

A Chinese export black and gilt lacquered chest-on-stand, with acanthus scroll carved X-shaped supports joined by stretchers, early 19thC, 42in (106.5cm) wide.
£650–750 *S(S)*

A hardwood side cabinet, the cleated top with raised sides, 3 frieze drawers, 2 doors to the panelled front, on square supports, 19thC, 85in (216cm) wide.
£600–700 *Bea*

A hardwood cabinet, early 19thC, 40½in (103cm) wide.
£600–700 *SLN*

An elm storage cabinet, c1860, 76in (193cm) high.
£2,000–2,250 *ORI*

An elm cabinet, in 2 sections, the wood of rich honey colour with a strong grain pattern, the upper section with panelled doors mounted with a brass escutcheon and bar locking system, above a similar arrangement in the base, the apron carved with sprays of flowers and foliage, on short legs carved with scrolls, Qing Dynasty, 19thC, 92in (233.5cm) high.
£800–900 *S*

An ebonised padouk wood side cabinet, inlaid with copper wire, mother-of-pearl, ivory and bone, with brass flat hinges and door plates, on key pattern carved bracket feet, late 19thC, 46in (117cm) wide.
£700–800 *HSS*

A part lacquered wood display cabinet, inlaid with ivory, supported on a matching stand, some pieces lacking, 19thC, 96in (244cm) high.
£14,500–16,000 *S*

The Influence of Fashion

Unlike European furniture, Chinese domestic furniture was not influenced by fashion. The same style of furniture was made over a vast period of time, using the same materials and manufacturing techniques. This can make accurate dating of furniture very difficult.

l. A pair of *zitan* wood side cabinets, inlaid with silver wire, the carved panelled doors depicting sea serpents, on square legs, 19thC, 16in (40.5cm) wide.
£3,000–3,500 *CSK*

A pair of red lacquer cabinets, the interior with drawers and shelves, 19thC, 41in (104cm) wide.
£3,500–4,000 *LR*

A black lacquer cabinet, set with hardstones and mother-of-pearl, late 19thC, 38½in (98cm) wide, with later ebonised stand.
£650–750 *Bea*

A coromandel cabinet, with carved ivory and shell inlay decoration, late 19thC, 60in (152cm) wide.
£5,000–5,500 *RBB*

A red wood table cabinet, with applied hardstones, ivory and mother-of-pearl, the silver mounts marked London 1894, 12½in (32cm) wide.
£1,800–2,000 *AH*

Chairs

A pair of *tielimu* spindleback armchairs, 17th/18thC.
£3,500–4,000 *CNY*

A pair of black lacquer armchairs, each with a scrolled crest-rail with a bowed, panelled splat and panelled seat, Shaanxi Province, 18thC.
£1,800–2,000 *S(NY)*

A mandarin chair, 17thC.
£720–800 *AWH*

l. A pair of horseshoe-back chairs, each splat carved with a central cloud-form medallion, restored, 18th/19thC.
£1,600–1,800 *SK*

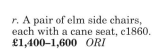

r. A pair of elm side chairs, each with a cane seat, c1860.
£1,400–1,600 *ORI*

A *hongmu* deck armchair, 19thC.
£1,000–1,200 *CNY*

Hongmu is a type of Chinese hardwood.

An elm 'official's hat' armchair, with plain back splat and cane seat, c1870.
£1,000–1,100 *ORI*

An elm horseshoe-back open armchair, with plain splat and cane seat, c1870.
£750–900 *ORI*

A pair of *hongmu* armchairs, the backs and sides carved with *linghzi* clusters growing on contorted branches, some repair, 19thC, 39in (99cm) high.
£3,000–3,500 *CNY*

A pair of *hongmu* spindleback armchairs, 18thC, 33in (84cm) high.
£4,500–5,000 *CNY*

A pair of carved and gilt red lacquer armchairs, slight damage, 19thC, 40in (101cm) high.
£500–600 *CNY*

Chinese Chairs

Chinese round-back or horseshoe-back armchairs are considered to be more important than the traditional upright style of chair. These chairs would be reserved for important guests and are often featured in ancestral portraits. Horseshoe-back chairs are usually slightly oversized, again indicating their importance.

The majority of Chinese domestic chairs were made in pairs. They would usually be placed against a wall, each side of a small table upon which tea would be served.

Two black lacquered armchairs, gilt-decorated with figures and flowers, 19thC, and a square table.
£1,300–1,500 *CAm*

Desks

An ebonised wood desk and chair, on dragon-carved cabriole legs, 19thC, 52in (132cm) wide.
£600–700 *Bea*

A hardwood desk, the top with inset central panel, with butterfly-shaped bronze lock plates, the legs joined by stretchers enclosing a 'cracked ice' pattern shelf, Qing Dynasty, 47½in (121cm) wide.
£850–1,000 *S*

A carved *huanghuali* davenport, with a pen drawer above 8 opposing drawers and pierced dragon brackets, some damage, late 19thC, 33in (84cm) wide.
£550–650 *S(S)*

Jardinière Stands

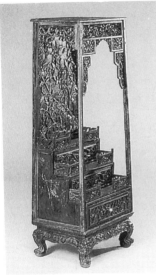

A polychrome hardwood altar stand, with pierced foliate carved apron and backplate, 3 shelves above a drawer, 18thC, 52in (132cm) high.
£800–900 *SLN*

A pair of rosewood vase stands, c1870, 33in (84cm) high.
£1,100–1,300 *ORI*

A pair of hardwood jardinière stands, the marble tops above carved friezes, on cabriole supports headed by masks and ending in claw-and-ball feet, 19thC, 18in (46cm) diam.
£700–850 *CS*

A pair of carved hardwood jardinière stand, with inset rouge marble top, the circular legs with claw-and-ball feet, 19thC, 16in (41cm) square.
£350–400 *GH*

A carved hardwood jardinière stand, with inset rouge marble top, pierced side aprons, shaped legs and cross stretcher, 19thC, 10in (25.5cm) diam.
£200–250 *GH*

A carved hardwood jardinière stand, with inset rouge marble top, floral carved side apron, shaped legs and pierced floral gallery, 19thC, 36in (91.5cm) high.
£350–400 *GH*

A pair of two-tier hardwood urn stands, the aprons, legs and edges carved to simulate bamboo, 19thC, 18in (46cm) square.
£800–1,000 *P(S)*

A *huanghuali* jardinière stand, the rimmed top above a beaded edge, pierced frieze and bowed supports, 19thC, 16½in (42cm) wide.
£700–800 *CSK*

A carved hardwood plant stand, with inset marble panel, on cabriole legs, 19thC, 19in (48.5cm) high.
£250–300 *GAK*

A pair of crimson lacquer hexagonal stands, decorated in gi[?] c1900, 38in (96cm) high.
£700–800 *S(S)*

Screens

coromandel screen, the 12 leaves
rming a continuous scene with
vilions, trees, figures and animals
thin a fenced garden, the border
nelled with fantastic animals,
rds, flowers and utensils, late
thC, 108in (274.5cm) high.
,000–8,800 *DN*

black and gold lacquer
ur-leaf screen, early 19thC,
½in (192cm) high.
,500–3,000 *C*

Tables

black and gold lacquer table, with
vin stretchers, decorated with gold
cquer scrolling stylised lotus,
anli period, 36in (91.5cm) high.
,000–4,500 *C*

bamboo table, with pierced
tticework frieze and recessed
gs, 18thC, 64in (162.5cm) long.
,400–4,000 *S(NY)*

A coromandel lacquer four-leaf
screen, decorated with figures amid
a mountainous river landscape,
within a foliate scrolled inner
border, the outer border with vases
of flowers and foliate sprigs, 18thC,
each leaf 19½in (49.5cm) wide.
£1,800–2,000 *CSK*

A Chinese export black and gilt
lacquer eight-leaf screen, with a
panoramic scene, the broad foliate
scroll-filled panelled border with
smaller scenes and foliate panels,
the reverse with bamboo, trees and
birds amid a broad foliate border,
mid-19thC, 83½in (212cm) high.
£6,500–7,500 *C*

A stepped low table, inlaid with
mother-of-pearl, fitted with a
single drawer, pierced apron below,
some damage, late Ming Dynasty,
40in (102cm) wide.
£2,800–3,000 *CNY*

r. A hardwood table,
carved and painted
with central bird
issuing from foliate
decoration, on carved
block legs, 18thC,
79in (200.5cm) long.
£2,400–2,800 *SLN*

A painted hide four-fold screen, with
pagodas, figures, boats and vases,
within a gilt hide border, distressed,
19thC, 75in (190.5cm) high.
£1,800–2,000 *S(S)*

A two-fold screen, with a design of
birds among flowering branches
carved with ivory, bone, wood and
mother-of-pearl, on black lacquer,
within a carved frame of dragons,
late 19thC, 73in (185.5cm) high.
£600–700 *RBB*

A pair of bamboo tables,
with black lacquer tops above
a latticework frieze, 18thC,
33in (84cm) wide.
£7,800–8,500 *S(NY)*

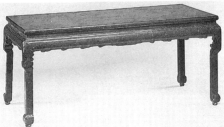

A Chinese export black lacquer and gilt work table, mid-19thC, 25in (64.5cm) wide.
£1,000–1,200 *Bea*

A *huanghuali* centre table, the top with burr wood panel within concentric bandings, carved and pierced frieze above 6 supports, joined by stretchers, on stylised carved feet, 19thC, 53½in (136cm) diam.
£1,500–1,700 *S(S)*

A Chinese export black lacquered and gilt work table, the interior fitted with compartments and removable trays above a well, mid-19thC, 25½in (63.5cm) wide.
£1,300–1,500 *S(S)*

r. A nest of 4 hardwood occasional tables, 19thC.
£650–750 *Bea*

A Canton gilt and black lacquer sewing table, with hinged cover, fitted interior with pierced ivory accessories, slight wear, mid-19thC, 28in (71cm) high.
£2,000–2,200 *CNY*

A hardwood corner table, with inset serpentine marble top, above a carved and pierced frieze, on 3 carved cabriole supports and claw-and-ball feet, tied by a roundel and curved stretcher, 19thC, 41½in (105cm) wide.
£800–900 *Bon*

A Manchurian table, in two halves, inlaid in parquetry style with a central figured medallion, some damage, 19thC, 54½in (138cm) diam.
£1,800–2,000 *CNY*

l. A hardwood centre table, with inset rouge marble top and undertier, 19thC, 24in (61cm) high.
£700–800 *LRG*

An Anglo-Chinese rosewood hall table, with pink veined marble inset top, on cabriole front supports, with carved ornament, scroll toes, on serpentine fronted plinth base, 19thC, 50in (127cm) long.
£2,000–2,200 *CAG*

A Chinese export black and gilt lacquered tilt-top tripod table, mid-19thC, 36in (92cm) wide.
£2,500–3,000 *C*

A lacquered sewing table, with fitted interior, lyre-shaped end supports, and turned stretcher, 19thC, 16in (40.5cm) wide.
£500–600 *Bon*

A padouk wood altar table, 19thC, 48in (122cm) wide.
£1,200–1,500 *N*

A rosewood side table, the panelled top with scroll ends above a pierced apron, Qing Dynasty, 50in (127cm) wide.
£650–750 *S*

A side table, with pierced carved apron, the legs joined by stretchers, top damaged, late 19thC, 21in (53.5cm) wide.
£500–550 *CAT*

A *huanghuali* altar table, the cleated top above a stylised pierced and carved frieze, on square legs with scroll feet, late 19thC, 53½in (136cm) wide.
£1,000–1,200 *S(S)*

l. A pair of walnut tea tables, with railed shelf, c1880, 33in (84cm) high.
£800–900 *ORI*

A Chinese export brown lacquer and gilt work table, decorated with figures and scrolling foliage, fitted interior and upholstered well, 19thC, 25in (63.5cm) wide.
£1,200–1,400 *CSK*

A rosewood table, carved to simulate bamboo, Qing Dynasty, 19thC, 60in (152cm) wide.
£1,400–1,600 *S*

A Chinese export twin-flap gateleg games and tea table, with black and polychrome lacquer, slight damage, 19thC, 32in (81cm) wide.
£1,500–1,700 *C*

A Chinese export marquetry-inlaid table, 19thC, 54in (137cm) diam.
£1,000–1,200 *CSK*

JAPANESE FURNITURE
Cabinets & Chests

r. A black lacquer cabinet, decorated in *hiramakie*, inlaid with mother-of-pearl, damaged, late 17thC, 20in (52cm) wide.
£2,500–3,000 *C*

A cabinet-on-stand, decorated in *hiramakie*, damaged, late 17thC, stand late 18thC, 36in (91.5cm) wide.
£8,500–10,000 *C*

An export lacquer cabinet, enclosing one long and 9 short drawers of various sizes, with engraved gilt copper mounts, the lacquer and handles probably later, early Edo period, 17thC, 36in (91.5cm) wide.
£6,500–7,500 *S*

Japanese Furniture

The exquisite workmanship of furniture from the Meiji period (1868–1911) is much admired. Although considered by some to be over-decorated, the export display cabinets with their intricate lacquer and ivory inlay are very good value and are ideal display cases for fine collections of *objets d'art* . Most Japanese furniture is lacquered and is therefore easily marked and distressed. If a piece has been relacquered it is advisable to check that it has not been altered in any way.

A hardwood *shodana*, decorated with *shibayama* panels depicting birds, flowers and parcel gilt, late 19thC, 53in (135.5cm) high.
£5,000–6,000 *CSK*

A pair of lacquer cabinets-on-stands, each with an arrangement of drawers, hinged compartments and doors, decorated with birds and poultry in landscapes, metal mounts, late 19thC, 19in (48.5cm) wide.
£850–1,000 *P*

A padouk wood collector's cabinet, late 19thC, 38in (96cm) wide.
£1,300–1,500 *HSS*

A carved hardwood and lacquer side cabinet, with pagoda pediment, galleried shelves, cupboards and drawers each with a lacquer panel and mounted carved ivory, decorated with open carved phoenix and flowering branches, Meiji period, 84in (213cm) high.
£2,300–2,600 *P(S)*

A wood and cloisonné enamel cabinet, enclosing 9 panels, Meiji period, 31in (79cm) high.
£4,500–5,000 *S*

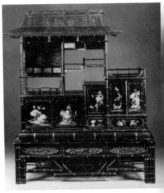

A wood and lacquer display cabinet, the panels decorated in *iroe hiramakie* and *takamakie* and various inlays, the stand modelled as a bamboo frame, slight damage, Meiji period, 70in (178cm) high.
£2,500–3,000 *C*

A lacquered and inlaid wood cabinet, with silver mounts, damaged, Meiji period, 25in (63.5cm) wide.
£2,200–2,500 *S*

A gold lacquer *shodana*, inlaid with ivory and horn, metal mounts and a wood stand, restored, later hinges, late 19thC, 22in (56cm) high.
£3,000–3,500 *S*

A padouk wood and lacquer cabinet, decorated with bone, mother-of-pearl and abalone shell, late 19thC, 44in (112cm) wide.
£1,700–2,000 *HSS*

l. A lacquer cabinet, decorated in gold, slight damage, 19thC, 30in (76cm) high.
£2,500–3,000 *S*

A lacquer table cabinet, with bronze foliate mounts, decorated in *iroe hiramakie* and *takamakie*, slight damage, late 19thC, 10½in (26.5cm) high, and another, with geometric decoration.
£350–400 *CSK*

Tables

A black lacquer temple table, with gold floral design, incised foliate scrolling on metal mounts, restored, 17th/18thC, 36in (91.5cm) wide.
£1,800–2,000 *SK*

A lacquered table, c1900, 23½in (60cm) diam.
£200–250 *TAR*

Relacquering

Beware of relacquered furniture. At best relacquering can hide replaced doors or drawers, and at worst the piece could be a complete fake. Also, be suspicious of new brass lockplates or handles. It is advisable to buy antiques from recognised dealers, and be sure that you are given the approximate date of the item you purchase.

Screens

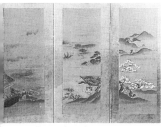

A carved wood and *Shibayama* screen, inlaid with mother-of-pearl and hardstone, late 19thC, 11½in (29.5cm) high.
£2,500–3,000 *Bea*

A six-panel screen, painted in ink and colours on silk, depicting the 4 seasons, Meiji period, 38½in (98cm) high.
£1,300–1,500 *SK*

A carved wood and *Shibayama* screen, late 19thC, 28in (71cm) wide.
£200–250 *CDC*

Shibayama

Shibayama was produced by applying pieces of mother-of-pearl, ivory and stones to a surface, then surrounding them with lacquer.

CHINESE ROBES & TEXTILES

Textiles and costume from the Chinese Ming (1368–1644) and Qing (1644–1916) Dynasties are now considered works of art in their own right. Their appeal is twofold – visual aesthetics and availability – although the latter is a perpetual challenge owing to increased demand. Interestingly, items from a period such as the 18th century, when the Emperor's influence created a cultural, political and spiritual stability, are most rare.

A collection can be sorted into categories: robes, rank badges, accessories, even colours. Colour denoted rank within the Imperial court: yellow for the Emperor and his first wife; orange for the secondary consort and first son; and green, brown and blue for lower ranks. During the Ming Dynasty, red was the colour of royal rank. As with any up-and-coming market, reproductions are appearing, and particular care should be taken when purchasing rank badges and 'lotus' shoes.

The market for Chinese textiles is predominantly in the West, with very little interest in mainland China. However, when recently asked what will happen when the Chinese begin to buy back their textiles, my reply was that the market will explode and prices will rapidly rise to heights that were hardly thought possible 20 years ago.

As with all textile art, condition is most important, and the more perfect the piece the higher the premium. A few simple precautions will protect silk textiles: framing using UV glass or Perspex; storage in acid-free tissue paper; and the use of lavender or camphor to deter insects (although very few eat silk). Costume is best kept flat in boxes – hangers will stretch silk which never regain its original shape. Oriental textiles should not be washed without taking advice, as many of the dyes are not fast. To preserve textiles as wall art, make sure they are covered and protected from the light and dust.

Linda Wrigglesworth

A brocade canopy, woven in yellow with the Eight Buddhist Symbols on scrolling lotus, 16thC, 70in (178cm) square.
£3,500–4,000 *S(NY)*

An embroidered coral silk satin hanging, with a central roundel of 2 dragons, a lion in each corner, the upper section with a phoenix and lotus, 17thC, 108 x 78in (274.5 x 198cm).
£2,200–2,500 *CSK*

A child's rank badge, with silver pheasant and couched gold detail 18thC, 5½ x 6in (14 x 15cm).
£3,500–4,000 *S(NY)*

A silk robe, embroidered with Buddhist Emblems on a blue ground, the applied hems on a darker blue ground, Qing Dynasty.
£3,200–3,800 *S*

Miller's is a price GUIDE not a price LIST

A blue brocaded robe, 18thC.
£7,000–8,000 *CSK*

A blue Imperial twelve-symbol robe, worked with couched metallic gold dragons, satin-stitched bats, clouds, rolling waves and a typical wavy stripe, the symbols arranged in 3 groups of 4, the *fu* symbol and other decoration in fine satin-stitch, 18thC, 56in (142cm) long.
£30,000–35,000 *S(NY)*

This type of robe is extremely rar

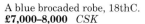

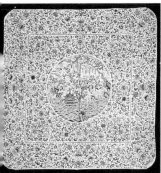

An Imperial cover, of golden yellow silk satin embroidered in coloured silks, the central roundel with cranes flying over sea waves, fruit trees and a pagoda in the distance, with lotus flowers and scrolling stems, backed with silk damask, 1800, 58in (147.5cm) square.
£2,800–3,200 *CSK*

A winter formal robe, of dark blue padded silk satin embroidered in coloured silks and gilt threads, with a later sea wave border, lined in blue silk, c1800.
£5,000–6,000 *CSK*

An Imperial cover of yellow gauze, finely embroidered in coloured silks, lined in yellow silks, c1800, 50 x 36in (127 x 91.5cm).
£3,000–3,500 *CSK*

An image robe for the Tibetan market, green silk, embroidered in coloured silks and couched gilt threads, the lining with inscription, early 18thC.
£4,500–5,000 *CSK*

The inscription translates: 'This robe was offered on the 2nd day of the 2nd month, the 6th year of Qianlong (ie 1741), followed by a list of the officers and the signature of the person who prepared the offering note.

A lady's stole, of black silk satin with couched silver and gilt-metal threads with dragons over a sea wave border, 7th civil rank badges of the Mandarin duck, with coral beaded sun, fringed, lined with salmon pink silk damask, late 19thC.
£2,500–3,000 *CSK*

A red/orange silk satin robe, embroidered in coloured silks and couched gilt threads, with blue satin borders, lined in pale olive silk damask, 19thC.
£2,500–3,000 *CSK*

This type of robe was traditionally part of a Chinese lady's bridal dress.

A pair of 'lotus' shoes, for bound feet, 19thC.
£280–350
Two Mandarin hat buttons, worn on the top of hats to represent rank by their colour, 19thC.
£65–75 *LW*

An ivory satin coverlet, embroidered with a central tree peony, pheasant and other birds, 19thC, 110 x 71in (279.5 x 180.5cm).
£1,700–2,000 *CSK*

A robe of bronze-coloured silk, embroidered in coloured silks and gilt threads on a lattice ground, with inscription in lining, fastened by ribbons, 19thC.
£2,500–3,000 *CSK*

Storing Costume

Chinese costume should be stored flat, with acid-free tissue paper between the folds.

r. A formal robe, of blue *kossu* silk, woven in coloured silks and gilt threads, mid/late 19thC.
£8,000–9,500 *CSK*

An informal robe, of dark blue silk satin embroidered in white and shades of blue, the pale blue damask sleeve bands worked in coloured silks with blossom, lined in blue silk, 19thC.
£1,700–2,000 *CSK*

An informal coat, of dark blue silk satin embroidered in white and shades of blue, with ivory satin sleeve bands, and black satin embroidered borders, lined in pale blue silk damask, 19thC.
£1,000–1,200 *CSK*

An informal coat, of dark blue silk satin embroidered in brightly coloured silks, worked in Peking knot stitch with the peony and cicada design on the centre front and back, with embroidered ivory satin borders, 19thC.
£800–1,000 *CSK*

A summer dragon robe, of blue gauze woven with ivory silk, the horseshoe cuffs with silk brocade trimming, 19thC.
£2,000–2,500 *CSK*

A dragon robe, of blue silk worked with couched gilt threads with 9 dragons among clouds and emblems, over a sea wave border, with horseshoe cuffs, 19thC.
£1,700–2,000 *CSK*

A semi-formal coat, of dark blue silk satin embroidered in coloured silks with roundels, the centre with a vase of flowers enclosed within a border of cranes and blossom, over a sea wave border, the cuffs with roundels and narrow sea wave border, lined in blue silk damask, buttons replaced, 19thC.
£4,500–5,000 *CSK*

l. A pair of embroideries on white silk, showing figures in gardens, couch work, watercolour and bullion work, framed and glazed, 19thC, 15½ x 30½in (39.5 x 77.5cm).
£400–450 *WL*

l. A priest's silk robe, with 7 gold couched dragons in shaped cartouches, the reverse with a Buddha on a lotus throne, the base bordered with dragons and phoenix, the neck with floral roundels, 19thC, 51in (129.5cm) long.
£1,700–2,000 *SK*

A semi-formal robe, of red/orange silk satin embroidered with flower sprigs and a sea wave border in white and shades of blue silks, flying birds in coloured silks, the front and back worked with the 7th civil rank Mandarin Duck, lined in emerald green silk, 19thC.
£2,000–2,500 *CSK*

A dragon robe, of brown summer weave gauze embroidered in coloured silks and gilt threads, the border of charcoal grey embroidered gauze, the pair of horseshoe cuffs loose, 19thC.
£2,500–3,000 *CSK*

An Imperial cover, of yellow silk satin couched with coloured twisted silks and metal threads, backed with silk damask, 19thC, 44 x 41in (112 x 104cm).
£2,500–3,000 *CSK*

A dragon robe, of chestnut-brown silk gauze worked with 9 dragons chasing flaming pearls in couched metal thread, amid cloud bands above a deep sea wave border, 19th
£3,500–4,000 *Bon(C)*

A brown satin semi-formal robe, embroidered in coloured silks and couched gilt metal threads, lined in blue silk damask, 19thC. **£1,500–1,800** *CSK*

An aubergine silk jacket, embroidered with flower-filled baskets, the borders with figures, 19thC, 38in (96.5cm) long. **£1,700–2,000** *S(NY)*

A lady's formal robe, the pale green silk woven with prunus and butterflies, late 19thC. **£1,700–2,000** *CSK*

An informal robe, the lilac silk damask trimmed with a cutwork collar and woven ribbons, late 19thC. **£1,300–1,500** *CSK*

A red silk complete bridal trousseau, 19thC. **£3,500–4,000** *CSK*

A black silk satin semi-formal coat, with embroidered dragon roundels, lined in blue silk, late 19thC. **£3,500–4,000** *CSK*

JAPANESE ROBES & TEXTILES

Collecting Japanese Costume

Japanese textiles have been avidly collected over the years in Japan. Kimonos are highly prized and considered treasured items in their cultural heritage. Most kimonos for the aristocracy were made of silk, while household textiles were mostly made of cotton and are generally easier to acquire.

Japanese kimonos made in the 20th century are still undervalued and are only just becoming collectable, so it is safer to collect examples from the 19th century or earlier.

r. A midnight blue silk *furisode*, embroidered in gilt threads and coloured silks, lined iwth red silk crepe, with padded hem, mid/late 19thC. **£650–750** *CSK*

An embroidered silk picture of a peasant woman carrying a bundle of reeds, Meiji/Taisho period, 19 x 12in (48.5 x 30.5cm), framed and glazed. **£500–600** *S(S)*

An embroidered hanging, with dragons, phoenix and cloud scrolls, within a brocaded border, 19thC, 84 x 55in (213 x 139.5cm). **£2,500–3,000** *CSK*

A hanging, worked in coloured silks with a dragon confronting a tiger, among cloud scrolls, 19thC, 58 x 36in (147.5 x 91.5cm). **£2,200–2,500** *CSK*

CHINESE SNUFF BOTTLES & GLASS

There has been a tremendous explosion in the price of Chinese snuff bottles over the past decade or so, largely because of the wealth of freshly published works on the subject that has encouraged a new breed of collector who is looking for quality. No longer are snuff bottles regarded as a minor Chinese decorative art; they are now appreciated as having played an important role in the development of all the Chinese arts of the Qing Dynasty (1644–1916).

The pivotal role that snuff bottles played was due entirely to the predilection of the great early Qing emperors for taking snuff. This led to a large proportion of the resources available for art production being chanelled into the manufacture of exquisite snuff bottles for the court, initially made in special workshops established within the palace in Beijing and later, as demand grew, at various centres throughout China, notably in Guangzhou and Suzhou.

During the 19th century the habit of snuff-taking spread down the social scale, and the huge increase in demand for snuff bottles inevitably led to a decline in quality. Thus today there is an increasing gap between the value of the outstanding snuff bottles produced for the court and the lesser items made for common use.

Snuff bottles were produced in a great variety of materials, including jade, glass, porcelain, chalcedony and coral. It is the variety in shape, colour, texture and design that gives snuff bottles their great appeal – an appeal that is further enhanced by their pleasant feel, as they were made to be handled and treasured.

The manufacture of glass and that of snuff bottles are closely related. The Chinese had been aware of the existence of glass since around the 2nd century BC, but they did not become glass enthusiasts until the late 17th century, when the Emperor Kangxi (1662–1722) was given gifts of glass by visiting Jesuit missionaries. He became fascinated by the possibilities of the medium, with its fiery colours and plastic nature, and the Jesuits, sensing an opportunity for influence at court, offered to send trained glassmaker priests to China. The offer was accepted, and Father Kilian Stumpf was sent from Bavaria to establish a glassworks within the palace precincts in Beijing.

For the next 150 years these glassworks produced a vast variety of wares, in particular snuff bottles, vases, bowls and dishes, many engraved with Imperial seal marks on the base. Snuff bottles constituted by far the largest proportion of Chinese glass made and are therefore much more readily found than other items.

Over the past 30 years or so snuff bottles and other Chinese glass items have been collected largely in the UK and the USA, but the position is changing rapidly. As China begins to play an increasingly important role in the world economy there is no doubt that a new breed of Chinese collectors will emerge who will draw the bulk of Chinese art, at present in private hands in the West, back to their homeland.

Robert Kleiner

Snuff Bottles

An amber snuff bottle, 18thC, 2in (5cm) high.
£850–1,000 *Bon*

A soapstone snuff bottle, carved with 2 archaistic dragons in pursuit of a flaming pearl, the reverse with bats and clouds, early 18thC, 2¾in (7cm) high.
£1,000–1,200 *S(NY)*

A macaroni agate snuff bottle, supported on a flattened footrim, 1780–1850, 2in (5cm) high.
£500–600 *Bon*

A glass snuff bottle, with carved red overlay fish amid bubbles, 18thC, 2½in (6.5cm) high.
£2,600–3,000 *RHa*

r. A Peking glass snuff bottle, imitation nephrite, of finely polished rounded form, 18thC, 2in (5cm) high.
£750–850 *S(S)*

r. A chalcedony snuff bottle, with ochre and brown inclusions in the front, carved in deep relief with a cat below a butterfly, 1800–50, 2in (5cm) high.
£550–650 *Bon*

r. A red overlay glass snuff bottle, carved with animals of the Chinese Zodiac over a bubble suffused ground, c1780, 2in (5cm) high.
£450–550 S(S)

A moulded porcelain snuff bottle, finely modelled with 9 dogs of Fo gambolling with brocade balls, against a cloud-pierced ground, all coloured cinnabar red with gilt detail, mark and period of Jiaqing, 2in (5cm) high.
£500–600 S(S)

A double-overlay glass snuff bottle, carved with stylised discs, and a pair of glass *chilong*, chipped 18thC, 2½in (6.5cm) high.
£1,500–1,800 S

A blue overlay glass snuff bottle, decorated with figures beneath bamboo and prunus over a bubble suffused ground, c1800, 2in (5cm) high.
£650–750 S(S)

A dark amber glass flattened table snuff bottle, with gilt metal filigree stopper, spoon missing, 1750–1820, 5½in (14cm) high.
£450–500 CSK

An agate snuff bottle, carved with a sage beneath a willow tree, the reverse with figures and peaches, mask and ring handles carved in low relief, 1750–1850, 2in (5cm) high.
£850–1,000 S(S)

Tips for Buying Chinese Snuff Bottles

When buying a snuff bottle check that there is no damage such as chips to the neck or footrim, which are very common. Hardstone snuff bottles should be well and evenly hollowed with a smoothly polished surface. Beware of hidden cracks in glass, which can be revealed by holding the object up to the light.

A chalcedony snuff bottle, carved with vertical reeding, gilt-metal mounted stopper, 1770–1850, 1¾in (4.5cm) high.
£550–650 S(S)

A puddingstone snuff bottle, the mottled stone with circular inclusions, c1800, 2in (5cm) high.
£850–1,000 S(S)

r. A chalcedony snuff bottle, carved using speckled brown and ochre inclusions with various animal subjects, c1800, 2in (5cm) high.
£650–750 S(S)

r. A cinnabar lacquer snuff bottle, carved with 2 panels of figures in landscape within floral meander borders, incised Qianlong seal mark, 19thC, 1¾in (4.5cm) high.
£300–350 S(S)

A macaroni agate snuff bottle, of flattened ovoid form, on an oval foot rim, 1780–1850, 2in (5cm) high.
£450–550 *S(S)*

An agate thumbprint snuff bottle, of pebble shape, with grey and white bands, c1800, 1¾in (4.5cm) high.
£350–400 *S(S)*

A faceted red glass snuff bottle, carved with shaped polygonal facets, 1750–1820, 2¾in (7cm) high.
£750–900 *S*

A Yixing pottery snuff bottle, brightly enamelled on a blue ground with a magpie and prunus, 1820–50, 3¼in (8cm) high.
£850–1,000 *S(NY)*

A cinnabar lacquer snuff bottle, carved with Shou Lao standing beneath a pine tree, the reverse with a maiden, restored, c1800, 2½in (6.5cm) high.
£250–300 *S(S)*

A carved jade snuff bottle, the vessel well hollowed and carved in low relief overall with a fruiting double gourd vine, Qing Dynasty, 1780–1850, 2½in (6.5cm) high.
£1,700–2,000 *S*

An overlay glass snuff bottle, the opaque white bottle overlaid in green, yellow, blue and pink, 19thC, 1¾in (4.5cm) high.
£750–850 *S(S)*

A red overlay glass snuff bottle, decorated to each side with a coiled *chilong* between mask ring handles, on a snowstorm ground, jadeite stopper, 1780–1850, 3in (7.5cm) high.
£650–750 *CSK*

r. A jasper snuff bottle, depicting an ochre monkey chasing a butterfly with a stick, small chip, 1780–1850, 2¾in (7cm) high.
£5,500–6,500 *S*

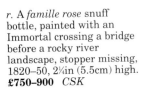

A red single-overlay glass snuff bottle, carved to the snowflake ground with 2 *chilong* chasing a flaming pearl on one side, the reverse with a further *chilong*, small chips, Qianlong period, 2¼in (5.5cm) high.
£650–750 *S(NY)*

r. A *famille rose* snuff bottle, painted with an Immortal crossing a bridge before a rocky river landscape, stopper missing, 1820–50, 2¼in (5.5cm) high.
£750–900 *CSK*

A puddingstone snuff bottle, of stout squared form, with mottled inclusions, 1800–50, 2¾in (7cm) hig
£300–350 *S(S)*

A porcelain snuff bottle, decorated in iron-red over yellow enamel with 5 bats around a *shou* medallion on each side, the neck and shoulders in blue and white with a brocade pattern, Qianlong mark and of the period, 2¼in (5.5cm) high.
£750–900 *S(NY)*

A porcelain snuff bottle, enamelled with 2 dragons chasing a flaming pearl, silver-coloured metal mount and stopper, six-character iron-red mark on base, Guangxu mark and of the period, 1874–1909, 2¼in (5.5cm) high.
£700–800 *S(S)*

A porcelain snuff bottle, formed as a folded lotus leaf with reeds and birds, c1850, 1¾in (4.5cm).
£250–300 *S(S)*

An ivory snuff bottle, carved as a giant double gourd, a crouching child clinging to one side, matching stopper, chipped, c1920, 2in (5cm) high.
£180–220 *S(S)*

A rock crystal snuff bottle, of flattened pear shape with a smoky hue, on a dimpled base, with a pink glass stopper, 1780–1850, 2¼in (5.5cm) high.
£600–700 *RHa*

An amber snuff bottle, with pale opaque inclusions, the shoulders carved with a mask and ring handles, 1800–50, 2in (5cm) high.
£450–500 *S(S)*

A glass overlay snuff bottle, with blue decoration of precious objects cut to clear glass, 19thC, 3in (7.5cm) high.
£280–300 *LHA*

A rock crystal snuff bottle, with brown inclusions, incised with bamboo, c1840, 1¾in (4.5cm) high.
£350–400 *Bon*

An amber snuff bottle, carved in the form of a pig, 1780–1850, 2¼in (5.5cm) long.
£7,000–8,500 *RHa*

A glass snuff bottle, of deep dark yellow colour, carved on one side with a lion-dog amongst cloud scrolls, the other with a temple emerging from clouds and flanked by birds, 1800–50, 2in (5cm) high.
£1,500–1,800 *S(S)*

A jasper snuff bottle, the mottled brown and yellow stone carved with lotus, 1800–50, 1½in (4cm) high.
£600–700 *S(S)*

An overlay glass snuff bottle, white overlaid in red, uncarved except the foot, chipped, 19thC, 2in (5cm) high.
£250–300 *S(S)*

l. A porcelain snuff bottle, painted in iron-red and gilt with dragons on each side, jadeite stopper, Daoguang two-character mark and of the period, 1¾in (4.5cm) high.
£1,500–1,800 *Bon*

l. A *famille rose* porcelain snuff bottle, moulded in relief with the 18 *lohan* on a green wave ground, minor chips, four-character Qianlong seal mark, 1800–50, 2in (5cm) high.
£1,300–1,500 *S(S)*

A jasper snuff bottle,
mottled green and ochre
with red inclusions,
1750–1850, 2in (5cm) high.
£600–700 *S(S)*

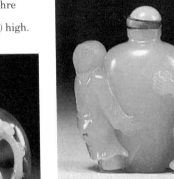

A *famille rose* porcelain figure-shaped
snuff bottle, modelled as a reclining female,
wearing a blue jacket and green trousers,
with her head resting on one hand and one
leg crossed over the other, the stopper in
the form of her left foot, restored, 1800–50,
3½in (9cm) high.
£1,200–1,400 *S(S)*

A lacquered wood snuff bottle,
in the form of a purse,
1780–1850, 2in (5cm) high.
£1,000–1,200 *RHa*

A Suzhou School nephrite
snuff bottle, 1780–1850,
2⅜in (7cm) high.
£25,000–30,000 *RHa*
*It is unusual to find a two-colour
jade bottle of this quality, where
the outer colour has been used
entirely in the decoration leaving
the base colour solely for the bottle.*

A celadon jade snuff bottle, shaped
as a vase with 2 boys either side,
1780–1850, 2in (5cm) high.
£1,700–1,900 *S(NY)*

A rock crystal snuff bottle, in the
form of a mallow flower, carved
in the centre of each side with
radiating flower petals, the stone
of smoky grey tone, slight damage
Qianlong period, 2⅜in (6cm) high.
£2,300–2,600 *S*

A fossiliferous limestone
snuff bottle, slight damage,
1780–1850, 2½in (6.5cm) high.
£1,000–1,200 *S*

A snuff bottle, decorated
in *famille rose* enamels,
rim slightly worn, Qianlong
seal mark and of the period,
2¼in (6cm) high.
£500–600 *S*

Fakes

The enormous increase in value
of Chinese snuff bottles has
inspired numerous fakes in the
past ten years, particularly those
of glass and hardstone. The
colours of fakes tend to be much
brighter, and the carved detail is
usually sharp to the touch, unlike
the smooth finish of the originals.

r. A chalcedony
snuff bottle,
the reverse with
pomegranates
picked out using
the ochre colours in
the stone, 1800–60,
1½in (4cm) high.
£250–300 *Bon*

l. A cinnabar lacquer snuff
bottle, carved with 4 fighting
dragons on a ground of waves,
lacking stopper, 19thC,
2in (5cm) high.
£350–400 *S(S)*

A silver snuff bottle, chased with
Manchurian script on one side, and
Mongolian on the other, the matching
stopper encrusted with coral and
turquoise, 1800–70, 2¾in (7cm) high.
£480–550 *S*

r. A white glazed ovoid porcelain snuff bottle, encased in a yellow glazed two-handled open basket, minor chip, 1800–50, 2in (5cm) high.
£600–700 *S(S)*

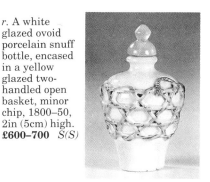

A seal-type glass snuff bottle, opaque white overlaid in brown, Yangzhou School, 1800–50, 1¾in (4.5cm) high.
£3,500–4,000 *S(S)*

A porcelain snuff bottle, covered in a speckled Robin's egg blue glaze, 19thC, 2in (5cm) high.
£400–450 *S(S)*

A glass snuff bottle, of deep dark yellow colour, carved on either side with fish, 1770–1850, 2in (5cm) high.
£1,500–1,800 *S(S)*

A cloisonné enamel snuff bottle, decorated in coloured enamels with butterflies and plants against a dark blue ground, 1820–50, 2½in (6.5cm) high.
£1,000–1,200 *S(HK)*

A porcelain snuff bottle, moulded in the form of a leaf, decorated in iron-red and gilt, reserved on each side with a large panel of diaper pattern in blue, Daoguang/Xianfeng period, 2½in (6.5cm) high.
£1,000–1,200 *S*

A rock crystal snuff bottle, carved with a magpie on a prunus branch, Daoguang period, 2½in (6.5cm) high.
£350–400 *S*

A porcelain snuff bottle, in the form of the Immortal Li Tieguai with a yellow double gourd tied to his back, 19thC, 3in (7.5cm) high.
£1,000–1,200 *S(HK)*

r. A porcelain snuff bottle, painted in underglaze blue with a five-clawed dragon chasing a flaming pearl, silver jadeite stopper, 1800–50, 3in (7.5cm) high.
£800–900 *Bon*

A porcelain snuff bottle, covered in a white glaze, foot and rim chipped, 1800–60, 1½in (4cm) high.
£70–100 *Bon*

A single-overlay snuff bottle, carved with stylised *shou* characters, 1800–50, 2¼in (5.5cm) high.
£450–500 *S*

An agate snuff bottle, with russet thumbprint patterns, 1770–1850, 1½in (4cm) high.
£350–400 *Bon*

An enamelled snuff bottle, moulded as an olive green squirrel on a fruiting vine, the flat base carved with leaves in varying shades of green with finely etched details, slight damage, c1880, 3in (7.5cm) long.
£850–1,000 *S(NY)*

l. A chalcedony snuff bottle, carved with a camel, monkey and lynx, yellow metal and jadeite stopper, 1820–80, 2in (5cm) high.
£720–800 *Bon*

l. A seal-type glass snuff bottle, overlaid in red, Yangzhou School, 1800–50, 2in (5cm) high.
£1,200–1,500 *Bon*

A chalcedony snuff bottle, the smoky stone with brown inclusions, c1800, 2½in (6.5cm) high.
£350–400 *Bon*

A porcelain snuff bottle, painted in *famille verte* enamels, Daoguang mark and of the period, 2in (5cm) high.
£350–400 *Bon*

A chalcedony snuff bottle carved with dragons, the reverse with an inscription, 19thC, 2in (5cm) high.
£130–150 *Bon*

An agate snuff bottle, supported on a neatly finished footrim, 1800–50, 2in (5cm) high.
£220–250 *Bon*

An enamelled glass snuff bottle, enamelled on a turquoise ground, with coral stopper, 1800–50, 2in (5cm) high.
£900–1,100 *Bon*

An agate snuff bottle, the white, honey and grey striated stone carved with figures on rocks, 1800–60, 2in (5cm) high.
£250–300 *Bon*

An amber snuff bottle and stopper, modelled as a finger-citron, 19thC, 2½in (6.5cm) high.
£250–300 *CSK*

Base Marks

Many items made in the Palace workshops were inscribed with the Imperial reign mark on the base. However, marks continued to be used long after the emperors to which they related had died. A reign mark on the base does not necessarily mean, therefore, that the piece dates from that reign.

A porcelain blue and white snuff bottle, with carved dragon decoration on white ground, inscribed seal mark, 19thC, 3in (7.5cm) high.
£350–400 *LHA*

A chalcedony snuff bottle, the darker skin in relief with a horseman holding a banner, 1800–50, 3in (7.5cm) high.
£650–800 *CSK*

A porcelain snuff bottle, moulded in the form of a corn on the cob, on a circular footrim, covered overall in blue, Daoguang period, 2¾in (7cm) high.
£250–300 *S(NY)*

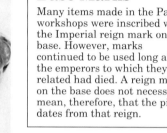

A *famille rose* porcelain snuff bottle, moulded and highlighted with iron-red and gilding with the 18 *lohan*, Qianlong four-character seal mark, 1800–50, 3in (7.5cm) high.
£250–300 *S*

A porcelain double snuff bottle, decorated with birds and dogs, Daoguang two-character mark, 2in (5cm) high.
£700–800 *POA*

r. An enamelled snuff bottle, moulded in the form of an artemisia leaf, the base with a four-character mark, c1850, 2¾in (7cm) high.
£350–400 *S(NY)*

A porcelain snuff bottle, decorated in *famille rose* enamels with warriors fighting outside a city wall, some wear, Tongzhi/Guangxu period, 3in (7.5cm) high.
£250–300 *S*

A shield-shaped snuff bottle, moulded with lions and brocade balls between *ruyi* head borders, covered in blue, late 18thC, 2½in (6.5cm) high.
£700–800 *S*

A snuff bottle, incised on each side with a dragon in flight, covered in a crackled white glaze, slight wear, the base incised with 3 characters '*cun de tang*', Jiaqing/Daoguang period, 2¾in (6cm) high.
£1,750–2,000 *S*

A snuff bottle, decorated in *famille rose* enamels with figures and a horse in a garden, Daoguang period, 2¼in (6cm) high.
£800–1,000 *S*

A porcelain snuff bottle, decorated in copper-red with a dragon on a blue and white ground, some damage, Jiaqing period, 3¼in (8.5cm) high.
£350–400 *S*

A porcelain snuff bottle, painted in *famille rose* with a grasshopper, slight wear, 1820–50, 3in (7.5cm) high.
£350–400 *S(NY)*

A porcelain pear-shaped snuff bottle, painted in iron-red with demons, worn, Daoguang/Xianfeng period, 2¾in (7cm) high.
£450–550 *S*

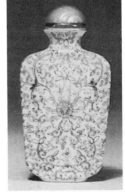

A *famille rose* snuff bottle, enamelled on a yellow ground with stylised lotus, lip worn, four-character mark in iron-red on the base, c1880, 2¼in (6cm) high.
£350–400 *S(NY)*

A porcelain snuff bottle, moulded in the form of a monkey, the eyes highlighted in black, slight damage, Jiaqing period, 3in (7.5cm) high.
£350–400 *S*

r. A white jade snuff bottle, late 18th/early 19thC, 2in (5cm) high.
£500–600 *C*

l. An inside-painted glass snuff bottle, by the Ye Family, with a scene of boys dressed in bright colours, playing in a tree-lined field, signed and dated, 1914, 2¼in (6cm) high.
£1,200–1,400 *S(NY)*

A cloisonné enamel snuff bottle, decorated with scholarly objects on a powder blue ground, Qianlong mark on base, early 20thC, 2½in (6.5cm) high.
£350–400 *S(HK)*

Glass

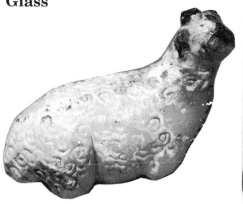

A glass model of a sheep, of pale celadon tone with amethyst coloured head, a whitish slightly degraded patination to most parts, incised underneath with small curls imitating wool, chips, probably Han Dynasty, 2½in (7cm) wide.
£2,500–3,000 *C*

A Peking red and yellow overlay glass vase, carved with flowers and birds with a rockwork ground, 18thC, 6in (15cm) high.
£2,500–3,000 *S(NY)*

A green glass bowl, with steeply rounded sides rising from a flat countersunk base, suffused with minute air bubbles, small chips to rim, four-character mark on the base, Qianlong period, 6½in (16.5cm) diam.
£1,500–1,800 *S(NY)*

A Peking red overlay 'snowflake' glass cup, with a band of dragons beneath a cloud collar border, Qianlong period, 2½in (6.5cm) high.
£1,350–1,500 *SK*

A pair of Peking red overlay 'snowflake' glass vases, decorated with dragons and phoenix, Qianlong period, 7½in (19cm) high.
£3,500–4,000 *SK*

A Peking deep red glass box and cover, incised with the *yin yang* symbols, Qianlong four-character mark and of the period, 5in (13cm) diam.
£3,500–4,000 *CSK*

A Peking yellow glass *zhadou,* with widely flaring neck, bulbous centre section, on a cylindrical foot, with four-character mark on base, Qianlong period, 4in (10cm) high.
£7,500–9,000 *S(NY)*

r. A yellow ground glass bottle, with red overlay, a *chilong* amid cloud swirls around the neck, carved flowers sprouting from rocks encircling the base, 1770–1820, 6¾in (17cm) high.
£5,000–6,000 *S(NY)*

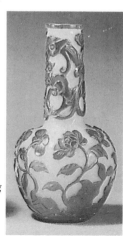

A turquoise glass vase, with yellow overlay, carved in deep relief with pheasants amid flowering branches, a frieze of rocks around the base, 18thC, 8½in (21.5cm) high.
£5,000–6,000 *S(NY)*

A Peking yellow glass vase, decorated in relief with birds among prunus, 1780–1850, 7in (18cm) high.
£2,500–3,000 *CSK*

A pair of opaque turquoise glass bottle vases, Qianlong marks and of the period, ½in (16.5cm) high.
£6,000–7,000 *CNY*

A reverse glass painting, depicting a maiden holding an oar in a boat, with vases of flowers, Daoguang period, c1830, 17½ x 12½in (44.5 x 32cm), framed.
£1,700–2,000 *S(S)*

A Peking turquoise glass vase, decorated with white circles and oblongs, 1750–1820, 9½in (25cm) high.
£1,500–1,800 *CSK*

A set of 4 glass cups, coloured red, blue, purple and turquoise, the steeply rounded sides flaring towards the rim, carved around the sides in deep relief with flowering branches, on short countersunk bases, 1800–60, 3¼in (8.5cm) diam.
£2,500–3,000 *S(NY)*

A pair of Peking red and white overlay glass vases, each decorated with female figures in a garden, late 19thC, 8in (20.5cm) high.
£1,200–1,400 *SK*

A Peking red overlay glass flared bowl, decorated to the exterior with flowering branches on a milky-white ground, late 19thC, 6in (15cm) diam.
£250–300 *CSK*

A rock crystal *koro* and cover, early 19thC, 5in (12.5cm) wide.
£750–900 *SW*

Collecting Chinese Glass

Chinese glass is still made by hand, so be careful – it can be difficult to distinguish between old and new wares. The value of Chinese glass is determined more by quality than age. Wear is not a reliable indication of age because many pieces were made simply for display. Copying in China is considered to be a mark of respect – even down to signatures and marks. Take care when evaluating any piece.

A pair of overlay glass vases, decorated in relief with birds and prunus, 1800–50, 9½in (24cm) high.
£800–1,000 *CSK*

r. A Peking blue and green overlay glass tapering vase, carved with birds among flowering prunus, 1820–80, 5in (12.5cm) high.
£500–550 *CSK*

A Peking yellow glass baluster vase, with flaring neck, carved with prunus, pine and bamboo issuing from rockwork, 1820–80, 6in (15cm) high, in a fitted box.
£850–1,000 *CSK*

CHINESE BRONZE

The first great age of bronze workmanship in China is associated with the Shang Dynasty (circa 1500–1050 BC), when bronze was valued as an elite symbol of royal power. Although mainly used for ritual objects, bronze was also used in the manufacture of bells and weapons. During the Zhou Dynasty (circa 1050–221 BC) bronze became more readily available and was used by a larger social group. Many fine objects such as lamps, tableware, mirrors and religious statues were made and subsequently buried with their wealthy owners. With the greater use of bronze came the expansion of the use of inscriptions, particularly on the larger and heavier pieces. These inscriptions often provide invaluable historical information:

what the object was used for, who it was made for and when it was made. Through the Ming (1368–1644) and Qing (1644–1916) dynasties bronze objects became more decorative and flamboyant, culminating in 19th-century bronzes that, at their worst, can be quite hideous.

Most early bronzes have been excavated from tombs and therefore have suffered surface degradation. This can be attractive in itself and, if left alone, best serves the interests of conservation. However, many old bronzes have been repatinated by selective polishing and staining. Bronzes with a good, original patination will always have a price premium over those with artificial finishes.

Bowls & Censers

A bronze footed bowl, with loose ring handles and animal masks, Han Dynasty, 10in (25.5cm) diam.
£650–750 *WW*

A bronze bombé tripod censer, with loop handles, traces of gilding, Xuande six-character mark within a coiled dragon to the base, 6½in (16.5cm) wide.
£500–600 *CSK*

A bronze tripod censer, cast with 3 panels of zoomorphic motifs among *leiwen*, some encrustation, late Shang/early Western Zhou Dynasty, 6in (15cm) high.
£850–1,000 *C*

A bronze bombé censer, with pierced handles and flattened rim, Xuande six-character mark, 12in (30.5cm) diam.
£420–480 *CSK*

A bronze tripod globular vessel and cover, with bird's head spout, handle inscribed, Ming Dynasty, 7in (18cm) wide.
£450–550 *CSK*

A bronze bombé censer, with mythical head handles, decorated with bands of stylised *taotie* masks on a key pattern ground, areas of malachite remaining, worn, Ming Dynasty, 7½in (19cm) diam.
£450–500 *CSK*

A bronze censer and joss stick holder, with handles modedlled as boys standing on rockwork above mythical deers, Ming Dynasty, 5in (12.5cm) high.
£575–650 *CSK*

A bronze censer, with high loop handles, the body cast with *taotie* between vertical flanges, early 17thC, 10in (25.5cm) high
£600–700 *CSK*

bronze tripod censer,
ith wood cover, elephant-
ead ring handles, inlaid
ith silver decoration on
key-fret pattern ground
bove flowersprays, 18thC,
⅜in (16cm) wide.
320–360 *CSK*

A bronze bombé censer, moulded
with twin Buddhistic lion handles,
18thC, 5⅛in (14cm) high.
£160–180 *CSK*

A pair of inlaid bronze censers,
modelled as Immortals, 19thC,
26in (66cm) high.
£2,000–2,500 *CSK*

A bronze tripod censer, the domed
cover with Buddhistic lion finial,
flaring foliate handles, decorated
with panels of lion masks and
scrolling foliage, on a raised stand
decorated with coiled dragons,
19thC, 21½in (54.5cm) high.
£500–600 *CSK*

bronze censer, on 3 lions'
ead feet, decorated with
central band of trigrams
etween borders of precious
bjects, seal mark, 19thC,
½in (9cm) high.
350–400 *CSK*

Bronze Censers

The bronze tripod vessel, *ding*,
was a cooking vessel in ancient
times but later took on an
important sacrificial role at
worship ceremonies. The number
of *ding* used and their size
indicated the power and status
of their aristocratic owner
(nine for an emperor, seven for
a duke or lord, etc).

r. A bronze censer and pierced cover,
modelled as a mythical horned beast,
19thC, 8¼in (21cm) high.
£700–770 *CSK*

Figures – Animals

l. A bronze weight,
modelled as a
reclining horned
mythical beast,
the tail flicked
over its back,
17thC, 3½in (9cm)
long, on a carved
wood stand.
£700–800 *CSK*

A pair of bronze mythical beasts, the tails resembling flames,
races of gilt and red lacquer, 17thC, 21in (53.5cm) high.
7,000–8,000 *C*

l. A gilt-bronze figure of a
recumbent unicorn, areas
of gilt rubbed, 17thC,
10½in (26.5cm) long.
£2,000–2,500 *C*

A bronze twin-headed duck,
inlaid with gilt and white metal,
late Ming Dynasty, 3½in (9cm) long.
£600–700 *CSK*

A bronze mythical beast, with long plumed tail, a snake on its haunches, old wear, 17th/18thC, 7in (18cm) long, on a wood stand.
£350–400 *CSK*

A pair of bronze ornamental elephants, each supporting a vase on its back, late 19thC, 10in (25.5cm) high, on hardwood stands.
£250–300 *PCh*

Miller's is a price GUIDE not a price LIST

l. A bronze model of a trumpeting elephant, 19thC, 32in (81.5cm) long.
£800–1,000 *CNY*

r. A group of gilt-bronze animal ornaments, Tang Dynasty, largest 2in (5cm) wide.
£1,800–2,000 *C*

Figures – People

l. A bronze figure of Buddha standing on a tortoise base, mandorla missing, late Ming Dynasty, 18½in (47cm) high.
£1,800–2,000 *CNY*

A Sino-Tibetan gilt-bronze figure of a monk, 17th/18thC, 6½in (16.5cm) high.
£1,300–1,500 *CNY*

A bronze figure of Buddha, with pendulous earlobes and tightly curled hair, the cloak falling over both shoulders, some degrading, late Ming Dynasty, 12½in (32cm) high.
£1,800–2,000 *CSK*

A gilt-bronze figure of an Immortal, wearing a leaf belt above a pleated skirt with decorated border, holding a censer in one hand, on a rockwork base, early 17thC, 13in (33cm) high.
£700–800 *CSK*

l. A gilt-bronze model of a bearded Immortal, wearing a tabbed hat and long flowing robes, early 17thC, 10in (25.5cm) high.
£300–350 *CSK*

l. A gilt-bronze figure of Buddha, some area regilt, early 17thC, 16½in (42cm) high.
£1,700–1,900 *CSK*

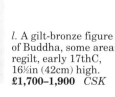

gilt-bronze model
f a seated Buddha,
ld wear, early 17thC,
in (18cm) high.
250–300 *CSK*

A bronze figure of Guanyin,
inlaid in silver with scrolling lotus,
one finger missing, 17thC, 11in
(28cm) high, on a wood stand.
£2,000–2,200 *C*

A gilt-bronze figure of Guanyin,
seated, with one had raised,
Ming Dynasty, 29in (73.5cm) high.
£24,000–28,000 *S*

gilt-bronze figure of a
odhisattva, Ming Dynasty,
in (23cm) high.
900–1,000 *Bon*

A bronze figure of a sage, his robes
cast with dragons, clouds and floral
designs, 19thC, 10in (25.5cm) high.
£450–500 *Bon*

A gilt-bronze figure of a
Bodhisattva, with jewels in her
hair and wearing a jewelled
necklace, 18thC, 6in (15cm) high.
£1,200–1,500 *P(S)*

Vases

r. A bronze *gu*-shaped
vase, decorated with
leaf-shaped panels of
stylised *taotie* on key
pattern grounds
interspersed with
flanges, some wear,
Ming Dynasty,
13in (33cm) high.
£180–200 *CSK*

l. A bronze trumpet-
shaped vase, decorated
in relief with flowering
prunus branches, some
wear, Kangxi period,
11in (28cm) high,
on a wood stand.
£350–400 *CSK*

A bronze *gu*-shaped beaker vase,
17thC, 10in (25.5cm) high.
£200–250 *CSK*

A gilt-splashed bronze vase, moulded with 2 scrolls, the neck flanked by dragon loop handles, Qing Dynasty, 4¾in (12cm) high.
£1,400–1,600 *S(HK)*

A pair of bronze pear-shaped vases, with garlic necks, decorated in relief with coiled dragons to the neck and 2 bands of flowering branches, old wear, early 17thC, 10in (25.5cm) high.
£450–550 *CSK*

A bronze vase, with 2 animal mask loose ring handles, the body with raised mask and cloud collar designs, the base of the neck with a band of stylised dragons, 19thC, 21½in (54.5cm) high.
£125–140 *SK*

Miscellaneous

A gold and silver-inlaid bronze wheel fitting, Warring States, 4½in (11.5cm) long.
£2,200–2,500 *C*

A bronze arrow vase, damaged, possibly 16thC, 20½in (52cm) high.
£2,200–2,500 *C*

A bronze bell, with double inter-twined dragon handle, decorated with various miscellaneous objects, 17th/18thC, 17½in (44.5cm) high, with beater and wooden stand.
£1,000–1,200 *CSK*

A bronze double gourd vessel, on 2 feet cast as branches, decorated in relief with numerous squirrels among fruiting vine, some wear, probably Qianlong period, 7in (17cm) high.
£350–400 *CSK*

A bronze seven-tier pagoda, late 18thC, 100in (254cm) high.
£8,500–9,500 *CNY*

A pair of bronze candlesticks, in the form of 2 boys holding lotus shaped torches, riding on an elephant and a mythical lion, 18th/19thC, 12½in (32cm) high.
£1,100–1,300 *S(NY)*

CHINESE CLOISONNE

Cloisonné decoration consists of different coloured glass pastes (enamels) contained within enclosures of copper wire, applied to the surface of metal vessels, fired in a kiln and then polished. Early cloisonné had heavy cast bronze or brass as the base material, but by the late Qing Dynasty copper was used, resulting in much lighter pieces. The wire fields, or *cloisons*, were glued on with vegetable glue rather than being soldered, and a much wider variety of colours was used.

Early cloisonné is not technically perfect and the surface can be quite rough, but the varied designs are bold and vigorous. Later designs became more standardised, and the techniques and styles reflect the move towards quantity rather than quality. At the end of the 19th century large amounts of cloisonné were exported to the West to meet demand created by international exhibitions. Although some of these pieces are of sufficiently high quality to merit attention, the majority are not.

Bowls

A pair of cloisonné bowls, decorated with lotus flowers and scrolling foliage, the undersides with 'cracked ice' pattern, 18thC, 5in (12.5cm) diam.
£750–850 *CSK*

A cloisonné bowl, decorated with a band of stylised scrolling lotus and foliage above a band of lappets, on a turquoise ground, Ming Dynasty, 5in (12.5cm) diam.
£700–800 *CSK*

Boxes

A cloisonné box and cover, made for the Tibetan market, pitted and restored, 17thC, 6¾in (17cm) diam.
£800–900 *CSK*

A cloissoné box and cover, with pierced celadon jade inset top, carved with trumpet-shaped flowers and leaves on a pierced trellis ground, the sides decorated with stylised peony flowerheads on a turquoise ground, incised Qianlong four-character mark, 11½in (29cm) wide.
£550–650 *CSK*

A cloisonné box and cover, decorated with bands of stylised lotus surrounding a central character, 18thC, 2in (5cm) diam.
£230–280 *CSK*

Censers

A cloisonné censer and domed cover, with elephant-head handles, damaged, Jiaqing period, 12in (30.5cm) high.
£1,200–1,500 *CSK*

A pair of cloisonné censers and covers, modelled as quails, Qianlong period, 5⅝in (14cm) high.
£2,000–2,200 *CSK*

l. A cloisonné enamel censer and cover, surmounted by a pierced dragon knop, decorated with birds, Kangxi period, 14¾in (37.5cm) high.
£1,800–2,000 *CNY*

Vases

A cloisonné bottle vase, decorated on a turquoise ground, Qianlong period, 5½in (14cm) high.
£350–400 *CSK*

A cloisonné flattened quatrefoil vase, with flaring neck, decorated with buildings and pagodas, trees and rockwork, on a turquoise ground, Jiaqing period, 13in (33cm) high.
£800–900 *CSK*

A cloisonné vase, mid-19thC, 14in (36cm) high.
£500–600 *Wai*

A cloisonné baluster vase, of diamond cross section, with mask ring handles, decorated on a turquoise ground, 19thC, 19in (48.5cm) high.
£650–750 *CSK*

A pair of cloisonné wall vases, modelled as baskets with overturned rims, decorated with rural scenes within central cartouches surrounded by a turquoise ground of lotus flowers, 19thC, 9in (23cm) high.
£500–600 *CSK*

A cloisonné baluster vase, decorated with scrolling lotus and leafy tendrils on a turquoise ground, damaged, 19thC, 17in (43cm) high.
£450–500 *CSK*

A cloisonné bottle vase, decorated on a turquoise ground reserved with key frets, slight damage, 19thC, 16in (40.5cm) high.
£850–1,000 *CSK*

A cloisonné bottle vase, decorated on a dark blue ground with stiff leaves to the shoulder, *ruyi* heads to the neck, 19thC, 16in (40.5cm) high.
£250–300 *CSK*

A cloisonné waisted baluster vase, with flaring neck, decorated with flowers issuing from rockwork, on a turquoise ground, early 20thC, 10in (25.5cm) high.
£100–120 *CSK*

Miscellaneous

A cloisonné octagonal stand, the top decorated with figures on a terrace, supported by a gilt stand on 8 scrolling legs joined at the feet, some enamel losses and gilding rubbed, 17thC, 13in (33cm) diam.
£2,300–2,800 *C*

A cloisonné tripod dish, decorated with entwined flowers and foliage on a turquoise ground, Ming Dynasty, late 16th/early 17thC, 6in (15cm) diam.
£600–700 *CSK*

cloisonné enamel and gilt-etal clock, the domed top with on finial, the edges applied ith prunus branch mounts, the des with panels of flowers, the ase with a pierced apron, Qing ynasty, 19¼in (49cm) high.
1,800–2,200 *S*

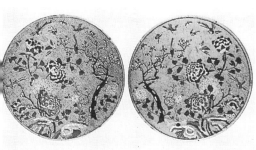

pair of cloisonné enamel plaques, decorated with flowers ssuing from ornamental rockwork, beneath a magnolia ree, rims gilt, late 18thC, 23⅓in (59.5cm) diam.
900–1,000 *Bon*

A pair of cloisonné and gilt-bronze jardinières, decorated in blue and white, a *ruyi* collar at the shoulder, applied with loose ring handles beneath double animals' heads, pitted, late Qing Dynasty, 22in (56cm) diam.
£3,200–3,600 *C*

Cloisonné

Cloisonné is considered to have reached its peak in terms of quality during the reign of the Ming Emperor Jingtai (1450–57). Objects were mostly of a blue (*lan*) colour, so cloisonné is known in China as *Jingtailan*.

CHINESE SILVER

silver bowl, early 20thC, in (23cm) diam, 24oz.
850–1,000 *SK(B)*

A pair of silver inlaid joss stick holders, modelled as cranes perched on lotus pods, the heads lowered, early 20thC, 11⅓in (29.5cm) high.
£450–500 *CSK*

l. A silver tripod lobed teapot and domed cover, decorated in relief with butterflies among flowerheads, the handle with ivory insets, signed, late 19thC, 7in (17.5cm) long.
£850–1,000 *CSK*

A silver stem cup, decorated with a continuous band of figures, surrounding a monogram 'The Banker's Cup, Hong Kong Nov 1866, Victoria Regatta Club', above a coiled dragon among cloud scrolls, 8½in (21.5cm) high.
£850–1,000 *CSK*

JAPANESE BRONZE

The earliest Japanese figurative bronzes to surface on the market are mostly Chinese-influenced Buddhist sculpture from the 8th to 18th centuries. The modelling is generally stiff or clumsy, the result of a tendency to replicate images. It is not until the Meiji period (1868–1912) and increased Western contact that a new approach to sculpture emerges. Given that the metalworkers were largely targeting export markets, they were naturally interested in Western models, and it is certain that the Italian sculptor Vincenzo Ragusa, who taught at the Tokyo Art School, had a huge influence in transmitting a taste for naturalism at the end of the century. The most common subjects are animals and genre. The often exotic animals sculpted do not occur naturally in Japan, but would have been seen at the newly established zoological gardens. Typical animalier compositions are dramatic struggles to the death of the type produced by such French sculptors as Antoine-Louis Barye earlier in the century. The genre subjects tend towards sentimentality, but whatever the subject these bronzes are well-observed naturalistic representations, with scrupulous attention to anatomical and other detail, and often finished with beautiful patination.
It should be pointed out that many of the animalier subjects cast by Genryusai Seiya, one of the most prolific foundries, exist to this day in large numbers, in particular the smaller elephant groups and the individual

lions and tigers. Good as they are, they are not obvious investment material, and often make lower prices at auction than expected. In general it is recommended to buy larger unusual compositions, particularly those without gory subjects.

Japanese engraving, too, can be impressive. Look in particular for variations of surface textures and cutting techniques, with the use of different chisels and stamps. The best work will include some cuts at a slant, as well as lines that vary in thickness along their length. The most impressive metalwork from the Meiji period tends to be that with mixed inlays, sometimes in combination with engraved elements. Some of the patinations on such works are not only sophisticated but also vulnerable, particularly the beautiful jet-black alloy called *shakudo*: if rubbed too vigorously or, even worse, cleaned with an abrasive or solvent, it may disappear to leave a disappointing copper in its place. On the whole such pieces should only be cleaned by an expert, and it is worth consulting a conservator who understands Japanese metalwork.

Past demand for Japanese metalwork has resulted in an abundance of poor-quality work on the market. However, the experience that comes from handling and looking at metalwork over a period of time will help the collector to tell the good from the bad.

Max Rutherston

Figures – Animals

A bronze eagle, perched on rockwork, looking at a coiled dragon, 19thC, 22in (56cm) high.
£2,500–3,000 *CSK*

A bronze hawk, perched on rockwork, mid-19thC, 12in (30.5cm) high.
£1,200–1,400 *ChC*

A bronze lion, naturalistically detailed, the eyes inlaid with mother-of-pearl and horn, seal mark, 19thC, 17½in (44.5cm) long, on a wood stand.
£600–700 *CSK*

A bronze crayfish, late 19thC, 17in (43cm) long.
£2,500–3,000 *P(M)*

A bronze model of a swimming carp, supported on its fins the eyes inlaid with gilt, 19thC, 8in (20.5cm) long.
£550–650 *CSK*

bronze terrapin with 2 babies,
9thC, 10in (25.5cm) long.
1,300–1,500 *HSS*

A bronze monkey, perched on a
persimmon fruit, slight damage,
19thC, 11½in (29cm) high.
£750–850 *CSK*

A gilt-bronze eagle with
outstretched wings,
alighting on a branch,
19thC, 27½in (70cm) wide.
£2,500–3,000 *CSK*

A bronze model of a snarling tiger,
he stripes well defined, signed,
ate 19thC, 11½in (29cm) long.
£350–400 *CSK*

A bronze rabbit, the fur
markings well delineated,
19thC, 8in (20.5cm) long.
£1,300–1,500 *CSK*

r. Two bronze crayfish, with
their tails tucked underneath
their bodies, old wear, 19thC,
8½in (21.5cm) long.
£350–400 *CSK*

Two bronze quails, probably by Yukiyasu,
Meiji period, 5in (12.5cm) wide.
£1,300–1,500 *WW*

r. A bronze hawk,
perched on a tree-
stump base, 19thC,
13½in (34.5cm) high.
£1,000–1,200 *CSK*

A bronze articulated crab, with naturalistic
details, 19thC, 4in (10cm) wide.
£500–600 *CSK*

A pair of bronze pigeons, the eyes gilt, possibly replacement feet, late 19thC, 4in (10cm) long.
£600–700 *CSK*

A bronze lion, its teeth bared in a roar, impressed seal Seiya saku, late 19thC, 20in (51cm) long, with wooden base.
£700–800 *S*

A pair of bronze elephant-head bookends, with deep red patinated decorated ears, undersides of trunks and tusks, signed, late 19thC, 6in (15cm) high.
£450–500 *GC*

A patinated bronze group of quail, coloured in copper, *shakudo* and gilt, mounted on a carved wood base, signed 'Yoshitani sei', late 19thC, 14in (35.5cm) long.
£1,800–2,000 *S*

l. A bronze model of a growling tiger, late 19thC, 26in (66cm) long.
£1,000–1,200
r. A bronze elephant being attacked by a pair of tigers, the elephant with ivory tusks, late 19thC, 17in (43cm) long.
£700–800 *Bon*

l. A bronze model of a seated monkey, holding a peach and gazing upwards, wearing a short jacket decorated with geometric patterns, 19thC, 7in (18cm) high.
£700–800 *CSK*

Figures – People

A bronze figure of Fugen Bosatsu, seated on the back of a recumbent caparisoned elephant, 19thC, 10in (25.5cm) high.
£500–600 *CSK*

l. A bronze figure of a warrior, decorated in relief with dragons among clouds, pole missing, late 19thC, 24in (61cm) high.
£1,700–2,000 *CSK*

A bronze figure of a seated smoker, signed 'Kaneda chu zo no ki', late 19thC, 17in (43cm) high.
£1,800–2,000 *S*

A bronze group, modelled as a young boy with a tortoise, stamped seal mark, 8in (20.5cm) high.
£1,500–1,800 *CSK*

A bronze figure of a woman feeding a pigeon, signed 'Kazumasa', late 19thC, 20in (51cm) high.
£1,300–1,500 *S*

parcel-gilt bronze figure f a rice farmer, by Miyao, igned with seal, on a gilt acquered wood stand, late 9thC, 8in (20.5cm) high.
1,300–1,500 *S*

A bronze *okimono* of an archer, by Seiko, late 19thC, 16in (40.5cm) high.
£2,200–2,500 *S*

parcel-gilt bronze model of mask carver, by Miyao, signed ith seal, mallet replaced, n a gilt lacquered wood stand, ate 19thC, 7in (18cm) high.
1,300–1,500 *S*

A bronze figure of a warrior, sword possibly restored, signed 'Miyao' with seal, late 19thC, 15in (38cm) high, on a giltwood base.
£2,500–3,000 *S*

A pair of ronze figures of vorkmen, with ilt details, signed Miyao' with seal, n giltwood bases, ate 19thC, 8in 20.5cm) high.
2,200–2,500 *S*

Okimono

Japanese *okimono* (literally meaning 'put thing/s') are sculpted figures, made during the Meiji and Taisho (1912–26) periods as ornaments for the home and for export to Europe and the USA. Many *okimono* are signed, but only a few of their makers are considered important.

l. A bronze figure of a fisherman, with gilt details, signed on a rectangular tablet 'Miyao' with seal, possibly a weighing stick missing from one hand, on a gilt wood base, late 19thC, 12in (30.5cm) high.
£1,600–1,800 *S*

An inlaid bronze figure of a warrior, signed 'Miyao zo', late 19thC, 7in (18cm) high.
£1,700–2,000 *S(NY)*

Incense Burners

A bronze incense burner and cover, modelled as a *shishi*, with green patination, 18th/19thC, 14¼in (36cm) high.
£650–750 *MSW*

A bronze incense burner, on 4 feet, top section missing, damaged, 56in (142cm) high.
£1,500–1,800 *CSK*

A bronze incense burner, in the form of a seated *shishi,* 19thC, 18in (45.5cm) high.
£1,500–1,800 *P(S)*

A bronze incense burner and cover, shaped as a persimmon, with a monkey holding a branch, his coat engraved with gilt birds and leaves, late 19thC, 12in (30.5cm) high.
£2,200–2,500 *S*

l. A bronze incense burner, cast as a caparisoned trumpeting elephant, minor damage, incised two-character mark on an applied plaque, inscribed 'Shomin', late 19thC, 24½in (62cm) high.
£1,000–1,200 *CNY*

A green patinated bronze incense burner, and pierced domed cover, one leg loose, one *karashishi* missing from base, old damage, 19thC, 47in (119cm) high.
£3,500–4,000 *CSK*

A bronze incense burner and cover, modelled as 2 carp, one leaping up and the other lying flat with its tail flicked up, 19thC, 6½in (16.5cm) long.
£600–700 *CSK*

A bronze two-handled incense burner and domed cover, seal mark, 19thC, 36in (91.5cm) high.
£2,500–3,000 *CSK*

l. A pierced bronze lantern, decorated with bamboo and flowers, chipped, late 19thC, 12in (30.5cm) diam.
£350–400 *CSK*

A bronze lantern, modelled as an owl, the hollow body with stylised pierced feathers, slight damage, late 19thC, 14½in (37cm) high.
£600–700 *C*

Jardinières

A bronze jardinière, minor damage, signed 'Dai Nihon Genryusai Seiya zo', late 19thC, 19½in (50cm) diam.
£2,500–3,000 *C*

A bronze jardinière, cast in relief with several monkeys playing, some holding persimmon, signed 'Genryusai (Seiya Zo)', late 19thC, 14in (36cm) diam.
£1,500–2,000 *CSK*

A bronze lobed jardinière, on 8 elephant-head feet, inscribed 'Dai Nippon, Bunsei Nensei, Sei Minju', early 19thC, 24½in (60cm) diam.
£3,500–4,000 *CSK*

A bronze jardinière, on 4 feet, with mythical head handles, decorated with birds and hares above breaking waves, seal mark, 19thC, 16in (40.5cm) wide.
£450–500 *CSK*

A bronze globular jardinière, on 5 feet, decorated in relief with a continuous procession of elephants, signed 'Seiya', late 19thC, 8in (20.5cm) wide.
£500–600 *CSK*

Vases

A pair of inlaid bronze vases, late 19thC, 13½in (34.5cm).
£1,700–2,000 *C*

A pair of bronze vases, decorated in silver, gilt and copper inlay with cranes, a kingfisher and a swallow in flight among lotus and reeds, damaged, one signed, 19thC, 6½in (16.5cm) high.
£450–500 *CSK*

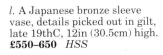

A bronze vase, with flaring neck, decorated in relief with carp and a crayfish among simulated waves and aquatic plants between foliate and geometric borders, old wear, signed, late 19thC, 24½in (62cm) high.
£1,200–1,400 *CSK*

l. A Japanese bronze sleeve vase, details picked out in gilt, late 19thC, 12in (30.5cm) high.
£550–650 *HSS*

r. A Japanese red and green patinated bronze baluster vase, inlaid in gilt and silver, damaged, 19thC, 14½in (37cm) high.
£350–400 *CSK*

A pair of bronze pear-shaped hexagonal vases, with foliate rims, decorated and patinated in green relief with irises issuing from streams, signed, both drilled, 19thC, 14in (36cm) high.
£450–500 *CSK*

A pair of green patinated bronze vases, with everted leafy necks, relief-decorated in silver with irises above ropes tying the stems, signed 'Seiya', late 19thC, 11in (28cm) high.
£1,000–1,200 *CSK*

A bronze vase, by Genryus Seiya, applied in high relie with vessels, an elephant and a hawk, signed, late 19thC, 18in (45.5cm) high
£4,500–5,500 *S*

Miscellaneous

An inlaid bronze bowl, of flower form, the exterior decorated in low relief with egrets wading among lotus, heightened in gilt, signed, late 19thC, 8in (20.5cm) diam.
£600–700 *S(S)*

A bronze bowl, with 3 panels depicting interior scenes with figures, silvered mounts, raised on 3 silver feet, late 19thC, 5in (12.5cm) high.
£1,000–1,200 *FBG*

A bronze cauldron, decorated with figures and clouds, having elephant mask and trunk handles 19thC, 18in (46cm) diam.
£300–350 *RBB*

A bronze tripod censer, inlaid with silver and gilt, with flowers and birds, above a band of key pattern, late 19thC, 9in (23cm) wide.
£600–700 *CSK*

A bronze teapot and cover, with loop handle applied with gilt, silver, copper and bronze insects and butterflies, signed, late 19thC, 4⅓in (11cm) high.
£800–900 *CSK*

A bronze dish, inlaid in brass with a writhing dragon, the details in black and red, signed 'Inoue' and 'Ariake', late 19thC, 11in (28cm) diam.
£1,000–1,200 *CSK*

l. A bronze teapot and cover, decorated in soft metal inlay with fruiting vine, the finial with a squirrel, signed 'Dai Nihon Kyoto Goro zo saku', late 19thC, 7in (18cm) high.
£1,000–1,200 *C*

A bronze inkwell, in the form of a helmet, late 19thC, 3in (7.5cm) wide
£1,300–1,500 *C*

JAPANESE CLOISONNE

A cloisonné vase, decorated with birds and flowers on a blue ground, slight damage, late 19thC, 21in (53cm) high.
£7,000–8,000 *LRG*

A cloisonné vase, decorated with a hen and a cockerel on a light green ground, late 19thC, 7in (18cm) high.
£200–250 *SK*

A pair of cloisonné vases, decorated with birds in flight among bamboo and flowering daisies on black grounds between bands of stiff leaves, late 19thC, 10in (25.5cm) high.
£400–500 *CSK*

A pair of cloisonné vases, decorated in wireless technique with irises on a pale cream ground, inlaid mark of Ando Jubei, late 19thC, 9½in (24cm) high.
£1,000–1,200 *S*

A pair of wireless cloisonné vases, each decorated with egrets on lime green grounds, restored, late 19thC, 5in (12.5cm) high.
£100–120 *CSK*

A cloisonné vase, decorated in gold wire on a black ground, slight damage, mark for Miwa Tomisaburo, late 19thC, 8in (20cm) high.
£6,000–7,000 *S*

JAPANESE IRON

l. An inlaid iron *tetsubin*, 19thC, 7in (18cm) wide.
£450–550 *S(S)*

Japanese Iron

The development of iron in Japan is linked intimately with that of armour. The best iron has a reddish (russet) tone and appears naturally wet or oiled. Alloys peculiar to Japan are *shakudo* (jet black), *shibuichi* (dull grey) and *sentoku* (yellow bronze).

An iron *tetsubin* and bronze cover, inlaid in silver and gilt with a flowerspray, the body decorated with Kinko on the back of a carp above waves, and a panel of calligraphy, with loop handle, the cover signed, 19thC, 8in (20.5cm) wide.
£350–400 *CSK*

l. Two articulated models of insects, one signed (Miochin) 'Muneyoshi', 19thC, 2½in (6.5cm) long.
£2,000–2,200 *S*

JAPANESE SILVER

A pair of silver presentation
vases, each with chrysanthemums
above a butterfly and lilies,
Meiji period, 11¾in (30cm) high.
£2,500–3,000 *Bon*

A silver-mounted pipe, applied in *takazogan* with
small birds above peonies, rubbed, signed 'Terumichi
saku', Meiji period, 10⅝in (27cm) long.
£700–800 *S*

Two silver bowls, decorated with flowering peonies
and irises issuing from rockwork on stippled grounds,
the interiors gilt, one rubbed, stamped 'Arthur &
Bone, Yokohama, Sterling', 5in (12.5cm) diam.
£450–550 *CSK*

A silver bowl, decorated with
irises on a stippled ground,
the interior plain, early
20thC, 7in (17.5cm) diam.
£550–650 *CSK*

A Japanese punch bowl, the body
applied with chrysanthemums
and mon, 3 foliate scroll feet,
two-character marks, early
20thC, 13in (33cm) diam, 97oz.
£1,200–1,400 *P(S)*

A silver-plated copper model
of a hawk, slightly worn,
signed 'Hidenao', late 19thC,
19in (48cm) overall.
£1,800–2,200 *S*

A silver pipe and case, the pipe engraved with bamboo,
chrysanthemum and grasses, the case with similar
motifs, signed 'Wakayama Hidemasa zo', worn,
Meiji period, 9in (23cm) long.
£850–1,000 *S*

A silver vase and
domed cover, base
missing, c1900,
12½in (31.5cm) high.
£1,300–1,500 *C*

A silver and *Shibayama* tray, late 19thC,
10in (25.5cm) wide.
£2,200–2,500 *HSS*

l. A silver and *Shibayama* vase, cover and
liner with mother-of-pearl and polished
hardstones, on a gold lacquered ground
applied with 2 dragon-shaped metal
handles, damaged, indistinct seal mark
to base, late 19thC, 10½in (26cm) high.
£2,500–3,000 *HSS*

JAPANESE ARMS & ARMOUR

The Samurai were originally bodyguards of the Japanese Emperor and came from well-to-do families. Their armour may appear very theatrical and somewhat insubstantial for the fighting man, but closer examination reveals sound construction: the plates are made of thin sheets of iron, which are protected from rusting by black lacquer. The *mempo* (face mask), used from the 15th century, covered the lower half of the face but sometimes a full mask was fitted. Although the masks were very devil-like in appearance and were, no doubt, intended to strike fear into the enemy, they were often styled on traditional folk heroes. The large arm panels attached to the shoulder, known as *o-sode* ('big sleeve'), acted as a shield.

Red was the favourite colour of the Samurai warrior and is often found in the laces of the suits of armour or on the trim of panels. The warrior's weapons usually consisted of a bow and arrows, and a *katana* and *wakizashi* (large and small sword). The Japanese sword blade is of laminated construction, and one piece of metal can be folded and refolded many times to achieve the required strength.

The various parts of the Japanese sword are a very popular and rewarding collecting niche. The small charms (*menuki*) in the hand grip under the binding come in an immense variety of designs, ranging from imps peeping out from under mushrooms to lobster pots. The collar and pommel caps (*fuchi kashira*) are also much sought after by collectors and again are decorated with Japanese flowers, insects, people etc. One of the important parts of a sword that has great collector appeal is the *tsuba*, the circular bronze guard, often inlaid with silver and gold figures and objects, and sometimes with complete scenes containing trees, birds, waterfalls, rivers etc.

It is possible to take a rubbing or impression of the signature on the *tang* (the part of the blade that is covered by the hilt). The small bamboo peg in the hilt must be removed first, and then the *tsuba* can be pushed upwards away from the hilt to free it from the *tang*. If there is an incised inscription on one or both sides it can be filled with white chalk and, after removing any surplus chalk, the hilt can be placed on a photocopying machine to produce a clear-cut result.

Roy Butler

Armour

An iron *myochin* helmet bowl, the gilt peak carved with peonies, late16th/17thC.
£3,000–3,300 *C*

A 62-plate *hoshi bachi*, the russet iron helmet bowl with raised rivets, russet iron peak, c1650.
£3,500–4,000 *C*

r. A Chinese-style *kawari kabuto*, of 6 plates, each with an additional decorated plate, with silver *nunome* characters riveted, the top with *kiku* form *tehan* of iron attached with decorative rivets, c1700, early Edo period.
£12,000–14,000 *C*

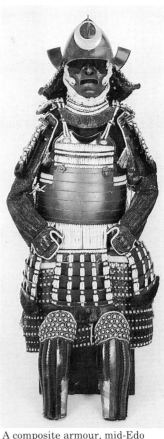

A composite armour, mid-Edo period, mostly associated.
£16,000–18,000 *C*

A russet iron *mempo*, of four-part construction with detachable nose and horsehair moustache, the teeth and interior lacquered, chipped and restored, Edo period, 10in (25.5cm) high.
£1,000–1,200 *S*

A russet iron *so-men*, the upper part and nose section detachable, ears riveted, horsehair moustache, chipped, one fixing lost, probably 18thC, 13in (33cm) high.
£2,500–3,000 *S*

An *eboshi*-style *kawari kabuto*, the 2 plates black lacquered, damaged, Edo period.
£5,000–6,000 *C*

A repoussé iron *do*, formed as a human torso, the ribs and nipples embossed, interior lined with lacquered cloth, 18th/19thC.
£6,000–7,000 *C*

A pair of inlaid iron *kaga abumi*, decorated with birds and netting, the underside with rafts and flowers on water, interior lacquered red, slight damage, signed, 18thC.
£5,000–6,000 *S*

A russet iron *mempo*, with detachable *tengu* nose, the interior lacquered in red, four-plate *yodarakake*, chipped, Edo period, 9in (23cm) high.
£1,300–1,500 *S*

A *hoshi-bachi*, with 24-plate bowl, by Miochin Munenaga, signed, dated '1812'.
£3,200–3,800 *S*

r. A russet iron *mempo*, with detachable nose, horsehair moustache, the interior lacquered in red, two-plate *yodarakake*, Edo period, 9½in (24cm) high.
£850–1,000 *BWe*

An Asagi composite armour, signed 'Myochin Muneyoshi saku', 19thC.
£7,500–9,000 *C*

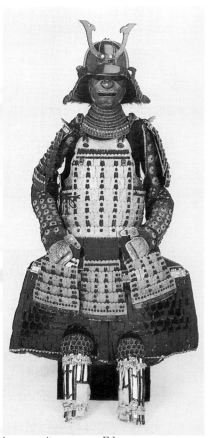

A composite armour, Edo period, helmet probably late Muromachi period.
£5,000–6,000 *C*

A composite armour, late Edo period, c1800.
£7,500–9,000 *C*

A lacquered helmet, decorated with dragonflies, 19thC.
£3,000–3,300 *C*

Japanese Helmets

The helmet, or *kabuto*, is sometimes quite heavy, and can be surmounted by a central crest. Crests usually take the form of a family crest (*mon*), animals, insects or even fish.

A black lacquer iron helmet of basic three-plate construction, with matching seven-piece hip guards and thigh protectors, old wear, with a black wooden box, 19thC.
£2,200–2,500 *C*

A white-laced *tosei gusoku*, the hip guards fur-trimmed, the armoured sleeves with pierced design of blossoms, associated iron chainmail thigh guard and shin guards, mid-Edo period, helmet 19thC.
£9,000–10,000 *C*

l. A composite armour, mid-Edo period, 18thC.
£17,500–20,000 *C*

The half mask and cuirass match each other, as do the armoured sleeves, the thigh guards, and the shin guards.

A composite armour, black and russet lacquered, laced in dark blue, with a wooden armour box listing contents, c1900.
£6,000–7,000 *S*

Edged Weapons

The long-standing tradition and excellence of Japanese metalwork is intimately linked with the history of the sword. Early Japanese swordsmiths produced steel blades of a quality that far surpassed those produced in other contemporary civilisations, and beside which most European swords look decidedly crude. It is not unusual to find a Kamakura period (1185–1333) blade that would lead the amateur to take it for a 19th-century example. Before the 17th century such blades were fitted with plain lacquer scabbards with iron fittings of sober, though often pleasing, design. Gradually, a taste developed for increasingly intricate fittings in soft metals (including alloys) with varied inlays and sophisticated engravings.

In 1876, following the reopening of Japan to unrestricted foreign contact and trade, the Samurai class was forbidden to carry swords in public. This edict threatened the livelihood of the fittings makers, since their works were largely for public show, but fortunately they found employment for their skills in the production of elaborate works for export to the West, where they found a ready market. Actively encouraged by the restored Meiji Emperor, many top craftsmen participated in the great international exhibitions, where they won praise, medals and commissions.

Max Rutherston

An *aikuchi*, the blade 16thC, the mounts 19thC.
£1,400–1,600 *S*

A *wakizashi*, the blade banded with black lacquer, signed 'Isshi hitsu', 16thC, mounts 19thC, 13in (33cm) long.
£1,300–1,500 *S*

A *wakizashi* blade, by Wakasaka Fuyuhiro II, c1615, 20⅛in(52cm) long.
£1,000–1,200 *S*

A *wakizashi* blade, ascribed to Umetada Yoshinobu, 17thC, 13¾in (35cm) long.
£1,400–1,600 *S*

A *wakizashi* and mount, the blade carved with a dragon, signed 'Echigo no Kami Fujiwara Kunitomo', early 17thC, 15¾in (40cm) long.
£8,500–9,500 *C*

The swordsmith Echigo no Kami Fujiwara Kunitomo, from Yamashiro Province, was a distinguished student of Horikawa Kunihiro, and his blades were famed for their exceedingly sharp cutting edges.

A silver-mounted *aikuchi* blade by Yamato Daijo Masanori, surface scratches, 17thC, mounts 19thC, 12in (30.5cm) long.
£5,000–6,000 *S*

A *shinto wakizashi* blade, ascribed to Omi (no) Kami Tadatsugu, 18thC, 20¾in (52.5cm) long.
£850–950 *S*

A *shin-shin to wakizashi*, in a *same* scabbard inlaid with the moon and flowers, late 18thC, blade 16in (40.5cm) long.
£850–950 *C*

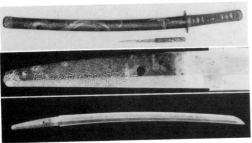

A *wakizashi*, the blade by Kazuma (no) Kami Munemichi, late 17th/early 18thC, mounts 19thC, 15¾in (40cm) long.
£6,000–7,000 *S*

A *shin-shin to tanto*, in a black lacquer mounting sprinkled with gold, 19thC, blade 8½in (21.5cm) long.
£1,750–2,000 *C*

A *wakizashi* blade, 18th/19thC, 20in (51cm) long, in *shirasaya*.
£1,400–1,700 *S*

A *tanto* and *kozuka*, mounted in ivory, signed 'Shungyoku', late 19thC, 19in (48.5cm) long.
£1,800–2,000 *C*

A *tanto*, the blade after Shinkai, 19thC, 10in (25.5cm) long.
£2,700–3,000 *S*

A *wakizashi*, blade 17thC, mounts 19thC, 18in (45.5cm) long.
£1,500–1,800 *S*

A lacquered wood sword stand *kake*, decorated with peonies and butterflies among rockwork in gold and silver, 2 hinged side plates for 3 swords, old wear and damage, 19thC, 16¾in (42.5cm) wide.
£2,000–2,200 *C*

A *nashiji* ground sword stand *kake*, decorated in gold and silver with cranes, the reverse decorated with *aoi mon*, some wear, 19thC, 20in (51cm) wide.
£3,500–4,000 *C*

A lacquered wood sword stand *kake* for 3 swords, decorated with chickens and pheasants in gold and coloured *takamakie*, chipped and faded 19thC, 20½in (52cm) wide.
£1,600–1,800 *S*

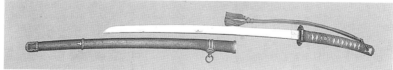

Japanese Sword Blades

Never touch the blade of a Japanese sword with your uncovered fingers, as the acids in your skin can damage the metal. It is advisable to always wear a pair of white cotton gloves when handling weapons. The To-Ken Society provide publications on how to look after Japanese weapons, and recommend the use of Chogi oil and Uchiko powder to protect the blades. Although some collectors use Oil of Cloves BP it is not advisable as it can stain the blades. Do not attempt to clean weapons without sound advice as you may do irreparable damage.

A *tachi*, signed, 19thC, 25in (63.5cm) long, in a black lacquered *saya* with gilt and embossed cherry blossom.
£2,800–3,200 *C*

An *aikuchi*, blade ascribed to Tadayoshi, mounts by Harunaga, 19thC, blade 9½in (24cm) long.
£3,500–4,000 *S*

A *ken*, with a Masamune signature and dated '1329–30', late 19thC, 8in (20.5cm) long, in a wood mounting carved and inlaid with dragons in ivory, mother-of-pearl and ebony.
£1,700–1,900 *C*

Pseudo archaic blades were not uncommon in the Meiji period, made by smiths such as Miyamoto Kanenori and Hayama Enshin among others.

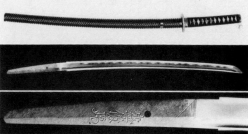

A silver and enamel-mounted *aikuchi*, signed 'Yoshimitsu', 19thC, blade 8in (20.5cm) long.
£4,200–5,000 *S*

l. An *aikuchi*, 19thC, blade 11in (28cm) long.
£1,300–1,500 *S*

An *aikuchi*, blade attributed to Kotaro Moritoshi, mounts by Goto Sei-i, 19thC.
£7,500–9,000 *S*

This item has a Hozon Token certificate, No. 312045, 1988, attributing the blade to Kotaro Moritoshi.

A *shin-shin to katana*, blade by Moritoshi, dated '1840', mounts late 19thC, 24in (61cm) long.
£7,000–8,000 *S*

A *katana*, blade by Nyudo Shoken Motooki, dated '1861', mounts late 19thC, 26in (66cm) long.
£4,500–5,000 *S*

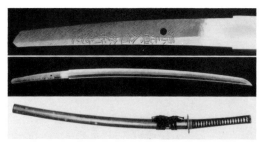

A *tanto*, the blade inscribed 'Yoshimitsu', 19thC, 8in (20.5cm) long.
£1,500–1,700 *S*

r. A *shin-shin to aikuchi*, blade by Yoshitsugu, mounts by Hirotaka, 19thC, 7in (18cm) long.
£4,500–5,000 *S*

A Goto-style mounted *daisho*, the *dai* after Tadatsuna, 18th/19thC, the *sho* by Kanesada, 19thC, blade 18in (45.5cm) long.
£10,000–12,000 *S*

Tsuba

An *owari* or *kyo-sukashi tsuba*, late Muromachi period, 16thC, 2½in (6.5cm) diam.
£780–820 *S*

A *ko-kinko yamagane sukashi tsuba*, of *mokko* form, carved and pierced as a stylised flower, with *tomobako* and certificate, Muromachi period, 16thC, 2½in (6.5cm) wide.
£600–700 *S*
The certificate describes this tsuba as tachi-shi *and dates it 1470–1570.*

An iron *tsuba*, decorated in brass, the ground with vine leaves, 17thC, 3in (7.5cm) wide.
£3,000–3,300 *C*

A *kyo-shoami tsuba*, carved and pierced with a bird among branches, *hakogaki* by Dr K. Torigoe, early Edo period, 3in (7.5cm) diam.
£500–600 *S*

An iron *mokume tsuba*, signed 'Kuminaga', probably 18thC, 3in (7.5cm) wide.
£350–400 *POA*

An *akasaka tsuba*, carved and pierced with birds, mid-Edo period, 18thC, 3in (7.5cm) diam.
£860–920 *S*

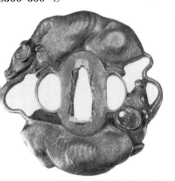

An associated pair of *sukashi tsuba* for a *daisho*, each in the form of oxen, 18thC, 3in (7.5cm) wide.
£850–1,000 *S*

A Goto-style *shakudo nanako tsuba*, with warriors of the Mongolian war in silver, 18thC, 3in (7.5cm) diam.
£2,300–2,500 *C*

An iron *tsuba*, carved in relief, inscribed 'Hamano Noriyuki', 19thC, 3½in (9cm) diam.
£1,800–2,000 *S*

An iron *tsuba*, by Otaka Masateru, signed, late Edo period, 19thC, 3in (7.5cm) wide.
£220–250 *Bon*

A *sentoku tsuba*, in the form of a badger teapot, signed 'Yasuchika', Meiji period, 3¼in (8.5cm) wide.
£4,000–4,500 *S(NY)*

A copper *tsuba*, decorated in *iroe takazogan* with a fish, signed 'Iwamoto Chokan', Meiji period, 3½in (9cm) wide.
£2,000–2,200 *S(NY)*

INDEX TO ADVERTISERS

BIBLIOGRAPHY

Carswell, John: *Chinese Blue and White and its Impact on the Western World* (Chicago, 1985)

Fuller, R.: *A Dictionary of Japanese Sword Terms* (To-Ken Society, Kent, 1986)

Fuller, R. & Gregory, R.: *Military Swords of Japan, 1868–1945* (Arms & Armour Press, London, 1986)

Garner, Sir Henry: *Chinese and Japanese Cloisonné Enamels* (Faber & Faber, London, 1970)

Howard, David S.: *A Tale of Three Cities: Canton, Shanghai and Hong Kong* (Sotheby's Publications, London)

Hutt, Julia: *Understanding Far Eastern Art* (New York, 1987)

Kerr, Rose: *Later Chinese Bronzes* (London, 1990)

Klein, Adalbert: *A Connoisseur's Guide to Japanese Ceramics* (Alpine Fine Arts Collection (UK) Ltd)

Lawrence, Louis: *Satsuma* (London, 1991)

Macintosh, Duncan: *Chinese Blue and White Porcelain* (Antique Collectors' Club, Woodbridge, 1997)

McKillop, Beth: *Korean Art and Design: The Samsung Gallery of Korean Art* (London, 1992)

Medley, Margaret: *The Chinese Potter* (Phaidon Press Ltd, London)

The Oriental Ceramics Society and The British Museum: *Chinese Ivories* (Sotheby's Publications, London)

Peterson, Harold, ed.: *Chinese Jades: Archaic and Modern* (London, 1977)

Rawson, Jessica, ed.: *British Museum Book of Chinese Art* (London, 1992)

Robinson, B. W.: *Arts of the Japanese Sword* (Faber & Faber, London 1970)
Schaap, Robert, ed.: *Meiji, Japanese Art in Transition* (Haags Gemeentemuseum, The Netherlands)

Schiffer, Nancy: *Japanese Porcelain, 1800–1950* (West Chester, 1986)

Shimizu, Yoshiaki, ed.: *Japan, The Shaping of the Daimyo Culture 1185–1868,* (National Gallery of Art, Washington)

Shixiang, Wang: *Classic Chinese Furniture* (Art Media Resources Ltd, Hong Kong)

Smith, Harris and Clark, *Japanese Art: Masterpieces in the The British Museum* (British Museum Publications, London)

Smith, Lawrence and Harris, Victor: *Japanese Decorative Arts from the 17th to the 19th Centuries* (London, 1982)

Watson, William, ed.: *The Great Japan Exhibition: Art of the Edo Period, 1600–1868* (London, 1981)

Whitfield, Roderick, ed.: *Treasures from Korea: Art Through 5000 Years* (London, 1984)

Wojciechowski, Kathy: *Nippon Porcelain* (West Chester, 1992)

GLOSSARY

We have defined here some of the words and terms used in this book, together with others that are in common use today.

Arita: the centre of Japanese porcelain production, on Honshu island.

aikuchi: a dagger without a guard.

aoi mon: 'blue crests' mark.

anhua: hidden decoration on Chinese porcelain.

bajixiang: box-form decoration.

bianco-sopra-bianco: white enamel decoration on Chinese porcelain.

bidong: a brush pot, see also **pitang**.

bijin: a beautiful woman.

bixie: a mythical composite figure resembling a feline; a guardian figure.

blanc-de-Chine: white porcelain from Dehua, China.

Bodhisattva: a potential Buddha.

bundai: a low writing table.

celadon: a green-glazed porcelain or stoneware, mostly of Chinese origin.

cha-ire: a Japanese tea caddy.

chawan: a Japanese tea bowl.

chilong: a small lizard.

clobbered: overglaze enamelling on simple Chinese blue and white porcelain by Europeans during the 18thC to enhance its value.

daimyo: the Samurai governor of a province.

daisho: a pair of swords, **katana** and **wakizashi**.

Dehua: see **blanc de Chine**.

dhoti: a loin cloth.

ding: a Chinese three-legged vessel.

Ding ware: porcelain of a creamy-white tone made in Hebei province.

do: a corselet.

dog of Fo: a Buddhist guardian lion.

doucai: decoration on porcelain using five colours.

eboshi: a stiff cap worn by Japanese nobility.

fu: see **fuku**.

fuchi kashira: a sword hilt fitting.

fuku: happiness, usually associated with a porcelain mark.

gaolin: a type of china clay from the Jiangxi mountains, also known as *kaolin*, used in the manufacture of porcelain.

grisaille: monochrome decoration.

gu: a bronze shape, also applied to the shape of porcelain items.

guan: a large Chinese storage jar.

guri: layered lacquer or metalwork, carved to reveal the separate layers.

hanaike: a flower vase.

hakeme-e: thigh guards.

hanabishe: floral decoration.

hare's fur: a variant of black glazed wares in which the iron precipitates from the edge towards the centre of the bowl, producing an effect resembling animal fur.

heaping and piling: an effect produced by cobalt burning through the glaze on blue and white Chinese porcelain, usually associated with the Ming period.

Henan: a province in China where stoneware with a shiny black glaze decorated with russet brown splashes was produced.

himotoshi: a type of wood used in the manufacture of Chinese furniture.

hiramakie/togidashi: flush lacquer, the latter beneath the surface.

ho-o: a mythical bird similar to a phoenix, symbolising wisdom and energy.

hongmu: a type of wood used in the manufacture of Chinese furniture.

hoshi bachi: rivets on a helmet.

hoshi bachi kabuto: a helmet with many protecting rivets.

hozuki: winter cherries.

hu: a bronze vessel for ritual use.

huanghualia: a type of wood used for making Chinese furniture.

huluping: a double gourd flask.

huyi huyi qing: cobalt imported from the Middle East during the Yuan Dynasty and early Ming Dynasty, known as 'Mohammedan Blue'.

ikebana: Japanese flower arranging.

inro: multi-compartmented container suspended from the sash of the kimono.

iroe hiramakie: a type of lacquer.

iroe takazogan: inlay in relief decoration.

Jingdezhen: the centre of Chinese porcelain production.

kabuto: a helmet.

kaga abumi: a stirrup.

kagamibuta: a shallow bowl with a decorated metal lid.

kake: a Japanese sword stand.

kakemono: a Japanese hanging scroll.

kao: a mark in the form of a face.

karakusa: 'Chinese grasses', a common decoration on Japanese ceramics.

karashishi: a lion dog – see also **shishi**.

katana: a long Japanese sword.

ken: a type of old sword.

kendi: a type of drinking vessel with a spout.

Kenjo Imari: presentation ware.

Ki-Seto: 'Yellow Seto', a type of celadon from the Seto kiln in Japan.

kiku: a chrysanthemum.

kinji/fundame: decoration with an even gold ground.

kinrande: brocade decoration.

kiri: a Paulownia flower.

kirigane: rectilinear cut gold foil particles.

kirin: a mythical beast.

ko: Japanese for old.

kobako: an incense box.

kodansu: a perfume cabinet.

kogai: a skewer.

kogo: a small incense box.

koro: an incense burner.

koto katana: armoured sleeves.

kozuka: a utility knife.

kraak porselein: Chinese blue and white export porcelain.

kylin: a Chinese mythical beast.

kyo-yaki: Kyoto enamelled pottery.

lac burgauté: lacquer wares inlaid with mother-of-pearl.

leiwen: a Chinese pattern, known as 'thunder pattern', used as a decorative motif, usually on bronzes.

lian: a small cosmetic vessel.

lingzhi: a type of fungus or mushroom, used as a motif on Chinese porcelain.

lianzu: a shape of a bowl, also known as a 'lotus bowl', thought to be symbolic of the opening of a lotus.

lohan: a saintly or worthy Chinese man.

lokapala: the Guardian Kings of the Buddhist faith.

long: a Chinese dragon.

longpao: 'Dragon Robes', Chinese Imperial Court dress.

luoping: a type of cobalt used in porcelain production.

mandorla: in sculpture or paintings, an area of light usually surrounding a person.

manjua: a round bun filled with sweet bean paste, now appled to the shape of a *netsuke*.

meiping: a Chinese vase of inverted shape.

mempo: a half mask.

menugi: a bamboo pin in a sword hilt.

menuki: hilt ornaments for Japanese sword mountings.

mizusashi: a water jar, used in the tea ceremony in Japan.

mokko: a sword guard with four lobes.

mokume: a pattern on sword blades resembling wood grain.

mon: a Japanese crest, or coat-of-arms.

mudan: a Chinese peony.

mukozuke: a dish.

nashiji: a multitude of gold flakes in lacquer, known as pear skin.

netsuke: a decorative toggle for securing personal possessions in traditional Japanese dress.

Noh: traditional Japanese masked drama with dance and song, evolved from Shinto rites.

nunome: false damascening or inlay.

o-sode: upper arm guards on Japanese armour.

oil-spot: a lustrous effect on a black glaze, imitating spots of oil on the glaze, produced by a short period of reduction-firing that allows small amounts of iron to precipitate out into the black glaze.

ojime: a small bead for tightening cords holding personal possessions in traditional Japanese dress.

okimono: a small, finely carved Japanese ornament.

oni: a devil.

palanquin: a covered litter for one.

petunze: a china stone from the Jiangxi mountains, used in the manufacture of porcelain.

pitang: a brush pot – see also *bidong*.

polychrome: decoration executed in more than two colours.

punch'ong: greyish-green celadon stoneware, with stamped decoration filled with slip.

qilin: an alternative name for *kylin*.

qilong: an alternative name for *chilong*.

qingbai: a white ware produced by potters in the Jingdezhen area throughout the Song Dynasty.

raden/aogai: inlaid shell, the latter smaller and more colourful.

rakkan: a legendary disciple of the historical Buddha.

reduction-firing: a reduction of oxygen to the kiln during firing.

roiro: black.

roironuri: black ground, fading to brown.

rouge de fer: iron-red colour produced with iron oxide.

ruyi: a presentation sceptre.

sage-jubako: a type of lacquer box.

sake: Japanese rice wine.

same: shark or ray skin used for sword hilts.

samurai: the Japanese hereditary military class.

sancai: three-colour decoration on porcelain.

sei: Japanese for made.

sentoku: a form of yellow brass.

sentoku tsuba: a brass sword guard.

shakudo: an alloy of copper with a small percentage of gold.

shakudo nanako: *shakudo* worked with a punch into a 'fish roe' pattern.

Shibayama: lacquer applied with semi-precious stones and ivory.

shibuichi: an alloy of copper and silver.

shibuichi migaki-ji kogo: an incense box made of *shibuichi*.

shikoro: the neck guard of a helmet.

shinto: sword blades made after c1600.

shippo: a type of Japanese cloisonné enamel.

shirazaya: plain wood mounting for storing sword blades.

shishi: a lion dog.

sho: Japanese for small.

shodona: a cabinet for writing utensils.

shoji: Japanese paper sliding doors.

shou: a decorative motif, symbolising longevity.

Shoulao: the Star God of Longevity.

shufu: 'Imperial Palace'. Character used to mark the Imperial porcelain of the Yuan Dynasty.

stupa: a pagoda.

sukashi: ornmamental piercing or openwork.

suneate: shin guards.

suzuribako: a writing utensil box.

tachi: a slung sword.

takabori: relief decoration.

takamakie: high-relief lacquer.

takazogan: high-relief inlay.

tang: the part of a Japanese sword blade covered by the hilt.

tanto: a dagger.

taotie: a monster face shown from the front, popular decoration on ancient Chinese bronzes.

tengu: mythical forest gnomes often portrayed on armour and sword mounts.

tetsubin: a Japanese tea kettle.

tanlu: a heavenly deer.

tielimu: Chinese hardwood often used for making the backs of furniture.

togidashi: a lacquer technique in which further layers of lacquer are added to **hiramakie** then polished flush with the original surface.

tosei gusoku: a corselet maker.

tsuba: a sword or dagger guard.

usagi: a Japanese rabbit or hare.

wakizashi: a sword shorter than a **katana**.

wawa: 'hundred children at play', decorative Chinese motif.

Willow pattern: 18thC English decoration on blue and white porcelain, associated with Chinese wares, but the legend portrayed is not of Chinese origin.

wucai: a type of five-colour porcelain decoration executed in a vigorous style.

Wu Xing: the Five Elements.

yakiba: the tempered edge of a blade.

yamagane: an alloy of copper, zinc and tin.

yanyan/yenyen: a Chinese vase shape.

yin yang/yinyang: a circle divided into two equal parts by a curving S-shaped line.

yodarakake: the laminated neck guard of a face mask.

Yue: high-fired green wares.

yuhuchunping: a pear-shaped vase.

zhadou: a particular shape of vessel.

zitan: a type of dense wood used for making Chinese furniture.

zushi: a portable shrine with doors, used to hold religious images.

INDEX

Italic page numbers denote colour pages; bold numbers refer to information and pointer boxes.

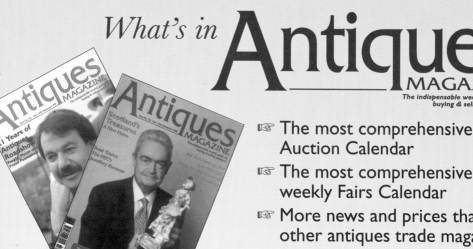